Intellectuals and Cultural Policy

Intellectuals and policy analysts might appear to inhabit two different worlds. Intellectuals aspire to articulate issues of universal concern; policy analysts attend to the detail of specific measures and programmes. Intellectuals point to the kingdom of ends; policy analysts to that of administrative means. Intellectuals speak truth to power; policy analysts sharpen the instruments of government. Intellectuals clash ostentatiously on the stage of politics; policy analysts, when they are drawn into government, pull hidden levers in the corridors of power. Intellectuals stand accused of seeking self-publicity; policy analysts of eluding public scrutiny. But how far do these common assumptions match up to reality? What happens when intellectuals engage with cultural institutions and the machinery of government? And how far is cultural policy connected to a history of ideas?

The essays brought together here attempt to answer these questions. From the English Romantics to Lenin's wife, from Plato to Herbert Schiller, this book offers new insights into how intellectuals from Europe, Canada and North America have sought over time to assert their cultural values in public life.

This book was previously published as a special issue of the *International Journal of Cultural Policy*.

Dr Jeremy Ahearne is Reader in the Department of French Studies at the University of Warwick.

Professor Oliver Bennett is the Director of the Centre for Cultural Policy Studies at the University of Warwick.

Intellectuals and Cultural Policy

Edited by
Jeremy Ahearne & Oliver Bennett

LONDON AND NEW YORK

First published 2007 by Routledge
2 Park Square, Milton Park, Abingdon, Oxfordshire OX14 4RN

Simultaneously published in the USA and Canada by Routledge
711 Third Avenue, New York, NY 10017

First issued in paperback 2014

Routledge is an imprint of the Taylor & Francis Group, an informa business

© 2007 Jeremy Ahearne & Oliver Bennett

Typeset in Myriad by Genesis Typesetting Ltd, Rochester, Kent

All rights reserved. No part of this book may be reprinted or reproduced or utilised in any form or by any electronic, mechanical, or other means, now known or hereafter invented, including photocopying and recording, or in any information storage or retrieval system, without permission in writing from the publishers.

British Library Cataloguing in Publication Data
A catalogue record for this book is available from the British Library

Library of Congress Cataloging in Publication Data
A catalog record for this book has been requested

ISBN 13: 978-1-138-86463-4 (pbk)
ISBN 13: 978-0-415-42090-7 (hbk)

Contents

Introduction
Jeremy Ahearne and Oliver Bennett — 1

1 **Intellectuals, Romantics and Cultural Policy**
Oliver Bennett — 3

2 **Knowing Her Place: Jane Addams, pragmatism and cultural policy**
Chris Bilton — 21

3 **A Pragmatic Intellectual: Dutch Fabians, Boekman and cultural policy in the Netherlands, 1890–1940**
Harro Maas — 37

4 **Harold Innis, Cultural Policy, and Residual Media**
Charles R. Acland — 57

5 **Fernand Dumont and the Vicissitudes of Cultural Policy in Québec**
William J. Buxton — 73

6 **Richard Hoggart: Public intellectual**
Jim McGuigan — 85

7 **Notes from the Number One Country: Herbert Schiller on culture, commerce and American power**
Graham Murdock — 95

8 **The Unacknowledged Legacy: Plato, the *Republic* and cultural policy**
Eleonora Belfiore — 115

9 **Krupskaya, Proletkul't and the Origins of Soviet Cultural Policy**
Christopher Read — 131

10 **Georg Lukács: Cultural policy, Stalinism and the Communist International**
W. John Morgan — 143

11 **The Urge to Judge: Intellectuals and communism in postwar Poland, past and present**
Laurie Koloski — 159

12 **Intellectuals as Cultural Agenda-Setters in the Federal Republic?**
Rob Burns and Wilfried van der Will — 177

13 **Public Intellectuals and Cultural Policy in France**
Jeremy Ahearne — 209

14 **Intellectuals and Cultural Policy in France: Antoine Hennion and the sociology of music**
David Looseley — 227

Index — 241

INTRODUCTION

Intellectuals and policy analysts might appear to inhabit two different worlds. Intellectuals aspire to articulate issues of universal concern; policy analysts attend to the refractory detail of specific measures and programmes. Intellectuals point to the kingdom of ends; policy analysts to the netherworld of administrative means. Intellectuals speak truth to power; policy analysts sharpen and recalibrate the instruments of government. Intellectuals clash ostentatiously on the stage of politics; policy analysts, when they are drawn into government, pull hidden levers in the corridors of power. We accuse intellectuals of seeking self-publicity and policy wonks of eluding public scrutiny.

This framework of commonplaces is not entirely misleading. Its principal interest, however, resides in the incitement it provides to seek interferences between the poles of such manifest dichotomies. The purpose of this and the next issue of the journal is to explore, precisely, instances where public intellectuals complicate these apparently clear-cut divisions between critical and practical thought, or between cultural politics and cultural policy.

The papers in these issues have their origin in a conference on "Intellectuals and Cultural Policy", funded by the Centre for Cultural Policy Studies at the University of Warwick and held at Coombe Abbey, Coventry, in September 2005. The conference was a natural development of the Centre's research interests and was also to some extent inspired and provoked by an earlier conference on arts policy and the history of economic thought, hosted by Duke University, North Carolina, in 2002. A selection of papers from the Duke conference have recently been published in a special edition of the *History of Political Economy* (vol. 37, no. 3, 2005), which in some respects can perhaps be read as a companion volume to these issues of the *IJCP*.

The papers presented here offer a series of case studies across different historical epochs and national contexts (the USA, Canada, Western and Eastern Europe, Russia). Some contributions analyze general tendencies within given national historical contexts (the UK, France, Poland). Most focus on individual figures while taking care to account for these within the national and historical settings in which they have operated (Richard Hoggart, Jürgen Habermas, Hilmar Hoffmann, Antoine Hennion, Emanuel Boekman, Plato, Jane Addams, Herbert Schiller, Harold Innis, Fernand Dumont, Nadezhda Krupskaya, Georg Lukàcs). These studies do not necessarily seek to collapse all distinctions between the practices of critical reflection and policy engagement. Some, on the contrary, accentuate points of incompatibility.

It does not make much sense at this stage to set up overarching meta-definitions of "the intellectual" and "cultural policy". Among the most interesting things revealed by the collection as a whole are the different kinds of socially and politically definitional work that has gone on around such terms in different national contexts. Moreover, the discussion between contributors around preliminary versions of their articles revealed considerable and stimulating divergences of view. It is worth, however, articulating something of the sentiment that encouraged us to collect together these articles in the first place. Where public intellectuals take up cultural policy positions with little sense of the constraints that bear down upon the policy field, their pronouncements are prone to lapse into vapid generality. On the other hand, without the abrasive and essentially non-expert input of autonomous public intellectuals, the cultural policy process is liable to become an altogether more arid and sterile affair, a simple means to a means.

Jeremy Ahearne
Oliver Bennett
Editors

INTELLECTUALS, ROMANTICS AND CULTURAL POLICY

Oliver Bennett

Introduction

In this paper, I shall be looking at the relationship between intellectuals, Romantics and cultural policy in England, with particular reference to the work of William Wordsworth (1770–1850) and Percy Bysshe Shelley (1792–1822). Before I do this, however, I would like, by way of introduction, to rehearse the general questions that this cross-national study of "intellectuals and cultural policy" throws up. Some of these questions are addressed explicitly in this and other papers in these two issues of the journal; others will arise implicitly in the contrasts and the comparisons that emerge from our combined efforts.

First of all, it is necessary to determine what one means by "intellectual" and why the person or persons under discussion merit the denomination. It is also necessary to make explicit the sense in which one is using the term "cultural policy" – a fairly recent construction, which has different associations in different languages and is often applied anachronistically. The coupling of "intellectuals" and "cultural policy" assumes that there is actually a relationship, but this needs to be established. If it can be established, what is its nature? Is it a relationship circumscribed by its time or has it left a legacy? If the latter, what is the nature of the legacy? Is it explicit or have the ideas persisted only in unstated institutional assumptions? How can such legacies be explained?

The comparative questions probably go beyond the scope of any one paper, but nevertheless present themselves as a result of the diversity and range of our collective enquiry. What, for example, are the various notions of "intellectual" that have been constructed across different nations and in different periods? How can these differences be accounted for? To what extent can we generalize about the role intellectuals have played in the development of policies for culture? Are there discernible models? Are the relations between intellectuals and cultural policy comparable to those between intellectuals and other forms of policy-making? Or does the nature of the cultural field involve some kind of "special relationship"? And how can the influence of intellectuals, or the absence of influence, be accounted for? What are the factors that determine whether a set of ideas takes root and persists in future generations?

It is also worth asking whether these questions matter. On the face of it, a study of intellectuals and cultural policy does not seem very promising. In England, cultural policy, at least if one were to understand it in a pure sense as governments supporting culture for its own sake, has never been a political priority. Indeed, according to Jim McGuigan (2004, p. 1), cultural policy in this sense has virtually disappeared, eroded by the dominance of economic reasoning and now so marginalized that it lives on only as a branch of economic policy. As for intellectuals, they have rarely had a good press in England and it seems to be getting worse.

In 1992, John Carey published his *Intellectuals and the Masses* – a savage indictment of how some of the most canonized intellectuals of the twentieth century, such as Virginia Wolf, George Bernard Shaw and Aldous Huxley, harboured a deep revulsion towards common humanity. Seeing themselves as "natural aristocrats", they used their culture to distinguish themselves from the "masses", whom they repeatedly characterized as a kind of semi-human swarm (Carey 1992, pp. 1–90). While Carey does not suggest that this quasi-fascist tendency is prevalent amongst today's intellectuals, he nevertheless leaves us in no doubt that intellectuals continue to display their assumptions of cultural superiority. In academia, for example, he sees the rise of "theory", with the impenetrable jargon of its various manifestations, as the appropriation of popular culture by intellectuals in order to re-process it and "take it out of the reach of the majority" (Carey 1992, p. 215).

For Frank Furedi (2004), on the other hand, the pressing question is the one he poses in the title of his recent book: *Where Have All the Intellectuals Gone?* For Furedi, it is not the assumption of cultural superiority that is the issue, but, on the contrary, the intellectual's abandonment of his or her historic mission as fearless investigator of the truth. Furedi sees many of today's intellectuals as so compromised by an instrumentalist approach to knowledge that they hardly deserve to be called intellectuals. Moreover, they are so fearful of the charge of elitism that the imperative to appear relevant and accessible assumes paramount importance. Not only do they not resist the forces of "dumbing down" that Furedi sees as triumphant throughout the educational and cultural spheres, but they are actually complicit in it. As a result, intellectuals lose their special status, their social role is devalued and their work is no longer endowed with "a unique significance" (Furedi 2004, pp. 8–9).

It does not take much to see that Carey's and Furedi's positions are directly contradictory. Carey distrusts the cultural authority that intellectuals have claimed for themselves; furthermore, assuming the absence of God, he sees no basis on which such authority can be legitimately claimed. In a later book (Carey 2005), he develops this position into one of full-blown relativism. "A work of art", he says, "is anything that anyone has considered a work of art"; and the true value of a cultural experience can only be known by the person experiencing it (Carey 2005, pp. 29, 23). This is anathema to Furedi. For him, the acquisition of authority is part of what constitutes an intellectual; and the failure to exercise it culturally, educationally or politically amounts to a dereliction of duty. He sees the intellectual as the true inheritor of Enlightenment ideals, committed to a universalist vision and willing "to wage a battle of ideas for the hearts and minds of the public" (Furedi 2004, pp. 43–46, 156).

These conflicting visions reflect not only a lack of consensus on what the role of the intellectual should be in matters of culture, but also a deep unease about how intellectuals have actually been performing this role. If this is what we learn from intellectuals (as Carey and Furedi indisputably are) reflecting upon other intellectuals, then it is hardly surprising that intellectuals as a group are not held in high esteem by the general public – that is, if the idea of "the intellectual" is even recognized at all. Even in relation to cultural policy, as defined above, some observers (Schuster 2002; Selwood 2006) have more or less concluded that intellectuals have nothing to offer. A sceptical observer might therefore dismiss a study of intellectuals and cultural policy by a group of academics as little more than a self-interested study of a marginalized group within a marginal area of government policy.

This is not a criticism I accept, nor to my knowledge, one that has actually been made, but it nevertheless constitutes a case that needs to be answered. As we shall see, cultural policy is a field that goes well beyond the pragmatic concerns of government policy and concerns itself with broader questions around the conditions of culture – "culture" being used here in the sense of more than the arts and extending to what Raymond Williams (1981a, p. 13) described as a "signifying system". If we think the signifying practices of our societies are important, which I do not see how we can fail to do, then a study of the conditions that influence them is clearly worthwhile. And despite the deeply contested status of the intellectual in England, it is difficult to see how cultural policy can be understood without examining the ways in which intellectuals have been so strongly implicated in it.

Even if we take cultural policy in its most limited sense, as a set of practical measures taken by governments either to regulate or support the arts, then we will almost certainly find that these measures reflect assumptions about the role of art in society that intellectuals have formulated, often in a quite different historical context. This may seem an obvious point, but many practitioners and policy-makers working in the cultural field today seem unaware that they are even making assumptions and appear almost to endow their pronouncements with the status of natural law. John Tusa, for example, Managing Director of London's Barbican Centre, tells us that the arts matter because, among other things, "they present a vision of integration rather than disintegration" and "they embrace, express and define the soul of a civilisation" (Tusa 1999, p. 22). Such a bizarre statement, which apart from anything else appears to suggest that Modernism never happened, only becomes comprehensible if we see it in relation to the ideas developed by those we now describe as Romantics.

However, at least Tusa is attempting to articulate some kind of philosophical basis to the work with which he is engaged. There is another tendency within cultural policy that abandons the attempt altogether and sees culture in predominantly instrumental terms. In other words, it is not culture *per se* that is important, but the contribution it can make to the economy or to other government objectives such as social inclusion. There are also researchers and policy analysts who follow this trend, either as consultants or in academia, and who see cultural policy as an exclusively operational matter, without reference to values, meaning or ideology. This has led to much debate about the relative merits of administrative and critical research (Bennett 2004; Nielsen 1991; McGuigan 1996, pp. 12–29).

So, if we think that the forces that shape culture and influence its reception are worth investigating, and if we acknowledge that intellectuals have been deeply implicated in this shaping, then a study of the relations between the two begins to look more promising. It is, of course, an extremely complex relationship and one that goes both ways: intellectuals are shaped by the conditions of culture as much as they contribute to the shaping of those conditions. Before we look at how this works out in the case of Romanticism, however, the notions of both "the intellectual" and "cultural policy" require a sharper definition.

The Idea of the Intellectual

The word "intellectual", used as a noun to denote a particular kind of person, first emerged in the early nineteenth century. Raymond Williams (1981b, p. 141) notes that "there was a distinct formation of unfavourable implications" around the word, particularly when used in the plural. He attributes this to the association of intellectualism, and therefore intellectuals, with rationalism and its corresponding connotations of coldness and abstraction. This was reinforced by the Romantic opposition to the separation of "reason" and "feeling" or "head" and "heart". The idea of the intellectual was also associated with practical ineffectiveness in social and political matters. This arose from a deep distrust, which had been popularized, amongst others by Edmund Burke, of those of an intellectual disposition who elevated theory over practical experience.

These early formulations have survived in the modern characterization of the intellectual as disassociated from feeling and lacking in practical common sense. On the other hand, a more positive valuation also survives as a result of the early identification of intellectuals with independent thinking and freedom from the orthodoxies of established institutions. Indeed, modern attempts to define and defend the role of the intellectual are still cast very much in these terms.

What emerges from these attempts is a "heroic" model of the intellectual: a repository of moral authority, but one that belongs, as we have seen from Furedi's observations, to a seriously endangered species. What are the attributes of this model? Well, first of all, an intellectual has to be deeply engaged with ideas. However, just to be involved in the production of ideas, as, for example, an architect will be in the designing of a building, is not enough. Intellectuals must be capable of stepping outside their own specialization and relating their intellectual labours to matters of general interest. As Zygmunt Bauman (1987, p. 2) has observed, the intellectual must "rise above the partial preoccupation of one's own profession or artistic *genre* and engage with the global issues of truth, judgement and taste of the time". Richard Posner (2003, p. 20) goes further, though this is implicit in Bauman's definition, and suggests that an intellectual will be explicitly engaged in addressing political and ideological matters.

Related to the "generality" of the intellectual's ideas is the notion that the intellectual also holds a universalist perspective. Although this has been challenged by Michel Foucault's concept of the "specific intellectual" (see McGuigan 1996, p. 186; Furedi 2004, p. 45), the "traditional" or "critical" intellectual is still held up as the exemplary model. Edward Said (1994, p. 9) tells us that the intellectual conducts his or her work "on the basis of universal principles"; while Furedi (2004, p. 34), deploring what he sees as Foucault's down-sizing of intellectual authority, claims that the intellectual is "the personification of the Enlightenment legacy and has traditionally sought to represent the standpoint of universality". For him, this means rising above any particular identity or interest and, through adherence to universal values such as rationality, science and freedom, aiming to work on behalf of society as a whole. Posner (2003, p. 22) argues that another attribute of the intellectual is his or her commitment to communicating directly with the general public. Scholars writing for other scholars, professional consultants and technocrats, advisers working exclusively within government or industry and those just incapable of expressing themselves clearly to a non-specialist audience all fail to qualify. To reinforce his point, though he acknowledges that it may be tautological, Posner prefers to use the term "public intellectual".

Furedi (2004, p. 36), as we have seen, wants to "capture the hearts and minds of the public", and he sees this desire to influence the world as a common goal of all intellectuals. Given that only a very small minority of people actually get to communicate with the general public, let alone influence the world, we can see how intellectuals can come to see themselves and be seen as an elite group. This was foreseen by Adam Smith, who, in *The Wealth of Nations*, wrote that in wealthy, commercial societies: "To think or reason comes to be, like every other employment, a particular business, which is carried on by a very few people, who furnish the public with all the thought and reason possessed by the vast multitudes that labour" (Williams 1979 [1958], p. 52).

What, of course, is missing from Smith's formulation, but which developed in the nineteenth century and survives strongly in contemporary accounts of the intellectual, is the emphasis on autonomy, independence of mind and a generally "oppositional" tendency. Said (1994, pp. 8–9) suggests that the role of the intellectual is "to raise embarrassing questions, to confront orthodoxy and dogma (rather than to produce them) [and] to be someone who cannot easily be co-opted by governments and corporations". An oppositional stance, of course, is not a virtue in itself, as it depends upon what is being opposed. Posner (2003, p. 31) argues that the oppositional reflex has sometimes led Western intellectuals into perverse attachments to untenable positions, such as support for communist regimes long after the evidence of their abuses had become known. The novelist Philip Roth (2000), in a fictional comment on America's "culture wars", gives a compelling account in *The Human Stain* of how, in the academy, the oppositional reflex can itself become hardened into an orthodoxy.

Although intellectuals are often seen as the conscience of society, living on the margins and upholding its true values and ideals (Furedi 2004, pp. 31–32; Posner 2003, p. 32), the academization of intellectual life has made it difficult for intellectuals to play this role convincingly. As Posner points out, it is not easy for insiders to be convincing outsiders when safely ensconced in highly paid and tenured university professorships.

Intellectuals, of course, have always been socially situated and viewed the world through the prism of their own formative experiences. There has never been an "outside" that they can inhabit, independent of social processes, and in this respect absolute autonomy is a myth. However, intellectual life has arguably become significantly more institutionalized through the growth of universities since the 1950s. Throughout the nineteenth century and the first half of the twentieth, the intellectual was more likely to be found outside the academy than within it. Burke, Coleridge, Carlyle, Bentham, Mill, Marx, Dickens, Freud, Orwell, Shaw, Eliot, to name just a few, were never employed as salaried academics.

But since the 1950s, the number of non-academic intellectuals shrunk dramatically (Posner 2003, p. 28). Few were willing to resist the opportunity of a clearly defined career path, good conditions of service and secure employment. Parallel opportunities arose for "media intellectuals". Had these opportunities been available in earlier periods, it seems unlikely that intellectuals would have refused them. Marx, for example, would almost certainly have found university tenure a more congenial way of making ends meet than relying on hand-outs from Engels and gambling (without much success) on the stock exchange. But it is difficult to imagine him, as a young man, enrolling on one of the growing number of graduate courses that are now being designed to produce intellectuals, such as the "Public

Intellectuals Program" offered by the Dorothy E. Schmidt College of Arts and Letters at Florida Atlantic University.

While all these developments reflect a growing employment market for intellectuals, they have almost certainly been accompanied by some erosion of intellectual autonomy. Universities have been increasingly subject to greater bureaucratic control in the name of accountability and quality assurance, while media intellectuals work within the framework of a highly competitive commercial market. To succeed in this environment requires the adoption of the appropriate professional behaviour. For Said (1994, p. 55), this means "not rocking the boat, not straying outside the accepted paradigms or limits, making yourself marketable and above all presentable, hence uncontroversial and unpolitical and 'objective'".

From these brief reflections we can begin to get a sense of the ambivalence that has gathered around the notion of the intellectual in the Anglophone world. On the one hand, he or she is variously seen as impractical, unrealistic, blinded by theory, self-important, emotionally repressed, possessed of a sense of cultural and moral superiority, and as compromised as anyone else; on the other hand, he or she is also seen – mainly, it has to be said, by intellectuals themselves – as the conscience of society, an investigator of truth, a source of cultural and moral authority, possessed of a holistic vision, an independent thinker, politically engaged and working on behalf of all people – in short, the personification of the Enlightenment.

This compressed portrait necessarily involves some simplification, but I believe that it nevertheless accurately represents the two main clusters of opinion that have formed round the idea of the intellectual in England at the present time. As we shall see, Romantics, though sometimes placed in opposition to intellectuals, also share many of the characteristics of this double image. Before we explore this further, however, it is necessary to define briefly what we mean by "cultural policy".

The Idea of Cultural Policy

As suggested above, the term "cultural policy" has a relatively short history, but has nevertheless acquired a number of different meanings. In one of its first appearances in English, it was defined in a UNESCO (1969) publication as "a body of operational principles, administrative and budgetary practices and procedures which provide a basis for cultural action by the state". In Britain, the "cultural action" referred to usually related to the arts. Indeed, when Britain got its first minister for culture in 1964 (Jennie Lee), at that time based in a "Branch" of the Department of Education and Science, she was entitled the "Minister for the Arts"; and when the "Branch" was upgraded to an "Office" in 1985, it was named the "Office of Arts and Libraries". Its policies, insofar as it actually articulated them, were restricted to the arts, libraries and museums; other areas that could be considered cultural, such as commercial film, broadcasting and the press, were specifically excluded from its sphere of influence. It was not until 1992 that all these policy areas were brought together in one department of state, and it was not until 1997 that the word "culture" actually appeared in the department's name.

For many years, therefore, as far as public policy was concerned, "culture" was synonymous with "the arts" and "cultural policy" meant "arts policy". In fact, the term "cultural policy" was rarely used in practical policy discourse. It was not until the 1980s that the first decisive moves were made from an arts policy towards a more broadly based cultural policy;

and it was a local authority – the Labour-controlled Greater London Council (GLC) – that made the break.

The GLC recognized that, if its cultural policy was to connect with the majority of its voters, then it would need to engage with the kind of culture that most people "consumed" – that is to say, the products of the commercial cultural industries that state policies for the arts had generally ignored. For Geoff Mulgan and Ken Warpole (1986, p. 1), both working for the GLC at the time, traditional arts policies were becoming progressively marginal while, as they put it, "the corporate planners and the strategy executives of the multinationals [were] only too keen to write the real cultural policies for themselves". The GLC thus became the first public authority to develop a "cultural industries strategy" of its own. Nicholas Garnham, one of the GLC's advisors, has suggested that this marked a significant departure from arts policies based on the "tradition of idealist cultural analysis" (Garnham & Epstein 1985, p. 145) – a tradition which, as we shall see, owes a great deal to English Romanticism.

Although the GLC was abolished before it was able to put much of its strategy into action, its conceptual innovations and public use of the term "cultural policy" had a lasting effect. It took another decade for central government to adopt these practices itself, but adopt them it did, albeit in a less radical form. By 1997, New Labour had established a Department of Culture, Media and Sport, set up a Creative Industries Task Force and within a few years would be announcing "cultural policies" of its own.

The term "cultural policy" thus came to encompass all those elements that made up Williams's "signifying system", such as broadcasting, film, design, publishing and recording as well as the live performing arts, museums and heritage. It is now routinely defined as "the totality of actions taken within these sectors, together with the measures adopted by both central and local government to support or regulate them" (Bennett 1995a, p. 111). However, despite these conceptual shifts, there is some evidence to suggest that the arts, traditionally defined, retain their central position both in cultural policy itself and in the preoccupations of analysts of cultural policy (Stanbridge 2005; Lewis & Miller 2003, p. 4).

The above account of the evolution of the term "cultural policy" refers more or less to the world of practical policy-making. However, it has had a parallel and arguably more interesting life in academic discourse, particularly within the humanities and critical sociology. While policy-makers are inevitably circumscribed by institutional and political imperatives, academic analysts of cultural policy have a greater opportunity to stand back and examine those imperatives, to question assumptions and imagine alternatives. For Jim McGuigan (1996, p. 1), therefore, "cultural policy is about the politics of culture in the most general sense: it is about the clash of ideas, institutional struggles and power relations in the production and circulation of symbolic meanings".

Following Williams, McGuigan (2004, pp. 61–91) also draws a distinction between cultural policy as display and cultural policy "proper". The former refers, in Williams' words, to "the public pomp of a particular social order" – such as royal or military displays; the latter to the explicit policies for various forms of culture that have been discussed above. This has similarities, though is not identical with, Jeremy Ahearne's (2004, p. 114) distinction between "implicit" or "effective" cultural policy and "explicit" or "nominal" cultural policy. The difference lies in Ahearne's rather broader notion of "implicit cultural policy", which he uses to denote "any political strategy that looks to work on the culture of the territory over which it presides (or on that of its adversary)" (Ahearne 2004, p. 114).

Usage of the term "cultural policy", in the sense of McGuigan's general politics of culture, was not common until the late 1970s, and then only among a very small number of academics such as Raymond Williams. It did not even make much headway in the field of cultural studies until the 1990s, when Tony Bennett (1992, p. 25) called for more attention to be paid to "the institutional conditions that regulate different fields of culture". However, the *idea* of cultural policy is much older. So, even though the term is an invention of the late twentieth century, it provides a useful way of conceptualising all those attempts that have taken place over time to assert or prohibit particular cultural values and practices. If cultural policy is viewed in this light, we will see that what came to be called "Romanticism" has played a significant part in its history.

Romantics and Romanticisms

In a much cited paper written in 1941, the historian of ideas, Arthur O. Lovejoy (1941, p. 258) observed that in its relatively short life the word "Romanticism" had accumulated so many incongruous and opposed meanings that "it had therefore come to be useless as a verbal symbol". This has not inhibited scholars from using it and, indeed, by 1966 Isaiah Berlin (1999 [1966], p. 1) was telling us that "the literature on romanticism is larger than romanticism itself".

Lovejoy prefers to think in terms of a plurality of "Romanticisms". Many of them nevertheless share a few common features, which are well known and can probably be re-stated without too much argument. Broadly speaking, "Romanticism" refers to a period of European thought and art, running from the middle to late eighteenth century through to the 1840s. Within music, it is said to have had a later trajectory, taking it from the early 1800s through to the first decade of the twentieth century. By extension, the term also gets applied to any set of ideas that resembles those of the original Romantics. Scruton (1983, p. 414) notes that it has variously been applied to the writings of the Frankfurt School, to the early Marx and to the "irrationalist" philosophy of Sartre. Herbert Read and Kenneth Clark saw it as a permanent state of mind that might be found anywhere (Berlin 1991 [1966], p. 5).

Romanticism is generally seen to be a response to Enlightenment rationality, though the precise nature of that response is strongly contested. In art, it is associated with the rejection of artistic and literary conventions, in particular Neoclassicism. In both art and thought, imagination is elevated over reason, or, at the very least, given equal status. Emotion is celebrated over logic and intuition over science. There is a new emphasis on subjectivity. Romanticism is also widely associated with both the cult of nature and profound spirituality.

More than this, it is difficult to generalize. Romanticism is alternatively seen as a rejection of Enlightenment or as a further manifestation of it (Halsted 1969, pp. 1–15; Day 1996, pp. 175–176). Romantics are both revolutionary icons and conservative reactionaries, socially engaged or wallowing in introspection (Williams 1979 [1958], pp. 48–49; Eldridge 2001, p. 5). They are both anti-bourgeois and bourgeois through-and-through (Hobsbawm 2003 [1962], p. 314; Eldridge 2001, pp. 6–7). They are heralded as artistic innovators, yet exposed as derivative (Day 1996, p. 38). Romanticism represents "the greatest single shift in the consciousness of the West" (Berlin 1999 [1965], p. 1), or it is a male appropriation of the feminine so that the "male poet could claim to be God" (Day 1996, p. 191). It has been variously shown to underpin Russian communism, Nazi nationalism and the modern liberal democratic state (Lovejoy 1941, pp. 270–279; Abrams 1971 [1953], pp. 333–334; Day 1996, pp. 90–94).

The diversity of Romanticisms arises, of course, from the diversity of the Romantics themselves and from the different conditions to which they were, in part, responding. For example, the Romanticisms of Britain, a nation-state undergoing a rapid process of industrialization, were inflected very differently from those of a largely pre-industrial Germany, ruled by a number of petty courts and still a long way from nationhood. Nor was Romanticism a homogenous movement within individual countries. Romantics took up positions against other Romantics, as in the case of Shelley and Southey in England, and sometimes against themselves, as both Coleridge and Southey had done, in order to retract views expounded in an earlier life. In England, in contrast to Germany, Romantics did not even call themselves "Romantics" and the notion of a "Romantic Movement" did not really begin to take shape until the second half of the nineteenth century (Day 1996, p. 87).

Relating all these Romanticisms to cultural policy is clearly beyond the scope of one paper. I am therefore going to focus on three essays, which capture what we might call "moments" of English Romanticism – namely, Wordsworth's *Preface to the Lyrical Ballads* (1800), Wordsworth's *Essay, Supplementary to the Preface* (1815) and Shelley's *A Defence of Poetry* (1821). These essays are often held up as Romantic manifestos. More importantly for our purposes, in their assertion of particular cultural values and practices, they articulate a cultural policy which can still be seen to resonate today. They may even bear some responsibility for the prominence of the arts in the model of cultural action favoured by the state. Before we consider this, however, it is necessary to look briefly at the extent to which Wordsworth and Shelley, on the evidence of these essays, conform to the idea of the intellectual discussed above.

Romantics as Intellectuals

The *Preface to the Lyrical Ballads* is a short introduction to a collection of poems by Wordsworth and Coleridge. The collection necessitated a preface, according to Wordsworth, because it represented a radical new departure in the writing of poetry, which required some explanatory comment. Much of the *Preface* is taken up with a fairly technical discussion of stylistic matters, but Wordsworth also takes the opportunity to set out what he sees as the purpose of the poems, the nature of the poet and the function of poetry in society. The *Essay, Supplementary to the Preface* is an extended discussion of the relations between poets and the public, with particular reference to cultural populism and the operation of the market.

Shelley's *Defence of Poetry* was written in response to a semi-comic attack on poetry by his close friend, Thomas Love Peacock (1921 [1820]), who argued that although poetry might have served a useful function in the past, its importance in the new scientific age was now negligible. While scientists, historians and philosophers were engaged in the serious business of advancing knowledge, poets such as Wordsworth and Coleridge were, according to Peacock (1921 [1820], p. 15), "wallowing in the rubbish of departed ignorance ... to find ... rattles for the grown babies of the age". Shelley responded with an impassioned defence, developing Wordsworth's ideas on the function of poetry, advocating its moral power and articulating its value in advanced civilizations.

If we examine these essays, we find that both Wordsworth and Shelley share many of the characteristics of both the "heroic" intellectual and the "double image" discussed above. First of all, although they are both primarily concerned with poetic questions, they relate these to precisely those "global issues of truth, judgement and taste of the time" that Bauman considered to be essential to an intellectual's perspective. Those issues inevitably related to politics and ideology, with which, it will be recalled, Posner argued that intellectuals were always in some way engaged. Furthermore, both writers attempted to conduct their work, as Said and Furedi argued that intellectuals should, from "the standpoint of universality".

In Wordsworth's case, the object of poetry was "truth, not individual and local, but general, and operative". Moreover, the poet was to be "the rock of defence for human nature … [binding] together by passion and knowledge the vast empire of human society, as it is spread over the whole earth and over all time" (Wordsworth 1969 [1800], pp. 737–738). For Shelley, a poem was "the very image of life expressed in its eternal truth" and "ever still the light of life" (Shelley 1988 [1821], pp. 281, 286).

With these highly ambitious claims, both writers were ascribing to poetry healing and regenerative powers that they believed performed a vitally important role in all societies. They attempted to demonstrate this historically and at the same time show how these powers were never more needed than in the period through which they were living themselves. For Wordsworth, the development of industrial society and, in particular, the dehumanising nature of employment in the rapidly expanding cities, was having a deleterious effect on the mental faculties of the population. These developments, which were historically unprecedented, were acting "to blunt the discriminating powers of the mind, and … to reduce it to a state of almost savage torpor" (Wordsworth 1969 [1800], p. 735). The poet, speaking to the whole man rather than to his specialized and fragmented function, could have the effect of restoring him to himself.

Shelley pushed the analysis much further and in a more radical direction. How could it be, he asked, that science and economics could make such extraordinary advances in material productivity while the end result was only to increase rather than lighten the burden of most peoples' lives? What could explain "the exasperation of the inequality of mankind"? Shelley's answer was a failure of imagination – a failure to imagine what was rationally known and a failure to act on what could be imagined. "Our calculations have outrun conception", he argued. "The cultivation of those sciences which have enlarged the limits of the empire over the external world, has … proportionally circumscribed those of the internal world; and man, having enslaved the elements, remains himself a slave" (Shelley 1988 [1821], p. 293).

Shelley went on to argue that it was only through a development of the imagination that human beings would fully develop their sense of moral responsibility. "To be greatly good", he suggested, a man "must imagine intensely and comprehensively. … The pains and pleasure of his species must become his own." And it was, of course, poetry that would strengthen the faculty of imagination – in much the same way as exercise strengthened a limb. Poetry thus came to perform a vital social and moral function.

Shelley's claims did not end here. Poetry was not just one form of knowledge, it was the highest form of knowledge, which, by virtue of its identification with the imagination, lay behind all knowledge. Without the promptings of poetry, Shelley argued, the human mind could never have been awakened to what he called the "invention of the grosser sciences" and the application of analytical reasoning. Poetry was thus "the centre and circumference of knowledge; it is that which comprehends all science, and that to which all science must be referred. It is at the same time the root and blossom of all other systems of thought" (Shelley 1988 [1821], p. 293).

We can begin to see from these arguments how closely Wordsworth and Shelley also conformed to some of the other aspects of the "heroic" intellectual we outlined above. As poets, they saw themselves as a source of cultural and moral authority, identifying social ills and acting as the conscience of society. As such, they necessarily assumed an oppositional role, but it was a role for which only a few exceptionally gifted people were properly equipped. The poet might only be "a man speaking to men", as Wordsworth observed, but he is "endowed with more lively sensibility, more enthusiasm and tenderness ... [and] has a greater knowledge of human nature, and a more comprehensive soul" (Wordsworth 1969 [1800], p. 737). For Shelley, poets were not just the "the institutors of laws and the founders of civil society"; they were "the mirrors of the gigantic shadows which futurity casts upon the present" (Shelley 1988 [1821], pp. 279, 297).

Romantic poets, therefore, like intellectuals, were members of an elite group, and like intellectuals, they were engaged, to use Furedi's words, in a struggle to "capture the hearts and the minds of the public". But how were they to do this when they shared, also with intellectuals, one serious problem – namely, that the general public often either did not understand or was not interested in what they had to say?

Wordsworth devotes much of his *Essay, Supplementary to the Preface* to addressing this question. He sets out to demonstrate through historical example how the literature most highly valued by posterity was invariably not properly recognized in its own time. Moreover, it usually attracted fewer readers and sold less well than the work of inferior writers. Thus, for example, the poems of John Milton were far less popular in the seventeenth century than those of now little-known poets such as Cowley, Flatman and Waller. Neither popular taste nor contemporary criticism nor volume of sales could therefore be considered a reliable judge of quality. The kind of literature that received popular approbation was, according to Wordsworth, sensationalist, superficial or mindless. Shelley was even more scathing. "Accept no counsel from the simple-minded", he urged. "Time reverses the judgement of the foolish crowd. Contemporary criticism is no more than the sum of the folly with which genius has to wrestle" (Williams 1979 [1958], p. 51).

But how could this contempt for the opinions of the public be reconciled with the avowed aims of serving the public? Wordsworth's answer was to draw a distinction between the "public" and the "people". The "public" was characterized as those fallible people who made up the bulk of the actual reading public, buying the wrong books and promulgating the wrong standards of taste. The "people", on the other hand, represented what it was possible for people to become – that is to say, human beings with all their most noble potentialities realized. To the public, wrote Wordsworth, the writer would give as much deference as it was entitled to; but "to the people, philosophically characterised", he or she would give "devout respect and reverence" (Wordsworth 1969 [1815], p. 751). Wordsworth thus got round the problem of an indifferent or hostile "public" by appealing to an idealized and nonexistent "people". It was an ingenious answer, but not, of course, a solution.

On the basis of these essays, we can conclude that the Romantics, at least, as personified by Wordsworth and Shelley, were indeed intellectuals in the "heroic" mould. But it is also possible to see how those "unfavourable implications", which have long been associated with intellectuals, might also attach themselves to Romantics and produce that "double image". Of course, it is hardly possible to level the charge of emotional repression and cold rationalism when Romanticism is so deeply associated with the celebration of feeling, but in all other respects, the negative connotations of "the intellectual", which we identified above, apply equally to the Romanticism of Wordsworth and Shelley.

First of all, however much we might see the Romantic claims for the imagination as a humane and genuine response to the sufferings of the age it is difficult to avoid the conclusion that it was a hopelessly impractical response. There is even an implicit recognition of this, which can be painful to read, in Wordsworth's (1969 [1800], p. 735) own description of his "feeble endeavour" to counteract the tendencies of the age and in Shelley's (1988 [1821], p. 297) famous cry that "poets are the unacknowledged legislators of the world". They remained unacknowledged because they could not, in practice, fulfil the role that had been prescribed for them. Wordsworth and Shelley had produced embryonic theories of art and society that had considerable rhetorical power, but they remained at the level of theory.

Secondly, these essays reflected a powerful – if defensive – sense of self-importance, which, it will be recalled, was another of those "unfavourable implications". When Wordsworth tells us that a poet is a very special kind of person with "a more comprehensive soul" than other people, he is, of course, telling us that *he* is a very special kind of person. Shelley does the same when he tells us that poets "sound the depths of human nature with a comprehensive and all-penetrating spirit". But there was more than a personal self-aggrandisement going on here. At the same time, a defensive ideology was being constructed in which creativity and imagination were being hived off from other spheres of life in an attempt to claim them for the exclusive province of art.

Thirdly, in these essays Wordsworth and Shelley displayed the assumption of cultural and moral superiority that Carey and others had identified in so many modern intellectuals. We have already seen how dismissive they were of popular taste. In the *Preface to the Lyrical Ballads*, we were also given a very explicit statement of how a particular kind of cultural refinement was associated with social superiority. "The human mind", Wordsworth (1969 [1800], p. 735) suggested, "is capable of being excited without the application of gross and violent stimulants". And "one being", he went on to say, "*is elevated above another* [emphasis added], in proportion as he possesses this capability". It was the task of the poet (at least that of the poet who wrote the kind of poems that Wordsworth did) "to endeavour to enlarge this capability". For Shelley, as we have seen, poets were engaged in an essentially moral enterprise. Inevitably, they thus inhabited a morally superior world to those who went about the more mundane business of making money. "Poetry", he told us, "and the principle of self, of which money is the visible incarnation, are the God and Mammon of the world" (Shelley 1988 [1821], p. 293).

There was, of course, some irony in Shelley's lofty attitude towards money. As the only son of a wealthy baronet, he was a man of independent means who could be assured of his inheritance, even though the relationship with his father had broken down altogether (Holmes 1995, pp. 110–111). His autonomy as an intellectual was therefore a product of precisely those unequal class relations that he ostensibly rejected. Indeed, there is some evidence to suggest that he was not even as free from the prejudices of his class as he liked to think (Holmes 1995, p. 151).

Wordsworth, on the other hand, suffered financial problems for a good part of his life and needed to make his accommodations if he was to provide adequately for his family. As is well known, he moved from the radicalism of his youth to various degrees of reactionary conservatism in his middle and late years. By 1818 (he was born in 1770), he was campaigning tirelessly for the Tories. By the time of the 1832 Reform Bill, he was writing that in setting the nation on the path to universal suffrage, the authors of the Bill were "committing a greater political crime than any recorded in History" (Gill 1990, p. 363).

In their different ways, therefore, Wordsworth and Shelley were reflecting the contradictions and compromises inherent in the idea of the autonomous intellectual. In this, as we have seen in so many other respects, they were sharing that double image that appears to be bound up with the very idea of the intellectual itself. On the one hand, these Romantics were engaged in a "heroic" intellectual struggle against what they perceived to be the iniquities of the age; on the other, they were fallible human beings, exaggerating the importance of their own role in response to a deeply felt sense of marginality in a rapidly changing world.

As Williams (1979 [1958], p. 63) observes with characteristic generosity, when we consider the lives of these men it is unlikely that we will be "betrayed into the irritability of prosecution". Their pretensions, with hindsight, may only be too easy to mock. But the project on which they were engaged was informed by principles that were deeply and widely humane.

Romantics and Cultural Policy

It will already be obvious to the reader that if cultural policy is understood as "the politics of culture in the most general sense", then Wordsworth and Shelley were both deeply implicated in it. Let me try and recapitulate the key themes that have emerged from the essays we have been discussing.

First, the poet is a special kind of person with a superior understanding. He or she is more sensitive and imaginative, has quasi-mystical powers and sees things that other people do not see. Because he or she is in touch with the most profound and unchanging elements of the human spirit, the poet speaks to all people across all time and space. He or she is therefore both a universal and a unifying figure.

Secondly, poets are not in control of their own creative processes. Poetry comes into being through inspiration and cannot be composed through an act of the will. It would be more accurate to say that the poem speaks through the poet than the poet speaks the poem.

Thirdly, poetry, by virtue of its imaginative power, has the capacity to awaken the imaginative potential of others. Because imagination is at the root of empathy, and because empathy promotes moral conduct, poetry thus fulfils a vital moral function.

Fourthly, the role of poetry becomes even more important with the development of modern, industrial societies. As the division of labour grows and the manufacturing cities expand, people become fragmented and alienated. They are seen more as specialized instruments of production than as human beings. Poetry can counteract these tendencies with its holistic power.

Fifthly, the growth of inequality and all its attendant problems is the consequence of the application of an unimaginative rationality. Poetry provides the imaginative resources for a moral re-ordering of society.

Sixthly, the kind of poetry that will achieve these aims is of a higher order than the ordinary, popular culture that is supplied by the market. Furthermore, poetry of this order does not lend itself to easy and immediate "consumption"; it requires a cooperating effort on the part of the reader, who has to work if the poetry is to yield up its full effect. Popular culture, on the other hand, tends to be superficial and basic, designed to appeal without effort to people whose tastes have been degraded by the conditions of modern, industrial society. Great art is rarely properly appreciated in its own time; however, it speaks to and realizes the ideal self that exists inside every person.

Finally, the spirit of poetry does not only inhabit its own domain. It is synonymous with creativity and therefore underpins all other knowledge. It thus occupies the primary position in any account of a general culture.

This brief summary cannot, of course, do justice to the complexity, allusions and sheer intensity of the essays themselves. But I think it conveys enough to show how, in their assertion of particular cultural values and practices, Wordsworth and Shelley were, at this point in their lives, deeply involved in the articulation of what we would now call cultural policies. Their aim was no less than a transformation of society; the means were to be a revolution of the imagination. But, as noted earlier, these "policies" remained at the level of theory only. There was no strategy for putting them into practice, nor was it possible to see how one might be developed.

As far as state cultural policy was concerned, the English Romantics had little influence in their own time. Governments of the day rarely engaged with culture in an explicit way and, when they did, the political and financial investment was minimal. It is perhaps possible to see echoes of Romanticism later in the century in the debates around government support for a National Gallery. Robert Peel and William Gladstone, for example, Conservative and Liberal prime ministers respectively, both justified support for the arts on the grounds of their civilising potential. Yet the kind of "civilization" that politicians had in mind had far more to do with the maintenance of public order at a time of political unrest than with the project of social transformation envisaged by Wordsworth and Shelley (Bennett 1995b, pp. 201–210).

However, the influence of these writers worked itself through in other ways. Raymond Williams (1979 [1958], p. 58), for example, saw their particular brand of Romanticism as initiating a way of thinking about the arts that became highly influential with other intellectuals. This was not, of course, to claim that they were without their own intellectual influences. The connections with other Romanticisms, particularly those of Rousseau, Goethe and Schiller, can be clearly seen. If the ideas are taken in the abstract, they can also be related to a number of classical texts. But in the positioning of poetry, and by extension the arts, as a humanizing power that works against the disintegrating tendencies of the age, these writers were laying down a significantly new emphasis.

The extension of the case for poetry into one for the arts in general was begun by Wordsworth and Shelley themselves. Poetry might reflect the faculty of the imagination in its purest form, but this faculty could also manifest itself through the other arts. In Shelley's view, this was because all artists were, at root, poets and their art was but another expression of the spirit of poetry (Shelley 1988 [1821], p. 293). What started, therefore, as a defence of poetry in particular ended up as a general theory of the arts and society, which took off in a number of different directions as the century progressed. This is what Nicholas Garnham, mentioned above, referred to as "the tradition of idealist cultural analysis". In its English form, its most prominent exponent was probably Matthew Arnold, whose connections with both Romanticism and modern forms of cultural policy I have explored elsewhere (Bennett 2005).

What is interesting is not only the degree to which this tradition, and the Romantic ideas that stand at the head of it, appear to have inspired the architects of modern forms of state cultural policy, but also that these ideas continue to exert their influence. Perhaps the most striking example of the former was the separating out of a particular notion of art from culture and then according it a privileged institutional position. The construction of a state cultural policy based on the arts, which we noted earlier, can in many respects be seen as an institutional reflection of the status accorded to poetry by Wordsworth and Shelley.

The creation by government of the Arts Council of Great Britain in 1946 was an illustration of precisely these tendencies. If we exclude the British Broadcasting Corporation, it was the first organization to be formed with a national remit for the promotion of culture, and what was to be promoted was a high-minded artistic culture. In a radio broadcast by its first chairman, John Maynard Keynes, to mark the Council's inauguration, the debt to English Romanticism could not have been clearer. "The artist", he told us, "walks where the breath of the spirit blows him. He cannot be told his direction; he does not know it himself. But he leads the rest of us into fresh pastures and teaches us to love and enjoy what we often begin by rejecting, enlarging our sensibility and purifying our instincts" (Keynes 1946, p. 21). In 1989, in his introduction to the Arts Council's Annual report, the then Chairman, Peter Palumbo (1989, p. 3), renewed the debt with a deliberate re-statement of Keynes's words. In many respects, post-war cultural policy in Britain was itself a Romantic project.

As noted earlier, the Greater London Council in the 1980s and New Labour in the 1990s, through its new Department for Culture, Media and Sport, both attempted to expand the scope of their cultural policies so that they engaged with popular culture and the so-called "cultural" or "creative" industries. On the face of it, this did indeed mark a significant shift away from Garnham's "tradition of idealist cultural analysis", but at the same time, it by no means signalled its extinction. For example, the Arts Council of Great Britain, now expanded into separate councils for England, Scotland, Wales and Northern Ireland, continues to exist. Between 2003 and 2006, the English Council alone will spend over £2 billion of public funds on the arts that it considers to have an inherent value, but which are not able to survive through the operation of the market alone. These arts, according to the Council, "have the power to transform lives and communities". Moreover, in an extension worthy of Shelley himself, the Council tells us that it will bring this "transforming power to bear on issues of crime, health, education and inclusion". In this enterprise, the artist is described as the "life source" of the Council's work (Arts Council England 2002, pp. 2–10).

Chris Smith (1998), New Labour's first Minister of Culture (who, incidentally, wrote a doctoral thesis on Wordsworth and Coleridge), also continues the Romantic tradition. "The arts", he claims, "fire the imagination and inspire the intelligence. ... They lead us into a world unknown to previous perception. ... They are one of the main factors by which we assess a civilization" (Smith 1998, pp. 43, 49). He even goes so far as to suggest, with an almost explicit reference to Shelley, that the Industrial Revolution went wrong "when people forgot about the empowering process of ideas and relied on mechanical development to bring improvement" (Smith 1998, p. 29).

I hope these few examples are enough to show how the influence of English Romanticism can still be read into the cultural policy debates of today. There are many other different ways in which it can be seen to manifest itself, but space does not permit a full exploration. It can be read, for example, into the fashion for seeing "creativity" as the answer to problems in all departments of life; it can be seen in the endless fascination of the public with the celebrity artist as a special kind of person; and it can be read into the many – and often defensive – pronouncements of artists and arts organizations as they seek to persuade us of their value to society.

The question remains of why. Why should these Romantic ideas still continue to resonate two hundred years after they were written? They have, after all, as we have seen, been subject to some very robust challenges – in particular, from those seeking a more materialist analysis of culture. The answer perhaps lies in the knowledge that the world evoked so powerfully by the Romantics, and with which they often struggled so hard, is still in many respects recognizably our own. We live, in Britain as elsewhere, in what appears to be a permanent condition of accelerating industrial revolution. It is driven, as so many have observed, by new and more aggressive forms of global capitalism (Bennett 2001, pp. 178–197). What Shelley described as "an unmitigated exercise of the calculating faculty" has arguably intensified, leaving large numbers of people with the sense that society exists more for the economy than the other way round.

Williams (1979 [1958], p. 271) criticized nineteenth-century idealist thinkers for separating out their moral and intellectual concerns from the fundamental questions of economic organization. It is a charge that can be levelled at both Wordsworth and Shelley, whose "ideology of the imagination" might seem a hopelessly inadequate response to the conditions of industrial capitalism. Nevertheless, alternative economic systems that better meet the needs of their societies have proved obdurately difficult to create and sustain. In this respect, it is the writings of the "materialist" Karl Marx or William Morris that might appear the more-old fashioned.

Wordsworth and Shelley did not offer economic prescriptions; they sought to respond on entirely different terms. What Williams and others have perceived as their greatest deficiency may in fact have been the very characteristics that have ensured the longevity of their ideas. When economic reasoning dominates, the desire to find other logics can become very strong. It is this, above all, that perhaps explains why the Romantic "revolution of the imagination", which embodies those other logics so powerfully, continues to remain seductive.

REFERENCES

ABRAMS, M. (1971 [1953]) *The Mirror and the Lamp*, Oxford University Press, Oxford.

AHEARNE, J. (2004) *Between Cultural Theory and Policy: The Cultural Policy Thinking of Pierre Bourdieu, Michel de Certeau and Regis Debray*, Centre for Cultural Policy Studies, University of Warwick, Coventry.

ARTS COUNCIL ENGLAND (2002) *Ambitions for the Arts, 2003–2006*, Arts Council England, London.

BAUMAN, Z. (1987) *Legislators and Interpreters: On Modernity, Post-modernity and Intellectuals*, Polity Press, Cambridge.

BENNETT, O. (1995a) 'Cultural policy and management in Europe', *Tidskrift för Kultur Studier*, vol. 1, pp. 108–120.

BENNETT, O. (1995b) 'Cultural policy in the United Kingdom: Collapsing rationales and the end of a tradition', *European Journal of Cultural Policy*, vol. 1, no. 2, pp. 199–216

BENNETT, O. (2001) *Cultural Pessimism: Narratives of Decline in the Postmodern World*, Edinburgh University Press, Edinburgh.

BENNETT, O. (2004) 'The torn halves of cultural policy research', *International Journal of Cultural Policy*, vol. 10, no. 2, pp. 237–248.

BENNETT, O. (2005) 'Beyond machinery: The cultural policies of Matthew Arnold', *History of Political Economy*, vol. 37, no. 3, pp. 455–482.

BENNETT, T. (1992) 'Putting policy into cultural studies', in *Cultural Studies*, eds L. Grossberg, C. Nelson & P. Treichler, Routledge, London, pp. 23–27.

BERLIN, I. (1999 [1965]) *The Roots of Romanticism*, ed. H. Hardy, Chatto & Windus, London.

CAREY, J. (1992) *Intellectuals and the Masses: Pride and Prejudice among the Literary Intelligentsia, 1880–1939*, Faber & Faber, London.

CAREY, J. (2005) *What Good Are the Arts?*, Faber & Faber, London.

DAY, A. (1996) *Romanticism*, Routledge, London.

ELDRIDGE, R. (2001) *The Persistence of Romanticism: Essays in Philosophy and Literature*, Cambridge University Press, Cambridge.

FUREDI, F. (2004) *Where Have All the Intellectuals Gone? Confronting 21st Century Philistinism*, Continuum, London.

GARNHAM, N. & EPSTEIN, J. (1985) 'Cultural industries, consumption and policy', in *The State of the Art or the Art of the State: Strategies for the Cultural Industries in London*, Industry and

Employment Branch, Department for Recreation and the Arts, Greater London Council, London, pp. 145–165.

GILL, S. (1990) *William Wordsworth: A Life,* Oxford University Press, Oxford.

HALSTED, J. (1969) 'Introduction', in *Romanticism,* Macmillan, London, pp. 1–42.

HOBSBAWM, E. (2003 [1962]) *The Age of Revolution, 1789–1848,* Abacus, London.

HOLMES, R. (1995) *Shelley: The Pursuit,* Flamingo, London.

KEYNES, J. (1946) 'The Arts Council: Its policy and hopes', in *Arts Council of Great Britain: First Annual Report,* Arts Council of Great Britain, London, pp. 20–23.

LEWIS, J. & MILLER, T. (2003) 'Introduction', in *Critical Cultural Policy Studies: A Reader,* Blackwell, Oxford, pp. 1–9.

LOVEJOY, A. (1941) 'The meaning of Romanticism for the historian of ideas', *Journal of the History of Ideas,* vol. 2, no. 3, pp. 257–278.

MCGUIGAN, J. (1996) *Culture and the Public Sphere,* Routledge, London.

MCGUIGAN, J. (2004) *Rethinking Cultural Policy,* Open University Press, Maidenhead.

MULGAN, G. & WARPOLE, K. (1986) *Saturday Night or Sunday Morning? From Arts to Industry: New Forms of Cultural Policy,* Comedia, London.

NIELSEN, H. (1991) 'Critical public agent or hired hand? Perspectives for research on cultural policy', *European Journal of Cultural Policy,* vol. 5, no. 2, pp. 183–198.

PALUMBO, P. (1989) 'Chairman's introduction', in *44th Arts Council Annual Report,* Arts Council of Great Britain, London, pp. 2–3.

PEACOCK, T. (1921 [1820]) 'The four ages of poetry', in *The Four Ages of Poetry Etc.,* ed. H. Brett-Smith, Basil Blackwell, Oxford, pp. 3–19.

POSNER, R. (2003) *Public Intellectuals: A Study of Decline,* Harvard University Press, Cambridge, MA.

ROTH, P. (2000) *The Human Stain,* Jonathan Cape, London.

SAID, E. (1994) *Representations of the Intellectual,* Vintage, London.

SCHUSTER, J. (2002) *Informing Cultural Policy: The Research and Information Infrastructure,* Center for Urban Policy and Research, Edward J. Bloustein School of Planning and Public Policy, Rutgers University, New Brunswick, NJ.

SCRUTON, R. (1983) *A Dictionary of Political Thought,* Pan Books, London.

SELWOOD, S. (2006) 'A part to play? The academic contribution to the development of cultural policy in England', *International Journal of Cultural Policy,* vol. 12, no. 1, pp. 35–53.

SHELLEY, P. (1988 [1821]) 'A defence of poetry', in *Shelley's Prose,* ed. D. Clark, Fourth Estate, London, pp. 275–297.

SMITH, C. (1998) *Creative Britain,* Faber & Faber, London.

STANBRIDGE, A. (2005) 'Display options: Discourses of art and context in the contemporary museum', *International Journal of Cultural Policy,* vol. 11, no. 2, pp. 157–170.

TUSA, J. (1999) *Arts Matters: Reflecting on Culture,* Methuen, London.

UNITED NATIONS EDUCATIONAL, SCIENTIFIC AND CULTURAL ORGANIZATION (UNESCO) (1969) *Cultural Policy: A Preliminary Study,* UNESCO, Paris.

WILLIAMS, R. (1979 [1958]) *Culture and Society, 1780–1950,* Penguin Books, Harmondsworth.

WILLIAMS, R. (1981a) *Culture,* Fontana, Glasgow.

WILLIAMS, R. (1981b) *Keywords: A Vocabulary of Culture and Society,* Fontana, Glasgow.

WORDSWORTH, W. (1969 [1800]) 'Preface to the lyrical ballads', in *Wordsworth: Poetical Works,* eds T. Hutchinson & E. de Selincourt, Oxford University Press, Oxford, pp. 734–743.

WORDSWORTH, W. (1969 [1815]) 'Essay, supplementary to the preface', in *Wordsworth: Poetical Works,* eds T. Hutchinson & E. de Selincourt, Oxford University Press, Oxford, pp. 743–751.

KNOWING HER PLACE
Jane Addams, pragmatism and cultural policy

Chris Bilton

Introduction

Born in 1860, Jane Addams was an American social reformer best known for her practical contributions to educational and industrial reform, women's and children's rights and pacifism. She was the co-founder of Hull House in 1889, a "settlement house" in Chicago where she continued to be involved in practical politics, education and social work throughout her life. She was also linked to Theodore Roosevelt's Progressive Party in 1912, and to national and international campaigns for social justice, including the National Association for the Advancement of Colored Peoples, the American Civil Liberties Union and the Women's International League for Peace and Freedom.

Addams does not have a reputation as an intellectual, despite her links to American pragmatism and the philosopher John Dewey.[1] Indeed her mistrust of abstract thought and moral certainty can be seen to place her within a tradition of American anti-intellectualism (Lasch 1965a). Her legacy is considered, if at all, in relation to her practical contributions to social work, social reform, feminism and internationalism, not in terms of cultural policy.

In choosing to focus on Addams as an intellectual, this paper is concerned not with the intellectual content of her writings, but with an ongoing commentary on the meaning and value of "the intellectual" (both as a mode of thought and as a type of person) projected through Addams' life and work. Her two volumes of autobiography (Addams 1990 [1910], 1930) describe not only her own story as a young woman searching for her place in the world, but also offer an extended meditation on the role of the intellectual in society, written during a period of rapid social and political change.

In this paper I want to focus on two aspects of Addams' intellectual legacy for cultural policy, first as an early advocate of cultural reform and cultural democratization, and second as somebody whose doubts regarding the place of the intellectual in American society were integral to her intellectual development. These two themes converge in her own life history, leading to a series of questions she asked herself regarding the value and purpose of culture and her own place in the world as a "woman of culture". Her views on culture and society are entangled with her own emotional history and with a particular juncture in the development of the educated middle class in America and Britain. The self-doubt of the young Addams reflects a wider crisis in the nineteenth-century tradition of genteel, middle-class culture. Her self-discovery as a social reformer reflects the emergent contradictions in twentieth-century cultural democratization.

The Woman of Culture

Jane Addams was one of a generation of college-educated young women who inherited a classical liberal arts education. This tradition had evolved in the ancient universities of Britain to meet the needs of the clergy and nobility, furnishing their minds with knowledge of literature and the arts acquired through a study of classic texts. By the second half of the nineteenth century, this tradition of aristocratic "useless knowledge" was challenged first by an expansion in higher education as a result of successive educational reforms, and second by a growing emphasis on social utility. The new generation of civic colleges in Britain and the United States, alongside the research institutions in Germany, emphasized vocational education and applied research, geared to the new needs of industry and the rising middle class (Jarausch 1983). The new universities in Bristol, London and Chicago were geographically and intellectually distant from the ancient universities of Oxford and Cambridge or New England. By the late nineteenth century, the generalist curriculum of liberal arts education appeared out of step with the times.

The old traditions persisted in three areas. First, the established universities (Oxford and Cambridge in Britain, Harvard and the Ivy League colleges in the United States) remained defiantly attached to the old humanist curriculum, a result of vested interests and internal politics as much as any intellectual commitment. Second, smaller religious colleges in the United States also resisted reform, partly as a result of their religious affiliations. Finally, the expanded area of women's higher education in the United States maintained the "genteel" tradition of "culture studies" into the late nineteenth century (Garrison 1979).

Instead of abandoning the classical curriculum, the American women's colleges of the 1870s emphasized the social utility and vocational application of cultural education in preparing the female student to uphold the ideal of true womanhood both in the home and in society as teachers and missionaries. Smith College (founded 1875) hoped its graduates would influence society by "forming manners and morals, moulding society, and shaping public sentiment", while the founder of Wellesley (also 1875) described higher education as "putting on God's armour for the contest" in preparation for a life of "noble usefulness"

(Rousmaniere 1970, pp. 50–51). Thus while these new institutions continued to emphasize the value of liberal education, they did so in terms of its social purpose; "culture" was to be made useful in the home and the school, religion was to be applied to practical social problems. This combination of cultural idealism and social purpose inspired a range of outreach activities including university extension classes and missionary activities among the urban poor. These activities were seen by their founders as a necessary outlet for a redundant educational inheritance.[2]

The nineteenth-century settlement house was a product of this attempt to make "culture" useful, and attempted to give "extension classes" a permanent physical home. In 1882 the Oxford-educated clergyman Samuel Barnett led a colony of male Oxford graduates into London's East End and established Toynbee Hall.[3] The new institution was driven by Barnett's feelings of social obligation alongside his idealization of the transforming power of culture. These ideas resonated with the idealistic young graduates who took up residence in Toynbee Hall. Here they introduced a programme of cultural and educational activities designed to "improve" the urban poor by furnishing their minds rather than simply alleviating material poverty.

When Jane Addams established Hull House in Chicago seven years later, she too was influenced by her educational inheritance as a college-educated young woman, as well as by the example of Toynbee Hall. According to Addams, the settlement house was "an attempt to relieve, at the same time, the overaccumulation at one end of society and the destitution at the other; but it [the settlement] assumes that this overaccumulation and destitution is most sorely felt in the things that pertain to social and educational privileges" (Addams 1990 [1910], p. 86). In other words, the settlement house was intended not only to relieve poverty and cultural disenfranchisement, but also to provide a useful social purpose for the accumulated educational privileges of young graduates and, by extension, for the institutions which educated them. For Addams, the settlement house was a "subjective necessity", not just an objective response to social injustice.

It is tempting to see in the settlement house a last bastion of Arnoldian culture, a symbol of "sweetness and light" in the inner city, and to see the settlement workers themselves as Arnold's "apostles of equality", constructing an idealized classless society based around a programme of morally uplifting cultural activities.[4] Some of the literature on Addams and other pioneering cultural reformers is unashamedly sentimental and heroic in tone, singling out for special praise a handful of individuals who championed the cultural rights of the poor and the marginalized (e.g., see Davis 1967, 1973; Elshtain 2001). Another school of thought identifies the cultural missionaries as agents of social control, imposing normative values on the sub-cultures of the urban poor and especially on the young (Huggins 1971; Platt 1969; Gans 1962, 1964; Karger 1987). Both the heroic and the hegemonic accounts of Addams and the settlement movement underestimate the complexity of Addams' motives, in particular her doubts as to the meaning and value of "culture". These doubts were a product of her education. In Addams' characteristic tone of uncertainty and self-criticism, she was sounding a different note from the well-meaning confidence in the power of culture voiced by Barnett. To understand the origins of these differences we must examine Addams' education further.

Education and Crisis

For Addams, self-doubt and loss of faith in the cultural ideal were the starting point for her intellectual contribution to cultural policy and her work in the settlement project. As a child, Addams described her feelings of unworthiness, particularly alongside her father whom she venerated. She was even fearful of being seen with him in public, hoping that "the ugly, pigeon-toed little girl, whose crooked back obliged her to walk with her head held very much upon one side, would never be pointed out to these visitors as the daughter of this fine man" (Addams 1990 [1910], p. 11). When her father died in 1881, the young Jane Addams was plunged into depression, and referred to the "black days" which followed his death (Addams 1990 [1910], p. 39). At around the same time, treatment of her "crooked back" resulted in physical illness and "a state of nervous exhaustion with which I struggled for years" (Addams 1990 [1910], p. 48). Upon graduating in 1882,[5] like many educated women from wealthy American families at the time, she set off for Europe. Over the next seven years she embarked on two trips, taking in the expected stops on the grand European tour. It was during a visit to London in 1888 that Addams and her companion Ellen Starr encountered the English settlement movement, visiting Toynbee Hall in London's East End.

According to the heroic narrative of Addams' career, this was the moment of redemption, when she discovered a sense of moral purpose and embarked on her new life as a cultural missionary. The darkness of physical pain and psychological damage was lit up by the beacon of European culture. However, Christopher Lasch has introduced a very different explanation of what happened to Addams during her time in Europe. According to Lasch (1965a, pp. 25–29), Addams' decision to found Hull House in 1889 stemmed from a subjective sense of revulsion against her family, class and culture, sparked by her second visit to Europe in 1888. Her distress at the poverty she encountered there mingled with "a sense of futility, of misdirected energy, the belief that the pursuit of cultivation would not in the end bring either solace or relief" (Addams 1990 [1910], p. 51). Her firsthand encounter with European culture crystallized traditions and values she had previously experienced through the tradition of liberal arts education at the seminary, but now she felt "a moral revulsion against this feverish searching after culture" (Addams 1990 [1910], p. 53). The moment of epiphany came when she attended a bullfight in Madrid in April 1888. Here was a different, more visceral European culture. Instead of sweetness and light, Addams confronted a violence which at once fascinated and repelled her. In the disapproval of her companions, Addams felt herself "tried and condemned, not only by this disgusting experience but by the entire moral situation which it revealed" (Addams 1990 [1910], p. 60). That moral situation reflected the stark contrast between the aesthetic beauty and grandeur of the occasion and its underlying cruelty and suffering. The mix of attraction and repulsion she felt at the bullfight seemed to bring to a head her confused response to the useless beauty of European culture. The object of her disgust was partly herself, but it was also the pursuit of culture, "a hateful, vicious circle which even the apostles of culture themselves admitted" (Addams 1990 [1910], p. 51).

Lasch finds a biographical explanation for Addams' crisis of faith in culture, linking it to the depression following her father's death, her loss of religious faith while at the seminary and her childhood feelings of inadequacy. Four years later,[6] in "The Subjective Necessity for Social Settlements", Addams herself offers an alternative basis for her feelings of futility in the education of young American women: "We have in America a fast-growing number of cultivated young people who have no recognized outlet for their active faculties. They hear constantly of the great social maladjustment, but no way is provided for them to change it, and their uselessness hangs about them heavily." As in many of her writings, autobiography merges with third person narrative. When Addams describes seeing "young girls suffer and grow sensibly lowered in vitality in the first years after they leave school" and claims that "the sense of uselessness is the severest shock which the human system can sustain", she brings a vividly personal dimension to the crisis in the idea of culture. But these personal feelings of bitterness and self-recrimination are rooted in education. Prepared by her upbringing for a life of refinement as a "woman of culture" yet "taught to be self-forgetting and self-sacrificing", the college-educated young woman is held back by social conventions and family expectations. In the unresolved conflict between "the social claim" and "the family claim", Addams identified "all the elements of a tragedy" (Addams 1990 [1910], pp. 82–83).

Addams' self-doubt is in marked contrast to the confident pronouncements of Samuel Barnett, the founding father of the British settlement movement. Barnett and his wife Henrietta believed firmly in the saving power of culture. Activities at Toynbee Hall included university extension classes, debating clubs, art exhibitions and visits to "friends" in the country (Barnett 1888). Despite the emphasis on "practicable" interventions, notably in researching and publicizing the conditions of poverty and in pushing for social legislation and improved municipal provision, Barnett emphasized that poverty was not simply an aggregate of material wants. He focused instead on the "cultural" condition of poverty and its debilitating effect on the individual's "character" and capacities. At the individual level, the problem of poverty was to be addressed in cultural terms by restoring dignity, independence and self-respect to the working man. Barnett identified this "common culture" with the habits of thought and behaviour fostered by a classical liberal education, specifically with the "culture" of the male Oxford graduate. According to one commentator, the young men who came to Toynbee Hall were schooled in a tradition of "manly Christianity", which owed as much to Thomas Arnold, the headmaster of Rugby School, as to Matthew Arnold, the writer of *Culture and Anarchy* (Meacham 1987, pp. 1–9).

In contrast, Addams arrived at Hull House "without any preconceived social theories or economic views" (Addams 1990 [1910], p. 5). According to her, the American settlement worker was both the product of a liberal education and in revolt against it. The inspiration behind Hull House was not a faith in culture, but a crisis of faith and the settlement's promise of "social and individual salvation" (Addams 1990 [1910], p. 87) extended not just to the urban poor, but to the college-educated young woman. The settlement would provide the necessary outlet for her active faculties by applying her skills to real social problems, while the settlement's quasi-domestic context and its emphasis on "culture" would satisfy the claims of her family, her class and her "cultivated" background. While the residents of Toynbee Hall were all men, the American settlement movement was dominated by college women who (according to Addams) shared her more ambiguous relationship to their own cultural legacy.

Addams identified the displacement of the intellectual class from the realm of social action. Matthew Arnold described his men and women of culture as "aliens", not bound to any social class or personal interest, loyal only to the general perfection of culture. Addams identifies the alienation of these aliens. She describes young people who "bear the brunt of being cultivated into un-nourished, oversensitive lives. They have been shut off from the common labor by which they live which is a great source of moral and physical health. They feel a fatal want of harmony between their theory and their lives, a lack of coordination between thought and action" (Addams 1990 [1910], p. 80). This alienation was what bound them to the poor immigrants they claimed to help, whom Addams (1990 [1910], p. 70) described as "people of former education and opportunity who have cherished ambitions and prospects, but who are caricatures of what they meant to be". She likens her own sense of disconnection to observing a stream of working people through the plate glass window of a hotel. Intellectually, the settlement would aim to breach this division and reconnect thought and action, an impulse that would lead Addams towards the philosophy of pragmatism (Addams 1990 [1910], p. 81). Addams' plate glass window also served as a mirror, and the project of cultural democratization was directed inwards towards a crisis in the educated middle class as much as it was directed outwards to the immigrant poor. Addams and her co-workers saw in the Americanized immigrants and displaced intellectuals now living in Chicago's slums an image of their own disconnection, and through their interaction with these communities sought to reconstruct their own identity.

In terms of cultural policy, Jane Addams represents a certain type of intellectual, the product of a crisis in the nineteenth-century ideal of culture. This crisis was experienced by a new generation of educated young men and women at the turn of the century who could no longer believe in the saving power of culture, yet were bound to it by experience. The crisis was made immediate by changes in nineteenth-century universities, where the humanist generalist curriculum of "liberal arts education" was challenged by ideas of social reform and social change and by an emergent utilitarianism. The heirs to that tradition struggled to make sense of their contradictory inheritance.

The Contradictions of Cultural Outreach

These developments need to be seen in the wider context of late nineteenth-century cultural institutions and the "civilizing mission". This was the time when the museums and libraries were being created as a result of state intervention and private philanthropy. The infrastructure of much of our contemporary cultural life in Britain and America was laid down during the last thirty years of the nineteenth century. Useful culture was not just an outlet for disaffected, middle-class Oxford graduates and American college women. The settlement houses developed alongside other cultural institutions designed to civilize the newly enfranchised working class. Many settlement houses including Hull House and Toynbee Hall[7] have continued to provide a focus for local cultural activities and played a part in the community arts movement of the 1970s and 1980s.

The impulses behind the attempt to "democratize" culture in the late nineteenth century, and continuing into our own times, are as complicated and contradictory as Jane Addams' decision to set up Hull House. On the one hand, commentators see in the civilizing mission an attempt to legitimize bourgeois taste and values by imposing a normative "culture" on the working class. There were expectations that museums and art galleries would soften the masses, making workers more malleable and less rebellious, or that exposing artisans to classical art would help to improve design quality in manufacturing industry. Others saw in the cultural mission a religious duty, raising the best qualities in the ordinary working man and developing morality and self-discipline. Some, like Samuel Barnett and his wife Henrietta, believed that culture was a genuine source of good in its own right, a way of improving the whole person by presenting them with what Matthew Arnold called "a general perfection". In the United States, cultural institutions in general and settlement houses in particular were set to play an important part in "Americanizing" the new immigrant population. Over all of this hung an unresolved debate about the meaning and value of culture in society.

When we examine the motives and personal stories behind cultural democratization today, I believe the experience of Addams encapsulates some of the inherent contradictions of "outreach work" or making the arts "accessible". On the one hand, there is an attempt to make culture "useful" and democratic. This attempt is as much to do with rehabilitating a displaced "redundant" middle-class culture as with addressing any identifiable needs among the recipients of cultural largesse. On the other hand, there is a residual faith in culture which continues to pursue social change by cultural means, rather than addressing the material causes of social change by tackling poverty and social exclusion directly.

If culture is merely an instrument for social change, why not find a better instrument? Writing eleven years after Addams, in 1903, the young William Beveridge, then a resident of Toynbee Hall, dismissed the idea that "colossal evils" could be remedied by "small doses of culture and charity and amiability" and claimed to distrust the "saving power of culture and mission and isolated good feeling as a surgeon distrusts 'Christian Science'" (Meacham 1987, p. 137).[8] Beveridge was typical of a more pragmatic, progressive strain among the second generation of residents at Toynbee Hall. In Britain, Toynbee Hall and the English settlement movement evolved into a kind of alternative finishing school for educated young men like Beveridge and R. H. Tawney, helping to mould a new professional class who would eventually administer reform on behalf of the poor. The cultural missionary work was no longer directly relevant to the problem of poverty (other than as a "gap year" indulgence) and cultural democratization would eventually be replaced by political democratization and social reform.

The contradictions between cultural inheritance and social utility followed different trajectories at Hull House and Toynbee Hall. At Hull House, Addams continued to ask herself difficult questions about her own role and the role of culture in the life of the urban poor. What had started as a journey of self-discovery led her towards a re-evaluation of the value and meaning of culture. While the idealistic young graduates of Oxford and the female graduates of Vassar, Smith and Wellesley had been profoundly influenced by the cultural core of the "liberal" curriculum, they had also learned to distrust culture as an end in itself, seeking to offset their perceived "uselessness" by plunging into a socially useful, practical vocation. The liberal-utilitarian debate in British and American universities paved the way for the new public cultural institutions by creating this pool of culturally disaffected, culturally educated, reform-minded workers. Alienated from their class, their culture and their family, these cultural workers sought an outlet in the warm glow of "community" and plunged into the work of social reform by cultural means. However, the buried contradictions of their educational inheritance would re-emerge in their new role as cultural missionaries.

Redemption and Wholeness

Addams was inspired not only by a personal moral sense but by a belief that her own life story was part of a broader narrative of social division and disconnection between culture and experience. She felt that the fundamental problem both for herself as an educated woman of culture and for the immigrant poor lay in this "want of harmony" between their potential and their present, constrained experience. She was probably influenced in this by her readings of Ruskin and Arnold.[9] The initial challenge for the settlement was thus to reconnect people both with their own potential and with each other. Where Arnold finds this reconnection in the general perfection of culture, Addams eventually finds it in the diversity of immigrant cultures.

Initially then, Addams points to a society divided by social class and self-interest, and suggests that a redistribution of social and educational privileges might be a way of redressing the balance. The early programme at Hull House appeared to be modelled on Matthew

Arnold's analysis of social division healed through the general perfection of culture. Yet Addams also saw culture as essentially incomplete, an unfinished project. Only by exposure to cultural diversity could her own cultural inheritance be made whole. Emphasizing that the settlement aims to serve not one specific "needy" sector of the community, but the "whole neighbourhood", Addams (1893, p. 32) notes that: "This site for a Settlement was selected in the first instance because of its diversity and the variety of activity for which it presented an opportunity." The integration and harmony Addams sought for herself and others are in this argument found not in a single common culture, but in the interaction and interconnections between different classes and cultures: "Hull House was soberly opened on the theory that the dependence of classes on each other is reciprocal; and that as the social relation is essentially a reciprocal relation, it gives a form of expression that has a peculiar value" (Addams 1990 [1910], p. 64).

Gradually the emphasis at Hull House shifted away from "culture" in the aesthetic sense towards "cultures" in the anthropological or sociological sense. Addams found herself especially drawn towards the cultures of the European immigrants and encouraged them to rediscover and sustain their distinctive traditions. Following what Kett (1994, p. 181) calls her "decade-long dalliance with Arnoldian culture", Addams became interested in a new educational philosophy of "socialised education, addressed to immediate situations rather than the diffusion of ideal culture". Initially Hull House's cultural programme, like that of Toynbee Hall, had revolved around music and art exhibitions; an art gallery was established in 1891 and a music school in 1893. Over the next ten years, these classes were replaced by more participatory programmes such as the Hull House Labor Museum and the Hull House Players in which culture was rooted in immigrant traditions and practical tasks. The Hull House Labour Museum sought to reconnect Americanized children with the craft traditions of their immigrant parents through practical demonstrations, making the point "that culture is an understanding of the long-established occupations and thoughts of men, of the arts with which they have solaced their toil" (Addams 1990 [1910], p. 160). The new cultural programmes emphasized both the roots of culture in everyday life and the applications of culture to everyday problems. Artistic activities were valued not as an end in themselves, but as a medium for connecting experiences across generations and cultures.

Addams' interest in "socialized education" coincided with her association with the pragmatist philosopher John Dewey. In Addams' description of socialized education, she describes education as a process of exchange between cultures and implicitly distances herself from the cultural idealism of the English settlement house. Once again, she presents her own convictions obliquely, as the collective decision of the Hull House residents: "They feel that they should promote a culture which will not set its possessor aside in a class with others like himself, but which will, on the contrary, connect him with all sorts of people by his ability to understand them as well as by his power to supplement their present surroundings with the historic background" (Addams 1990 [1910], p. 280). If Addams was referring to new theories of culture and class articulated by the immigrant intelligentsia in Hull House, she expressed these arguments in characteristically non-intellectual, subjective terms. Socialized education, according to Addams, grew directly out of her experience of living and working with immigrant communities and continued forwards into her internationalism. The initial naïve faith in culture as a social solvent, represented in lectures and literary evenings, was replaced by an ideal of community based on cultural difference.

Addams' multiculturalism is the unexpected and overlooked aspect of her contribution to cultural policy. While the other settlement houses found themselves increasingly locked into a government agenda of "Americanization" of immigrants, Addams sought to maintain the integrity and diversity of immigrant cultures. Her scepticism towards a unifying ideal of culture was engrained in what she described as her "premature pragmatism" (Addams 1990 [1910], p. 43), which caused her to reject religious and political commitments from an early age. Addams presented her pragmatism as matter of innate character and experience, equating intellectual uncertainty with the crisis of religious faith which followed her father's death. But her pragmatism was also an intellectual position which owed much to John Dewey's theories of knowledge and value.

Addams, like Dewey, questioned the value of abstract ideas which had not been tested through practical experience, and believed that the value of an idea lay in its contribution to human progress. This philosophical pragmatism was linked to Addams' progressive optimism; by refusing to place their faith in any one ideological creed, the pragmatists believed that a dialectic between ideas and action would lead to intellectual and practical progress. Individual and collective knowledge was accumulated not by holding onto fixed beliefs, but in the exchanges between competing ideologies and in the testing of theories by experience. In the debating clubs of Hull House, Addams (1990 [1910], p. 128) found that "the abstract minds at length yield to the inevitable or at least grow less ardent in their propaganda, while the concrete minds, dealing constantly with daily affairs, in the end demonstrate the reality of abstract notions". Abstract ideas, including culture itself, are incomplete in themselves and only made whole through concrete action. The process of making culture "whole" was driven by Addams' sense of dissatisfaction with her own culture and drove her to engage with the cultures of others.

Politically, Addams' pragmatism prevented her from taking sides in political disputes or declaring her political affiliations. She saw herself and the settlement in the role of trusted intermediary, negotiating between striking workers and factory owners, or identifying common causes behind the personal fiefdoms and competing interests which characterized local ward politics. Addams believed that this consensual approach allowed her to be more effective in achieving long-term social reform "during the much longer periods between strikes" and described the labour movement as "a general social movement concerning all members of society and not merely a class struggle" (Addams 1990 [1910], pp. 150, 142).

Culturally, Addams' pragmatism led her in a similar direction away from the idea of the settlement house as a beacon of cultural excellence and towards the idea of a neutral forum within which cultural differences could be accommodated and connected. Cultural pragmatism tempered the cultural idealism of her youth, and was again arrived at through experience; the outcome was not so much a universal common culture as a search for common ground. In this sense, the settlement house anticipates contemporary cultural policy debates regarding multiculturalism. As with her political pragmatism, the attempt to create a neutral space within which cultural differences could be confronted, negotiated and eventually tolerated was idealistic and controversial.

Pragmatism for Addams did not mean mere instrumentalism or "getting things done"; indeed one of her later complaints against the social reforms of the 1920s was that practical problem-solving prevented a longer term, political approach to social change (Addams 1930, pp. 153–156). Pragmatism amounted to a sceptical conviction that every political ideology or cultural value system was necessarily incomplete, but could be built upon by combining it with something new. She was a reluctant sceptic; confronted with the chaos of poverty, she "longed for the comfort of a definite social creed" (Addams 1990 [1910], p. 125), but had been unable to find this in religion, culture or politics. Her immersion in the settlement house did not result in any conclusive answer to the problem of poverty or to her confused sense of her place in the world. But in pragmatism, she found a way of making sense of her intellectual uncertainties and turning them into a creative, practical process. Hull House remained her home, and in her interactions with diverse cultures, political beliefs and social groups, she found the fulfilment and purpose she had previously lacked.

Americanization and the Failed Idealism of the Settlement Movement

The faith placed by Addams and other social reformers in a benign social interaction between different cultures and classes has been criticized as a sentimental attachment to nostalgic forms of working-class community, the fantasy of an alienated middle-class imagination. There was no unified community among the urban poor. The immigrant communities were themselves divided and there was conflict between the generations. The settlement house seemed most successful in working with those who shared the residents' own sense of alienation from their native communities and cultures. They appealed disproportionately to the better-off immigrants who felt dissatisfied with their current situation, the so-called "upper tenth".[10] This has led several commentators to criticize the settlement movement as socially divisive, singling out gifted individuals and failing to recognize the integrity and diversity of the separate communities and sub-cultures in their neighbourhoods (Gans 1962, 1964; Lissak 1983; Platt 1969). The settlement appealed most strongly to those who, like the settlement residents, felt themselves marginal to their peer group, alienated from their culture, family and class. All of these criticisms converged on the American settlement movement's involvement in the "Americanization" of immigrants, a project which became increasingly central to American immigration policy in the early twentieth century. Different approaches to Americanization within the settlement movement in turn exposed some of the inherent contradictions in Addams' multiculturalism.

Criticism of the settlement movement's apolitical emphasis on "community" must be seen in the context of a revisionist attack on cultural institutions as centres of middle-class cultural hegemony in the 1960s and 1970s. Many of these accusations stemmed from the politics of the 1960s, not the history of the 1890s. Sociologists like Herbert Gans and Saul Alinsky saw in the American settlement house a symbol of conservatism which denied the legitimacy of class consciousness and class struggle in the 1960s "war against poverty" (Trolander 1987, pp. 145–151); the settlement was also accused of failing to take effective action in the struggle for black civil rights (Trolander 1987, pp. 94–108, 184–187; Karger 1987, pp. 114–120).

Nevertheless, criticisms like these also highlight problems in the settlement movement as a whole, and the extent to which Addams and Hull House had by the 1910s broken away from the mainstream of the American settlement movement. For Addams, one of the primary purposes of the settlement project was to provide a neutral, non-prejudicial site where different groups could engage in debate and exchange different ideas and values. Yet by the time of America's entry into the First World War, Addams found her emphasis on diversity and tolerance out of step with the prevailing orthodoxy in the settlement movement. As the United States began to prepare for the possibility of war, the settlement house's sociocultural missionary work was increasingly turned to wartime ends. The area of work most affected by the threat of war was the settlement house's "Americanization" of immigrants. Here the "multicultural" policy of Americanization through mutual respect and interaction between cultures, as it had developed at Hull House, was in many settlement houses replaced by a more aggressive approach, which effectively translated "Americanization" to mean the repression of immigrant cultures and the "regimentation"[11] of a diverse civilian population under the banner of American nationalism. Immigrant communities found themselves under suspicion as "nests of dissipation, of contagious disease, of crime, of disloyalty, of espionage, of actual resistance to the Government" (Woods 1970 [1923], pp. 213–217).

Wartime Americanization of immigrants exposed the dark side of the settlement house's unconditional faith in "community". In 1921, Robert Woods, the director of Boston's South End House, noted the emergence of "a wholly cosmopolitan composite with little or no regard to what America has been or now is" and argued that this multicultural mosaic was "in root and branch un-American" (Woods 1970 [1923], p. 269). The reference indicated how far Addams' cosmopolitan internationalism had fallen from favour. Addams would later be attacked for her pacificism and her membership of the board of the American Civil Liberties Union, and described her feeling of being "officially outlawed" (Addams 1930, pp. 135–138). Meanwhile Woods, whose rise in the settlement movement paralleled Addams' fall, wrote of "the elimination of the feeble-minded strain from our National stock" and argued for "the more effectual segregation of the unfit" (Woods 1970 [1923], pp. 217, 128); the "best results" in the search for "common ground" between human beings would come from "instilling into the minds of the newcomers and their children American political ideas and American national loyalties" (Woods 1970 [1923], p. 58). The common culture of the settlement house had become a form of American nationalism with no room for the "unfit" and "feeble-minded". The anti-immigrant backlash continued after the war with the quotas imposed under the 1921 Immigration Act and the deportation drives of 1919 and 1920.

Settlement workers' contributions to the Americanization process were from the outset contradictory, caught between a desire to steer the immigrant towards a vaguely conceived "universal" common culture, a desire to help the individual immigrant succeed in American society by assimilating American language, customs and values, and a desire to preserve and perpetuate the integrity of immigrant cultures. The contradictory nature of "Americanization" is summarized by Mina Carson (1990, p. 109) as "an ultimately untenable equilibrium between cultural autonomy and social assimilation". According to Addams, settlement workers were not attempting to impose a "middle-class" cultural heritage on the poor, or to dupe the workers into political inertia under the guise of "non-partisan" negotiation; rather they were attempting to mould their working-class "neighbours" in their own non-partisan image, as rootless, practical citizens seeking common cause with each other. In order to enter the idealized community of the settlement house, Addams herself sacrificed the ties to her culture, class and community. The denial of her middle-class cultural heritage represented a declaration of independence and a ritual act of self-abnegation. Self-sacrifice was the key to community, sweetness and light. Yet for the urban immigrant poor, this escape from the past was more complicated. They were not inclined to follow the settlement worker's lead and deny their own culture, class and history. Addams respected these attachments by insisting upon the integrity and autonomy of immigrant cultures. At the same time, the idealized community of the settlement house ultimately depended upon all the participants sacrificing their old attachments in pursuit of a common good.

The experience of the settlement movement during and immediately after the First World War indicates the vulnerability of its ideals. The idealized public sphere of the settlement house, within which cultural diversity and interaction were both possible, could be co-opted into the crude Americanization project advocated by Robert Woods. This gap between theory and practice is one of the criticisms directed at communitarian solutions to social inequality and cultural fragmentation. It also points to the fragility of Addams' intellectual definition of the cultural sphere, dependent upon an unstable equilibrium between integration and diversity. These inconsistencies continue to dog contemporary cultural democratization projects, from culturally driven "social inclusion" to educational and community outreach projects undertaken by arts institutions. They also continue to feature in debates over national, cultural and religious identity. Americanization involved a debate over the meaning of American culture. Addams' vision of national culture as a product of many distinctive cultures and beliefs was superseded by the regimented patriotism of Robert Woods. If Woods represented Addams' nemesis, he also embodied some of her contradictions, in particular the difficulty of combining cultural inclusion with cultural autonomy.

The Promise of Art and Education

Addams' intellectual contribution to cultural policy represents a transitional moment between the cultural idealism of the nineteenth century and twentieth-century America's faith in science, technology and progress. Her feelings of incompleteness and lack of fulfilment led her to question the value and meaning of her own inherited culture, and to argue that culture and society must continually evolve through an interaction between diverse communities and experiences. In the latter part of her career, from the end of the war to her death in 1935, this increasingly led her to examine the relationship between art and education. In the promise of art and education to deliver diversity and unpredictability, Addams found a riposte to the crude nationalism, cultural homogenization and social engineering which during and immediately after the First World War, had swept over not just the settlement movement, but the country as a whole.

Art, according to Addams (1930, p. 388), provided the "variation" which was suppressed by mechanized labour and was thus an essential part of education. Through the arts educational programmes at Hull House, she sought to challenge a system of industrialized education which "fitted" the individual to a specific job or position. As somebody who had never fitted into her own social niche, Addams hoped that education could instead provide the individual with the "space, time and tools" to think independently (Addams 1930, p. 346). Arts education aimed to develop a "play instinct" which would challenge and counterpose an educational system based on the needs of the employer. Addams also connected the play instinct to a society's capacity to interact and grow. When opportunities for play and "social intercourse" were blocked, the individual's educational deprivation would lead to a sick society based on narrow loyalties and blinkered vision.[12] Art and education were not presented as normative, fixed values, but as catalysts for individual change and for collective interaction.

Art and education were also Addams' means of challenging "the tyranny of the herd mind" (Addams 1930, p. 289). Here Addams seemed to criticize both the regimented patriotism of Woods and the rising tide of American nationalism following America's entry into the war. In art and education, Addams identified a way of re-injecting diversity into American culture and nationhood. For her idealized community to retain its dynamism and autonomy, the variation of art provided a necessary catalyst and challenge to cultural homogenization. Now Addams broadened her critique from the settlement house to the nation at large: "The patriotism of the modern state must be based not upon a consciousness of homogeneity, but upon a respect for variation, not upon inherited memory but upon trained imagination" (Addams 1930, p. 367).

According to Addams, the greatest gift of the modern city lay in its diversity, providing "the opportunity for varied and humanizing social relationships" as opposed to "those limited loyalties and that sense of restricted obligation which may prove so disastrous to the common good. It is always easy for a democracy which insists upon writing its own programs to shut out imagination, to distrust sentiment and to make short work of recreation. It takes something like a united faith and a collective energy to insist that the great human gifts shall be given the sort of expression which will develop into the arts" (Addams 1930, pp. 367–368). Art was the key to unlocking the diversity of the city through collective interaction and mutual self-discovery, through "recreation" and "imagination". At a time when many other settlement houses were specializing either in providing artistic opportunities for gifted individuals or taking on a professionalized approach to social work, Addams was insistent that art and social development should work in tandem and that art should be a public good, not a private achievement. Art was integral to her vision of community, disrupting fixed ideas and stimulating the diversity and interaction on which a healthy society depends, based on a continual rewriting of cultural identities through "variation" and interculturalism.

Addams' Legacies

According to Addams (1930, p. 381), the special role of the settlement house lay in its "unending effort to make culture and the issue of things go together". This unending effort was the story of her own life, a struggle to reinvigorate her own culture by reconnecting with the diversity and conflict of the immigrant communities in America's cities and with the necessities of social reform. There were contradictions and paradoxes in her effort; she could not resist connecting her new experiences back into her old ideals and retained her residual faith in the saving power of culture even as she embraced Dewey's pragmatism.

The most obvious connection between Addams' intellectual legacy and twentieth-century cultural policy lies in her insistence on cultural diversity as the basis for cultural democratization. This conviction stemmed initially from her own self-doubt and alienation, but was confirmed by her later experiences of settlement life and her intellectual commitment to pragmatism. In the settlement house, Addams discovered a space within which unexpected cultural connections could be made and where the narrow boundaries of culture, class and education could be expanded. The settlement houses of the late nineteenth century would later double up as community arts centres and social service facilities in the 1970s, although their separate fields of operation became specialized and professionalized. Addams and the American settlement house also laid the foundations for American civil society, a neutral space within which different communities and ideologies could learn from each other and seek common grounds for collective action. Her neutrality and refusal to take sides in political and social conflicts may have begun as a result of intellectual uncertainty, but would eventually become a deliberate stand against nationalism and self-interest. She followed "the women's club path from culture to civic activity" (Addams 1930, p. 97), turning her back on the "useless" culture of her youth, only to rediscover later in life the social usefulness of culture not in a narrow utilitarian sense, but as a symbol and mechanism for social "variation". What began as a tentative, paradoxical attempt to make culture useful, later became an analysis of the relationship between art, education and social development.

Finally, Addams embodied the "secret self-contempt" (Lasch 1965a) of the intellectual man or woman of culture. By describing her ideas in the subjective form of confessional autobiography rather than abstract theory, she pointed towards the emotional, personal motivations behind cultural policies and ideals. "Knowing one's place" is an ongoing challenge for intellectuals in cultural policy and for culture in society. By turning this feeling of uncertainty and self-rejection into an active process, Addams sought to find what Arnold would have called her "best self". In order to achieve this, she embarked on a journey of self-destruction and rebirth, abandoning her own social position and immersing herself in the lives of others. Through this process, Addams eventually found a new role for herself and a new sense of purpose. Ideas of self-denial and self-sacrifice form a recurring motif in her writings and in her childhood. Her emotional impulse may have been towards self-sacrifice, but intellectually she discovered in the settlement house a means of reinventing both herself and her cultural idealism. Addams' personal doubts and self-criticism were not only a motivating force, but represented a critical reflection on the general perfection of Arnoldian culture, reinvigorated through diversity and interaction.

ACKNOWLEDGEMENTS

Thanks to the participants at the "Intellectuals and Cultural Policy" conference and to two anonymous reviewers for help in developing this paper.

NOTES

1. More recently Addams' intellectual legacy as a Progressive thinker and a leading figure in the peace movement has been re-evaluated (see, e.g., Fischer & Whipps 2003; Seigfried 1996). From a feminist perspective, Addams' contribution to the intellectual reputations of male contemporaries such as John Dewey (a friend and a board member at Hull House) has been underestimated. According to Christopher Lasch (1965b, p. 176), "it is difficult to say whether Dewey influenced Jane Addams or Jane Addams influenced Dewey. They influenced each other and generously acknowledge their mutual obligations."
2. This intention was made explicit not only by Addams, but also by Samuel Barnett, the founder of Britain's first settlement house, Toynbee Hall, in 1882.
3. Toynbee Hall was the inspiration and practical model for most of the settlement houses which followed, including Hull House. The settlement took its name from Arnold Toynbee, an idealistic young graduate of Balliol College, where the Master, Benjamin Jowett, inspired many of his students with ideals of social responsibility. Most of the early British settlements were affiliated to one or other of the Oxford and Cambridge colleges; American settlement houses were more reliant on private benefactors and recruited from a broader range of graduates.
4. For example, Mina Carson (1990, p. 198) describes the settlement houses as "powerful conduits of Victorian social thought into the twentieth century"; see also Garrison (1979).
5. She completed her studies in 1881, but was awarded her BA the following year when Rockford Seminary became Rockford College. She then enrolled in medical school, but was too ill (and perhaps too emotionally and intellectually depleted) to continue.
6. Reproduced in its entirety in *Twenty Years at Hull House* (c. 1910), but first delivered as a lecture in 1892 in Plymouth, Massachusetts, on the theme of "Philanthropy and Social Progress".
7. Other examples of community arts centres which began as settlement houses include Henry Street Settlement in New York and Oxford House in London.

8. Meacham, however, also points out that Beveridge's claimed "distrust" of culture needs to be taken in context in a letter to his parents reassuring them of his "practical" future career plans.
9. Addams read Ruskin, Arnold and Carlyle at Rockford Seminary. Although the language and rhetoric of her writing suggest a familiarity with these intellectual traditions, she brusquely denied any link between her reading and her "philosophy" (Addams 1990 [1910], p. 36).
10. Toynbee Hall was committed to saving the "worthy poor" among its neighbours (Barnett 1888, pp. 48–49). In the United States, the man who would eventually succeed Addams as the leading figure in the settlement movement, Robert Woods, saw the settlement as an experiment in social engineering, a means of "shielding the better grades of labor from the disastrous competition" of the underclass while writing off the "residuum" of the extremely poor who were "characterised by some chronic form of dependence or degeneracy" (Woods 1902, pp. 370–372; see also Huggins 1971, p. 77).
11. "The Regimentation of the Free" was the title of Robert Woods' 1918 chapter on wartime immigration policy quoted in the next paragraph (Woods 1970 [1923], pp. 207–219).
12. There is no evidence that Addams knew of Freud's work on these themes, or vice versa. Where Freud's *Civilisation and Its Discontents* applies a psychoanalytic model to a sick society, Addams approaches the problem in reverse, applying social theory and sociological observations to individual psychology.

REFERENCES

ADDAMS, J. (1893) 'The objective value of social settlements' in *Philanthropy and Social Progress*, Tomas Crowell, New York, pp. 27–56.

ADDAMS, J. (1990 [1910]) *Twenty Years at Hull House: With Autobiographical Notes*, University of Illinois Press, Urbana, IL.

ADDAMS, J. (1930) *The Second Twenty Years at Hull House: September 1909 to September 1929 – With a Record of a Growing World Consciousness*, Macmillan & Co., New York.

BARNETT, REV. & MRS S. A. (1888) *Practicable Socialism: Essays on Social Reform*, Longmans, Green & Co., London.

CARSON, M. (1990) *Settlement Folk: Social Thought and the American Settlement Movement, 1885–1930*, University of Chicago Press, Chicago, IL.

DAVIS, A. F. (1967) *Spearheads for Reform: The Social Settlements and the Progressive Movement, 1890–1914*, Oxford University Press, New York.

DAVIS, A. F. (1973) *American Heroine: The Life and Legend of Jane Addams*, Oxford University Press, London.

ELSHTAIN, J. B. (2001) *Jane Addams and the Dream of American Democracy*, Basic Books, New York.

FISCHER, M. & WHIPPS, J. D. (2003) *Jane Addams's Writings on Peace*, Continuum, Bristol.

GANS, H. J. (1962) 'The caretakers: Missionaries from the outside world', in *The Urban Villagers: Group and Class in the Life of Italian-Americans*, Free Press, New York, pp. 142–162.

GANS, H. J. (1964) 'Redefining the settlement's function for the war on poverty', *Social Work*, vol. 9, no. 4, pp. 3–12.

GARRISON, D. (1979) *Apostles of Culture: The Public Librarian and American Society, 1876–1920*, Free Press, New York.

HUGGINS, N. I. (1971) *Protestants Against Poverty: Boston's Charities, 1870–1900*, Greenwood Press, Westport, CT.

JARAUSCH, K. A. (1983) *The Transformation of Higher Learning, 1860–1930: Expansion, Diversification, Social Opening and Professionalization in England, Germany, Russia and the United States,* University of Chicago Press, Chicago, IL.

KARGER, H. J. (1987) *The Sentinels of Order: A Study of Social Control and the Minneapolis Settlement House Movement, 1915–1950,* University Press of America, Lanham, MD.

KETT, J. F. (1994) *The Pursuit of Knowledge Under Difficulties: From Self-improvement to Adult Education in America, 1750–1990,* Stanford University Press, Stanford CA.

LASCH, C. (1965a) *The New Radicalism in America, 1889–1963: The Intellectual as a Social Type,* Alfred A Knopf, New York.

LASCH, C. (ed.) (1965b) *The Social Thought of Jane Addams,* Bobbs-Merrill, Indianapolis, IN.

LISSAK, R. (1983) 'Myth and reality: the pattern of relationship between the Hull House Circle and the "new immigrants" on Chicago's West Side 1890–1919', *Journal of American Ethnic History,* vol. 2, no. 2, pp. 21–50.

MEACHAM, S. (1987): *Toynbee Hall and Social Reform, 1880–1914: The Search for Community,* Yale University Press, New Haven, CT.

PLATT, A. M. (1969) *The Child Savers: The Invention of Delinquency,* University of Chicago Press, Chicago, IL.

ROUSMANIERE, J. (1970) 'Cultural hybrid in the slums: The college woman and the settlement house, 1889–1894', *American Quarterly,* vol. 22, no. 1, pp. 45–66.

SEIGFREID, C. H. (1996) *Pragmatism and Feminism: Reweaving the Social Fabric,* University of Chicago Press, Chicago, IL.

TROLANDER, J. A. (1987) *Professionalism and Social Change: From the Settlement House Movement to Neighbourhood Centers, 1886 to the present,* Columbia University Press, New York.

WOODS, R. A. (ed.) (1902) *Americans in Progress: A Settlement Study,* Houghton, Mifflin & Co., Boston, MA.

WOODS, R. A. (1970 [1923]) *The Neighborhood in Nation-building,* Arno Press/New York Times, New York.

A PRAGMATIC INTELLECTUAL
Dutch Fabians, Boekman and cultural policy in the Netherlands, 1890–1940

Harro Maas

This paper examines the work of a self-made social democrat, Emanuel Boekman, whose dissertation "Government and the Arts in the Netherlands" (1939) still serves as a benchmark for defining the goals and limits of cultural policy in the Netherlands. I will discuss Boekman's ideas against the background of wider debates between social democrats and others (Catholics, in particular) on the relation of culture and society. In the first decades of the twentieth century, the aesthetic-, Fabian- and Morris-inspired socialist ideal became the dominant view of the Amsterdam cultural elite. This ideal centred around one central notion – *gemeenschapskunst* (community art) – that was fleshed out in debates in the journal *De Kroniek* (*The Chronicle*) in the early 1890s.

Boekman, I will argue, was a pragmatist – in a commonsense understanding of the word. His turning to the Social Democratic Party and his early training in statistics made him wary of deep philosophical disquisitions of any sort – factual evidence and circumstances served as the canvass in which analyses of social policy, including cultural policy, should be played out. Boekman's pragmatism was perfectly fitted to neutralizing the ideological and theological divisions along which Dutch society was organized. His analysis of the relation of the state and the arts thus extended the aesthetic socialist views on the role of art and culture in society on a nationwide scale. His pragmatic attitude essentially identified the ideal of community art with the dissemination of culture over all layers of society.

Boekman's views on the role of culture in society and its relation to state interference became the benchmark to which the whole political spectrum in the Netherlands would take recourse after the Second World War – even to the extent that a newspaper columnist in 1998 reproached the Social Democratic secretary of state and neo-liberalist economist Rick van der Ploeg for the fact that his alleged new plea for the greater accessibility of the arts for "youngsters, the lower educated and immigrants" was nothing but "freewheeling" on an "old ideal" for which Boekman in 1939 had written the blueprint (Blokker 1998).[1] Because of its substantial neutrality, Boekman's politics of dissemination paradoxically boiled down to a cultural policy of experts that was inherently biased towards the new and avant-garde. The resulting tension between "quality" and "accessibility" haunts cultural policy in the Netherlands to this day. Boekman did not live to see this fruit of his work: a Jew, he committed suicide with his wife and their close friends the Van Gelderens shortly after the Dutch government surrendered to the Germans in the Second World War.

Dutch Fabians: Social Ideals in Brickstone and Stained Glass

Of importance to my story is that Dutch social democrats at the turn of the nineteenth century were rather more inspired by socialist movements in England than in Germany or France. The socialism of the Fabians and William Morris's Arts and Crafts movement, in particular, shaped Dutch socialists' attitudes towards the relation of state, culture and the economy. At first glance, there could not be a greater difference between William Morris, the late Romantic poet and Utopian socialist, and the pragmatic Fabians, and so their combination by Dutch socialists seems highly unlikely. Yet, for them, this combination followed as a matter of course. As best explained by E. P. Thompson, the nub of the difference between the Fabians and Morris resides in their different conceptions of "community" and its consequences for the relation of state and society.[2]

Fabianism has been described as socialism "from above" rather than "from below". Well known is Beatrice Webb's snub that "hard thinking" of experts was greatly to be preferred to "all this nonsense about Democracy". In the 1908 re-issue of *Fabian Essays*, Shaw (1962, p. 291) wrote that if the Fabians could redo their work, they would have aimed their essays straight away at "administrative experts … bankers, lawyers and constructive statesmen" rather than at the general public. Fabianism clearly perceived itself as an upper- or middle-class socialist movement that aimed for the improvement of the condition of the working class through a state-controlled politics of social engineering, rather than by any revolutionary socialism from below. Socialism, for the Fabians, was distributive justice, enforced by the state on a market society that essentially was left unaffected. Morris, by contrast, perceived an irresolvable conflict between the competitive pressures of market society and the communal form of living he pictured in *News from Nowhere*. One of his lifelong frustrations was that his art strived to express a sense of community for the whole population, especially the working poor, but in fact only reached the wealthy and better off. The Fabians and Morris thus represent two seemingly irreconcilable poles in which society was made from above or emerged out of an allegedly revolutionary movement from below.

The Dutch social democratic movement of the end of the nineteenth century happily reunited these two diverging poles of British socialism as its sources of inspiration, even though the tension between state intervention for the enforcement of equality and grassroots culture in opposition to existing capitalist institutions has haunted it through much of the twentieth century. It certainly characterizes the episode at which I will be looking: the interwar period in which social democrats effectively took on governmental responsibilities, at least at a local level.

The kind of people involved in the early social democratic movement were of upper- or middle-class origin and held liberalist sympathies before becoming socialists. Some of them cherished the same idea of social engineering as the Fabians. But they also importantly aimed to materialize the ideal of communality that was contained in Morris's *News from Nowhere*, which hinged on cooperation rather than on competition. One might think of people like F. M. Wibaut, who had made a comfortable living in business before becoming one of the important leaders of the Social Democratic Labour Party (SDAP), H. P. Berlage, the architect famous for the early twentieth-century city extension of Amsterdam (Plan Zuid) and for his designs for the Amsterdam Stock Exchange and the General Dutch Diamond Cutters Union (ANDB) buildings, the artists Jan Veth and Richard Roland-Holst, the latter's wife, the poet and (in later years) Marxist theoretician Henriette Roland-Holst, Henri Polak, first head of the General Dutch Diamond Cutters Union, or Frank van der Goes, one of the founders of the SDAP and one of its important early theoreticians.

In the 1890s these people functioned as a group organized to some extent around the journal *De Kroniek* (*The Chronicle*), which was run by Wibaut's longstanding friend, P. L. Tak. Wibaut and Tak came from Middelburg, the capital city of the southern archipelago of The Netherlands (flooded in 1953 by the combination of a springtide and a furious storm). They spent most of their active political life in (or closely around) Amsterdam. Tak himself was a liberal with a social bent, who gradually turned towards socialism – or rather was seduced by Wibaut to join the SDAP, where he would serve in the executive committee before becoming a Socialist MP.

The influence of the Fabians and the Arts and Crafts movement on this group (and on the journal) was considerable. Wibaut translated *Fabian Essays* as *Socialisme* (socialism), and his foreword to the translation reads like a genuine "coming out" of a bourgeois for the Fabian socialist creed. Wibaut was particularly taken with the Fabians' idea of a gradual reform of society that should start locally, and thus fit local needs. This emphasis on the needs of local communities provided the ground for a reconciliation of Morris's grand utopian vistas with Fabian pragmatism. Henri Polak translated Sydney and Beatrice Webb's history of trade unionism, Jan Veth published an adaptation of Walter Crane's *The Claims of Decorative Art*, Hugenholtz translated lectures of William Morris and Henri Polak wrote a short sketch of Morris's life to introduce this volume. There was a similar emphasis on the unity of design and execution of the work, and on the enjoyments of life that could only be obtained from redressing the existing monotony in society resulting from the ever more refined division and mechanization of labour. Architecture and the arts should strive to the monumental and the decorative. In doing so, they showed Morris's community of mankind.

At the time, one of the issues where opinions of intellectuals and artists in the Netherlands critically diverged was how the dawning day of the community of mankind was to be conceived – as a utopia of the mind, as it was envisaged by some of the more religiously and mystically inclined contributors to *De Kroniek* like the catholic composer Alphons Diepenbrock and the Catholic (stained glass) painters, Antoon Derkinderen and Jan Toorop; as a genuine social utopia that would be reached only once socialism had overhauled the capitalist mode of production as conceived by Morris himself and in the Netherlands by communists like David Wijnkoop; or as something that could be thought of in less revolutionary terms that could be obtained by gradual improvements in labour conditions on a local level – rather more the pragmatic stance of the Fabians and of Dutch social democrats.

These differences in opinions were particularly provoked by a glorifying description of the coronation of the Russian Tsar written by the painter Marius Bauer and published in *De Kroniek*. In an editorial, P. L. Tak severely criticized Bauer for completely ignoring the brutal conditions of oppression and impoverishment in which the common Russian people found themselves. Subsequent contributions revealed that the different valuations of the coronation were motivated by different implicit meanings of the notion of community art.

The phrase *gemeenschapskunst* (community art) was first used by Jan Veth in the early 1890s in a laudatory comment on a mural of Antoon Derkinderen for the city hall of Den Bosch (see Figure 1). The concept of community art has a close and a remote history. Its close history refers to Wagner's notion of a *"Gesamtkunstwerk"* – a community of the arts – lacking any specific reference to a social community. But it also refers to the medieval days in which art was made in the service of the religious, catholic community. Community art was subservient to the community of believers. Both aspects (the integration of different art forms and art subservient to a social or religious community) were present in ideas about community art in the last decades of the nineteenth century. P. J. H. Cuypers' neogothic Rijksmuseum (1885) and Central Station (1889) in Amsterdam aimed to integrate different forms of art: wall paintings and stained glass, in particular. Derkinderen, one of the emancipating Catholics at the end of the nineteenth century, refused to work for Cuypers because he was not allowed to unite design and execution and so could not effect a true community of the arts.

FIGURE 1
Fragment of Antoon Derkinderen's murals in the Den Bosch town hall. The fragment shows the Duke of Brabant. In the background are workmen building the new fortress of Den Bosch. The whole is stylized to static, thus elevating the event from historical turmoil to a new eternal order. Commenting on this work, Jan Veth argued that it was an expression of community art (*gemeenschapkunst*) – a notion he developed in close cooperation with Derkinderen himself. In contrast to *art for art's sake* that, according to Veth, was only an expression of the individual, community art referred to (and incorporated) a higher ideal that showed the binding elements of society expressed in an idealized and stylized way. For the Catholic Derkinderen, this higher ideal found its best expression in the religious art of the Gothic. Veth, and his socialist contemporaries like Richard Roland Holst, his wife Henriette Roland Holst-van Schaik, and others like the increasingly radical Berlage, considered this higher ideal to be found in the expression of the socialist ideals of justice and equality in *this* world, rather than in the imagined order of the eternal God. With kind permission of the Rijksmuseum, Amsterdam.

Veth admired in Derkinderen's murals their expression of "general thoughts of humanity". Derkinderen (and Veth) thus referred to a symbolic, as opposed to concrete, existing community and it was just this issue that was at the centre of the controversy in *De Kroniek* over Bauer's description of the coronation of the Tsar. It became very clear that for symbolists (and Catholics) like Derkinderen, the composer Diepenbrock and others, there was nothing offensive in Bauer's words to be found because he spoke to an imaginary community – and the coronation itself revealed to the existing community the idea of beauty, and to do so was exactly the purpose of art.

Veth's early use of the phrase "community art" was criticized for being a hollow word "that as an apple dumpling fell from the hollow mouth of Jan Veth on this poor country" (Boot & van der Heijden 1978, p. 37, citing P. Tideman), but Bauer's account of the Tsar's coronation made Veth realize that he actually shared sides with the socialists against any reference to a merely imaginary community. In subsequent issues of *De Kroniek*, fragments of Morris were translated with comments by Veth. From the exchange of contributions in *De Kroniek*, it emerged that social democrats thought about community art in terms of art made by and for existing communities. The symbolists' retreat to the "gloomy glow" of medieval Catholicism with its "mumbles of devotion and community sense" gave way to a forward-looking conception of social democratic art that was monumental in design and intended to morally and culturally elevate the masses. Art should be sociable and further moral progress. It should guide and fulfil the aesthetic and social needs of the masses. It should express the unity of mankind not in the abstract, but in the concrete.

The generation of the 1890s combined the ideal of community art with a Fabian sense of practicality. In the first decade of the twentieth century, and largely through the continued pressure of people like Wibaut, social democrats abandoned their resistance to taking on governmental responsibilities – though not without inner party conflicts. Henriette Roland Holst sided with the more radical factions of the socialists (and later communists), to the regret of her husband who reproached her for political naivety (Etty 1997). In line with his Fabian sympathies, Wibaut accepted administrative responsibility in 1914 and became alderman for the city of Amsterdam for public housing and labour issues (on Wibaut, see especially Borrie 1968).

The outbreak of the war itself was an important factor for Wibaut in making the decision that it was no longer possible for socialists to wait until capitalism would destroy itself – rather it was the task of social democrats to actively engage in the furthering of social progress, even by taking part in institutions that had been, and sometimes still were, used to oppress the working class.[3] This pragmatism became a defining characteristic of social democracy in the Netherlands. With short intermezzos, Wibaut remained alderman until 1931 when he retired from active politics. In this period, Wibaut was responsible for various offices, in the years of the First World War for food supply and then after the war for financial affairs and for education and culture. It is hardly possible to exaggerate the importance of Wibaut in city politics in this period.

The social democratic idea of community art – that is, the emphasis on the value of cooperation and community values – is expressed best in two of Berlage's buildings: the Stock Exchange and De Burcht (see Figure 2). It found its most enduring and grand scale expression in the implementation (after the First World War) of the new Amsterdam city extension to the south – the internationally acclaimed "Plan Zuid" designed by Berlage and executed by several architects of the so-called "Amsterdam School", like De Klerk. Its spectacular use of brickstone (criticized severely as well) and its overall design was meant to show

FIGURE 2
De Burcht: the building for the Dutch Diamond Factory Worker's Union (ANDB). Today, it serves as the National Trade Union Museum. With kind permission of De Burcht, Amsterdam.

uniformity and harmony of the social fabric. Ornamental elements were repeated in style, but not in full detail, in all its parts (see Figure 3). The bridges ornamented by Hildo Krop are a fine example of how a sense of social community was revealed through the sculptures, giving a sense of harmony and unity to the whole of the city extension.

Berlage's design of the Amsterdam Stock Exchange echoes the mediaeval (Italian) past that, in line with Morris's Romanticism, was considered to embody this same sense of harmony and beauty. His design of the General Dutch Diamond Cutters Union Building befittingly is called "De Burcht" (the bastion) and similarly refers to the alleged merits of the age of guilds. Richard Roland Holst designed a series of wall paintings based on the past, present and future of the modern labour movement, which clearly show the influence of Morris and pre-Raphaelites like Ford Madox Brown and Edward Burne-Jones and reflect a similar message of solidarity (see Figures 4 and 5). Roland Holts's work in De Burcht is accompanied by texts of his wife Henriette and the overall intention may be well summarized by one of them: "Once dawn will find labour and beauty united"[4] (see Figure 5).

"Plan Zuid" was the most visible realization of the social democratic conception of community art. Berlage's architectural design created a communal space that fitted local needs: a space that showed the superiority of community values over that of competition.[5] In 1926, Roland Holst succeeded Derkinderen as professor and director of the Royal Academy of Arts in Amsterdam, the most prestigious arts school in the Netherlands.

FIGURE 3
Photograph of the early 1920s of De Klerk's design for the P. L. Takstraat in Berlage's city extension "Plan Zuid" in Amsterdam.

Under Wibaut's aldermanship, city intervention in the funding of culture became a matter of routine. He aimed at the dissemination of culture by direct stimulation of cultural productions and by a politics of, basically, price discrimination. The city council agreed to support so-called "people's concerts" or "people's shows" at the concert hall or theatre. The defence of this politics would become an important element of Boekman's own aldermanship. The concerts and theatre plays showed "the best" performances of "high art". Given the strong ideological tradition of government abstinence in matters of culture in the Netherlands that goes back to the liberalist statesman Thorbecke (on which more anon), this politics met with remarkably little resistance in the city council (Jansen & Rogier 1983, p. 143). The aesthetically driven socialist ideas of the generation of *De Kroniek* had found their way into the establishment, and, importantly, determined how the relation of art and society was perceived in the capital of the Netherlands and allegedly its most cultured city.

Originating from sympathies with Morris, Crane and the Arts and Crafts movement, and from sympathies with the Fabian version of socialism, this aesthetic socialism became a largely Amsterdam-based creed. Just this Amsterdam provincialism provides the context in which Emanuel Boekman formulated his ideas on cultural policy. Before turning to Boekman's thesis on cultural policy, let us first have a look at Emanuel Boekman himself and the social environment into which he was born.

Jewish Corner: Emanuel Boekman, Amsterdam and the Culture of Statistics

Internationally, Boekman is best known because of the Boekman Foundation, the centre for arts, culture and policy in the Netherlands, and its publications, among which is

FIGURE 4
One of Richard Roland Holst's murals in De Brucht, depicting a working man who resists the temptation of gold because he is firmly committed to solidarity with his fellow workmen. The background consists of grey brickstone walls, above which can be seen the scaffolding of a new building; the new fabric of society, based on strength (left panel) and solidarity (right panel). This mural is the centrepiece of the assembly hall of the union, which is abundantly decorated in its totality. With kind permission of Thijs Quispel.

Boekman, successor of the *Boekmancahier*. The centre is to be credited for having provided one of its former directors and one of its staff members, Jan Rogier and Tony Jansen, the opportunity to write a truly monumental biography on its eponym. Inevitably, this section will draw heavily on their work.[6]

In the early decades of the twentieth century, Amsterdam regained some of its long lost splendour, particularly due to the rich cultural climate of the large Jewish population of the city, which for the most part was not rich in a material sense. Music halls, theatres, *cafés chantants*, and other outlets of culture and semi-culture were flourishing in the east side of the city centre, and though the artists as well as visitors importantly belonged to the Jewish part of the population, it is commonly held that the sort of entertainment provided was not particularly of Jewish signature (on vanished Jewish Amsterdam, see, e.g., Bloemgarten & Velzen 1997; Bregstein & Bloemgarten 2004; Multatuli *et al.* 1993; Stoutenbeek & Vigeveno 2003; Verhoeff *et al.* 1999).

Apart from theatrical and musical entertainment, there were many (second hand) bookstores and market stalls on the Waterlooplein flea market and, close to the University, at the Oudemanhuispoort covered arcade. Jews lived in highly packed areas of the city, close

FIGURE 5
Mural by Richard Roland Holst. The text, by his wife Henriette Roland Holst-van Schaik, reads: "Eens zal de dag – opgaand – vinden Arbeid en Schoonheid vereend" ("Once dawn will find labour and beauty united"). Henriette was an important poet in her own right, and one of the most outstanding socialist theorists the Netherlands has ever seen. As the phrase indicates, she was much more inclined towards a revolutionary interpretation of socialism than her contemporary social democrats, including her husband. She consequently moved towards increasing sympathy with the communist movement in the Netherlands to the point of breaking off her linkages with the SDAP in the 1920s. This painful episode is best described in Elsbeth Etty's monumental biography of her life and work (see Etty 1997). With kind permission of Thijs Quispel.

to the Central Station, though there was never a formal ghetto. In later life, Boekman wrote extensively on Jewish demographical issues for Jewish periodicals as well as periodicals for a more general public. His first major publication was a book-length examination of Jewish demography he submitted as his master's thesis in social geography at the City University of Amsterdam in 1933.

Emanuel Boekman was born on 15 August 1889, son of a Jewish shopkeeper in first- and second-hand books in the "De Pijp" district of Amsterdam. Though the family was poor, it formed part of the social scenery of poor men's philosophers that was widely spread in the Jewish community at the turn of the century (Jansen & Rogier 1983, p. 72). Culture in early twentieth-century Jewish Amsterdam was culture from below. The family was not orthodox and did not go to the synagogue except for special occasions, but nevertheless considered itself to be Jewish rather than assimilated.

In the beginning of the twentieth century, the struggle for economic and cultural emancipation of the Jews was emphasized and organized by the ANDB: the diamond workers' trade union. Henri Polak, who I mentioned above, advocated in particular the unity of economic and cultural emancipation. The improvement of the aesthetic tastes of the working class was an important issue as witnessed from Polak's answer to objections of union members with respect to the costs of the new trade union building. Polak countered that "workers were in need of education … [the building] will give us a moral rent". After 1918, social democrats organized nationwide in this typical Dutch model of pillarization in which the four different "pillars" of society (Catholics, Protestants, social democrats and liberals) organized around their own economic (trade union), political (party) and cultural institutions.[7] Such organization was particularly apt for the Amsterdam Jewish population, among others, because of its intense engagement with culture and trade unionism (Jansen & Rogier 1983, p. 145).

At the age of twelve Boekman started work as a typesetter. In the ensuing years, Boekman managed to learn English through self-study, passed the examination for telegraphy and followed courses in political economy at the City University with Professor van Embden. On his advice, Boekman continued his studies in political economy in The Hague. There he met his lifelong friend Bob van Gelderen, then already an active member of the SDAP. It is quite conceivable that Van Gelderen's influence was instrumental in shifting Boekman's early radical, rather more anarchistic, political sympathies towards the SDAP.[8]

After his studies in The Hague (which he combined with his work as a typesetter), Boekman entered the administrative bureaucracy, first as an inspector of harbour labour in Amsterdam, and later as head of statistics of the mathematics and statistics department of the State Insurance Bank. He wrote articles on the social organization of a market for harbour labour in Amsterdam for popular and scientific periodicals like the *Economic Journal* (Boekman 1917). These articles have a largely descriptive, rather than theoretical character. This was in conformity with the common practice among statisticians to limit oneself to a description of states of affairs, rather than to make theoretical inferences. In line with the Victorian split between political economic theory and statistics, statisticians refrained from theory; statistics were used to describe the social world and make policy recommendations on its basis (Goldman 1983, 2002; Maas 2005; Porter 1986).

In the first decades of the twentieth century social democrats used statistics as a lever for social change. Boekman's thoughts went in the same direction. His new experiences in administration had opened his eyes to the importance of state legislation to the benefits of the working class, and confirmed the importance of the collection of statistical materials for effective government intervention in and regulation of the economy and of society more generally. In line with the perceived emancipatory role of statistics, Boekman's articles combined descriptive statistics with policy recommendations. He presented his facts "objectively" – his statistical publications were guided by what he called the "common sense of numbers" rather than by speculative theory or idealism.[9] Hence, although numbers were presented "objectively", the very fact that they were gathered was not neutral at all; statistical data could serve emancipatory socialist politics.

In an article of November 1921 in *Het Volk* (*The People*), Boekman wrote in alarming terms about the budget cuts that affected the collection of statistics, and which would result in the worst possible outcome for the working class. He observed that

> [T]he truth that statistics is an indispensable element of all effective guidance to economic policy, has now gradually been implanted into the most stubborn and backward heads. In earlier days considered as an innocent pastime, it has been acknowledged for long as an indispensable instrument. (Boekman, quoted in Jansen & Rogier 1983, p. 83)

For that reason, cutting the budgets of statistical institutions could only be seen as an implicit recognition on the part of the government that they were no longer interested in the effective regulation of social affairs. Such an attitude might be in conformity with the opinions of contemporary entrepreneurs, but it was opposed by Boekman. According to him, statistics were not objective in the sense of neutral; its end-purpose was the regulation and control of social and economic life through the state.

Boekman, as in fact all other statisticians of his day, including someone like Verrijn Stuart, could not avoid searching for explanations in the data they collected. Boekman's "common sense" extended to the search for causal explanations from the data. There was no "deep theory" to which he referred, rather Boekman searched for an obvious cause that could explain patterns found in the data. On this basis, he then made policy inferences. A good example of Boekman's approach to statistics can be found in his demographic study of Jews in the Netherlands. He wrote this study in the early 1930s, and initially hoped to submit it as a doctoral thesis in social geography, but it was only accepted as a master's thesis. By that time Boekman had already become active in Amsterdam municipal politics as leader of the social democratic fraction in the city council and as a councilman for culture and education from 1931 onwards (a position he held until 1940, with the exception of 1933–1935 when the Social Democrats were in the opposition).

In his biographical sketch of Boekman, Abel J. Herzberg characterized *Demografie van de Joden in Nederland* (demography of the Jews in the Netherlands) as a book "full of numbers, a collection of minutely controllable materials", but without any "speculative ideas" (quoted in Dulken & Jansen 1989, pp. 28–29). The numbers (and graph) showed that the percentage of Jews in the total population declined from 1870 onwards. Boekman inferred that observed data patterns could be attributed to the low frugality of mixed marriages (i.e., of Jews with non-Jews). Combining historical and demographical statistics, Boekman argued that some of the problems encountered by Jews in Amsterdam, like their devastating housing conditions, were social and economic in character – that is, largely due to decisions made by Jews themselves: they did not want to live in other city areas, they cultivated Yiddish as their language – and in all this, there was no enforcement from city politics involved. Boekman's use of numbers thus extended to low-key explanations that might have important policy implications, however.

Herzberg's assessment of Boekman's statistical work is therefore completely justified: Boekman's rejection of speculation and his predilection for arguments on the basis of facts set him apart from those social reformers who placed ideology over and above "facts". This clearly was not because he flinched from conflict; quite the contrary, Boekman was feared for his sharp and sometimes even arrogant tone. It was rather because he felt a profound contempt for those who put ideology over factual evidence. Boekman perceived this attitude most clearly with Dutch communists with whom social democrats (as everywhere in Europe) held tensioned relations. In the Amsterdam city council, Boekman bullied the communist David Wijnkoop, himself an eloquent orator, for his unwillingness to tally his demands on politics and society with the (in Boekman's eyes) irreducible constraints of circumstances (on David Wijnkoop, see Harmsen 1966; Koejemans 1967). For Boekman, facts were the stuff social democrats had to engage with to improve the condition of the working class; politicians should refrain from making blueprints from scratch. Wibaut and his generation served as the example that improvement through existing institutions was not only possible, but also the most desirable way to proceed. The dawn of a community of mankind could be reached by a politics of pragmatism. Statistical evidence served as the vehicle to obtain this result. This was Boekman's inheritance from his formal education in statistics and of social democracy of the blend of the Fabians and Morris combined.

Boekman on Cultural Policy

Let us now turn to Boekman's still much cited PhD thesis *Overheid en Kunst in Nederland* (Government and the Arts in the Netherlands). Boekman defended his thesis on 6 June 1939 at the auditorium of the City University in the old Lutheran Church at the Spui (see Figure 6). His thesis supervisor was the Professor of Demography Ter Veer, who had refused to accept Boekman's study on Jewish demography in the Netherlands as a doctoral thesis. The thesis defence was a public event. The floor and the balcony were all packed with people. Among the audience was the Secretary of State for Education, Arts and Sciences, the director-general of this department, the Major of Amsterdam, an array of Social Democrat MPs, Kautsky's widow and a list of professors, artists and others spanning the political spectrum from left to right, with an emphasis on social democrats, of course, and Catholics.

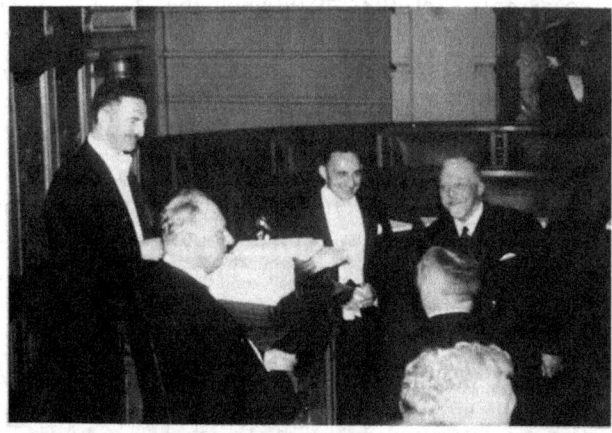

FIGURE 6
Public dissertation defence by Emanuel Boekman in the Aula of the Amsterdam City University (now University of Amsterdam). (From left to right) upper photograph: Emanuel Boekman, E. van Hinte, S. Mok, G. de Vlught (major of Amsterdam); lower photograph: first row: G. de Vlught, Slotemaker de Bruine (secretary of education), second row: unknown, prof. J. van Gelderen, unknown, Henny Boekman (daughter of Emanuel Boekman), Mrs. Boekman-Nerden (Boekman's wife). From Jansen and Rogier (1983), p. 287. With kind permission of Boom publishers.

Romanticizing Boekman's poor background and downplaying his formal education, the socialist A. B. Kleerekoper wrote in *Het Volk* (The People) that the thesis was a "a piece of writing, witnessing of such a wide reading and knowledge, as a man can savour, whose only school has been life itself" (Jansen & Rogier 1983, p. 286). Anton van Duijnkerken, editor of the Catholic daily *De Tijd* (The Time) heralded it as one "for which artists and society should be grateful to the author" (Jansen & Rogier 1983, p. 286). Even the right-wing and increasingly antisemitic daily *De Telegraaf* (The Telegraph) sourly admired the considerable work that had been accomplished in this thesis.

Indeed, it was not an ordinary thesis. First because of the person who wrote it, and second because of the period in which it saw light: the end of the great crisis and the dawn of a new world war. At the end of the 1930s, Boekman unquestionably had become one of the leading figures in the Social Democratic Party. As alderman for culture and education, he steered Amsterdam for much of the 1930s through a very difficult period of repeated budget cuts in the arts and education by central government. Forcefully hit by the crisis, the attendance of the Amsterdam population at theatre, music and museums declined considerably and funding possibilities increasingly diminished.

Under Wibaut's aldermanship in the 1920s, city intervention in the sponsoring of the arts had become a regular business. The (now Royal) Concert Hall, for example, had been financed by private money, but it became increasingly clear – and to a broad political spectrum – that support for the arts could not be left to private initiatives alone. Wibaut had an important ideological impetus to hand over the management of the arts from bourgeois individuals to the municipal government. Art and culture were not the property of a small elite, they were, following Morris's and the Fabians' creed, meant to be enjoyed by all, including the working (and jobless)[10] poor.

Boekman set clear limits to the subject of his thesis; it was about the state and the arts. It has been argued that Boekman made the first sociological analysis of the relation of the state to the arts (Oosterbaan Martinius 1990, p. 12), and indeed, he suggested it was but a small step from sociographics (a branch of geography) to descriptive sociology (Boekman 1939, thesis III appended to the body of the text). Boekman emphasized the descriptive nature of his study. He would only consider "facts and opinions" as he found them, but would not enter into any fundamental discussion of the relation of the state to the arts. In line with the perceived role of the statistician, he limited himself to a description of factual evidence and then drew policy inferences from it in the third part of the thesis entitled "Perspectives". He thus followed more or less the same format as his Master-thesis in Jewish demography; a descriptive account was followed by a part in which inferences and policy conclusions were drawn from this description. The last part of his thesis did so in a manner, however, that read like a proposal for future state policy towards the arts – something that was not to be expected in such an explicit form in a thesis (Jansen & Rogier 1983, p. 328).

From these limitations it followed that "general considerations on aesthetics, on the social function of art, on the philosophy of the state or of art or of both in their mutual relations" would be excluded from the book, not because these considerations were unimportant, but because their importance asked for a much more thorough discussion than he could provide in a thesis that was in its essence "sociographic" (Boekman 1939, p. 5). Lack of empirical evidence also explains his decision to leave out a substantial discussion of the new media of radio and cinema. Boekman argued that "both inventions certainly have promising possibilities, that may bring them to the realm of the arts", but it was as yet unclear if both media would develop into that direction and so, from a descriptive point of view, he could safely dismiss engagement in a discussion of their merits as a means of artistic expression and of any role of the state in their regard (Boekman 1939, p. 10).

As we have seen when discussing Boekman's opinions about the aims of statistics, a presentation of the facts as they are did not prevent him from taking a political stance. This also holds for his thesis. His historical discussion of the role of the state in the arts abounded with expressions of amazement and indignation about the neglect of the arts by not only the government, but other segments of society as well. With clear agreement, Boekman quoted the important nineteenth-century German Museum director Wilhelm Bode who wrote that "was nicht niet- und nagelfest war, ist mit den zahllosen holländischen Privatsammlungen bis auf einen geringen Bruchtheil in das Ausland verschachert" (Boekman 1939, p. 24).[11] The gist of Boekman's book was to show how this squandering of Dutch national art treasures gradually came to a halt, and how in the process the attitude of the government (and the economic elite) towards the arts changed from one of non-intervention to that of active support not only of historical treasures, but also of contemporary art and artists. The aim of this active support became concerned not only with conservation of cultural inheritance, but also with a policy to "spread" the arts over all layers of society – what is referred to in Dutch as "*spreidingsbeleid*".

The captions to the different chapters and the numerical evidence showed this developments in tandem, with the exception of the period of decline that yet again seemed to have started from the 1930s onwards. This downturn was due to the crisis of the 1930s rather than that there being a return to the nineteenth-century (deliberate) neglect of the arts. Table 1, which Boekman included near the end of the descriptive part of his thesis, summarized in his own words the historical development of state expenditure on the arts from 1870 until the (then) present. Combined with data on city expenditure on the arts, Boekman could make the argument that even though it had never become a substantial part of central government budget, city expenditure had become clearly significant, thus confirming the

TABLE 1
Nominal and relative expenditure of the central government on the arts. The column headings read (from left to right): Year, Total Nominal Amount on Central Government Budget, Expenditure on the Arts, and Percentage (of the total budget). From Boekman (1939, p. 167).

VERHOUDING VAN DE UITGAVEN VOOR KUNST OP HET TOTAAL DER STAATSUITGAVEN

Jaar	Totaalcijfer Rijksbegrooting	Uitgaven voor Kunst	Percentage
1870	99.107.000	99.000	0.099
1875	118.911.000	178.250	0.149
1880	113.051.000	264.650	0.234
1885	122.158.000	280.202	0.229
1890	165.938.000	292.240	0.176
1895	133.297.000	326.190	0.244
1900	154.161.000	368.590	0.239
1910	203.947.000	574.713	0.281
1920	911.228.000	1.511.707	0.165
1931	838.850.000	2.306.812	0.274
1939	744.830.000	1.626.617	0.218

overall impression that active government intervention for the arts had become an irreversible part of government politics.

Boekman's explanation for this development was divided into two parts. In the first part of his thesis, he discussed the three main "spiritual currents" of the nineteenth century in the Netherlands. He did so in an order that developed the scenery for the second part, in which recognition of the importance of integrating the working class within the cultural fabric of society first came to be recognized by social democrats, but then was accepted as being of general concern to the government. The chapter entitled "Spiritual Currents and the Arts" ("Geestesstroomingen en kunst") discussed three nineteenth-century attitudes towards the arts that, according to Boekman, typified the Dutch case: Liberalism, Calvinism and Catholicism. The order of his discussion also revealed the merits of the stance of the generation of the 1890s on community art. Boekman discussed liberalism, Calvinism and Catholicism in a logical, rather than chronological, order: a choice that was rhetorically highly effective in bringing out the message that at the end of the nineteenth century, the government could no longer refrain from active politics towards the arts.

Boekman started with the great liberalist statesman of the mid-nineteenth century, Thorbecke, who famously was deemed to have said that "the state has no role to play in the arts".[12] Using parliamentary proceedings, Boekman could easily point out that this famous saying in fact was a serious misquote of Thorbecke's more refined statements, even though it was a fitting description of his practical politics.[13] Thorbecke actually said that the state should refrain from any *judgement* in relation to the arts. This did not entail, so Boekman argued correctly, that the arts were excluded from government's financial support – quite the contrary.

Boekman then used his discussion of Calvinism and Catholicism to first show that with the turn towards neogothic, conservation of national monuments for the general public had become a matter of political concern. Though Calvinism and liberalism were united in a plea for government financial abstinence in matters of the arts (though for different reasons), the emancipation of the Catholics importantly changed this attitude for the better. Boekman continued to discuss the "revolution" in the attitude of the state towards the arts when "radical voices" came to the fore. The rebuilding of the Amsterdam theatre after it had been burned to ashes at the turn of the nineteenth century was a matter of debate because it was brought into connection with the "social issue": it could not be made clear to the members of the city council why the city should help rebuilding the theatre if it could not be guaranteed that it would truly become a theatre for the general public. For that reason the theatre should be the property of the city rather than of a wealthy minority. Boekman continued that these voices became even stronger in discussions about one building in Amsterdam: Berlage's Stock Exchange. Indeed, no debates had been more heated than these.

It is worth quoting Boekman at length here because he makes explicit what motivates and underscores the question of the relation of state and the arts:

> Criticism [of this building] declined over the years, the admiration of many, the appreciation of all increased. Today, the Stock Exchange is one of the monuments of Dutch architecture. … The Stock Exchange has its unique and special character for another reason as well. More consistently than with any other building of the nineteenth century, the purpose has been from the very start to attain a community of the arts. Architecture, poetry, architectural sculpture and painting unite harmoniously. The building that gloriously brings the history of Dutch nineteenth-century art to a close, received the best of the young artists of those days,

Berlage, Derkinderen, Mendes da Costa, Roland Holst, Toorop, Verwey en Zijl. Its finish opens a new era, in which the government, the municipal government in particular, no longer could persevere in its indifference and aloofness to the arts. (Boekman 1939, pp. 77–78)

Boekman's choice of the Stock Exchange not incidentally gave prominence to the generation of the 1890s, as in fact many of the captions to the chapters of his thesis were taken from this same generation. The Stock Exchange most clearly showed a unity of the arts in the sense of a "Gesamtkunstwerk", but it also revealed a sense of community, which showed the important role of the government in furthering the arts. It fell to the state to further the sense of community entailed in the social conception of art as it was developed by the generation of the 1890s that lay at the root of an essentially aesthetic conception of socialism. Art should express a sense of social harmony, and it was the job of to the state to further such expressions. Through the promotion of culture, the state not only furthered a sense of beauty in separate individuals, but it also furthered a sense of social cohesion.

The second part of the thesis, in which he turned to the twentieth century, emphasized the important role that social democrats had played in stabilizing the interventionist role of the state with regard to the arts. As Boekman's comparative statistics for the years 1931 and 1939 showed, this was particularly so on the more local level of the cities, most prominently in Amsterdam. The generation of the 1890s had opened a "new era" indeed, in which the state could no longer rest indifferent to the integrative role of the arts for society. For this reason it was no coincidence that Catholic commentators as well as socialists gave such high praise to Boekman's thesis. As a typical social democrat of the 1930s, Boekman replaced the role of the old ecclesiastic institutes in furthering culture by that of the state.

The emphasis on the role of the state did have (and still has) a paternalistic aroma; those that had been excluded from the arts should be given greater opportunities for their enjoyment, but such an argument presupposes that there are expressions of arts of high quality that one could single out to subsidize one way or another. Boekman's annoyance as alderman of education and culture with communists like David Wijnkoop was precisely about the latter's denial that such artistic expressions existed. For Wijnkoop, any support for the arts from the state was only support for biased forms of art – art that obeyed capitalist criteria and so was unfit to fulfil the true needs of the working class. Only when social conditions had been revolutionized would art surface that genuinely expressed the interests of the working class. For him, it was only wasting energy and money to support existing bourgeois culture and its dissemination over the working class against its own interest. One might even infer that for this reason Wijnkoop did not even bother to know the facts and circumstances of concrete cases of city intervention – something for which Boekman always took him to task. Boekman's reference to statistical evidence made sense on the assumption that the furthering of *existing*, traditional artistic expressions was to the benefit of the working class and would contribute to their social emancipation.

In their monumental biography, Jansen and Rogier considered it one of the weaknesses of Boekman's thesis that he almost exclusively based his investigations into the relation of the state and the arts on official reports and statistics. Through his life as an active politician, and through his increasing commitment to a Fabian version of social democracy, Boekman had come to place increasing emphasis on the role of the state in social and economic policy. It was, we have seen above, no different for culture. Therefore it was natural for him to look at the state's role in this regard on the general and on the lower levels. In a sense, Boekman thus perfectly fits the early nineteenth-century idea of the statistician as a "statist" or "political arithmetician": someone who uses factual evidence in relation to the state to improve its politics.

Boekman's alleged weakness thus is intimately linked to his belief in state intervention as the road to general social progress. In relation to the ambitious plan of the social democrats to use state intervention to further economic growth (the famous "Plan van de Arbeid" (Labour Plan) of 1936 designed by Jan Tinbergen, Hein Vos and Bob van Gelderen among others – De Jong remarks that "Boekman thinks like them" (quoted in Dulken & Jansen 1989, p. 41). This is true for his views on culture and the arts as well.

News from Nowhere

In 1934 Boekman gave an obituary on William Morris to the VARA-radio – the radio broadcast association (not company) of the Social Democrats. Boekman referred to Ruskin as being "in many ways Morris's example", protesting against the "uniform, nasty-deadly products" that were so characteristic of the "modern, capitalist, commercial mode of production" and retreating to a romanticized past: the middle ages of the Gothic. As a typographer, Boekman was clearly much impressed with Morris's revolutions in press-editing at Kelmscott House. He praised the translation of *News from Nowhere* by the early foreman of the Social Democrats, Frank van der Goes, who promised the "utopia of a delightful art, made by the people for the people, a happiness to its maker and user" (Dulken & Jansen 1989, p. 129).

As the protagonist of his novel, Morris was a dreamer rather than a scientist, and the novel should not be judged as a work of science, so Boekman told the audience. But Boekman clearly showed sympathy for the way in which Morris turned his visionary ideals into practice. It was the same sympathy he showed for the Dutch generation of the 1890s. Their vision underscored his efforts to stake out a field for cultural policy, particularly on the local, city level. As a practical politician, Boekman put trust in numbers to give flesh to these efforts.

But whatever numbers give, they cannot tell you what Ithaca looks like. The vision contained in a descriptive analysis is inherently received from the past. And so it may well be that those who have a clear vision of how the future should look consider such a description to only lead down a false trail. One might think of politicians like the communist Wijnkoop, for whom all received culture was just that and therefore one needed no factual information.

One might also think of those avant-garde movements in the interwar period that struggled as much with the relation of art and society as the generation of the 1890s discussed above for the Dutch case, and which aimed at the instalment of radically new criteria to assess the aesthetic. This impressive group of avant-garde intellectuals gathered around the international journal *i10* that was edited at the end of the 1920s by the anarchist Arthur Lehning. Members of *De Stijl*, like Mondriaan, Oud, Rietveld, Van Eesteren, Stam, and artists and essayists like Pijper, Ter Braak, Moholy-Nagy, Arp, Kandinsky, Bloch, Benjamin, Schwitters and many others contributed to this short lived journal which genuinely showed radically new visions of community art: sociable art – on the relation of art and society. In this journal, film and radio were embraced as new means of artistic expression; Mondriaan developed a radically new vision of the city; and, on a somewhat smaller scale, Van Eesteren and Stam designed radical reconstructions for one of the oldest parts of Amsterdam – the Rokin – which would meet the future needs of traffic and trade. These designs for the Rokin were heavily criticized by Boekman for putting the needs of the economy over those of the social fabric of the city.

In a similar tone to Boekman, Richard Roland Holst reproached *De Stijl* for embracing the cold mechanistic conditions of modern industrial society rather than criticizing them, while members of *De Stijl* accused the aesthetic socialists of the 1890s of randomly taking recourse to the medieval past for their symbolisms rather than trying to find solutions to concrete problems in architecture and design in terms of its contemporary techniques. The architect Van Eesteren wrote dismissively about the "brickstone puzzles" and "false romanticism" of the Amsterdam School. Just like Mondriaan, he rejected its emphasis and use of the closed housing block as "Kulissenstädtebau" (an unmistakable reference to Potemkin's long overdue Russian quasi-villages) and instead preferred open and transparent housing blocks. These voices found a sympathetic hearing with the more radical socialist, communist and anarchist currents that had more structural difficulties with the idea that under the present conditions of society, art and culture could be an appropriate expression of the needs of the working class.

Such mindsets were alien to Boekman, who strongly believed that the fabric of society could only gradually be transformed, or better: improved. State support for the arts served to enhance the sociability of society. He shared this belief with the older generation of the 1890s, and presented his evidence for it in his sociographic, descriptive analysis of the relation of the state to the arts. While the generation of the 1890s had materialized their vision in brickstone and glass, Boekman's message was much more neutral, however. He refrained from making substantial claims about which specific works of art should or should not be supported by the state because judgements on the arts fell outside the scope of government intervention. In that sense, Boekman was as much in agreement with Thorbecke as were the other pillars of Dutch society. Boekman's descriptive approach to government intervention could gain the status of reference point after the Second World War just because the only substantial claim he defended after all was that there was no way back in state support for the arts. For Boekman, government policy for the arts was about the conservation and the dissemination of culture over all layers of society. What choices to make and how remained unstated, but would become a matter of heated policy debates after the war (see in particular Oosterbaan Martinius 1990). Boekman placed these debates outside the scope of his thesis, as they were placed outside the reach of his life because of his untimely death.

ACKNOWLEDGEMENTS

I would like to thank Oliver Bennett, Jeremy Ahearne, and Ruth Leary for organizing an intense seminar on intellectuals and cultural policy. I thank all participants, and Oliver Bennett in particular, for their comments on an earlier version of this paper. The usual caveat applies.

NOTES

1. Van der Ploeg turned out to be quite persistent in his references to Boekman, as witnessed from a presentation on cultural education of 22 March 2000 (Van der Ploeg 2000). Since presentations of members of the government are normally written by civil servants, one can safely infer that Boekman's ideas on cultural policy were still prominent within the administrative domain, even in 2000.
2. There is a wealth of literature on Morris and the Fabians. Apart from his own writings, E. P. Thompson's biography (Thompson 1988) is a must. See Kinna (2000) and Upchurch (2002) for recent accounts relevant to this paper and for further references. On the Fabians, see McBriar (1962) and Cole (1961), as well as *Fabian Essays* itself (Shaw 1962).
3. The party leader of the SDAP, Willem Troelstra, notoriously proclaimed revolution in the Netherlands in 1918 after the outbreak of the Bolshevik Revolution. This episode served as

catalyst for a definitive break between social democrats and communists in the Netherlands as it also enforced a break within the SDAP itself; some important members of the SDAP, such as Henriette Roland Holst-van Schaik and Herman Gorter, two of the most distinguished Dutch poets, definitively came to side with the communist party.
4. "Eens zal de dag, opgaand, vinden Arbeid en Schoonheid vereend."
5. And highly successfully so. The city extension "Plan Zuid" has become one of the neighbourhoods most in demand in Amsterdam, and still shows signs of very strongly felt community, though its inhabitants now primarily are part of the wealthy middle and upper class compared to its first inhabitants who belonged to a large extent to the working class.
6. Jan Rogier was director of the Boekmanstichting from 1978 to 1986 when he unexpectedly died.
7. The central text on Dutch pillarization is Lijphart (1968). For a recent assessment of the usefulness of this term, see Blom (2000).
8. In later life, Van Gelderen became professor of political economy. One of his first studies, published in the socialist and radically inclined periodical *De Nieuwe Tijd* (the new era) in 1913, was on business cycles. The article attracted international scholarly attention and still is considered a classic contribution to the study of business cycles (Freeman 1996).
9. This conception of statistics was also embraced by the Dutch Central Bureau of Statistics (CBS), and by one of the prominent Dutch professors of political economy and statistics in the early decades of the twentieth century, C. A. Verrijn Stuart, who wrote the first Dutch handbook in statistics (Verrijn Stuart 1910) – a book Boekman certainly would have known.
10. The social democrats (and trade unions) had a betwixt attitude towards the unemployed. An unemployed person could not become a member of the SDAP, for example. In fact, the unemployed were treated like untouchables. This attitude only gradually changed in the interwar period.
11. "What was not pinned or nailed down has been squandered up to small exceptions from the innumerable Dutch private collections to foreign countries."
12. "Kunst is geen regeeringszaak."
13. For a brief overview of Thorbecke's views on the relation of state and the arts, see Kempers (1994). A biography of Thorbecke, commissioned by the Royal Dutch Academy of Sciences (KNAW) to Remieg Aerts, is scheduled to appear in 2008.

REFERENCES

BLOEMGARTEN, S. & VELZEN, J. VAN (1997) *Joods Amsterdam in een bewogen tijd, 1890–1940,* Waanders, Zwolle.
BLOKKER, J. (1998) 'Klutsei', *De Volkskrant* (daily newspaper), 5 September, p. 7.
BLOM, J. C. H. (2000) 'Pillarisation in perspective', *West European Politics,* vol. 23, no. 3, pp. 153–164.
BOEKMAN, E. (1917) 'The problem of casual dock labour in Holland', *Economic Journal,* vol. 27, no. 105, pp. 115–118.
BOEKMAN, E. (1939) *Overheid en kunst in Nederland,* Hertzberger, Amsterdam.
BOOT, C. & HEIJDEN, M. VAN DER (1978) Gemeenschapskunst, in *Kunstenaren der idee: Symbolistische tendenzen in Nederland, c. 1880–1930,* ed. C. Blotkamp, Staatsuitgeverij, Den Haag, pp. 36–47
BORRIE, G. W. B. (1968) *F. M. Wibaut: mens en magistraat. Ontstaan en ontwikkeling der socialistische gemeentepolitiek,* Van Gorcum & Co., Assen.
BREGSTEIN, P. & BLOEMGARTEN, S. (2004) *Herinnering aan Joods Amsterdam,* De Bezige Bij, Amsterdam.
COLE, M. (1961) *The Story of Fabian Socialism,* Heinemann, London.

DULKEN, H. VAN & JANSEN, T. (eds) (1989) *Het leven als leerschool: portret van Emanuel Boekman,* Van Gennep, Amsterdam.

ETTY, E. (1997) *Liefde is heel het leven niet: Henriette Roland Holst, 1869–1952,* Balans, Amsterdam.

FREEMAN, C. (1996) *Long Wave Theory,* Edward Elgar, Cheltenham.

GOLDMAN, L. (1983) 'The origins of British "social science": Political economy, natural science and statistics, 1830–1835', *Historical Journal,* vol. 26, no. 3, pp. 587–616.

GOLDMAN, L. (2002) *Science, Reform and Politics in Victorian Britain: The Social Science Association, 1857–1886,* Cambridge University Press, Cambridge.

HARMSEN, G. J. (1966) *Voorspel, ontstaan en verloop van het schisma in het Nederlandse communisme; de geschiedenis van de CPH-CC (de Wijnkoop-partij), 1926–1930.*

JANSEN, T. & ROGIER, J. (1983) *Kunstbeleid in Amsterdam, 1920–1940: Dr E. Boekman en de socialistische gemeentepolitiek,* Sun, Nijmegen.

KEMPERS, B. (1994) *Het kunstbeleid kan het wel zonder Thorbecke stellen,* NRC, Handelsblad.

KINNA, R. (2000) 'William Morris: Art, work and leisure', *Journal of the History of Ideas,* vol. 61, no. 3, pp. 493–512.

KOEJEMANS, A. J. (1967) *David Wijnkoop: een mens in de strijd voor het socialisme,* Moussault's Uitgeverij, Amsterdam.

LIJPHART, A. (1968) *The Politics of Accommodation: Pluralism and Democracy in the Netherlands,* University of California Press, Berkeley, CA.

MAAS, H. (2005) *William Stanley Jevons and the Making of Modern Economics,* Cambridge University Press, Cambridge.

MCBRIAR, A. M. (1962) *Fabian Socialism and English Politics, 1884–1918,* Cambridge, Cambridge University Press.

MULTATULI, C. T. H., TER HAAR, C. & VAN VOOLEN, E. (eds) (1993) *Verhalen uit Joods Amsterdam,* Meulenhoff, Amsterdam.

OOSTERBAAN MARTINIUS, W. (1990) *Schoonheid, welzijn, kwaliteit: kunstbeleid en verantwoording na 1945,* Schwartz-SDU, 's-Gravenhage.

PORTER, T. M. (1986) *The Rise of Statistical Thinking, 1820–1900.* Princeton University Press, Princeton, NJ.

SHAW, G. B. (1962) *Fabian Essays,* Allen & Unwin, London.

STOUTENBEEK, J. & VIGEVENO, P. (2003) *Joods Amsterdam,* Ludion, Amsterdam.

THOMPSON, E. P. (1988) *William Morris: Romantic to Revolutionary,* Stanford University Press, Stanford, CA.

UPCHURCH, A. (2002) *William Morris and the Case for Public Support for the Arts,* paper presented at Duke University/Luce conference "Public Support for the Arts", Berry Hill Centre, Virginia.

VAN DER PLOEG, F. (2000) Address as secretary of culture to forum "Cultuureducatie: franje of fundament", The Hague, 22 March.

VERHOEFF, M. & WIEREMA, T. (1999) *Ochenebbisj: verhalen en geintjes over het Amsterdamse getto, 1870–1925,* Lubberhuizen, Amsterdam.

VERRIJN STUART, C. A. (1910) *Inleiding tot de Beoefening der Statistiek. Eerste Deel,* De Erven F. Bohn, Haarlem.

HAROLD INNIS, CULTURAL POLICY, AND RESIDUAL MEDIA

Charles R. Acland

Few statements depict the backdrop to Canadian cultural policy conundrums as evocatively as Harold Innis's (1956, p. 405) wry assessment that Canada's maturation went "from colony to nation to colony". Describing the economic and psychological reorientation of the first decades of the twentieth century, Innis was alluding to the rapid shift of Canada's imperial center from the UK to the USA. With the swapping of colonial masters, and with the project of cultural and economic sovereignty perpetually unfinished, came successive waves of nationalist hand-wringing and hair-pulling, some legitimately pessimistic, some inexcusably elitist, and some just plain neurotic. The Canadian "national insecurity state" helped launch decades of critical ferment and energetic advocacy, leaving a tangled knot of defensive and avant-gardist ideas acting as ballast against imported and commercial culture.[1] Lasting national bodies that followed include the Canadian Broadcasting Corporation (est. 1936), the National Film Board of Canada (est. 1939), the National Library of Canada (est. 1953) and the Canada Council for the Arts (est. 1957). These ambitious cultural initiatives, and others like them, put in place, for better or worse, many of the dominant institutional entities and mandates that continue today in variously tinkered and tattered forms.

These policy endeavors sought the appropriate cultural and educational conditions for modern democratic citizenship. They have been responsible for advancing core ideas about democratic spaces for free expressive exchange, carrying a liberal-rational model that hopes to produce "citizens", "cosmopolitans" and "artists". But it would not be accurate to say that this has been the only product of cultural policy initiative. Cultural policy was equally concerned about a nation-building project. In this respect, the Canadian cultural establishment has displayed a conservative heart split between the desire for a *familiar* "distinctive" and "unique" Canadian cultural language and a defensible national union. These two tendencies of conservative-distinctive and liberal-rational cultural policy objectives, far from contradictory, have been responsible for our current patchwork of uneven support for industrial sectors and artist-oriented enterprises. Indeed, it is not a stretch to see a certain "Red Tory" stripe running throughout the history of Canadian cultural policy, a term describing a longstanding tradition of collectivism or soft leftism displayed by the variously named conservative parties (though not evident in the current incarnation of the federal conservative party). Similarly, a bargained relationship has attempted to promote those defensive nationalist goals alongside a desire to be a credible participant in and beneficiary of a transnational cultural market. Such a balancing act has meant that cultural policy tends to be oriented toward Ottawa and Washington, but with Hollywood (in the case of film and television) acting as the true magnetic north. This is to say that a political and ideological hodgepodge was built into the root sensibilities of the Canadian cultural project. Indeed, Innis's "colony to nation to colony" epigram was part of an argument about the ideological uncertainty of nationalism, pointing out how protectionist measures such as tariffs had actually benefited foreign industrialists. "Canadian nationalism", he wrote, "was systematically encouraged and exploited by American capital" (Innis 1956, p. 405) – a truism about cynical nationalism adaptable to many current conditions of globalization and policy formation.

Harold Innis (1894–1952) developed his ideas about economic history and media systems at exactly the same time as this messy Canadian cultural framework was being consolidated. Innis was both a product of and sharp contributor to this intellectual and political context. It is possible to assess his contributions to cultural policy studies by itemizing Innis's participation in an emerging national policy network for social science and humanities research and adult education. Alison Beale (1993), for instance, has done just that, drawing our attention to Innis's important role as a liaison between the Canadian scene and US philanthropies, especially the Rockefeller Foundation. This role assisted in decisions to fund and develop the Canadian arts and research environment, in particular the Canadian Social Science Research Council (est. 1940). Suffice it to say that for years, this aspect of Innis's work had been downplayed, leaving an erroneous portrait of a distant, ivory tower critic.[2] This view notwithstanding, I propose to consider his conceptual legacy for cultural policy. In this respect, I see as fundamental in Innis's writings a historiographic argument about knowledge and power, a critical tact that deserves special scrutiny and will be the focus of the following account of the advantages Innis provides cultural policy studies.

Innis resides as a defining figure for the disciplinary coherence of communication studies, economic history and cultural history in Canada. As a case in point, the *Literary Review of Canada* published a list of the 100 most important Canadian books, on which Innis was one of only four authors who had two entries (the other three were Margaret Atwood, Mordecai Richler and Northrope Frye) (Taylor 2005).[3] And yet, he remains largely unknown abroad. Even in Quebec, his presence beyond anglophone intellectual circles is a fairly recent development. The notable exception to the apparent immobility of Innisan thought is the work of James Carey (1989), who has assured an enduring, if marginal, influence of Innis in US communication studies. Essential in Carey's interpretation is the identification of Innis not only as an alternative to certain dominant strains of communication studies, but also as someone who prefigured North American cultural studies.

Anyone who has taken on the work of Innis has, no doubt, found it to be an exceedingly difficult and, at times, frustrating read. For all of the sheer originality of his writings, he is far from inviting as a prose stylist. Even in his day, his peers commented on his obtuseness. J. B. Brebner (1953, p. 172) called him "always a man in a hurry and ... not a little careless of sustained logic". Brebner (1957, p. 52) later wrote: "[W]hile occasionally he [Innis] gave himself time to write brilliantly, with ample guidance to others, he was usually in too much of a hurry to unburden himself of the products of research and insight to care enough about communication. As many have testified, you had to read Innis, but he made it unnecessarily hard work".

In the rush to unburden himself, a good deal of Innis's later research is weighted toward the suggestive rather than a single linear course of argumentation. Marshall McLuhan (1953, p. 392) described Innis's "roving mental eye, an intellectual radar screen" and James Carey (1967, p. 7) saw his work as a "psychedelic delicatessen". Though this adds to the task of decoding him, strangely enough, his evocativeness may go a long way in explaining the continuing interest in Innisian thought. The ambiguities built into his research have inspired subsequent interpreters to construct multiple incarnations for him, and we have witnessed him dressed up as the proto-Marxist, the anti-Marxist, the liberal economist, the conservative nationalist, the technological determinist, the intellectual activist and the media historian – to name just some of the more prominent appearances. This disciplinary adaptability in Canada responds to the scope of his writing. His early staples studies, exemplified by *The Fur Trade in Canada* (Innis 1930a) and *The Cod Fisheries* (Innis 1940a), focused on particular commodities and their related technologies of extraction, manufacture and transportation. His work for Royal Commission, Provincial Economic Inquiry (1934) brought his geographical and historical analysis of the economy to bear upon state policy. Innis's massive body of texts includes lesser know contributions like his biography of fur trader Peter Pond (Innis 1930b) and the elliptical *Idea File* (Christian 1980). Most prominently, his communication essays and lectures, notably collected in *The Bias of Communication* (Innis 1951a) and *Empire and Communications* (Innis 1950), launched a formidable critique of contemporary civilization. In these works, Innis proposed that media have relative predispositions toward lightness, transportability and impermanence or toward heaviness, immobility and permanence – that is, respectively, space and time bias. The former is best suited to political and cultural control over distances, and becomes essential to the construction of empires. The latter assists in continuity through time, and becomes a stabilizing and conservative force in society.

His later media works, composed during the last decade of his life, are typically what people continue to read today. For most students of cultural and communication studies, these works *are* Innis. Occasionally, they act as an entry point to his economics research, if those earlier texts are read at all by said scholars. I would venture that this truncated encounter with Innis may be partly responsible for the reigning view that there were essentially two Innis's: the economic historian and the communication historian. More recent scholarship has begun to reason that the split was not so dramatic and that the lessons of each phase of his life fed subsequent ones. Even in his more disjointed and unfinished efforts, interpreters are finding surprising consistency. For instance, William Buxton (200, p. 105) has offered points of contact between Innis and the *Annales* historians in his (Innis's) own version of the *longues durées*. Buxton does this through a reassessment of Innis's immense unpublished "History of Communication" manuscript, which previously had been seen as rough notes and drafts for his communications essays, but which Buxton convincingly proposes Innis designed as a comprehensive and integrated study.

To extend such claims, the complete Innis comes into focus when we treat him as a materialist historian, rather than choosing sides between economics and communication. A special critical valence in Innis's work involves cultural history. Since the 1980s, there has been an enlivening of cultural history, with its attention to the everyday and the attendant relations of power (e.g., Hunt 1989; Chartier 1988). Victoria Bonnell and Lynn Hunt (1999) typify this as part of a wider "cultural turn" taking place in the social sciences and humanities over the last few decades. Running parallel to, and at times directly informed by, cultural studies, this turn valorizes "history from below" and the "thick description" of context, and has been vital to the problematization of narrative and representation in historiography. Some, however, have seen the renewed historiographic investment as a corrective to certain "presentist" and "immaterial" strains of cultural studies, where "[p]remature anti-disciplinarity is a major problem when it leads to the abandonment of the archive and the object, to ignoring traditional cultural forms, to the shunning of close reading, and to the forgetting of anything but the currently or formerly popular" (Czaplicka *et al.* 1995, pp. 5–6). Most assuredly, cultural history is less concerned with sweeping monolithic narratives or the history of events (*histoire événementielle*), and more interested in the connections between the micro- and macro-historical – "a methodological swing ... between close-ups and extreme long shots" (Czaplicka *et al.* 1995, p. 11; cf. Lethun 1995; Burke 2001).

Any move between the detail and the panorama poses analytical quandaries, and productively so. Bonnell and Hunt (1999, p. 26) suggest that one of the lasting influences of the "cultural turn" has been a rethinking of causality such that we "no longer assume ... that causal explanation automatically traces everything cultural or mental back or down to its more fundamental components in the material world of economics and social relations". So where does Innis fit here as a precursor to this turn, given that he has been seen as relentlessly economistic, deterministic and causal in his logic? And not without reason have these labels been affixed to him, for it is possible to read "Minerva's Owl" and come to the unfortunate conclusion that he argued that Charlemagne owed his reign to changes in animal husbandry (Innis 1951b, pp. 15–16)! Sections do seem to be of a piece with the "Guns, Germs and Steel" school of historical writing. In that same essay, he skips from the Phoenicians to the Americans with scant reference to more than the alphabet and newspapers. Though it is my assessment that the charge of determinism is an unsatisfactory one to level at Innis, and that it is the juxtaposition of evidence that advances his novel claims, we nonetheless must account for the fact that Innis has inspired rigid technological determinism among his admirers, including McLuhan.

Innis's own cultural turn was an unusual intellectual path for an economist. He did not stay within the bounds of his training, taking inspiration from the iconoclastic Thorstein Veblen and choosing to seek interdisciplinary cross-pollination. On this topic, Innis (1940b, p. vi) wrote: "I find it difficult to conceive what useful purposes the formal definition of the scope of a discipline can serve, except the purposes of editors of encyclopaedias and administrators of educational institutions". In his 1944 essay "On the Economic Significance of Culture", we do not encounter what we might expect an economist to write under such a title; it is not about the marketing of cultural commodities or the effects of theater festivals, say, on local businesses and tourism. Rather this paper sketches a research program for "a sociology or a philosophy of the social sciences and particularly of economics, an economic history of knowledge or an economic history of economic history" (Innis 1944, p. 80). In it, he decried the limited explanatory power of quantitative economics, worried about our obsession with the immediate at the expense of reflection, and studied how the technologies of modernization have not led to democratic freedoms, but to centralized political and cultural power. As Judith Stamps (1995) has elaborated, attention to these issues has legitimately earned Innis a place parallel to that of some of the Frankfurt School. By the end of his essay, it is evident that the title is to be read as "on the significance of economic history for cultural critique".

To elucidate Innis's analytical method, one needs to be alert to the impressive range of evidence on which he relied. He skipped easily between legal, governmental, technological, institutional, geographical, economic and – something typically downplayed by interpreters of his writings – literary formations. "On the Economic Significance of Culture" drew from Veblen, Adam Smith and Polanyi, as well as Freud and Marx. He quoted Oscar Wilde and Victor Hugo as he discussed telegraphy and architecture. The expansiveness of this relatively compact essay consists of commentary upon economic forces (business cycles, price liquidity, postal subsidies), media (textbooks, newspapers, film), technological changes (moveable type, electric light, gunpowder), commodities (timber, cotton, wheat, patent-medicine), and cultural and social formations (religion, censorship, advertising, public opinion, national consciousness). Each point interrelates with another and none arise from a single source nor has a singular effect. Such a critical approach, driven by juxtaposition, seems to be a near perfect example of what others would call over-determination, steering wide of anything that might be mistaken for a crude economism. In fact, his consistent assessment of multiple forces of determination draws him close to the materialism of Raymond Williams, especially as exemplified by Williams's (1980 [1973]) revised base/superstructure model, which challenged the more static qualities of the traditional Marxist base and expanded the very idea of productive forces.

Innis was forging a similar path. Taking an especially Innisian statement, again from the same essay, one sees how qualified his claims were. Innis wrote: "Geography has been effective in determining the grooves of economic life through its effects on transportation and communication" (1944, p. 85). This is a deceptively careful sentence in so much as it does not propose that geography determines *tout court* transportation or the economy, but that it is one element that comprises a foundation upon which economic life develops. Typical of Innis's spatial consciousness, the assertion reflects a theorization of *distance*, not as some essential characteristic, but as a varying feature mediated by the technologies of communication and transportation. With imperial and industrial expansion as the engine, mediating technologies re-write and re-direct the exigencies of distance. Speedier vessels and advanced navigation draw continents closer together. Railways and canals cheapen, and hence foster, links to the interior of continents. And beyond resource extraction and the building of markets, such pathways spread government, religion, ideas and communal awareness. As the structure of economic and civic existence is modified, so too is the experience of distance. He left us with an axiom for cultural analysis: the historical process involves thinning or widening the grooves that cultivate social relations.

Innis was most taken with the structuring function of those grooves. This is made clear in a tribute essay written by his contemporary W. A. Mackintosh (1953, p. 187) on the occasion of Innis's death, in which he characterized Innis's "cautious groping toward generalizations which would illuminate the pattern of historical development". Here, a program for cultural history might be marked out. Though culture may be contradictory and always mutating, one must be attentive to efforts to restrict this. As cultural historian William H. Sewell, Jr (1999, p. 56) puts it:

> The typical cultural strategy of dominant actors and institutions is not so much to establish uniformity as it is to organize difference. They are constantly engaged in efforts not only to normalize or homogenize but also to hierarchize, encapsulate, exclude, criminalize, hegemonize, or marginalize practices and populations that diverge from the sanctioned ideal. By such means, authoritative actors attempt, with varying degrees of success, to impose a certain coherence onto the field of cultural practice.

Regardless of overarching objectives to create lively, diverse and sustainable cultural environments or industries, cultural policy is a domain that participates in this inscription process. Initiatives promote and lend advantage to certain tendencies, setting a course for the selective blossoming of some practices and agents over others. It behoves us to examine seriously the lasting consequence of the grooves in social existence as scratched out by policy programs. In the end, we need to ask not only about the decisions taken, but what manner of *cultural coherence* is being fabricated, fortified and advanced by said decisions.

What Innis (1944, p. 96) described as the "search for patterns rather than mathematical formulae" was a chronicle of the imposition of this coherence. Identifying the agencies, logics, technologies and locations engaged here, Innis helps us understand the administrative function at work – that is, the relationship between policy choices, governing agendas and the technological apparatus available to enact the ensuing decisions. As he saw it – and he came back to this conclusion time and again – the most pronounced features of that function are patterns of centralization. These patterns assist the establishment of "monopolies of knowledge", fortified by dominant technologies that manage or limit the storage and dissemination of culture, information and ideas. In Innis's view, such monopolies invariably "organize difference", as Sewell would put it, and promote anti-democratic conditions. For instance, here is Innis commenting upon the role of archival storage and historiography:

> The mechanics of archival organization have given enormous impetus to the writing of history from the standpoint of centralized power. Administrative machinery and preservation of records have impressed on historical writing the imprint of the state and fostered the bias which made history the handmaid of politics. (1944, p. 83)

Thus, bureaucratic rationality enforces patterns of historical memory and a conservative rigidity in which alternative practices might be effectively limited. Crucially, the focus of core/periphery relations means that Innis was never only concerned with the effects of technology or media, but how cities exercise command over vast terrains, how monopolies of knowledge differentially shape the thinking of a time and place, and how empires rise and fall. Jody Berland (1999) explored this dimension, with the goal of speculating upon the space of the "margin" for criticism, and showing, among other things, Innis's contemporary applicability to an analysis of globalization.

For Innis, the patterns of centralization (i.e., the administration of core/periphery relations) result in different rates of development in metropolitan centers and hinterland regions. The sliding scale of uneven development has many consequences for Innis's ideas. It means that he did not present the periodization of historical change without also delimiting location. History bumps along irregularly, corresponding to a host of factors from the particular routes administering ruling monopolies of knowledge to what previous infrastructure had been in place. Mackintosh made this point, noting how Innis's (1936) *Settlement and Mining Frontiers* covers the full life-cycle of the mining industry showing the subsidiary consequences for a region, including how subsequent industries take advantage of the rail and hydroelectric operations left in place, even after mining has declined (Mackintosh 1953, p. 191). The historical process is one that leaves deposits and produces layers of sediment constituting the new geography for future activities and investments. With this sedimentation in mind, we come to understand that the re-inscription of grooves cannot be precisely predicted, indicating that the supports and incentives of policy have an impact upon tangential practices and economies, all of which need to be assessed and imagined, whether geographically proximate or temporally distant.

On the point of new relations encountering the old, advantageous links are to be made with Raymond Williams, something Sut Jhally (1993) has discussed in reference to Williams's work on television and technology. A further connection can be made with Williams's efforts to give us a vocabulary for the vicissitudes of material cultural life. His concepts captured, in a fittingly loose fashion, the systematicity of culture, its dominant strains and its dynamism. In this outlook, the dominant does not form culture unequivocally like some fixed machine press. Instead, to appreciate the system-in-process model, Williams talked about temporal lags of the varying stages of cultural change, defining residual, emergent and prefiguring formations (cf. Williams 1977). Of the residual, Williams (1980 [1973], p. 40) wrote: "I mean that some experiences, meanings and values, which cannot be expressed in terms of the dominant culture, are nevertheless lived and practised on the basis of the residue – cultural as well as social – of some previous social formation", using certain religious values as a case in point. The emergent takes account of the fact "that new meanings and values, new practices, new significances and experiences, are continually being created" (Williams 1980 [1973], p. 41).

Among these concepts, residual formations are where Williams's programme for cultural materialism resonates with Innis's earlier project. In Innis, it is essential to remember that spatial and temporal biases of media technologies were relational. They were not inherent a-historical attributes, but were drawn out as technologies move into dominance, always in reciprocity with other existing and circulating technologies and tendencies. For example, Innis wrote about the role religious orders played, along with their numerous periodicals, in developing an advertising industry at the turn of the twentieth century. Advertising's role in the establishment of national markets in turn emerged from several other coinciding factors, including a willingness to believe the miraculous claims of patent-medicine advertisers, the accelerated distribution of newspapers and advertisement copy via railroad and telegraph, and even the particular architectural presence of large department stores whose image radiated beyond their city locations. As he summarized: "The phenomenal increase in the production of goods and the demands of more efficient methods of distribution stimulated the expansion of newspaper production, and newspapers stimulated production by widening and intensifying the market" (Innis 1944, p. 90). Note, then, that this is not about the new. Almost all of these factors predated the end of the nineteenth century, save department stores. A dialectical method is being employed whose analysis presumes confrontations among the already operating and the already radiating. As Stamps (1999) has addressed, Innis's dialectical thinking assured his attention to the intricacies of causality and consequence such that he avoided bracketing off points of investigation from the world. It also assured he opened up the temporality of culture to cross-fading influences as opposed to the sudden revolutionary upheaval one continues to see in some media history. Innis offered what we might think of as a view to residual technology and media. The residual is part of the process of inscription that guides what can more easily emerge. Conversely, the sediment can act as a barrier to entry for alternate forms.

I have chosen to spend time with this argument because I am convinced that an inappropriate and excessive amount of energy – and this is the case in many areas, but especially in policy circles – has gone into the study of new media, new genres, new communities, new industries and new bodies – that is, into the emergent forms. Often, the methods of doing so have been at the expense of taking account of continuity, fixity and dialectical relations with existing practices, systems and artifacts. Moreover, there is critical hubris in this work, one that is symptomatic of what Innis called our obsession with the immediate. At every turn – policy, budget, pedagogic – we seem to confront yet another grand proclamation about our age of freshly minted media trinkets. The mythologization of new media would not be surprising, but for the fact that it appears among scholars and agenda-setters who, well, should know better. One finds shocking continuity between the manifestos of aesthetic avant-gardists and the glossy pages of free business inserts to daily newspapers. Reading these sources, one might imagine that mobility, miniaturization, decentralization, media self-referentiality, blurred relations between copy and original, confounded distinctions between producer and consumer, even the very possibility of the storage and transport of ideas and expressions apart from the singular human form only appear after 1994. Thinking about residual media, then, resonates with an Innisian plea for balance in cultural analysis against the reigning "present-ism".

Some of these claims about historical critique may sound familiar. Comparable approaches, and what we can loosely identify as Innisian concepts, can be found in recent scholarship – a testament to the enduring nature of their problematics as much as their malleability. And yet I often find certain key elements do not make as forceful an appearance as they do in Innis. Greg Urban (2001) attempts to construct an anthropological model for cultural change in which "newness", quite accurately, is one of the dominant metacultural discourses of modernity. His compelling argument pays special attention to the material cultural artifact, or what he calls the "ceramicized" aspect of culture, alluding to the inscription of stories upon pottery. This material, and hence exterior and potentially public element, corresponds to an interior and immaterial sense of affiliation – that is, the shared in culture. He sees the operation of cultural *replication* – carrying versions of stories forward through time – as being overtaken with *dissemination* – in other words, a metacultural valuation of the new that carries versions through space. Though without Urban's specific interest in the re-telling of culture, this conclusion echoes a key, overarching claim of Harold Innis, who similarly worried about the time-bias of media (for Urban, "replication function") succumbing to the "present-mindedness" of space-bias (or Urban's "dissemination function"). Critically absent from Urban, Innis added that this tilting toward spatial control is a characteristic of the growth of empires. This tilting, he argued, indicated an inherent instability in those empires as a lesser weight is placed upon continuity through time.

Even for those committed to the traces of historical determination, the lessons of Innis can go ill-considered. For example, there has been a rising interest in the materialities of communication as related to technological artifacts and writing systems, exemplified in the work of Hans Ulrich Gumbrecht, Ludwig Pfieffer and Friedrich Kittler. As Pfieffer (1994, p. 12) writes: "We are looking for underlying constraints whose technological, material, procedural, and performative potentials have been all too easily swallowed up by interpretational habits". In this, Kittler (1990 [1985]) seems uniquely compelling in that his historical expansiveness and attention to symptomatic products of technological systems is strongly reminiscent of Innis. In fact, in an essay that sketches his overarching project titled "The History of Communication Media", Kittler (1996) liberally itemizes some of the standard Innisian arguments about social and cultural shifts facilitated by changing storage and transmission materials. However, he misses the power of Innis's analysis due to his (Kittler's) primary attentiveness to technological systematicity, rather than the imperial organization and administration of power. For Kittler, historical patterns consist of repetitions traceable to notation systems without thorough attention to their spatial or temporal uneven development or to core/periphery distinctions. Admittedly, this characterization gives Kittler and his cohort short shrift; he and the others who have freshly "discovered" the materialities of communication offer a poststructuralism rarely engaged in the North American context, where some versions appear to be merely the latest incarnation of New Criticism. Nonetheless, my intent here is to remind of the legacy such claims are built upon and of the existing traditions of cultural materialism, and to caution that some of the most valuable aspects of Innis have tended to be discarded or neglected in favor of an enthusiasm for minutiae, certainty or novelty.

To recapitulate, Innis's contribution to cultural analysis has been to encourage us to pay attention to (1) the patterns of cultural life that arise from multiple forces, especially new formations encountering already existing patterns; (2) the spatial and temporal forms of uneven development that result; and (3) the way this uneven development, and the administration of core/periphery relations, is an operation of empire-building.

These aspects are relevant to contemporary policy studies, and they mark Innis's potential contribution to cultural policy specifically. In order to better delineate this, for the sake of argument, let me identify three orthodoxies of cultural policy. First, a dominant strain remains oriented toward forms of bureaucratic operationalization. This impulse works by schematizing culture, if only for the purposes of targeting and rationalizing decisions. Measurement and categorization of cultural activity are central obsessions. Of this bureaucratization, Virginia R. Dominguez (2000 [1992], p. 23) writes that: "[C]ultural policies presuppose 1) the objectification of 'the cultural'; 2) clarity in the reference to culture; and 3) the belief that government has a say in the shape of a country's culture and that nations are valued and identified by their cultural characteristics". Toby Miller and George Yúdice (2002) elaborate, indicating cultural policy tends to be invested with a functionalist reproduction of existing power ultimately geared toward the modern project of producing governable citizens. Taste, education and community identity become realms in which advanced capitalist states attempt to secure a steady hold on the social order. Curiously, appeals to the authentic, the fragile and the pure abound, and functionalist cultural policy that is necessitated by, and acts through, *Gesellschaft*, still harkens back to some irretrievable *Gemeinschaft*.

The upshot of bureaucratic pressures on the operation of cultural policy, and the reification of what is recognized as culture, is a tendency to reproduce the most basic of communication models: sender-message-receiver (variously becoming creator/industry-media/technology-consumer/audience). Interestingly, the most schooled of cultural theorists can find themselves echoing such proto-cybernetic models from the late 1940s, even as they propose more complex models for the categorization and flow of cultural life. For example, the demand to segment culture for the benefit of developing cultural indicators leads Colin Mercer (2005, p. 20) to propose the following categories: creation, production and reproduction, promotion and knowledge, dissemination and circulation, and consumption and usage. While designed as a practical "thinking machine" for the problem of statistical measures of policy activity, Mercer's categories still map rather neatly onto that more conventional communication model. Challenging the assumptions of this strain, an important work on the consequences of the bureaucratic mentality is Michael Dorland (1998) that examines the discourses of cultural measurement and assessment at the heart of Canadian film policy; Ira Wagman (2005) also takes up the history of knowledge producing formations and cultural policy.

Second, cultural policy, as a predominantly liberal-rationalist venture, is future-oriented, imagining a coming state of "development" with the connotations of "improvement" in full operation. Miller and Yúdice (2002) describe this as an assumption of the "ethical incompleteness" of cultural subjects, which creates a category of people who require ameliorative projects. This is certainly a convention of Canadian cultural policy, which systematically chooses to ignore actual cultural life in favor of some imagined ideal. For example, film policy has been, and continues to be, peppered with assertions about a missing national cinema, an absence built upon a wilful neglect of the popular cinematic practices, which are deemed to be either inappropriate, undesirable or not Canadian enough (cf. Acland 2003, Chapter 7).

Third, cultural policy is location-bound. Policy involves cultural life and institutions in and serving a designated locale, be it neighborhood, municipality, metropolis, region, nation or continent. This is where, yet again, it is evident that cultural policy is as much about governance through culture as it is, say, sovereignty or distinctive identity. Not surprisingly, "citizenship" functions as a core concept, the associated rights and responsibilities to democratic society supposedly blooming in the appropriately "developed" cultural environment. There is a double-edge to this dimension. Making citizens through culture involves governing cultural subjects, but it also produces discourses of agency and ownership of cultural life. Consequently, as citizens, people may demand a say in cultural organization, which can usefully unsettle the strictest categories of functionalist policy operations. Some recent work seeks to expand this aspect, while challenging the limits of the location-bound ideal. For example, Miller and Yúdice (2002) direct us toward an internationalist orientation in which "citizenship" may not exactly recede, but is revised.

Contestations to each of these three orthodoxies are routine enough among critical policy analysts. Canadian examples of these policy dispositions are easily found – for example in the essays in the *Canadian Journal of Communication* (1994) issue on cultural development and in Andrew *et al.* (2005). With a few exceptions, most of the articles gathered there frame their arguments or challenges with those three underlying claims. Overall, the results of the functional, ameliorative and location-bound aspects of cultural policy is that material demands, like the priorities of ad hoc committees and the whims of budgetary constraints, combined with the dominant thinking of the day about, say, technological convergence, drive program formation and limit policy imagination. In a way, cultural policy becomes a mechanism for the reproduction of existing social relations, contra the language of growth, advancement and change found in much of its rhetoric.

Innisian thought draws out these problematics, productively rattling those orthodoxies with the expectation of an expansive and progressive model for policy, or what Miller and Yúdice (2002) call "transformative" cultural policy. Innis's vision of the "good" and "balanced" society showed little resemblance to the bureaucratic schematics of first-level communication modeling called for by the reigning class of cultural functionaries. His model of culture saw the struggle for humanist values shaped or stifled by material conditions, especially cultural artifacts and their technologies of production and circulation. Indeed, he expressed suspicion that state and corporate efforts served centralizing monopolies of knowledge rather than democratic progress. He unambiguously supported an interventionist agenda to correct ill-considered market developments in the realm of culture, but not as a matter of course. His understanding of economic history informed his stance that development was not a neutral arena of progress, and that it could represent the extension of the reach of a particular elite faction's power, doing so at times through the discourse and logic of education and democracy.

Furthermore, he only moved to support *dirigiste* state action after a complete examination of the historical context, with special attention to the geographic and technological framework for social and economic relations. Exemplary in this respect is his "Strategy of Culture" (Innis 1952) essay that offered detailed historical rationale for the public culture programs recommended by the Royal Commission on National Development in Arts, Letters and Sciences (1951). Innis concluded that the "constant hammering from American commercialism" and the new horizon of American military adventure – the Korean War – had made state action essential. He wrote: "We can only survive by taking persistent action at strategic points against American imperialism in all its attractive guises" (Innis 1952, p. 20). His future-oriented analysis avoided the "present-mindedness" of merely reproducing dominant ideas about capital and commercial culture through an historical understanding of how empires emerge and operate. In sum, cultural policy has generally downplayed the historical, except as captured as a lineage of policy actions and by statistics-gathering agencies. Innisian analysis, in contrast, prods us to consider the place of cultural history in cultural policy.

Perhaps most characteristic of all, concerning the location-bound nature of cultural policy, no Innisian analysis can take place and space as given. He compels us to ask what produces those entities we think of as cities, nations and empires, and what experiences follow. Rather than serving an existing place, his thought directs us to examine how policy contributes to the emergence of a particular kind of place, especially through dominant technologies of the day. As Innis's exhaustive historical research shows, changing materials and practices of writing, and the process by which these varying materials and practices are taken up by societies, contributed to the uneven development characteristic of empires. In this way, inscription systems also inscribe the organization of difference and establish cultural coherence upon a governable population, producing those categories of location like colony, empire and nation along the way.

So here is a political economy that does not match the dominant issues and approaches of what we currently describe and recognize as political economy. Yes, he prioritizes the economic organization of industries and markets. But with Innis, the economies of culture are not really about ownership, but about *movement* and *durability* – how do things get from one place to another, by what mode do they travel, for what purpose, how quickly, transported by whom, lasting how long, accessible to whom and to whose benefit. Though he is a critic of mechanization and industrialization, he is also a philosopher of distance, both temporal and spatial. As such, he focuses upon the administration of the movement of culture, charting the radiating impact of centers of production, finance and consumption. In this way, his historical assessment of the shifting geographical dimensions of culture is fundamentally about uneven development. Why does this matter? Because, as technology, media, market forces and commodities change, so too does a center/periphery relation, either strengthening or weakening monopolies of knowledge and formations of empire. I emphasize this because it appears to be one of the most overlooked aspects of his thought as many interpreters drop the study of colonialism and power in favor of a crude determinism about media and technological forms. Moreover, cultural policy has found itself increasingly positioned close to the heart of modern governmentality, and as such, it plays an ever-more crucial role in the formation and administration of uneven development. To avoid confronting this dimension of policy is to risk reproducing a triumphalism in which "better" policy makes "better" and more ethical citizens, rather than systems of exclusions and historical blindspots.

Innis's method zeroed in on historical impressions – that is, the way cultural formations leave footprints and create the paths upon which we now try to make decisions for coming situations. What foundational or residual base has been and is being constructed? What groove has been and is being inscribed? In the most straightforward terms, he asks us to consider the collateral damage of policy initiatives. In the Canadian context, this means a half-fulfilled promise of a public culture, its institutional and textual products accumulating over the decades and serving as a sometimes prominent and sometimes neglected aesthetic and artifactual backdrop. It equally produced unintended consequences ranging from the impression of elitism to limited senses of an authorized multiculturalism.

His plea for historical consciousness, sounded at a moment when forces sought to stifle such thinking, was the most appropriate response of the modern engaged critic. Today, we still feel the need for this stance, if only to fight the industrial and technological Darwinism that makes up much of the discussion about convergence, synergy and globalism, and taints so much of our understanding about future cultural development, terms that do little to mask an obsession with the immediate. Is there a cultural policy context today that is *not* obligated to address, manage or exploit new technology or new media? And given this, is there a cultural policy context that is *not* pulled, reluctantly or otherwise, toward dominant presumptions and myths of the new? I believe the instances in which cultural policy has the luxury of avoiding this pull are rare, and this observation alone raises high a flag of suspicion about what much of our cultural policy is actually developing and promoting.

Innis's call for balance between space and time, present and past, oral and literate, in the end, was an effort to voice what he saw as the most likely conditions for democratic life. To quote Mackintosh (1953, p. 193) from his tribute to Innis: "It was the roots of the present that he was looking for, not the chronicle of the past". Leslie Pal (1977, p. 34), on the occasion of the 25th anniversary of his passing, similarly indicates: "Past activities and patterns were not entombed in dusty books, neither were they once-and-forgotten affairs. History for Innis was the accumulated structure of bias which shaped contemporary activity". Now, we continue to live with the cult of the immediate; many appear to envisage a world that constructs itself anew with every turn of the calendar's pages. The very concept of "change" is part of the folklore of our age. Some may debate whether or not our world has been given over to a new age of technology, but it is most assuredly the case that our daily lives are increasingly saturated with discussions about this new era. As a result, we prepare ourselves and our students to live with change, developing programs, institutions, departments and industries to acclimatize us to perpetual upheaval in social life. We, unfortunately, insist that policy – cultural, economic and education – help people and organizations keep pace with some imagined standard rate of modification, progress and development. "Change" is a dominant tale we tell ourselves. It is going to be disastrous if cultural policy formation and analysis continues to ventriloquize that tale, to be equally complicit in the fetishization of the emergent over the residual, and to legitimate myths of technological advantage. For all of Innis's many despairing moments, few seem as prophetic and ripe for reconsideration today as the closing statement to "Industrialism and Cultural Values": "Each civilization has its own methods of suicide" (Innis 1951c, p. 209). To this we might add: each, too, has its own methods of forgetting.

ACKNOWLEDGEMENTS

Earlier versions of this research were presented at the Special Panel in Honour of Harold Innis, University of Toronto, May 2002, and at the Intellectuals and Cultural Policy Symposium, Centre for Cultural Policy Studies, University of Warwick, September 2005. Discussion at each venue greatly assisted the development of the paper, particularly those with Jeremy Ahearne, Oliver Bennett, Jody Berland, Chris Bilton, Bill Buxton, James Carey, Heather Menzies, Graham Murdock and Will Straw. This essay is dedicated to James Carey, dear teacher and mentor, who inspired several generations of critical communication scholars, and whose work will no doubt inspire several more.

NOTES

1. Dowler (1999) is a perceptive commentary on these issues of policy, applying Wesley Wark's (1992) description of Canada as a "national insecurity state" to matters of culture.
2. Full documentation of Innis's wide-ranging policy and administrative work appears in several of the contributions to Acland and Buxton (1999); see also Paul Heyer's (2003) biographical reassessment of Innis.
3. Innis's *The Fur Trade in Canada: An Introduction to Canadian Economic History* (Innis 1930a) holds the number 16 spot and *Empire and Communications* (Innis 1950) comes in at number 27.

REFERENCES

ACLAND, C. R. (2003) *Screen Traffic: Movies, Multiplexes and Global Culture,* Duke University Press, Durham, NC.

ACLAND, C. R. & BUXTON, W. J. (eds) (1999) *Harold Innis in the New Century: Reflections and Refractions,* McGill-Queen's University Press, Montreal/Kingston.

ANDREW, C., GATTINGER, M., JENNOTTE, M. S. & STRAW, W. (eds) (2005) *Accounting for Culture: Thinking through Cultural Citizenship,* University of Ottawa Press, Ottawa.

BEALE, A. (1993) 'Harold Innis and Canadian cultural policy in the 1940s', *Continuum,* vol. 7, no.1, pp. 75–90.

BERLAND, J. (1999) 'Space at the margins: Critical theory and colonial space after Innis', in *Harold Innis in the New Century: Reflections and Refractions,* eds C. R. Acland & W. J. Buxton, McGill-Queen's University Press, Montreal/Kingston, pp. 281–308.

BONNELL, V. E. & HUNT, L. (eds) (1999) *Beyond the Cultural Turn: New Directions in the Study of Society and Culture,* University of California Press, Berkeley, CA.

BREBNER, J. B. (1953) 'Review of *Changing Concepts of Time*', *Canadian Historical Review,* vol. 34, pp. 171–173.

BREBNER, J. B. (1957) 'Review of *The Fur Trade in Canada: An Introduction to Canadian Economic History,* revised edition', *Review of Books,* pp. 52–53.

BURKE, P. (ed.) (2001) *New Perspectives on Historical Writing,* 2nd edn, Pennsylvania State University Press, University Park, PA.

BUXTON, W. J. (2003) 'Harold A. Innis's "History of Communications" manuscript', in *Harold Innis,* by P. Heyer, Rowman & Littlefield, Lanham, MD, pp. 103–111.

CAREY, J. (1967) 'Harold Innis and Marshall McLuhan', *Antioch Review,* vol. 27 (Spring), pp. 5–39.

CAREY, J. (1989) *Communication as Culture: Essays on Media and Society,* Unwin Hyman, Boston, MA.

CHARTIER, R. (1988) *Cultural History: Between Practices and Representation*, trans. L. Cochrane, Polity Press, London.

CHRISTIAN, W. (1980) *The Idea File of Harold Adams Innis*, University of Toronto Press, Toronto.

CZAPLICKA, J., HUYSSEN, A. & RABINBACH, A. (1995) 'Introduction. Cultural history and cultural studies: Reflections on a symposium', *New German Critique*, vol. 65 (Spring/Summer), pp. 3–17.

DOMINGUEZ, V. R. (2000 [1992]) 'Invoking culture: The messy side of "cultural politics"', in *The Politics of Culture: Policy Perspectives for Individuals, Institutions and Communities*, eds G. Bradford, M. Gary & G. Wallach, Free Press, New York, pp. 20–37.

DORLAND, M. (1998) *So Close to the State/s: The Emergence of Canadian Feature Film Policy*, McGill-Queen's University Press, Montreal/Kingston.

DOWLER, K. (1999) 'Early Innis and the post-Massey era in Canadian culture', in *Harold Innis in the New Century: Reflections and Refractions*, eds C. R. Acland & W. J. Buxton, McGill-Queen's University Press, Montreal/Kingston, pp. 229–354.

HEYER, P. (2003) *Harold Innis*, Rowman & Littlefield, Lanham, MD.

HUNT, L. (ed.) (1989) *The New Cultural History*, University of California Press, Berkeley, CA.

INNIS, H. (1930a) *The Fur Trade in Canada: An Introduction to Canadian Economic History*, Yale University Press, New Haven, CT.

INNIS, H. (1930b) *Peter Pond: Fur Trader and Adventurer*, Irwin & Gordon, Toronto.

INNIS, H. (1936) *Settlement and Mining Frontiers* (with Arthur Lower, *Settlement and Forest Frontier in Eastern Canada*), McMillan Co., Toronto.

INNIS, H. (1940a) *The Cod Fisheries: The History of an International Economy*, Yale University Press, New Haven, CT.

INNIS, H. (1940b) 'Foreword', in *Essays in Sociology*, ed. C. W. M. Hart, University of Toronto Press, Toronto, pp. v–viii.

INNIS, H. (1944) 'On the economic significance of culture', *Journal of Economic History*, vol. 4, pp. 80–97.

INNIS, H. (1950) *Empire and Communications*, Clarendon Press, Oxford.

INNIS, H. (1951a) *The Bias of Communication*, University of Toronto Press, Toronto.

INNIS, H. (1951b) 'Minerva's Owl', in *The Bias of Communication*, University of Toronto Press, Toronto, pp. 3–32.

INNIS, H. (1951c) 'Industrialism and cultural values', *American Economic Review*, vol. 41, pp. 201–209.

INNIS, H. (1952) 'The strategy of culture', in *Changing Concepts of Time*, University of Toronto Press, Toronto, pp. 1–20.

INNIS, H. (1956) 'Great Britain, the United States and Canada', in *Essays in Canadian Economic History*, University of Toronto Press, Toronto, pp. 394–412.

JHALLY, S. (1993) 'Communications and the materialist conception of history', *Continuum*, vol. 7, no. 1, pp. 161–182.

LETHUN, H. (1995) 'Kracauer's pendulum: Thoughts on German cultural history', *New German Critique*, vol. 65 (Spring/Summer), pp. 37–45.

KITTLER, F. A. (1990 [1985]) *Discourse Networks 1800/1900*, trans. M. Metteer & C. Cullens, Stanford University Press, Stanford, CA.

KITTLER, F. A. (1996) 'The history of communication media', *Ctheory* (July) [online], available at: http://www.ctheory.net.

MACKINTOSH, W. A. (1953) 'Innis on Canadian economic development', *Journal of Political Economy*, vol. 61, no. 3, pp. 185–194.

MCLUHAN, M. (1953) 'The later Innis', *Queen's Quarterly*, vol. 60, pp. 385–394.

MERCER, C. (2005) 'From indicators to governance to the mainstream: Tools for cultural policy and citizenship', in *Accounting for Culture: Thinking Through Cultural Citizenship*, eds C. Andrew, M. Gattinger, M. S. Jennotte & W. Straw, University of Ottawa Press, Ottawa, pp. 9–20.

MILLER, T. & YÚDICE, G. (2002) *Cultural Policy*, Sage, Thousand Oaks, CA.

PAL, L. A. (1977) 'Scholarship and the later Innis', *Journal of Canadian Studies*, vol. 12, no. 5, pp. 32–44.

PFIEFFER, K. L. (1994) 'The materiality of communication', in *The Materialities of Communication*, eds H. U. Gumbrecht & K. L. Pfieffer, Stanford University Press, Stanford, CA, pp. 1–12.

ROYAL COMMISSION ON NATIONAL DEVELOPMENT IN ARTS, LETTERS AND SCIENCES (1951) *Report*, King's Printer, Ottawa.

ROYAL COMMISSION, PROVINCIAL ECONOMIC INQUIRY (1934) *Report and Complimentary Report*, King's Printer, Halifax.

SEWELL, W. H., JR. (1999) 'The concept(s) of culture', in *Beyond the Cultural Turn: New Directions in the Study of Society and Culture*, eds V. E. Bonnell & L. Hunt, University of California Press, Berkeley, CA, pp. 35–61.

STAMPS, J. (1995) *Unthinking Modernity: Innis, McLuhan and the Frankfurt School*, McGill-Queen's University Press, Montreal/Kingston.

STAMPS, J. (1999) 'Innis in the Canadian dialectical tradition', in *Harold Innis in the New Century: Reflections and Refractions*, eds C. R. Acland & W. J. Buxton, McGill-Queen's University Press, Montreal/Kingston, pp. 46–66.

TAYLOR, K. (2005) 'What Howie Meeker and Atwood have in common', *Globe and Mail*, 18 November, p. A3.

URBAN, G. (2001) *Metaculture: How Culture Moves Through the World*, University of Minnesota Press, Minneapolis, MN.

WAGMAN, I. (2005) 'Back from the margins: The Royal Commission studies of Charles Siepmann and Dallas Smythe', paper presented at 'Tracking: A Symposium on the History of Communication Studies in Canada', Concordia University, Montreal, November.

WARK, W. (1992) 'Security intelligence in Canada, 1864–1945: The history of a "national insecurity state"', in *Go Spy the Land: Military Intelligence in History*, eds K. Neilson & B. J. C. McKercher, Praeger, Westport, CT, pp. 153–178.

WILLIAMS, R. (1980 [1973]) 'Base and superstructure in Marxist cultural theory', in *Problems in Materialism and Culture*, Verso, New York, pp. 31–49.

WILLIAMS, R. (1977) *Marxism and Literature*, Oxford University Press, New York.

FERNAND DUMONT AND THE VICISSITUDES OF CULTURAL POLICY IN QUÉBEC

William J. Buxton

Cultural Policy and Its Discontents

Cultural policy, as it is usually discussed, takes place within the framework of a political system capable of enacting legally binding legislation. A recent definition found in a discussion of Canada's cultural policy is a case in point:

> Cultural policy is the expression of a government's willingness to adopt and implement a set of coherent principles, objectives and means to protect and foster its country's cultural expression. The arts are the very foundation of this expression. In an age when countries are becoming increasingly interdependent economically and politically, promoting cultural expression by means of a coherent cultural policy for the arts is a valuable way to emphasize and define what distinguishes one country from another. (Canada 1999, p. 1)

While this definition in principle applies to regional entities (such as provinces) or local entities (such as municipalities), most discussions of cultural policy examine it at the nation-state level. This way of framing cultural policy certainly makes sense, given that intervening in the cultural sphere has become such a central feature of how the countries of the world identify and deploy the resources available to them. But it also is constricting in that it implies the nation-state framework provides a general model readily applicable to all instances of cultural policy. However, there are innumerable instances both above and below the nation-state level where cultural policy is implemented. In the international arena, UNESCO has been particularly important in this regard. Indeed, by virtue of the program it launched in the postwar period, its member nation-states were obliged to take stock of their cultural resources and implement programs geared to the preservation and development of culture (Valderrama 1995). Similarly, below the nation-state level, cultural policy takes place in a variety of arenas. In addition to regional and local authorities (Bianchini 1996; Martorella 2002), cultural policy can be found in a myriad of institutional settings including health, religion and education. While these agencies for cultural policy differ in scope and magnitude from those of the nation-state, they share in common with the larger entities the stability and routinization that comes with juridically based forms of authority.

However, there are innumerable instances below the nation-state level in which the range and nature of authority is contested, and where the policy-making structure is lacking both in stability and routinization. Possibly the most notable example of these are ethnic groups or nationalist movements that challenge the division of powers within the nation-state(s) they inhabit and are continually pressing for greater autonomy. These would include movements such as the Palestine Liberation Organization, the Zapatistas of Chiapas, Mexico (Vaughan 1997) and Shining Path of Peru. Arguably, a form of cultural policy is central to their struggle in that their success is predicated upon their ability to cultivate a sense of community and belonging within the group in question.

One of the most intriguing cases of a nationalist movement operating below the nation-state level is that of francophone (previously called "French-Canadian") nationalism, which has become identified with the province of Québec. What distinguishes this case from many other independence movements is the fact that Québec nationalists of various tendencies, over the course of the past fifty or so years, have been able to institutionalize their aspirations within the structure of the Québec provincial government – in effect, redefining the division of powers between the Québec state and the federal authority (Lacroix 1992; Bonin 1992). A particularly notable aspect of this reconfiguration of the Québec state has been the institutionalization of cultural policy enshrined in a series of ministries beginning with the Department of Cultural Affairs established in 1961 by the Liberal premier of the province, Jean Lesage[1] (Marsh 1988, p. 552). Over the subsequent years, the succeeding ministries have been extremely active not only in planning and implementing cultural policy, but orchestrating extensive research projects on the meaning and nature of culture; the latter have been crucial in providing the foundations for the various policy measures that have been enacted (L'Allier 1976; Québec 1978a, 1978b, 1992).

It should be emphasized that this provincial cultural policy has been exercised within the context of Canadian federalism. The Canadian state, of course, has become well known for its interventions into cultural life through major legislative measures such as the founding of the Canadian Broadcasting Corporation, the National Film Board and various funding agencies as a result of the 1949–1951 Massey-Lévesque Commission, including the Canada Council and the Humanities Research Council (Litt 1992; Van den Bosch & Beale 1998). Paralleling the Québec state's involvement in cultural affairs, the federal government has overseen cultural matters through a series of ministries, the current variant of which is called the "Department of Canadian Heritage" ("Patrimoine canadien").[2] Given the duplication and overlap between the two levels of government, inevitably there are clashes and disputes about how cultural policy is designed and implemented and, in particular, to what extent federal policies hold sway in Québec.

However, there is more at issue here than simply jurisdictional conflict – a state of affairs that is endemic in federal structures. What makes the Québec case particularly fascinating is the fact that the Québec state, in its coupling with the francophone nationalist movement, has not been a fixed entity; particularly since the Quiet Revolution, it has been almost continuously in flux.[3] This has involved both its continual redefinition in relation to the aspirations of francophone nationalists, as well as to the Canadian federal state (Allor & Gagnon 1994). In effect, Québec can be viewed as an instance of what Benedict Anderson (1983) called an "imagined community", in which both the act of imagining and what constitutes the community have been chronically contested terrains.

The case of Québec raises some important issues about the relationship between cultural policy and the intellectual. If we confine ourselves to the nation-state framework, we are obliged to ascribe a certain fixity to both the legislative body and to the role played by the intellectual in defining and shaping the cultural policy for which the state is responsible. That is to say, because the nation-state has reasonably clear lawmaking and administrative capacities, its policy framework tends to be stable and routinized. This means that the role of the intellectual in relation to the policy-formation process becomes similarly circumscribed.[4] However, if we are dealing with an "imagined community" that is emergent and inchoate, as in the case of Québec, the role of the intellectual is arguably much different from that found in relation to conventional nation-states. Above all, the intellectual – along with artists and other cultural figures – undoubtedly plays a much more central role in the cultural development of their inchoate national societies than does his or her counterpart in established nation-states. This is likely because the success of the collective project is predicated upon the cultivation and development of a common sense of culture, tradition and destiny. This is evident in the historical importance of intellectuals and cultural figures in the various movements for Québec independence, which had their embryonic form in the nineteenth century.[5]

Intellectuals and artists not only play an enhanced role in the cultural development of "imagined communities" such as Québec; the notion of culture to which they subscribe is generally broader and more wide-reaching than that serving as a point of reference within stable nation-states. As is evident in the earlier quote from a report on Canadian cultural policy, from the standpoint of the Canadian state, culture refers primarily to "creative expression" with particular reference to the arts. Cultural policy, then, is concerned with encouraging and developing this aspect of collective life. However, in Québec, culture has traditionally been used in a much broader and holistic sense, encompassing what former Québec premier Jean Lesage once called the "soul" of the French-Canadian people.[6] In this sense, culture has been viewed in terms of a bewilderingly wide range of phenomena including collective memory, language, identity, religion, education, rituals, folklore and the humanities, as well as forms of creative expression such as literature, poetry and music.[7] And since Québec has been viewed as a work in progress, the realm of culture is continually being recast and reformulated in relation to issues of national identity and policy. As key actors in the process, intellectuals, journalists and artists have enjoyed an elevated status within Québec society. It is difficult, for instance, to think of English-Canadian figures who figure as prominently in the national collective imagination as do Henri Bourassa, Lionel Groulx or Félix Leclerc in Québec.[8]

In effect, intellectuals and artists have had a recursive or reflexive relationship to the emergent Québec national community; the formation of their own identities has been closely bound up with their ongoing efforts to helping define culture in Québec. This broad project of cultural definition has taken place, of course, within the Canadian federal structure, and in relation to both the cultural mother country and to the cultural juggernaut to the south. Given the sheer numbers of intellectuals and artists who have taken part in the process of cultural definition, singling out any particular figure for closer examination is a perilous task. However, if one goes by criteria such as exploring epistemological and philosophical issues of culture with profundity, addressing cultural practices in a wide-ranging way based on a thorough understanding of cultural development in Québec, involving oneself intimately in questions of cultural policy, and gaining recognition as an eminent authority on cultural matters, one particular figure immediately jumps out: Fernand Dumont.[9] After an account of Dumont and his biographical trajectory, we will examine the relationship between his longstanding intellectual work as a cultural theorist and his involvement with Québec cultural policy.

Fernand Dumont and Québec Intellectual Life

Fernand Dumont (1927–1997) was arguably one of the greatest intellectuals produced by Québec in the twentieth century, making contributions in the areas of sociology, theology, philosophy and poetry. Born into a working-class family of modest means, he earned a master's degree at Université Laval's faculty of social sciences. In 1953, he began graduate studies at the Sorbonne in Paris, but returned to Laval to take up a professorship in 1955. He completed his doctorate at the Sorbonne in 1967 and later a second doctoral degree in 1987 in theology at Laval. His entire academic career was spent at Laval, from which he retired in 1995. Among his major accomplishments were the founding, with Jean-Charles Falardeau and Yves Martin, of *Recherches sociographiques* in 1960. This interdisciplinary journal gave particular attention to the study of Québec and francophone Canada. He also was active in policy matters, holding the chairmanship of the Commission sur les laïcs et l'Église from 1968 to 1970 and playing a central role in the drafting of Québec's cultural development policy in 1978. Following his stint in the Ministry of State for Cultural Development, he was appointed founding president of the Institut Québécois de Recherche sur la Culture, holding this position from 1979 to 1990. Following his death in 1997, the Chaire Fernand-Dumont sur la culture *INRS*-Urbanisation, Culture et Société was created in his honor (Langlois & Martin 1995; Harvey 2006).

Dumont wrote prolifically, authoring more than twenty books, along with many book chapters and articles. He also was the editor of numerous volumes and collections. He received numerous prizes and distinctions during his lifetime, including an officership of the Ordre national du Québec in 1992 and the governor-general's award for non-fiction.

While Dumont's contributions to the social sciences received national acclaim, the Canadian nation-state was far from being a point of reference for Dumont's life's work (except perhaps as an enduring irritant that he thought continually intruded upon the lives of francophones living in Québec). His Archimedean point, it goes without saying, was the French minority in Canada (who formed the majority in Québec) and its centuries-old struggle to overcome its colonial status and to control its own destiny within North America.

His upbringing could not have exposed him to the reality of colonialism any more directly. He was born and raised in the town of Montmorency, just outside of Québec City.[10] Montmorency, as was the case with many villages of Québec during the epoch, was a company town dominated by Dominion Textile – the largest employer across Québec during the period between the First World War and the end of the Second.[11] Dumont describes in detail how the plant's ownership and management was English-Canadian and American, with French-Canadians providing the labour power for the factory. At a young age, he bore witness to the strike of 1937, which was put down in a brutal fashion by company management. Dumont describes his own trajectory in vividly spatial terms as a form of emigration from popular culture to learned culture. In effect, Dumont reflexively saw his own cultural development as inherently bound up with the broader patterns of cultural change that he detected in Western civilization. He saw the popular culture of his childhood as an expression of various peoples' primordial efforts to define themselves by creating a common *sens* – "a dwelling where nature, our relations with the other, the weighty traditions of history could be confronted with conscious intentions in a never ending dialogue" (Weinstein 1985, p. 54). The primary culture was thereby broadly conceived and included a range of aspects such as "sensation, feeling, judgment, intelligence, meaning, interpretation, ... and perhaps most importantly, way and direction" (Weinstein 1985, p. 54).[12]

Dumont argues that culture develops through a process of *dédoublement*. This involves the abstraction from the immediacy of life and from primary culture into new realms of cultural practice, which come to relate to one another within an emergent complex. Contemporary cultural life, according to Dumont, is a matrix of various hermetic cultural worlds that intersect. He gives particular attention to three of these: the *culture savante*, the constellation of various other institutionalized cultural practices and the *culture populaire*. The *culture savante* refers to "a reconstitution of more primary cultures according to specialized, individualized or rationalized perspectives or postulations" (Weinstein 1985, p. 81). The cultural practices of professional groupings within such areas as law, religion, government, business and education draw on the *culture savante*, but have the specific purpose of emplacing members of society within particular webs of human relations. Finally, "popular culture" is composed of "those who receive the effects of hierarchical organizations and ... adapt to them by reworking traditional practices". In a manner somewhat akin to the approach developed by Karl Mannheim (1959) in *Ideology and Utopia*, Dumont saw these forms of culture as in dynamic relation with one another. Particular attention was given to how the social sciences, as the key sector of the *culture savante*, could help bring the other variants of knowledge/culture out of their narrowly conceived particularism, thereby raising the consciousness of members of society under the sway of these forms of cultural practice.

In Dumont's early work, these distinctions were discussed in a rather abstract fashion, referring to humankind and civilization in quite general terms (Dumont 1968). However, with the onset of the Quiet Revolution in 1960 and the massive changes attendant upon it, Dumont's cultural work became increasingly oriented towards the new reality that was taking shape within Québec.[13] In particular, in the wake of the crisis linked to the War Measures Act of 1970, Dumont began to systematically reflect upon Québec society and the direction in which it was headed (Dumont 1964; Dumont & Rocher 1964). In this regard, he took issue with those who believed that the state was to be the leading agent in the development of modernity. For *Cité Libre*[14] intellectuals such as Pierre Trudeau, it was the federal state that was to correct the twin evils of the church and nationalism; for the nationalist historians centred at the Université de Montréal, it was the Québec state that was to assume a *dirigiste* role not just in economic matters, but in cultural questions as well. By contrast, Dumont was of the view that real meaningful change could only take place through significant cultural change, involving a thorough abandonment of the widespread culture of defeat. He believed that the crisis experienced by Québec could be attributed to a failure of culture. Dumont's ambivalence about the role the state could play in the development of culture is evident in some of his reflections on cultural policy.

Dumont and Cultural Policy

Dumont's standpoint on cultural policy began to take shape during the Quiet Revolution, but was more proximately related to his direct involvement with the world of policy as well as his longstanding engagement with policy issues. He identified what he called *les politiques des cultures*, which referred to various efforts by the state to support the work or artists and creators. Dumont largely supported initiatives of this kind. However, he was much less sanguine about what he termed *la politique de la culture* – namely the state's project of incorporating the masses through its support for cultural initiatives. Indeed, as Dumont points out, state projects by their very nature had this cultural dimension.[15] What concerned him most of all was the tendency of *les politiques des cultures* to develop into *la politique de la culture*. This involved an instrumentalization of culture and its removal from public control and local expression. Given his views on cultural policy, where did Dumont then locate the creation and preservation of culture? Consistent with his commitment to popular culture, he put his faith in democratically organized social organizations that would serve as leading groups for cultural growth and preservation. Taking his cue from E. P. Thompson's *Making of the English Working Class* (Thompson 1964), Dumont felt that there were groups with similar predispositions and tendencies in Québec, such as the Catholic Workers Organization and the Association of Adult Education. In this regard he took issue with an official report on cultural policy (Québec 1991), which he felt did not adequately address the question of access to culture or of the role of popular groups in creating culture (Dumont 1995, pp. 116–123).

His reservations about cultural policy notwithstanding, Dumont was brought in as a consultant after the Parti Québécois election victory of 1976 to work in the newly formed Ministry of State for Cultural Development under the direction of Dr Camille Laurin, a psychiatrist by training and an *independentiste* by inclination. In this capacity, Dumont was responsible for producing a two-volume series on cultural development (Québec 1978a, 1978b). He also wrote the White Paper that accompanied Bill 101: the keystone of Québec's new language policy (Picard 2003, pp. 244–245). The conception of culture found in these documents was very much in line with Dumont's broad and holistic view of this phenomenon.[16]

That Dumont felt that his foray into cultural policy was not entirely successful is evident in his reflections on the experience as recorded in his autobiography (translation mine):

> The project was ambitious, and, as I was later to recognize, far too vast. In conjoining the policies of the Minister of Education with those of the Minister of Cultural Affairs, it was indispensable; the weight of the structures and the traditional boundaries did not allow it to reach its goal. To go any further than that was infinitely more risky. The intention was a worthy one: culture should not be limited to an elite with easy access to literature, arts and science; why shouldn't it penetrate into the daily existence of those who live on the margin of the cultural sanctuary? Perhaps I had let myself be influenced by the memory of my origins, of the time already a long time ago when popular culture still had a certain style, which was disappearing rapidly as a result of diverse influences, such as massive advertizing. The contributors to the White Paper produced texts of variable quality [Québec 1978a, 1978b]. The collection was unsatisfying. The question of cultural development remained in my view the most decisive for an intellectual who saw himself as responsible. The governmental arena is probably not the place most propitious for its elucidation.

After having collected the documentation useful for the elaboration of a policy of scientific research, I left the corridors of power with relief in order to return to the university and to the green pastures of theory. (Dumont 1997, pp. 199–200)

Around the same time that he was completing his stint with the government, Dumont published an essay that provides some insights into why he was less than satisfied with his experience as an architect of cultural policy (Dumont 1979). To be sure, he never mentioned his policy work directly in the article, which dealt with how cultural development had been conceptualized within sociological writings. But the fact that the expressions used and concepts deployed strikingly paralleled those of the cultural policy document, leaves little doubt about the connection between the two endeavors.[17] He argued that the concept of cultural development presupposed the notion of cultural production, based on a spurious economic model. As an alternative, he proposed that sociology should consider culture neither as a commodity nor a product, but rather as the local practice in institutions such as the school and the workplace. At first glance, it might seem that Dumont was contradicting himself. On the one hand, he had just orchestrated a series for the Minister of State for Cultural Development in which this leitmotif was front and center. On the other hand, he deconstructed and criticized cultural development policy for its instrumentalist tendencies. However, Dumont was actually being quite faithful to his own vision of how an intellectual should be involved in the making of cultural policy and in the creation of culture. He was disturbed at the tendencies he observed in Québec society following the failed referendum of 1980. In his view, echoing sentiments that had been expressed earlier by Harold Innis, intellectuals had become transformed into servants of the state and no longer were engaged in the grassroots movement of transforming the culture of Québec. Rather, the realm of cultural definition had been taken over by bureaucrats, technocrats, experts and politicians, who viewed culture in an instrumental manner (Dumont 1995, p. 241).[18] In his view, intellectuals and artists needed to maintain their practices in order to effectively intervene in questions of culture.[19] The full-time administrator did not have sufficient contact with the world of ideas and aesthetics to be in a position to deal with it in other than an instrumental and applied fashion. In effect, in deconstructing the same project for which he was responsible, Dumont was affirming himself as an intellectual, particularly one who was engaged in the production of knowledge for the sociological community. And by returning so quickly and resolutely to his practice as a sociologist, Dumont was consistent with his claim that intellectuals could only play a leading role in cultural policy matters if they maintained their status as practicing members of *la culture savante*.

Ultimately, nothing like the Dumontian vision of the working relationship between intellectuals and cultural policy-makers ever materialized in Québec. Recent ministries of culture have embraced wholeheartedly a "cultural industries model"[20] in which there is very little place for intellectuals such as Dumont and Guy Rocher (Allor 1993). And in any case, in line with tendencies remarked upon by Russell Jacoby (1987) in his jeremiad of almost two decades ago, the public intellectual in Québec is high on the list of vanishing species. Potential public intellectuals have largely eschewed the artisan-like engagement that Dumont so effectively carried out in favor of enthusiastically joining generously funded networks of researchers churning out studies within the policy frameworks defined by the new class of technocratic experts.

In sum, when reading Dumont's reflections on the role of the intellectual in relation to cultural life – against the backdrop of the various cultural policy initiatives in Québec during the last thirty years – one is struck by a strong sense of poignancy. For in his efforts to contribute, however reluctantly, to the cultural policy formation process, Dumont was undermining his own credo about what was at stake for those who saw themselves as members of the *culture savante*. For through his engagement in political life, Dumont helped to bolster and legitimate the very agencies whose assumptions and practices he had consistently impugned. And in helping Québec to achieve something approaching "normalcy" as a state and society, he unwittingly jeopardized the critical role of the intellectual that he so deeply cherished.

ACKNOWLEDGEMENTS
The author wishes to thank Martin Allor, Jean-François Côté, Christine Dancause and Manon Niquette for their assistance in the preparation of this paper.

NOTES
1. It began with a budget of CAN$3 million, which had increased to CAN$57 million by 1977 (Marsh 1988, p. 552).
2. The Department in turn comprises five sectors: Citizenship and Heritage, Cultural Affairs, International and Intergovernmental Affairs, Planning and Corporate Affairs, and Public Affairs and Communications.
3. The Quiet Revolution refers to the massive changes that took place in Québec during the period from 1960 to 1970. These included the decline of the church, greater urbanization, the growth of the state bureaucracy and educational reform (McRoberts 1988).
4. A number of my colleagues who have been invited to contribute to deliberations about communication policy have voiced their frustrations about how the issues they raised have been routinely ignored by bureaucrats running the programs.
5. They came into particular prominence beginning in the early 1960s when Québec sought to abandon its longstanding conservatism and traditionalism, embarking on a process of "*ratrappage*" ("catching up"). To a large extent, with the decline of religious authority, they began to assume the cultural leadership the church had long exercised in the province of Québec.
6. This broad notion of culture stands in contrast to the narrower focus on "the production of high culture" characteristic of the "Continental European model of cultural policy exemplified by the French case" (Toepler & Zimmer 2002, p. 36).
7. In this respect, cultural policy, as originally established in Québec, was quite similar to that of the postcolonial regimes of Malaysia and Indonesia, in which "culture was identified as a state-directed tool of national identity" (Lindsay 2002, p. 65).
8. A glance at the names of the *Métro* (subway) stations in Montreal compared to those in Toronto bears this out. By the same token, those who work in other languages, notably English, or are supportive of federal institutions are treated with indifference, as in the case of Pierre Elliot Trudeau, Sir Wilfrid Laurier, Roch Carrier and Père George-Henri Lévesque. Curiously, those who are successful in the United States – and by extension, the world market – are looked on with pride, as is the case with Céline Dion, Cirque du Soleil and André-Phillipe Gagnon.
9. One could also make a strong case for Marcel Rioux (1919–1992) as the intellectual having the most influence upon cultural policy in Québec. He not only wrote extensively on issues related to culture (Rioux 1979, 1981), but took part in the Federal Royal Commission

that examined bilingualism and biculturalism in the 1960s (Canada 1969). Above all, he chaired the provincial Royal Commission that produced an influential report on arts instruction in Québec schools with particular attention given to the teaching of music within the educational system (Québec 1968). The report's recommendations led to the establishment of vocational public music schools in Québec. However, unlike Dumont, Rioux did not participate in the actually drafting of cultural policies, and the socialist perspective that informed much of his work (e.g., Rioux 1978; Crean & Rioux 1983) was at odds with the more centrist vision of politicians and bureaucrats. Indeed, Rioux was not able to secure an academic position at Université Laval because of his radical views. For a discussion of the contributions made by both Rioux and Dumont to cultural theory in Québec, see Dandurand (1992).

10. The area is now best known for its majestic "Chutes Montmorency" ("Montmorency Falls").
11. Dominion Textile was given prominent mention in E. C. Hughes's classic study of Drummondville: *French Canada in Transition* (Hughes 1943).
12. Dumont's notion of popular culture emphasized the practices and rituals of everyday life (largely linked to the Catholic Church) and was mostly grounded in his own experiences growing up in the village of Montmorency. In distinguishing between popular culture and "l'actuelle culture de consommation" (Dumont 1997, p. 35), his account differs from the "cultural populism" described by McGuigan (2004, pp. 114–115), which stresses the close links between popular culture and mass culture (see also Dumont 1982; 1987; 2000).
13. Dumont's writings from the period of the Quiet Revolution and his commentary on the crisis leading to the War Measures Act of 1970 formed the basis of a text: *La Vigile du Québec* (English translation (*The Vigil of Québec*): Dumont 1974).
14. *Cité Libre* was a Montreal-based journal that was highly critical of the church and championed modernization and reform.
15. In this regard, Dumont was quite wary of how cultural policy was closely linked to cultural imperialism, particularly in its American variant. Coming from Québec, he was particularly sensitive to this issue as the United States has long pursued an aggressive policy of exporting its culture to the rest of the world, with the rest of North America singled out for particular attention because of its proximity.
16. Cultural policy, according to the report, "encompassed a wide field. In addition to the traditional sectors of preservation of our heritage, and arts and letters ... the policy deals with education, work structures, the implications of leisure, eating habits and drug use, problems relating to sex and age, regional limitations and strengths, decentralization and so forth" (Québec 1978a, pp. 2–3).
17. The first volume of the published version of the White Paper on cultural development was entitled *"Perspectives d'ensemble: de quelle culture s'agit-il?"*. Similarly, in the introduction to his 1979 article, he noted that he would be addressing the question "de quelle culture s'agit-il" (Dumont 1979, p. 8).
18. In this sense, he was quite critical of the direction taken by the report on administrative restructuring that appeared in 1986 under the direction of Paul Gobeil (Québec 1986). It called for eliminating or cutting back on the sorts of cultural institutions that were favored by intellectuals (Dumont 1995, pp. 252–253).
19. His model in this regard was André Laurendeau, a prominent writer and journalist who became best known for co-chairing the Royal Commission examining biculturalism and bilingualism (Canada 1967). Even though Laurendeau became very involved in administrative life, he continued to write poems and music (Dumont 1995, pp. 250–251)

20. In line with the corporatist "Québec Inc" orientation of the state that has become entrenched (Fraser 1987), the state views culture as a key sector of the economy, capable of producing a range of economic spin-offs such as job creation and increased tax revenues.

REFERENCES

ALLOR, M. (1993) 'Cultural *métissage*: National formations and productive discourse in Québec cinema and television', *Screen,* vol. 34, no. 1, pp. 69–75.

ALLOR, M. & GAGNON, M. (1994) *L'État de Culture: Généalogie Discursive des Politiques culturelles Québécoises,* GRECCO, Montreal.

ANDERSON, B. (1983) *Imagined Communities: Reflections on the Origin and Spread of Nationalism,* Verso, London.

BEAUCHEMIN, J., BOURQUE, G., DUMAS, B., DUMONT, F., GAGNON, A., NIELSEN, G. et al. (1995) 'Forum: la genèse de la société québécoise', *Recherches Sociographiques,* vol. 36, no. 1, pp. 77–120.

BIANCHINI, F. (1996) *Cultural Policy and Urban Regeneration,* Centre for Urban Studies, Liverpool.

BONIN, D. (1992) 'La culture au Québec à l'ombre de deux capitales', in *Canada: The State of the Federation, 1992,* eds D. Brown & R. Young, Institute of Intergovernmental Relations, Kingston, pp. 183–205.

CANADA (various years, 1967–). *Report of Royal Commission on Bilingualism and Biculturalism,* 6 vols, Queen's Printer, Ottawa.

CANADA (1999) *Cultural Policy in Canada,* prepared by J. Jackson & R. Lemieux, Social Affairs Division, Ottawa.

CREAN, S. & RIOUX, M. (1983) *Two Nations: An Essay on the Culture and Politics of Canada and Quebec in a World of American Pre-eminence,* J. Lorimer, Toronto.

DANDURAND, R. B. (1992) 'Marcel Rioux et Fernand Dumont: deux penseurs québécois de la culture, 1965–1985', in *Hommage à Marcel Rioux. Sociologie critique, création artistique et société contemporaine,* Les Éditions Albert Saint-Martin, Montreal, pp. 39–76.

DUMONT, F. (1964) 'The systematic study of the French-Canadian total society', in *French-Canadian Society,* vol. 1, eds M. Rioux & Y. Martin, McClelland & Stewart, Toronto, pp. 386–405.

DUMONT, F. (1968) *Le lieu de l'homme: La culture comme distance et mémoire,* Éditions H M H Ltée, Montreal.

DUMONT, F. (1974) *The Vigil of Quebec,* trans. S. Fischman & R. Howard, University of Toronto Press, Toronto.

DUMONT, F. (1979) 'L'Idée de développement culturel: esquisse pour une psychanalyse', *Sociologie et sociétés,* vol. 11, no. 1, pp. 7–33.

DUMONT, F. (1982) 'Sur le génèse de la notion de culture populaire', in *Cultures Populaires et Societés Contemporaines,* ed. G. Pronovost, Presses de l'Université du Québec, Sillery, pp. 27–42.

DUMONT, F. (1987) *Le sort de la culture,* Hexagone, Montreal.

DUMONT, F. (1995) *Raisons communes,* Boréal, Montreal.

DUMONT, F. (1997) *Récit d'une emigration,* Boréal, Montreal.

DUMONT, F. (2000) *Un Témoin de l'homme: Entretiens colligés et presentés par Serge Cantin,* Hexagone, Montreal.

DUMONT, F. & ROCHER, G. (1964) 'An introduction to a sociology of French Canada', in *French-Canadian Society,* vol. 1, eds M. Rioux & Y. Martin, McClelland & Stewart, Toronto, pp. 178–200.

FRASER, M. (1987) *Quebec Inc.: French-Canadian Entrepreneurs and the New Business Elite,* Key Porter Books, Toronto.

HARVEY, F. (2005) 'Fernand Dumont', *Canadian Encyclopedia* [online], available at: http://www.thecanadianencyclopedia.com/index.cfm?PgNm=TCE&Params=A1ARTA0002443 (accessed 6 June 2006).
HUGHES, E. (1943) *French Canada in Transition,* University of Chicago Press, Chicago, IL/W. J. Gage, Toronto.
JACOBY, R. (1987) *The Last Intellectuals: American Culture in the Age of Academe,* Basic Books, New York.
L'ALLIER, J.-P. (1976) *Pour l'évolution de la politique culturelle, document de travail, mai 1976,* Gouvernement du Québec, Ministère des Affaires culturelles, Québec.
LANGLOIS, S. & MARTIN, Y. (1995) *L'Horizon de la culture: Hommage à Fernand Dumont,* Les Presses de l'Université Laval/Institut Québécois de Recherche sur la culture, Ste. Foy.
LACROIX, J.-G. (1992) 'La culture québécoise face aux politiques culturelles canadiennes', in *Bilan québécois du fédéralisme canadien,* ed. F. Rocher, VLB éditeur, Montreal, pp. 302–322.
LINDSAY, J. (2002) 'A drama of change: Cultural policy and the performing arts in Southeast Asia', in *Global Culture: Media Arts, Policy and Globalization,* eds D. Crane, N. Kawashima & K. Kawasaki, Routledge, London, pp. 63–77.
LITT, P. (1992) *The Muses, the Masses and the Massey Commission,* University of Toronto Press, Toronto.
MANNHEIM, K. (1959) *Ideology and Utopia,* trans. L. Wirth & E. Shils, Harcourt, Brace, New York.
MARSH, J. (1988) 'Cultural policy', in *The Canadian Encyclopedia,* 2nd edn, vol. 1, pp. 551–553.
MARTORELLA, R. (2002) 'Cultural policy as marketing strategy: The economic consequences of cultural policy in New York City', in *Global Culture: Media Arts, Policy and Globalization,* eds D. Crane, N. Kawashima & K. Kawasaki, Routledge, London, pp. 118–131.
MCGUIGAN, J. (2004) *Rethinking Cultural Policy,* Open University Press, Maidenhead.
MCROBERTS, K. (1988) *Quebec: Social Change and Political Crisis,* McClelland & Stewart, Toronto.
PICARD, J.-C. (2003) *Camille Laurin: L'homme debout,* Boréal, Montreal.
QUÉBEC (1968) *Rapport de la Commission royale d'enquête sur l'enseignement des arts dans la province de Québec,* Gouvernement du Québec, Québec.
QUÉBEC (1978a) Le Ministre d'État au Développement culturel, *La politique québécoise du développement culturel. vol. 1: 'Perspectives d'ensemble: de quelle culture s'agit-il?',* Gouvernement du Québec, Québec.
QUÉBEC (1978b) Le Ministre d'État au Developpement culturel, *La politique québécoise du développement culturel. Vol. 2,* Gouvernement du Québec, Québec.
QUÉBEC (1986) *Rapports/Groupe de travail sur la révision des fonctions et des organisations gouvernementales,* Gouvernement du Québec, Québec.
QUÉBEC (1991) Le groupe-conseil sur la politique culturelle de Québec, *Une politique de la culture et des arts,* Les Publications du Québec, Québec.
QUÉBEC (1992) *La Politique Culturelle du Québec: Notre Culture, Notre Avenir,* Gouvernement du Québec, Ministère des Affaires culturelles, Québec.
RIOUX, M. (1978) *Essai de sociologie critique,* Hurtubise HMH, Montreal.
RIOUX, M. (1979) 'Pour une sociologie critique de la culture', *Sociologie et sociétés,* vol. 11, no. 1, pp. 49–55.
RIOUX, M. (1981) 'Fête populaire et développement de la culture populaire au Québec', *Loisir et société,* vol. 4, no. 1, pp. 55–79.
THOMPSON, E. P. (1964) *The Making of the English Working Class,* Pantheon, New York.

TOEPLER, S. & ZIMMER, A. (2002) 'Subsidizing the arts', in *Global Culture: Media Arts, Policy and Globalization,* eds D. Crane, N. Kawashima & K. Kawasaki, Routledge, London, pp. 29–48.

VALDERRAMA, F. (1995) *A History of UNESCO,* UNESCO, Paris.

VAN DEN BOSCH, A. & BEALE, A. (1998) 'Australian and Canadian cultural policies: A feminist perspective, in *Ghosts in the Machine: Women and Cultural Policy in Canada and Australia,* Garamond, Toronto, pp. 1–21.

VAUGHAN, M. K. (1997) *Cultural Politics in Revolution: Teachers, Peasants and Schools in Mexico, 1930–1940,* University of Arizona Press, Tempe, AZ.

WEINSTEIN, M. (1985) *Culture Critique: Fernand Dumont and New Quebec Sociology,* New World Perspectives, Montreal.

RICHARD HOGGART: PUBLIC INTELLECTUAL

Jim McGuigan

Introduction: Hoggart's Significance

Richard Hoggart is a principal founder of British cultural studies, perhaps the most important pioneer in carving out a space for the subject on the university curriculum, albeit modestly at the postgraduate level. He is barely remembered in the field these days and little honoured in consequence. In his late eighties, Hoggart is still writing and publishing – recently at the rate of a book a year: *Everyday Life and Everyday Language* (2003), *Mass Media in a Mass Society: Myth and Reality* (2004) and *Promises to Keep: Thoughts In Old Age* (2005). Yet, he is now a yesterday's man, a figure, most memorably, of the Swinging Sixties, although he entered the public arena to considerable acclaim in the previous decade: the Forgotten Fifties.

Hoggart burst into the limelight of public debate beyond academia with his book *The Uses of Literacy* (1957), which was very quickly seen as a key statement on the fate of the working class in the post-Second World War "affluent society". Hoggart examined the customs and mores with which he was familiar from his own working-class background. Ethnographically acute in an anthropological sense, this was not, however, a work of sociology so much as socially extended literary criticism. He analysed the publications of "mass culture", the reading matter of the working class, with the close reading techniques of a Leavisite critic. Because Chatto & Windus's over-zealous legal advisor was anxious about possibly offending the publishers of such magazines and novels, Hoggart had to discard the analysis of actual texts and fabricate his own such texts as illustration (Owen 2005). He was also obliged to change the title of his book from *The Abuses of Literacy* to *The Uses of Literacy*.

The whole process took several years of writing and rewriting. By the time of publication, Hoggart was on a teaching stint in the USA and missed the enthusiastic response the book instantly generated in Britain, which was sustained and expanded by swift republication as a Penguin paperback in 1958. Hoggart's message was clear: he believed that the new, "Americanized" mass culture was inferior to the lived popular culture of the traditional working class – especially the Northern English working class. That was, in fact, only just "traditional" historically, being a comparatively recent "way of life" formed in response to the harsh living conditions brought about by the industrialization and urbanization which had developed in the nineteenth century and matured in the twentieth.

In 1960, while still a senior lecturer in English at the University of Leicester, Hoggart was the outstanding defence witness in the prosecution of Penguin Book's paperback edition of D. H. Lawrence's *Lady Chatterley's Lover*. When asked by the prosecuting counsel if he thought the novel obscene, he replied that, quite to the contrary, it was in his opinion "puritanical". His famous retort was a kick-start for "the Swinging Sixties" in Britain. Hoggart served as a member of the Pilkington Committee on Broadcasting, which called for greater public control over "trivializing" commercial television and recommended that a second, publicly funded channel be given to the British Broadcasting Corporation, which became BBC2. Independent Television (ITV) was to be denied a second channel and its profits were creamed off in taxation by the 1964 Wilson Labour Government. Pilkington first mooted what eventually became Channel 4 in the 1980s, funded by advertising procured by the ITV companies and thus not a direct responsibility of the Channel and pressure on it. This is no longer the case since Channel 4 now sells its own advertising space, which has obvious implications for programming. Also, in the early 1960s, Hoggart became Professor of English at the University of Birmingham, where he set up the Centre for Contemporary Cultural Studies (CCCS) with the aid of Stuart Hall. Hall's fellowship and secretarial assistance were funded by a donation of £2,500 a year for five years plus a one-off payment of £500 from a grateful Allen Lane, the head of Penguin Books (Hoggart 1993 [1992], p. 90), Chatto & Windus and *The Observer*, which amounted to a "tidy sum" in those days, as Hoggart himself might have put it.

There is a problem with situating Richard Hoggart, particularly with regard to his founding role in cultural studies, due to a tendency to conflate him with Raymond Williams, fostering the still prevalent "myth of 'Raymond Hoggart'" (Jones 1994, 2004). Hoggart was very different from Williams. And, as far as I can gather, they did not get on well personally. In addition to Williams, Hoggart is also grouped with the historian E. P. Thompson by Stuart Hall (1980), no less, as the founders of British cultural studies in its "culturalist" mode. In actual fact, Hall himself is probably the more significant figure behind the spread and international diffusion of British cultural studies in the 1970s and '80s, but with a "structuralist" inflection, and was certainly the most influential of the four of them on developing the field intellectually, educationally and in publications. The one thing that Hoggart, Thompson and Williams did indeed have in common was that all three began their careers, and were known to one another, teaching adult education classes from the late 1940s and throughout the 1950s while, at the same time, writing their respectively classic books, apparently unbeknownst to each other: *The Uses of Literacy* (Hoggart 1957), *Culture and Society* (Williams 1959) and *The Making of the English Working Class* (Thompson 1963). According to Williams (1989), the actual breeding ground for the cross-disciplinary work that led to the discipline of cultural studies was these extension classes for mainly working-class people who had missed out on higher education (see Steele 1997). It is interesting to note that Williams,

Thompson and Hall were all, in some sense, Marxist, whereas Hoggart never was. The partnership with Hall, though paradoxical, is undoubtedly the most significant connection, at least institutionally, in founding cultural studies as an intramural university subject. Neither Williams (the cultural critic and guru of the British New Left) nor Thompson (the historian of the English working class and anti-nuclear weapons campaigner) did much in that respect.

When Hoggart went off to Paris at the beginning of the 1970s to become an assistant director of UNESCO, never to return to Birmingham, Hall succeeded him as director of the CCCS, upon which he stamped his personality firmly. Hoggart remarks that Hall was much more "theoretic" than he was (interview with the author). The intellectual gulf between them might reasonably be summed up in terms of the enduring philosophical tension between British empiricism and continental rationalism. It is Hall who should have gone to Paris.

Unlike Williams's cultural materialism, Hoggart never sought to produce his own brand of theory or to borrow much at all from other theorists as Hall has done – that is, if you do not regard Matthew Arnold and F. R. Leavis as theorists, of course. Arnold's cultural paternalism and Leavis's discriminating criticism were deeply influential on the young Hoggart and remained so throughout his entire career. In this sense, he is a figure of the core English literary and cultural policy traditions. Politically, he may be seen as rather more Fabian than Marxist in his socialism. I am inclined to characterize him as an exemplary public intellectual of the post-Second World War social-democratic consensus in Britain – and elsewhere – that has been usurped over the past thirty years by the encroachment of neo-liberalism in Labour as well as Conservative politics.

Public Intellectual

Here it is necessary to digress briefly on the debate concerning the role of the public intellectual in order to situate Hoggart's significance. Before the Second World War, Antonio Gramsci made an important distinction between "traditional" and "organic" intellectuals (see Hoare & Nowell-Smith 1971). Traditional intellectuals were men of the book, typically clerics. With the rise of capitalism, traditional intellectuals were losing their usefulness and being replaced by organic intellectuals – that is, those with a technical rather than doctrinal function with regard to the production and dissemination of knowledge. It would be trite to say that Gramsci's observations on the role of intellectuals anticipated the contemporary notion of a "knowledge" or "information" society. Nevertheless, there was indeed an explosion of routine intellectual work in the late twentieth century. Back in the 1930s, Gramsci had his critical eye on the kind of organic intellectuals that Pierre Bourdieu and Loic Wacquant (2001) have identified as the jobbing type who labours in, say, think-tanks like Demos and the Institute for Public Policy Research (IPPR); and a more elevated type who is, in their words: "the *communication consultant to the prince*" (emphasis in original). For Bourdieu and Wacquant, sociologist Anthony Giddens – Tony Blair's own Dr Pangloss – exemplified the exalted type close to the prince at the turn of the millennium. Actually, Gramsci did have in mind a variant of "the *communication consultant to the prince*", the organic intellectual of "the modern prince", that is, the communist party. This notion of a radical organic intellectuality was certainly played around with at the Birmingham Centre under Hall after Hoggart departed the scene. Hall's organic intellectual was the kind of figure who was to transmogrify into a slippery postmodern subject with an indeterminate political affiliation sometime later.

Hoggart fits none of these categories. He is more accurately seen as a descendant of a liberal tradition stretching from the Enlightenment *philosophes*. It is this kind of figure to whom the debate over the public intellectual usually refers. In the 1980s, Russell Jacoby (2000 [1987]) complained that the public intellectual had been sucked into academia, thereby losing the role of critical witness. Since then, Richard Posner (2003 [2001], albeit from an opposite point of view, more or less agrees with Jacoby, but qualifies the judgement by praising those intellectuals who manage to cross over between the university world and a wider public culture. Posner conducts a tortuous citation count for public intellectuals in academic publications, the media and on the World Wide Web. Hoggart does not figure in Posner's citation count. Although Posner is American, he does count some Europeans, albeit omitting Hoggart. Citations for Hoggart may have fallen away in his old age, but, I would hazard to guess his media counts match his academic counts. Hoggart's output of journalistic writing and broadcasting during his career has been immense – far too numerous to itemize here, but recorded and preserved in the Hoggart archive at the University of Sheffield. There is no doubt that Hoggart has functioned as a public intellectual beyond the groves of academe. In 1971, at the height of his fame, he delivered the Reith Lectures on BBC Radio 4 (Hoggart 1972).

However, the debate still rages about the fate of the public intellectual. Is Hoggart one of a dying breed? Recently, Frank Furedi (2004) has asked plaintively: "Where have all the intellectuals gone?" Steve Fuller (2005) replied, in effect saying: "Look, Frank, I'm over here!" To my mind, the public intellectual, like the public sphere itself, may be scarcely in evidence yet it is a necessary ideal and of practical consequence (McGuigan 2005). Richard Hoggart has sought to fulfil that ideal consistently not only in his critical writings and public statements, but also in the burdensome committee and administrative duties that he has undertaken over the years. Another Reith Lecturer, the late Edward Said, summed up the role of the public intellectual succinctly and in a form that certainly applies to Hoggart:

> [T]he intellectual is an individual with a specific public role in society that cannot be reduced simply to being a faceless professional, a competent member of a class just going about her/his business. The central fact for me is, I think, that the intellectual is an individual endowed with a faculty for representing, embodying, articulating a message, a view, an attitude, philosophy or opinion to, as well as for, a public. And this role has an edge to it, and cannot be played without a sense of being someone whose place it is publically to raise embarrassing questions, to confront orthodoxy and dogma (rather than produce them), to be someone who cannot easily be co-opted by governments or corporations, and whose *raison d'etre* is to represent all those people and issues that are routinely forgotten or swept under the rug. The intellectual does so on the basis of universal principals: that all human beings are entitled to expect decent standards of behaviour concerning freedom and justice from worldly powers or nations, and that deliberate or inadvertent violation of these standards need to be testified and fought against courageously. (Said 1994, pp. 8–9)

Cultural Studies and Policy

The Birmingham Centre for Contemporary Cultural Studies' first annual report in 1964 listed its initial seven projects:

1. Orwell and the Climate of the Thirties
2. The Growth and Change in the Local Press
3. Folk Songs and Folk Idioms in Popular Music
4. Levels of Fiction and Changes in Contemporary Society

5. Domestic Art and Iconography in the Home
6. Pop Music and Adolescent Culture
7. The Meaning of Sport and its Presentation (CCCS 1964, pp. 6–7)

This would be seen as a fairly uncontroversial and tame set of topics now; yet at the time, it was anything but, especially in a Department of English where the Centre was lodged with considerable misgiving. Some of the themes here were to develop into a distinctively Birmingham research agenda in cultural studies – most notably perhaps in the work of the youth sub-cultural theorists and ethnographers. However, over the next forty years, such innocuous topics would be to a great extent superseded by much more abstrusely political theorizing and arcane topics, influenced by a succession of continental and mainly French theorists such as Althusser, Lacan and Foucault – not Hoggart's terrain at all. However, as late as 1978, the greatest work of the Birmingham Centre – the Gramscian *Policing the Crisis* (Hall *et al.* 1978) – was published. This book was much more sociological and theoretically framed than Hoggart's work, though it is not unrecognizable in terms of the earlier agenda, tackling controversial issues of the day in a seriously academic manner. It developed from research on the "mugging" panic of the early 1970s into complex examination of a drift to the Right in British society that was manifest in "law'n'order" rhetoric and practice. *Policing the Crisis* was a prelude to Stuart Hall's writings on Thatcherism and authoritarian populism (Hall 1988).

This kind of work – scholarly research of a critical character in response to currently controversial issues in the wider society – in my opinion, has been and should be at the heart of cultural studies. Hoggart – and Hall – played no small part in establishing such a focus for cultural research. I fear it is too little in evidence today. Hoggart was interested in policy questions, particularly questions of cultural policy, though his work in Cultural Studies and with regard to practical matters of cultural policy were not as intimately connected to one another as you might expect.

Efforts have been made to connect cultural studies and cultural policy academically and with practical intent. However, in the case of the influential Australian school of cultural policy studies, this involved jettisoning the critical responsibilities of cultural studies and replacing them with an instrumental orientation to managerial usefulness (Bennett 1998) that has been criticized in detail elsewhere (McGuigan 1996, 2004).

In the 1970s, Hoggart was, in effect, cut off from what were becoming mainstream developments in cultural studies with his move from Birmingham to Paris. At the same time, his work with UNESCO brought him much closer to questions of practical policy than ever before. On leaving UNESCO, he wrote a book about it, *An Idea and Its Servants: UNESCO from Within* (1978). In the preface, Hoggart wrote of UNESCO:

> One of its great weaknesses is over-defensiveness, unwillingness to listen to criticism. ... This lesson – of the value of open, critical comment – is one UNESCO must at last learn, or it will become even more of an enclosed Byzantine system than it is at present. (Hoggart 1978, n.p.)

On returning from Paris, Hoggart became warden (effectively, vice-chancellor) of the University of London's Goldsmiths College, where he immediately set about introducing cultural studies into the curriculum. His role at Goldsmiths in that respect is much less well known than his role at Birmingham. However, with the effective closure of what was left of cultural studies at Birmingham in 2001/02, Goldsmiths achieved a virtually unchallenged standing as the leading centre for cultural studies in Britain. Even that can be traced back to Hoggart as a skilled institutional operator.

Hoggart's most public role towards the end of the 1970s was as Chair of the Drama Panel and then Vice-Chair of the Arts Council of Great Britain. Previously he had applied unsuccessfully for the post of Secretary General, which went to his close friend, Roy Shaw. This was a torrid time for both of them. The Shaw–Hoggart regime was attacked from the Left for cutting off grants to some alternative theatre companies and marginalizing community arts, later hiving them off to the Regional Arts Associations. Eventually, Hoggart was unceremoniously dumped from his position as Vice-Chair of the Arts Council at the personal instigation of the newly elected Conservative Prime Minister, Margaret Thatcher. Both Hoggart and Shaw had been busy fending off a full-frontal assault from the cultural Left when the Right crept up from behind to challenge their defence of social democratic arts policy. Hoggart and Shaw, however, were aware that they were facing a pincer movement and believed that left-wing populism was undermining the system of public arts patronage in wanting to revolutionize it.

A notorious passage in photographer and community arts activist, Su Braden's book, *Artists and People*, particularly incensed Roy Shaw (1978, p. 13). The passage reads:

> [I]t must be understood that the so-called cultural heritage which made Europe great – the Bachs and Beethovens, the Shakespeares and Dantes, the Constables and Titians – is no longer communicating anything to the vast majority of Europe's population. … [I]t is bourgeois culture and therefore only immediately meaningful to that group. The great artistic deception of the twentieth century has been to insist to *all* people that this was *their* culture. The Arts Council of Great Britain was established on this premise. (Braden 1978, pp. 153–154)

Shaw was right to remark that not even Karl Marx would have gone along with this ultra-leftist populism.

Battling Relativism

In 1980, the *New Universities Quarterly* hosted a conference on "Excellence and Standards in the Arts". Richard Hoggart delivered the opening keynote to the conference with his talk entitled "The Crisis of Relativism". At the outset of his talk, Hoggart (1980, p. 21) announced: "[T]here is today a sizeable attack, first, on traditional definitions of art and, second, on the idea of standards in arts; … this attack is usually made in the name of openness and democracy." Before counter-attacking what he considered the fallacies of the attack, Hoggart spelt out his own attitude towards the value of art – particularly his appreciation of literature, which he has a tendency to hold up as the finest of the arts. Cultural judgement, for him, is founded on the freedom of speech. Even more than the problem of relativism, Hoggart was troubled by the censoriousness of what would much later be called "political correctness" – most prevalent in feminist complaints against sexism. One can see how Hoggart became so unpopular in cultural studies.

To be fair to Hoggart, he made some interesting remarks in this keynote address in defence of art. For instance, he said: "[T]he call to produce an art starts by our being fascinated by a medium" (Hoggart 1980, p. 23). He goes on: "[N]ot all of us are equally gifted. Many are called but few are chosen" (Hoggart 1980, p. 23). This does not, of course, preclude the possibility of pleasure and self-expression in doing something that one is not very good at, as in sport as well as the arts. Just as importantly (perhaps more so now than in 1980): "Many are called but few are chosen". This observation makes me think not only of the reserve army of unemployed or otherwise employed fine arts graduates, but also of the great majority of fashion designers who never make it (McRobbie 1998) and all the young people exploited outrageously when trying to break into media industries, especially television (McGuigan, forthcoming). In the main, these are the consequence of marketplace judgement, not matters of cultural judgement in Hoggart's much more refined sense.

Hoggart (1980, p. 28) also notes "an anti-intellectualism, a fear of making discriminatory judgements". This, in general, was more astute an observation than merely fending off the excesses of what can be called the *"productionist populism"* of the community arts movement. His observation applies equally to what became much more widely significant – to whit: *"consumptionist populism"*. Consumptionist populism was at the heart of cultural studies during the 1980s and so, ironically, Hoggart himself might bear some of the blame for it (McGuigan 1992). That refusal of judgement would not have been so successful in an emergent and fairly marginal field of study if it did not represent a growing conventional wisdom that now seems virtually unassailable: that popular taste is the final arbiter of quality. If people like it, then it must be okay.

This is why, among other reasons, Richard Hoggart's book *The Way We Live Now* (Hoggart 1996 [1995]) was such a tonic. (Incidentally, the title was changed for the American publication of the book to *The Tyranny of Relativism: Culture and Politics in Contemporary England*.) As Hoggart (1996 [1995], p. 102) said in *The Way We Live Now*: "[I]t's enjoyable to lay about you." That he certainly did in criticizing various features of Thatcherite Britain, including "the tyranny of relativism". His constancy is very striking: he had more or less remained in the same place while there had been a headlong rush from Left to Right. Although Hoggart does not mention it, the trajectory of several *Marxism Today* writers, such as Charles Leadbeater (1999), from revisionist communism to advocacy of "New Times" capitalism was especially symptomatic, though bizarre, of the way things were going.

By the 1990s, the excesses of cultural leftism were nothing compared to the wholesale shift to the Right in England at large under the cover of "consumer sovereignty" and the like. Hoggart's critique of "relativism" was not so much epistemological – he was never much of a one for philosophy – but, instead, focused upon the flattening out of social and cultural values. He said: "[R]elativism leads to populism which then leads to levelling; and so to reductionism, to quality reductionism of all kinds – from food to moral judgements" (Hoggart 1996 [1995], p. 8). He recognized that this was reflected in cultural studies' unwillingness to criticize what is now most accurately called *mass-popular* culture. Hoggart's older distinction between mass and popular culture is no longer particularly useful. In that sense, populist cultural studies is right. Embrace of "populism", however, is a simple inversion of the dreaded "elitism", caught on the horns of a hopeless dilemma or, rather, binary opposition. Hoggart, unfortunately, is keen to deny the most obvious solution to this chronic problem: what he calls "the good of its kind" argument. His view is similar to David Hare's claim, asserted on a 1991 edition of BBC2's *Late Show*: "Finally, Keats is a better poet than Dylan" (see McGuigan 1997). Apparently, Keats was not quite heavy enough for Hoggart to make the case. He chose John Milton's *Paradise Lost* instead to compare favourably with Bob Dylan's lyrics (Hoggart 1996 [1995], p. 59).

Hoggart returned to the fray in his book *Mass Media in a Mass Society* (2004), where once again he discusses "relativism", which is, to quote him: "[T]he condition in which nothing really matters except those things which can be consumed without ever arising the question of whether some are better than others" (Hoggart 2004, p. 48). Relativism is the cultural expression of a dubiously "democratic" consumerist society.

It is worth quoting Hoggart at length on "the good of its kind" answer to questions of value:

> That favourite exculpatory phrase on the lines of "Agreed. It's not very high-brow but at least it's good of its kind" is especially tempting. It seems to avoid the awful business of having to say that some things might be better than others, that some things show the feebleness of their authors' talents and others are no more than market-invented hogwash. In such a world all products should be without distinguishing value-judgements, never set against any other things. All views are horizontal, never vertical. The excusing phrase above is used as a blanket acquittal to avoid any criteria of value being applied, especially to all of what could be called "the popular arts". This is a pity because it can have a valid as well an invalid use. (Hoggart 2004, p. 60)

The qualifying sentence at the end of this passage is a necessary one for Hoggart since it was he, more than anyone else, who was responsible for inserting "the good of its kind argument" into the cultural debate in Britain over forty years ago. He goes on to reiterate the reason for doing so now:

> A valid use of that "good of its kind" rule could start by recognizing just what in any particular popular art, other than the numbers who consume it, might actually make it good: verbal or musical inventiveness, say; that might do nicely. (Hoggart 2004, p. 60)

Hoggart then notes that some work defined as "highbrow" may be as meretricious as any "lowbrow" work. However, he goes on to qualify "the good of its kind" argument decisively: "The scales of value should run from the very top to the bottom of what is offered at any time, in any genre; but some scales reach higher, and some lower, than others" (Hoggart 2004, pp. 60–61). So we are back to the old argument that some art forms are inherently superior to others, which plainly contradicts Hoggart's somewhat bombastic statement first made in an *Observer* article of 1961:

> The crucial distinctions today are not those between the *News of the World* and the *Observer*, between the Third Programme and the Light Programme, between sex-and-violence paperbacks, between Bootsie and Snudge and the Alan Taylor lectures, between the Billy Cotton Band Show and the Brains Trust, between the Top Ten and a celebrity concert, or between "skiffle" and chamber music. The distinctions we should be making are those between the *New of the World* and the *Sunday Pictorial*, between "skiffle" and the Top Ten; and, for "highbrows", between the *Observer* and the *Sunday Times*, or, in "egghead" paperbacks, between Peter Townshend and Vance Packard. (Hoggart 1973, pp. 129–130)

In order to elaborate on these discriminations *within* rather than *between* genres and media, Hoggart distinguished between "the processed" and "the lived". Processed culture is utterly consumer-oriented – the audience typically conceived of as a homogeneous mass, whether large or small – whereas "living culture", to quote Hoggart (1973, p. 131), "recognises the diversity, the particularity, of all experience". These terms and the specifics of the distinction may be disputed in all sorts of ways, but the basic distinction is a powerful one. Moreover, it avoids having to make hierarchical claims regarding superiority or inferiority of different media and forms such as the pointless assumption that, say, theatre is inherently superior to cinema. Moreover, it does not necessarily undermine public support for a cultural heritage and experimental practice that may not suit the market.

Conclusion: A Blast from the Past

Richard Hoggart, after all is said and done, is a blast from the past. However, as he might agree, some of the older tunes are better than many of the newer ones. Hoggart writes in an older idiom, that of an English radical tradition that never would have been satisfied with speaking to academia alone. In terms of cultural analysis and public engagement, he has frequently asked the right questions. That I do not always agree with his answers is neither here nor there. He is a trustworthy voice and good to argue with. None of these questions will be resolved once and for all. The debate goes on. At present, cultural policy, however, seems to have been denuded of a distinctly *cultural rationale*. It is justified mainly on economically instrumental grounds and seen as a magical means of "regeneration" – the current buzzword. A rather implausible social inclusion rationale is also tagged on typically as an afterthought to economic reductionism. We need to think again about a specifically cultural rationale for cultural policy. Curiously, the British government's Secretary for Culture, Media and Sport, Tessa Jowell (2004) has said much the same. The trouble is, she quite possibly does not actually believe it.

REFERENCES

BENNETT, T. (1998) *Culture: A Reformer's Art,* Sage, London.
BOURDIEU, P. & WACQUANT, L. (2001) 'NewLiberalSpeak: Notes on the new planetary vulgate', *Radical Philosophy,* vol. 105 (January–February), pp. 2–5.
BRADEN, S. (1978) *Artists and People,* Routledge & Kegan Paul, London.
CENTRE FOR CONTEMPORARY CULTURAL STUDIES (CCCS) (1964) *First Report,* University of Birmingham, Centre for Contemporary Cultural Studies, Birmingham.
FULLER, S. (2005) *The Intellectual,* Icon, Cambridge.
FUREDI, F. (2004) *Where Have All the Intellectuals Gone: Confronting 21st Century Philistinism,* Continuum, London.
HALL, S. (1980) 'Cultural studies: Two paradigms', *Media, Culture & Society,* vol. 2, no. 1, pp. 57–72.
HALL, S. (1988) *The Hard Road to Renewal: Thatcherism and the Crisis of the Left,* Verso, London.
HALL, S., CRITCHER, C., JEFFERSON, T., CLARKE, J. & ROBERTS, B. (1978) *Policing the Crisis: Mugging, the State, and Law and Order,* Macmillan, London.
HOARE, Q. & NOWELL-SMITH, G. (eds) (1971) *Selections from the Prison Notebooks of Antonio Gramsci,* Lawrence & Wishart, London.
HOGGART, R. (1957) *The Uses of Literacy,* Chatto & Windus, London.
HOGGART, R. (1972) *Only Connect: Culture and Communication,* Chatto & Windus, London.
HOGGART, R. (1973) 'Culture: Dead and alive', in *Speaking to Each Other, vol. 1: About Society,* Penguin, London, pp. 129–132.
HOGGART, R. (1978) *An Idea and Its Servants: UNESCO from Within,* Chatto & Windus, London.
HOGGART, R. (1980) 'The crisis of relativism', *New Universities Quarterly,* vol. 35, no. 1, pp. 21–32.
HOGGART, R. (1993 [1992]) *An Imagined Life: Life and Times, vol. III: 1959–1991,* Oxford University Press, Oxford.
HOGGART, R. (1996 [1995]) *The Way We Live Now,* Pimlico, London.
HOGGART, R. (2003) *Everyday Life and Everyday Language,* Transaction, New Brunswick, NJ.

HOGGART, R. (2004) *Mass Media in a Mass Society: Myth and Reality,* Continuum, London.
HOGGART, R. (2005) *Promises to Keep: Thoughts in Old Age,* Continuum, London.
JACOBY, R. (2000 [1987]) *The Last Intellectuals: American Culture in the Age of Academe,* Basic Books, New York.
JONES, P. (1994) 'The myth of "Raymond Hoggart" founding father and cultural studies', *Cultural Studies,* vol. 8, no. 3, pp. 394–416.
JONES, P. (2004) *Raymond Williams's Sociology of Culture: A Critical Reconstruction,* Palgrave, Basingstoke.
JOWELL, T. (2004) *Government and the Value of Culture,* Department for Culture, Media and Sport, London.
LEADBEATER, C. (1999) *Living on Thin Air: The New Economy,* Viking, London.
MCGUIGAN, J. (1992) *Cultural Populism,* Routledge, London.
MCGUIGAN, J. (1996) *Culture and the Public Sphere,* Routledge, London.
MCGUIGAN, J. (1997) 'Cultural populism revisited', in *Cultural Studies in Question,* eds M. Ferguson & P. Golding, Sage, London, pp. 138–154.
MCGUIGAN, J. (2004) *Rethinking Cultural Policy,* Open University Press, Maidenhead.
MCGUIGAN, J. (2005) 'The cultural public sphere', *European Journal of Cultural Studies,* vol. 8, no. 4, pp. 427–445.
MCGUIGAN, J. (forthcoming) 'Culture and risk', in *Beyond the Risk Society,* eds S. Walklate & G. Mythen, Open University Press, Maidenhead.
MCROBBIE, A. (1998) *British Fashion Design: Rag Trade or Image Industry?,* Routledge, London.
OWEN, S. (2005) 'The abuse of literacy and the feeling heart: The trials of Richard Hoggart', *Cambridge Quarterly* (Spring), pp. 148–176.
POSNER, R. (2003 [2001]) *Public Intellectuals: A Study of Decline,* Harvard University Press, Cambridge, MA.
SAID, E. (1994) *Representations of the Intellectual: The 1993 Reith Lectures,* Vintage, London.
SHAW, S. (1978) 'Carried to an extreme, a passion for democracy in the arts does lead to the rejection of quality', *The Guardian,* 30 September, p. 13.
STEELE, T. (1997) *The Emergence of Cultural Studies, 1945–1965: Cultural Politics, Adult Education and the English Question,* Lawrence & Wishart, London.
THOMPSON, E. P. (1963) *The Making of the English Working Class,* Victor Gollancz, London.
WILLIAMS, R. (1959) *Culture and Society, 1780–1950,* Chatto & Windus, London.
WILLIAMS, R. (1989) 'The future of cultural studies', in *The Politics of Modernism: Against the New Conformists,* Verso, London, pp. 151–162.

NOTES FROM THE NUMBER ONE COUNTRY
Herbert Schiller on culture, commerce and American power

Graham Murdock

In his valedictory presidential address, delivered in January 1961, Dwight Eisenhower warned "against the growing acquisition of unwarranted influence … by the military-industrial complex" formed by the increasing integration of military capacity and corporate enterprise, and urged the American people to "never let the weight of this combination endanger our liberties or democratic processes" (Yale Law School 2005). Herb Schiller was one of the first commentators to recognize that the postwar information and entertainment industries developing around commercial television, satellite links and computerized data stores were pivotal to future of the "alert and knowledgeable citizenry" that Eisenhower had seen as democracy's last line of defence. The economic, political and cultural centrality of communications arose from three core features. Firstly, monitoring operating environments and coordinating geographically dispersed sites of activity increasingly depended on untrammelled access to state-of-the-art data processing capacity and telecommunications links. Secondly, the mobilization of popular support for corporate and military goals presupposed a mediated culture tilted towards the promotion of compliance and the sidelining of dissent. Thirdly, matching supply to demand required a cultural landscape in which conceptions of citizenship were continually countered by the consumerist vision of personal and collective freedom advanced by advertising and marketing. In a series of books written over two decades, Herbert Schiller set out to show how these processes were organized and how they combined to undermine a democratic polity anchored in a philosophy of the common good.

Public Interventions and Corporate Strategies

At first sight it seems odd to include Schiller in a collection on intellectuals and cultural policy since his work is little known or read in cultural policy circles. In the wider intellectual community, however, the clarity of his writing and the passion and wit of his lectures and public speeches confirmed his place as one of the most important critics of postwar American culture and its entanglements with the exercise of power. There are three major reasons to re-read his work now. Firstly, discussions of cultural policy have often been conducted in relative isolation from debates on media policy to the detriment of both. Schiller saw very clearly that in a situation where popular cultural experience is increasingly mediated, cultural policy needs to pay close attention to the ways communication systems are organized and changing. Secondly, "living in the number one country" (as he later put it; Schiller 2000), where public deliberation and intervention was continually pressured and often captured by commercial lobbies and interests, he was one of the first to analyse in detail both the ascendancy of market thinking and the quickening migration of key decisions from public committees to company boardrooms. For him, unpacking corporate decisions and the strategies that underpinned them was always an essential starting point for any attempt to map the shifting cultural landscape. Thirdly, in marked contrast to the solidly domestic focus of much cultural policy debate, Schiller situated national issues firmly in an international context.

He was one of the first to grasp that the locus of global power in the postwar era was moving from the appropriation of territory to the annexation of imagination. The bitter wars of decolonization fought out across the old European empires opened up unprecedented opportunities for American enterprise. Hollywood was already the dominant force in world film, and American jazz and popular music an established global *lingua franca*. Starting with his first book, *Mass Communications and American Empire* (Schiller 1969), his analysis of the connections between American-mediated culture and the new global economic order won him readers across the developing world, particularly in the major countries of Latin America, which had been grappling with the collision between economic dependence and cultural colonization for over a century. Argentina became an autonomous state in 1816 and Brazil broke away from the Portuguese empire in 1825. Having gained political independence from their former colonial masters, however, they found themselves within the new zone of US influence unilaterally declared by President Monroe in 1823. This pattern was repeated and generalized in the postwar period as more than 90 countries gained political independence only to enter a world system increasingly organized around American imperial interests and aspirations.

Critical Theory and Radical Populism

Reading Schiller can be a frustrating experience since he often borrows from sources and attacks opponents without naming them. His pages are peopled with unannounced guests. His critique of the commercial cultural industries as engines of mass deception owes much to Horkheimer and Adorno's analysis, developed while both were living in exile in the

United States. Versions of their claims that "the basis on which technology acquires power over society is the power of those whose economic hold over society is greatest" (Horkheimer & Adorno 1973, p. 121) or that "progress in the culture industry … mask(s) a skeleton which has changed just as little as the as the profit motive itself since the time it first gained its predominance over culture" (Adorno 1991, p. 87) recur throughout his work. His argument that the most important social effects of commercialized cultural artefacts are structural also picks up on their emphasis on repetitive patterns of expression that are "exclusive to none but shared by all" (Horkheimer & Adorno 1973, p. 127). Raymond Williams' later insight (developed while he too was resident in the United States) that the central experience of broadcasting is "one of sequence or flow" across the schedule rather than engagement with individual programmes (Williams 1974, p. 86) also finds strong echoes in Schiller's writings. While these intersections with European critical theory and radical British cultural analysis are certainly important for an understanding of his work, in the end his major debt is to the tradition of radical populism developed within the United States and represented in its most forceful form by Upton Sinclair.

Sinclair was an investigative journalist and writer who came to national attention with his 1906 novel, *The Jungle*, a savage exposé of labour and health conditions in the Chicago meatpacking industry, which played a major role in getting The Pure Food and Drug Act onto the statute books. In 1920, he turned his attention to the media system with *The Brass Check*, a scathing attack on the corruption of the American news system by corporate and governmental power. In 1934, he stood as the Democratic candidate in the election for Governor of California, proposing radical measures for ending unemployment. Despite a concerted media campaign of vilification which saw the film mogul, Louis B. Mayer, producing fake newsreels showing bearded actors endorsing Sinclair's proposals in Russian accents, Sinclair got 37% of the vote and might have been elected had not a third-party progressive candidate taken 13%.

The core themes in Sinclair's analysis of media power were later returned to by C. Wright Mills, who, although based in the academy, pursued the radical populist distrust of entrenched power. His claim, made in 1956, that the new "power elite" "have placed within their grasp historically unique instruments of psychic management and manipulation which include the media of mass communication" (Mills 1959, pp. 310–311) later provided the departure point for Schiller's second book, *The Mind Managers* (Schiller 1973). Mills' general critique was conventional wisdom on the Left, but no one else pursued it with the same attention to empirical detail.

As Edmund Wilson noted, in his writings and speeches Sinclair set out to "put to the American public the fundamental questions raised by capitalism in such a way that they could not escape them" (Social Security Online 1996, p. 1). This was an ambition that Schiller shared. Although he spent his adult career as a university teacher, his relationship with the academy was always uneasy. Even when he was securely established and widely published and translated, the University of California delayed his promotion to senior professor.[1] Academic titles were never important to him; rather he saw himself as a public intellectual, in the business of intervening in current debates by making ideas and analysis as accessible as possible in the hope not simply of understanding the world, but also of changing it.

Unlike American radical critics who concentrated on the state of the nation, however, he was from the outset concerned with the tensions between Republic and Empire, between the revolutionary impetus that created the United States as the first modern democratic polity and the continual push to colonize and control, both internally and externally. These tensions were written into the project from the outset. The United States was founded territorially on the systematic slaughter of the continent's indigenous peoples and rooted economically in the slave economies of the Southern plantations. Consequently, for Schiller, the central issue in contemporary cultural and communications policy was always "the struggle to overcome domination-external, where the power resides outside the national community; internal, where the power is exercised by a domestic ruling stratum" (Schiller 1976, p. 70). The career trajectory that led him to develop his distinctive approach to this project was by no means straightforward; rather it was the product of a series of formative, but largely serendipitous, experiences.

An Unsentimental Education

Schiller was born in 1919 into a New York Jewish family living in a one-bedroom apartment in the Washington Heights district of northern Manhattan. His father, a jewellery maker, was conservative and cautious in his political convictions. He voted for Hoover rather than Roosevelt, as did Herbert when he had the opportunity in a mock election in his high school. In 1929, at the onset of the Great Depression, his father was laid off and for the next decade the struggle to make ends meet dominated family life. They were kept afloat by his mother's job as a cleaner and his uncle's help with the monthly rent. His own earnings from odd jobs were enough to pay for his fares and lunches, and to see him through high school and a first degree from the free City College of New York. The family's sudden change of circumstances left him with a permanent sense of the precariousness of the "American Dream" and the constant prospect of crisis just below the surface. It also fostered a strong sense of anger at the injustice and inequality of an economic and political system that discarded and devalued people so easily and was unable to provide affordable "doctors, lawyers, dental care, adequate education, and other essential social services" to the poor while supplying the well-off with "mountains of absurd goods and innumerable unjustifiable services (such as tax shelter advisors [and] luxury kennels for pets" (Schiller 1969, p. 190). As he later recounted, seeing his father "not having any full-time employment for ten years … left very deep impressions and made me have an awful lot of questions about the social order". He had no answers since he had no access to "a thought-out or even partially organized view of the structure of society" (Lent 1995, p. 135). This was in marked contrast to Noam Chomsky, whose critical interrogations of American foreign policies and analyses of the American news media as a "propaganda" system intersected with Schiller's main concerns at a number of points.

Chomsky, seven years younger, was born into a Jewish intellectual family in Philadelphia. His father was a professional Hebrew scholar who ran the Hebrew school system in the city, in which his mother taught. His father's family were solidly orthodox, but his mother's family were radicals, and through working on his uncle's news stand in New York, Chomsky came into contact with a range of left-of-centre political positions. He later recalled "that newsstand became an intellectual centre for émigrés from Europe [and] was very lively – professors of this and that arguing all night" (Kreisler 2002, p. 2). By his early teens, influenced by George Orwell's *Homage to Catalonia*, he gravitated toward anarchism – a decision strongly reinforced by his conversations with the émigrés who clustered around the anarchist book shops off Union Square. "Talking to these people was", as he later put it, "a real education" (Kreisler 2002, p. 3). In contrast, Schiller's politics were largely self-taught. He acknowledged the transformative potential of the grassroots action at the heart of traditional anarchism, but saw socialist models of public intervention as the best hope of securing the preconditions for substantive institutional change.

He graduated from City College with a degree in social sciences and a major in economics, and went on the take a master's degree in economics from Columbia University, but the experience left him frustrated. He encountered a curriculum which paid little or no attention to the moral tensions between private interests and collective well being that had preoccupied earlier writers on the political economy of capitalism from Adam Smith to Marx. As he noted later, his real social science education only began when he was drafted for military service. He was posted to North Africa in the autumn of 1943 where, after brief periods in Algeria and Tunisia, he spent two years in Casablanca.

The wartime image of the city has been forever fixed in popular consciousness by Michael Curtiz's film starring Humphrey Bogart in his most famous role, released in 1942. Schiller's experience of being an American abroad was very different. Beyond the GI bars and enclaves of wealth and luxury in the expatriate community he glimpsed a great sea of destitution. Nothing he had seen in Depression America prepared him for the scale and depth of the poverty and deprivation he encountered in the "tin can settlements" that ringed the city (Schiller 2000, p. 17). This very concrete image of marginalization and disposability came to underpin his later writings. For him, the Third World was never simply an abstract concept; it was a palpable space filled with cries, stench and destitution, and with the resilience and resistance of the human spirit. Over time, as he later recounted, he came to realize that the tragic destinies of the shantytown dwellers were "ordered by foreign owners and investors, and local oligarchs, whose one public concern is undisturbed profit making" (Schiller 2000, p. 18). The dispossessed paid for the "advanced" world's affluence with their continuing poverty. He saw this burden, imposed on the world's poorest and weakest peoples, as the pivot of the imperial project.

With the notable exception of Japan, imperialism in the modern era was a mainly European affair culminating in the scramble for Africa between 1880 and 1914 in which Britain, Germany, Belgium, France and Portugal competed for control of the continent's key resources. As the Second World War drew to a close, however, it was clear that the baton of empire was passing to the United States. As Schiller (2000, p. 17) later noted: "Although the French were still the reigning colonial power across the rim of North Africa it was clear, even in 1943, their rule was coming to a close" and the USA was emerging as "the new pole of power" – a position consolidated through a combination of military intervention, the subversion of alternatives and the aggressive promotion of consumerism. Watching an outdoor screening of a Hollywood film with other GIs, he noticed that all around the edges "Moroccan kids and adults followed the images intently". This very concrete image of "[t]he new power, with its material riches and dazzling images, was nonchalantly elbowing out the once-dominating authority" played a central role in his later analysis (Schiller 2000, p. 18).

After a few months spent back in New York after his demobilization in the autumn of 1945, he accepted a civilian job with the US Military Government in Berlin. He arrived to find a city divided into zones governed by the four main Allied powers: the USA, the UK, France and the Soviet Union. As he later recounted, "there was something of a socio-economic political vacuum – how this vacuum was then refilled with the preferred kinds of institutional arrangements" would determine the subsequent outcomes "in terms of economic activity, in terms of political structure, in terms of social consciousness" (Lent 1995, p. 137). He was shocked at the aggression behind the American occupying power's push for a solution that reproduced the essential features of American capitalism and how quickly alternatives were discounted. Consequently, when the Western allies moved to outflank the Soviet Union in 1948 and create the basis for an independent West German state, he was not in the least surprised. Later, back home in New York, witnessing how "American business and governmental perspectives sought to reverse the mild postwar reforms of the British Labour Party", he concluded that: "The not-so-secret US objective" was to make the postwar world not simply safe for, but sympathetic to, "private corporate exploitation" (Schiller 2000, p. 25).

Underneath the obvious instrumentality of this project he saw a catastrophic failure of the imagination rooted in the American experience of the Second World War. Unlike many combatant countries in Europe and the Far East, the United States was never invaded or occupied or subjected to saturation bombing. Nor was its economy and infrastructure drained and devastated. On the contrary, the war was a time "of great economic growth and expansion and of corporate and individual enrichment" (Schiller 1984, p. 109). As he remembered from his time in army camps in southern California, when he was first drafted in 1942, with factories at full capacity "workers would come off their jobs at midnight, revved up and raring to join the nightlife that was organized on a round-the-clock schedule. Consumption needed no encouragement, coming after a ten-year depression. It was supported by full pay checks" and laid the basis for the postwar boom (Schiller 2000, p. 16). Looking out at the world from this "privileged material position" and served by a media system "sealed off surprisingly well from outside opinion" most Americans, Schiller argued, were unable to "comprehend or sympathize with the most elemental and powerful feelings and social movements" of the era or to "empathize with a huge, have-not world" (Schiller 1984, p. 109). Consequently, he found himself deeply at odds with both the economic order and dominant world view of the world's new "number one country" and set out to investigate how American power was deployed "to extract privilege and prevent social change that might limit that privilege". This overarching theme ran through all his subsequent work.

Throughout his working life, antagonism to communism, and by extension to socialism, ebbed and flowed through American popular culture and government rhetoric providing a ready-made rationale for the official equation of political freedom with free markets. Firmly entrenched in American popular culture and political rhetoric since the Bolshevik seizure of power in 1917, it was easily refurbished to construct a pervasive Cold War culture grounded in the enveloping fear of a full-scale nuclear exchange. Schiller saw things differently. His experiences in Berlin convinced him that American policy was based on "a terribly wrong and falsified assessment of Russian aims" (Schiller 2000, p. 19) and that the push to persuade "the American people that their daily existence was threatened by the war-devastated and totally drained Russian economy" (Schiller 1973, p. 6) was "a spectacular excursion into mind management" designed to advance the interests of the military-industrial complex, at home and abroad. His view was confirmed by Harry Truman's relentless attacks on the newly formed Progressive Party's campaign for active cooperation with the Soviets in the November 1948 election. From that point on, as he later put it: "A curtain had come down in America, smothering free discussion" and fostering a political atmosphere marked by "investigating commissions, firings, the blacklist, and generalized repression and coercion" (Schiller 2000, pp. 21–22).

His experiences in Berlin also furnished him with a method of inquiry. He held a relatively junior position, but "because of the kinds of chaos that existed and the lapses that frequently occur in large bureaucratic circumstances", he often found himself at high-level meetings and witnessed at first hand how "people in important positions behaved" and how they pushed their policies through to completion (Lent 1995, p. 136). He later turned this habit of eavesdropping on the powerful as they talked among themselves and went about their business into the major method he employed in his writings, combing through official reports, transcripts of government hearings, trade publications, and speeches to meetings and conferences for telling phrases and off-the-cuff remarks that revealed their world views and rationales.

In and Against the Academy

Schiller moved into academia in 1950 with a full-time position at the Pratt Institute, an art school in Brooklyn, supplemented by an evening job at the City College business school, paid by the hour. The punishing teaching load left little time for research and the climate created by McCarthyism proved inhospitable to critical analyses of American power, but he found another outlet for the radicalism that had grown out of his wartime experiences. In 1949–1950, when, as he later noted, "most middle-class professionals were scurrying as rapidly as they could away from anything they feared might bring them to the attention of the new vigilantism" (Schiller 2000, p. 22), he began to write weekly and bi-weekly commentaries on American foreign economic policy for the Labour Research Association under the by-line "LRA".

The Cold War provided the immediate day-to-day context for this work, prompting him to cover his face and worry incessantly about being photographed as he entered the LRA offices to deliver his weekly articles by hand. Surveying the postwar order, he saw "a world split as much by a North-South poverty line as by an East-West ideological divide" (Schiller 1969, p. 10) and he used the freedom offered by anonymous authorship to interrogate the performance of the key agencies the Allied nations had established at Bretton Woods in 1944 to manage the emerging global economic order. He was in no doubt that the International Monetary Fund and the International Bank for Reconstruction and Development (later to become the World Bank) operated as important levers of power for their main financial backer, the United States. In articles like "The World Bank: Agency for Wall Street's Cold War", he set out to show that their decisions to grant or withhold economic assistance were designed to reward compliance with American objectives and punish socialist-inclined states. He also saw very clearly that this pursuit of national interests by other means sat uneasily alongside the more cosmopolitan impetus of the other major postwar global agency – the United Nations. Because they were seen as central to the battle for hearts and minds, the educational and cultural activities of UNESCO became a particular focus of contention which later came to a head in the bitter debate over the "free flow" of communication, in which he was very much involved, and which provided the pretext for America's withdrawal of support for the Organization.

When the anti-communist witch hunts abated, Schiller diversified his journalism, writing regular signed articles for a range of other radical magazines and newsletters, including *The Nation*, *The Progressive* and the *Bulletin of the Atomic Scientists*. These pieces, designed to counter what he saw as the distortions and evasions of conventional press coverage, played an important role as first drafts of arguments and evidence that would later find their way into his books.

His critical stance towards the mainstream press also provided one of the key elements that made his teaching so magnetic to students. He would regularly begin lectures by selecting an article or quotation from the day's newspaper and then set about deconstructing it, laying bare the concealed mechanisms and unannounced motivations behind current events and policy initiatives. This practice later gained a wider public through the series of half-hour programmes made by the leading video activist, Dee Dee Halleck, and distributed by the Paper Tiger TV collective. Entitled "Herb Schiller Reads *The New York Times*", they featured him riding in a mock-up of a New York subway carriage commenting acerbically on the evasions and half truths of that day's coverage and offering alternative interpretations.

His commitment to making his work as accessible as possible was grounded in a lifelong conviction that intellectuals had a duty to "confront the day-in-day-out real tribulations and trials of people" and explain the hidden mechanisms shaping everyday experience in ways that anyone willing to make a modest effort could understand. For him, writing and teaching were weapons in a war of public enlightenment. He saw making "a nice little presentation that's going to be acceptable to a half dozen or two dozen types" who have had the same academic training but "eludes popular understanding" (Lent 115, p. 138) as at best a distraction and at worst a betrayal. His uneasy relation with academia was reinforced by his own experience of doctoral studies. As a part-time student with a family and a full-time job, he found himself very much on the margins, slipping through the institutional cracks. As he later remembered: "I was a sort of floating piece of flotsam in a huge educational factory, left to my own resources" (Lent 1995, p. 137) On reflection, he came to see his lack of integration into an ordered process of "being led, being told, being influenced ... being put into a mould" as a fortunate escape from academic processing (Lent 1995, p. 137). He graduated with a ticket to a better position, but with his world view and way of working untouched. Soon after gaining his doctorate he left New York to take a year's visiting position at the University of Illinois in 1961. After returning to teach at Pratt the following year, he moved to permanent position at Illinois in 1963 where he stayed until 1970.

He was appointed to the Bureau of Economics and Business Research directed by V. Lewis Bassie, who as a maverick himself, allowed him to tackle issues outside the Bureau's normal remit. He opted to focus on the allocation and control of natural resources, an interest that led him to examine the regulatory regime governing the radio spectrum – the resource base for both the domestic broadcasting industry and, with the development of satellite technology, for an increasingly important segment of transnational communications. In a key chapter in *Mass Communications and American Empire* (Schiller 1969), he details how the American government set out to exercise control over the future deployment of satellite technology by pressing the international Radio Administrative Conference in Geneva in 1963 to make a definitive allocation of frequencies. The aim was to use this emerging technology to reproduce the control over the global communications system once exercised by the British through their domination of the transoceanic cable network. This push, which was successful, gave the USA, which had invested heavily in research and development, substantial first-mover advantages and effectively locked less developed countries into a regime that could not be revised in the light of future technological developments. As the leader of the US delegation noted at the time, "many of the countries here were not as prepared as perhaps some of the rest of us in the overall space communication field, and we had quite a little discussion about this problem" (quoted in Schiller 1969, p. 132). Satellite technology offered enormous potential for addressing the core problems of literacy, training and education facing low-income countries. Schiller (1976, p. 76) saw its annexation by "a global system serving the interests of American equipment producers, electronics corporations, the military establishment, and the general advertising and commercial community" as a comprehensive betrayal of this promise.

He observed the same process whereby "power-wielders retain the inside track" and incorporate new technologies "as quickly as possible into their special needs and interests" (Schiller 1976, p. 76) at work within the USA in the struggle over the allocation of frequencies to television. The major equipment manufacturers had pursued research and development strategies that assumed that television broadcasting would employ the VHF portion of the spectrum, although it was very crowded. There was ample spare capacity in the ultra high frequency UHF band, but utilizing it would require them to produce sets that could accommodate both bands, which they saw as an unnecessary additional expense. Faced with concerted industry lobbying, in 1945 the national regulator, the Federal Communications Commission (FCC), placed commercial television in the VHF band reserving the UHF band for the 70 additional channels it licensed in 1952, most of which were educational channels. Because very few sets could receive UHF signals, 80% of the assigned frequencies went unused throughout the 1950s. By the time Congress passed legislation in 1964 requiring manufacturers to produce sets that could receive all channels, popular television viewing had become synonymous with watching the major commercial networks. Once again, Schiller argued, communications facilities, "which could be a vigorous mechanism of social change" had been "seized by the commanding interests in the market economy ... making alternate paths seen undesirable" and creating "a major obstacle to national reconstruction" (Schiller 1969, p. 29).

As Chief Economist at the FCC from 1943 to 1948, Dallas Smythe had witnessed this process of corporate capture unfolding at first hand and had seen his own arguments for non-advertising-supported channels comprehensively rejected (Smythe 1994, p. 73). When Schiller arrived at Illinois, Smythe had been teaching there since leaving the FCC and had established the first course on communications grounded in critical political economy rather than mainstream economics. Although Marx and later Marxist writers provided an essential starting point for this project, it also drew on the vigorous current of radical populism within the American critical tradition. Consequently, the intellectual thrust of new critical political economy centred on the structural contradiction between the public cultural resources required for a fully functioning democracy and the shortfalls in the performance of a privately owned communications system dedicated to profit maximization. Smythe departed soon after Schiller arrived to take up a position at the University of Saskatchewan, leaving Schiller to assume responsibility for graduate teaching in the political economy of communications. It provided him with a context in which he could legitimately focus on his primary interest and from that point on, as he later recalled, he considered himself "in the field of communications" (Lent 1995, p. 140).

In 1966 he began converting the essays already published in various radical journals into the manuscript of *Mass Communications and American Empire*. In developing this project, he relied more on his family than on the normal academic support systems, from which he was relatively disconnected. His wife Anita, a professional librarian, had joined the university's nationally known Library Research Centre when they moved to Illinois. Since libraries were in the front line of changes in the provision of information, they provided an early warning system of the shifts towards computerization, commodification and privatization that were later to restructure public information resources as a whole. Schiller (2000, p. 40) attributed his "own recognition of what was occurring completely to Anita's experiences, commentary and early writings on these trends" and relied on her professional knowledge throughout his career, particularly in his later work, *Information and the Crisis Economy* (Schiller 1984). He also drew on the expertise of his two sons. Dan (now a distinguished critical communications scholar himself) undertook the bulk of the basic research for the key chapter on the recreation and entertainment industries in his father's second book, *The Mind Managers* (Schiller 1973), and Zack, who became an economic journalist on *Business Week*, regularly supplied material on corporate activity.

Schiller's fractured postgraduate experience had left him without a senior academic figure who could sponsor the book when it came to searching for a publisher, and the manuscript was rejected by the nine or so commercial companies to which he sent it. It eventually found an unexpected home with Augustus Kelley: a small, independent publisher specializing in reprints of early works in political economy. As he later remarked, this chain of unplanned coincidences "was very similar to [his] experiences as an academic" (Lent 1995, p. 143). Serendipity also played a role in the book's subsequent success. Published in 1969, just before a crucial meeting on the New International Information Order in Montreal, its central arguments resonated strongly with the growing critique of American global cultural and communicative power. It received a further boost when the *Saturday Review* hailed it as the first book to challenge Cold War assumptions in the field of communications, and it was subsequently widely taken up in countercultural circles. Its growing reputation was one of the factors that helped secure him a job at the University of California at San Diego (UCSD) in 1970.

The Belly of the Beast

In response to student pressure the university administration agreed that the proposed Third College on the campus be dedicated to the needs of students from the black, Latino and Native American minorities. Communications was chosen as one of the four foci of teaching, and Schiller was invited to apply for the position of head of the communications programme. After a gruelling interview with student representatives, he was appointed to the post.

Living in San Diego provided Schiller with daily confirmation of his core analysis of American power and its contradictions. The university was located on a hill above the beach resort of La Jolla, which at the time had one of the highest concentrations of millionaires of any town in the USA. Half an hour's drive south, however, the other side of the border with Mexico stood as a stark reminder of the poverty and desperation that led illegal immigrants to risk their lives on a daily basis crossing over into the USA in the hope of finding work on construction sites or as gardeners or nannies. The city was a conservative stronghold, by tradition the last stop on the campaign trail for Republican candidates for President and one of the major bases for the Pacific Fleet. At the same time, the UCSD campus had seen some of the most concerted opposition to American foreign policy culminating in a student setting fire to himself in protest at the Vietnam War. These fault lines ran through Schiller's street. One of his neighbours was the disgraced former Republican Vice President, Spiro Agnew, who, after his resignation over allegations of tax evasion, built a second career as an international trade executive. Schiller, for his part, fitted perfectly into the role of "nattering nabob of negativity", one of Agnew's favourite terms of abuse for the radical intelligentsia.

Schiller remained at UCSD for the rest of his career, playing a major role in developing a programme, and later a Department, that became one of the most distinguished centres of communications scholarship in North America. It also became a key node in an international network of intellectual exchange, with a steady stream of researchers from Europe and elsewhere coming to teach for a semester or a year and Schiller himself accepting visiting positions at a number of overseas universities, including Amsterdam, Stockholm and Paris.

This intellectual traffic was consolidated and extended by the leading role he assumed in the International Association for Mass Communication Research (IAMCR), where he established a thriving Political Economy section and later accepted the position of Vice President. Unlike the other major professional body in the field, the International Communications Association, which was then overwhelmingly US-based in both its membership and choice of conference venues, IAMCR actively recruited members from both the "Third World" and the "Eastern Bloc", and sought to hold meetings in a range of venues, which included during Schiller's active involvement Prague and Delhi.

Schiller drew on his experience of living and working in San Diego and his overseas speaking and teaching engagements to develop his existing interests and extend them into new areas. Three central threads in his writing are particularly relevant to current debates; his work on the corporate takeover of public expression; his analysis of cultural imperialism; and his critique of the utopian promises made for the new digital technologies. He is often dismissed by contemporary critics as "yesterday's man": a scholar whose preoccupations have been overtaken by a recent events and new theoretical developments. I want to argue the opposite case; that a close reading of the entire corpus of his writings offers us an analysis that was often ahead of its time and more relevant than ever.

Culture Incorporated

His first two books, *Mass Communications and American Empire* (1969) and *The Mind Managers* (1973), provide a comprehensive critique of the American media system's failure to provide the cultural resources required for informed and active citizenship. No one had ever explored the chains connecting culture to economy with such clarity and thoroughness or mustered such a wealth of empirical detail and concrete illustration. For Schiller, the American system offered a perfect laboratory for investigating what happens when capitalist logics are allowed to dominate the cultural sphere with only minimal regulatory checks. The result, as he saw it, was the progressive concentration of symbolic production in the hands of major corporations whose first and last priority was to maximize returns to shareholders by creating cultural commodities that could be sold to the largest possible number of buyers. This requirement, he argued, put a premium on material that had already proved its market worth and militated against dissent and challenge. The result was a plurality of variations of conventional thinking and familiar themes rather than a genuine diversity of expression and contest of ideas.

This mainstreaming effect was most pronounced in the commercial television system, which was firmly entrenched as the central focus of the everyday cultural experience by the time he came to write. He saw reliance on advertising finance having three major impacts. Firstly, programming decisions were indelibly stamped by the need to assemble audiences that advertisers wanted to reach at the prices the networks were charging. As a consequence:

> Though no single program, performer, commentator, or informational bit is necessarily identical to its competitors, *there is no significant qualitative difference*. Just as a supermarket offers six identical soaps in different colours and a drugstore sells a variety of brands of aspirin at different prices ... (Schiller 1973, p. 20; emphasis in original)

Secondly, "the needs of the consumer economy to fill all communications space with commercial messages" meant that programmes were continually interrupted by advertisements making it next to impossible for programme producers to place events in context or develop the sustained exposition and argumentation that illuminated connections, causes and possible solutions. This disconnection from shared inquiry and debate was, in his view, further reinforced by the privatized nature of television viewing. The result was a virtuous commercial circle anchored in the core American value of individualism. By relentlessly addressing audiences as consumers with a sovereign right to realize their aspirations and re-make themselves through choices in the marketplace, commercial television reinforced an "American life style [which] from its most minor detail to its most deeply felt beliefs and practice, reflects an exclusively self-centred outlook, which in turn is an accurate image of the structure of the economy itself" (Schiller 1973, p. 10). In the process, the sense of shared responsibility for common problems that is central to the exercise of full citizenship was eroded and pushed to the margins.

He returned to this central theme in what is arguably his most important book: *Culture Inc: The Corporate Takeover of Public Expression* (1989). Written against the backdrop of the Reagan Government's relentless dismantling of public enterprise and continuous squeeze on public investment, it presents a detailed and damning critique of the impact of "expanded corporate power" on "cultural activity and the visions that sustain a people", and develops his earlier argument that "the drive to privatize and bring under corporate management as many elements of economic and social activity as possible ... has tipped the balance of democratic existence to an uncomfortable precariousness" (Schiller 1984, p. 3). He pursues the corporate takeover of public expression across the full range of cultural sites, moving from the mass media to museums, art galleries, public libraries and urban spaces. The result is one of the most powerful dissections we have of how "spheres of activity that historically have been public and non-commercial" have been pushed back and often eliminated (Schiller 1984, p. 28).

His earlier work had paid relatively little sustained attention to the workings of cultural institutions that operated outside the advertising and price systems. Despite his extensive knowledge of developments in Europe, he remained sceptical of the countervailing potential of public service broadcasting, seeing it as only a matter of time before it too was enveloped by corporate logics and subjected to market disciplines. In the 1970s, this looked like wilful blindness to many observers outside the USA. Commentators in Western Europe could point to fifteen nations where public service providers still enjoyed a monopoly, and British analysts could present the launch of Channel 4 in 1979 as an extension, rather than a contraction, of public service ideals. A decade later, privately financed cable and satellite services had broken public service broadcasting's monopoly in a number of its former citadels, including Sweden, Norway and West Germany. The BBC was being cajoled into behaving more and more like a private corporation seeking to maximize the commercial returns from its various activities. Channel 4 was selling its own advertising. Corporate sponsorship was establishing itself as an essential support for major public exhibitions and performances, and public information services were being privatized. Suddenly, Schiller's fierce and eloquent analysis of the corporate capture of cultural life and its attenuation of citizenship and the public domain had acquired a new and urgent relevance. A decade and half later, *Culture Inc.* remains an essential resource for anyone wanting to understand the cultural consequences of marketization. We can see a similar resurgence of relevance in his analysis of cultural imperialism.

Culture and Empire

To populations subjected to severe material deprivation and concerted propaganda and information control during the war years, the promise of a postwar order in which information and resources would flow freely across borders was deeply attractive, and as Schiller demonstrates in detail, US corporate and governmental interests were quick to seize the opportunity to promote the "free flow of information" as a core international policy objective (see Schiller 1976, pp. 24–45). As with free trade theory generally, this seemingly benign ambition carefully "set aside the structural and social divisions that characterize the global community" (Schiller 1969, p. 117). On the one side stood the depleted and war-damaged economies of Europe and Asia; on the other, the USA, emerging from the war physically unscathed and economically overpowering with its existing competitive advantages in world cultural trade consolidated by the artefacts and styles that American troops had brought to countries across the theatre of conflict. As Schiller had noted from his experiences in Casablanca, the way they looked, lived and took their leisure was a daily reminder of the comforts and pleasure of consumption, a vivid celebration of possession and display as the principle sphere of personal choice and freedom. Although the later debate on "free flow" in and around UNESCO focused primarily on information and news, Schiller argued from the outset that the primary problem was the promotion of consumerism.

He saw commercial broadcasting, and particularly commercial television, as the principle battleground. As he noted in a key passage in *Mass Communications and American Empire*,

> material from the United States offers a vision of a way of life. The image is of a mountain of material artefacts, privately furnished and individually acquired and consumed. The imagery envelops all viewers and listeners within the range of electronic impulses patterned after the American model. (Schiller 1969, p. 3)

This "stimulation to personal consumption", he argues, fosters a disposition that supports the diversion of "painfully scarce materials from group projects and [the] long range improvement possibilities" represented by "massive campaigns for literacy, manpower training programmes and honest forums for popular discussion" (Schiller 1969, pp. 115, 117). Faced with commercial broadcasting's wholesale disregard of these core priorities for development, Schiller saw the prospects for collective advancement and cultural diversity resting "largely on the willingness and ability of scores of weak countries to forego the cellophane-wrapped articles of the West's entertainment industries and persistently to develop, however much time it takes, their own broadcast material" (Schiller 1969, p. 122).

This analysis has been criticized on three main grounds. Firstly, it is argued that state-directed broadcasting services are all too easily commandeered to advance selective conceptions of "national culture" that serve the interests of ruling elites, and that the formats and styles introduced by commercial programming open up spaces that allow subordinated experiences and voices to enter the public domain. The experience of India, which moved from a television system monopolized by the state broadcaster to a competitive market built around competing cable and satellite services, is often cited as an illustration of this pluralizing process in action. Secondly, it is asserted that Schiller's model of cultural domination presupposes that global cultural flows move overwhelmingly in one direction, from the centre to the periphery, and ignores the complex collisions and integrations that are producing increasingly hybrid and heterogeneous cultures in the world's major metropoles. Thirdly, it is claimed that he sees Third World audiences as largely passive and defenceless in the face of US cultural imports and devalues the agency displayed by their active appropriation, reinterpretation and redeployment of narratives, images and styles.

In his later work – particularly, the provocatively entitled *Communication and Cultural Domination* (1976) and *Culture Inc.* (1989) – he replied to these criticisms in emphatic fashion.

He begins by arguing that "cultural imperialism today" has to be understood in the context of "a world system within which there is a single market" whose "terms and character are determined in the core and radiate outwards" (Schiller 1976, p. 5), and that it comprises "the sum of the processes by which [a society's] dominating stratum is attracted, pressured, forced and sometimes bribed into shaping social institutions to correspond to, or even promote, the values and structures of the dominating centre" (Schiller 1976, p. 9). At the end of the 1970s, this was very much a minority view among American commentators on international trade and foreign relations. By the beginning of the 1990s it could be re-read as a remarkably prescient description of a global order in the making. With the collapse of the Soviet Union, China's market reforms and India's move from self-sufficiency to a more open economy, the three major regions that had remained outside the capitalist world system since the Second World War were finally incorporated into it, creating a truly global market for the first time. Elsewhere, growing disillusion with state management in all it forms, the aggressive promotion of the benefits of privatization by President Reagan and Prime Minister Thatcher, and demands by the International Monetary Fund and the World Bank that countries wanting loans must "restructure" to become more business friendly, had combined to roll back public enterprise and massively increase both the operating space available to private corporations and the resources at their disposal. In the process, the relations between global cultural flows and local production were reconfigured and Western corporations have been obliged to take on local colouration. Local producers have adapted templates originating in the USA and Europe and invented new traditions tailored to major overseas markets.

China offers some paradigmatic recent examples. Disney has finally decided that Mickey Mouse will speak Mandarin in the relevant Asian markets. The Chinese version of the hit UK and US game show, *Pop Idol*, has been the country's biggest ratings success of 2005. *Crouching Tiger, Hidden Dragon*, which carefully reworks elements from Chinese folk tales and martial arts traditions for Western audiences, has been a critical and commercial success abroad, but widely criticized in China. The result is certainly more hybridity, but it is also a cultural system increasingly geared to maximizing market returns. Production may be local but the master templates and the meta-ideology of consumerism that underpins them are either made in the West or adapted to Western tastes and preconceptions.

It is not necessary to assume that audiences are passive and compliant in order to argue that this process is likely to have profound long-term impacts on popular consciousness. For Schiller, the perfectly valid argument that "audiences interpret messages variously [and] may transform them to correspond with their individual experiences and tastes" signally failed to address the cumulative impact of a consumerist vision of personal success and social progress "incessantly repeated in all cultural conduits" (1989, p. 156). On the one hand, by dissipating popular support for collective solutions to shared problems it clearly consolidated corporate control; on the other, "the consumerist model, carried into the world at large" also acted as "a radicalizing force". By "installing itself in all corners of the globe, and spreading the message of consumption through its advertising-supported media channels" and by "simultaneously feeding and thwarting human expectations", transnational corporations operating in impoverished and radically unequal societies were, Schiller argued, fermenting what they most feared: "future massive political instability" (Schiller 1984, p. 98). These upheavals have not taken the form that he envisaged, at least not yet, but growing opposition to Western consumerism's social, environmental and spiritual costs has found powerful expression in the campaign for global justice and contributed substantially to the resurgence of fundamentalisms across the world's major religions.

The extensive use of mobile phones and Internet websites and bulletin boards by both these movements alerts us to the fact that the rise of marketization and its discontents has coincided almost exactly with the continuing shift from analogue to digital communications technologies. Investigating how innovations in communications intersected with the dynamics of corporate enclosure and global markets was a continuing theme in Schiller's work and a major focus of his later writings.

Digital Deceptions

For Schiller, technological innovations never arise out of thin air. Their design, development and applications are always strongly shaped by the prevailing power structure. At the same time, this drive for control is never complete. There is almost always "a glimpse of new possibilities and social arrangements" alternative ways of organizing and operating (Schiller 1976, p. 76). As a consequence, technologies become the site of an intensifying battle for control. This struggle is particularly acute in the case of cultural and communications technologies, Schiller argued, because American corporations and governments have come to see innovations in this area as the major solution to both a gathering crisis of profitability and challenges to America's global hegemony. They therefore have a strong material interest in marginalizing dissenting views and arguing that new media will deliver unprecedented choice and control to audiences and users. This case is developed in detail in his book, *Information and the Crisis Economy* (1984), but debunking the dominant rhetorics surrounding new technologies was a prominent theme is his work from the outset. His attack focused on three issues: the resilience and reinforcement of structural inequalities, the concerted management of consumer choice, and the central role of communications technologies in supporting security and military agendas.

Since introducing new machines into societies characterized by deep-seated structural inequalities of access to essential material and cultural resources did nothing to address the underlying dynamics of exclusion, he argued, it was "cruel and deceitful … to suggest that ghetto children confronting computer consoles will magically overcome generations of deprivation" (Schiller 1973, p. 174). Indeed, their disadvantages are likely to be reinforced as access to hardware, connectivity, software and digital services becomes more and more commercialized and dependent on ability to pay and public provision is increasingly cut. As a result, "what hypothetically could be a truly information-rich society is on its way to becoming a community divided into information 'haves' and 'have-nots'" (Schiller 1984, p. 103). This trenchant analysis of what came to be called the "Digital Divide" was again ahead of its time, written a decade before the US government finally acknowledged the issue and commissioned the National Telecommunications and Information Administration to map its contours and the phrase became part of popular debate.

Schiller was also one of the first commentators to argue that the promise that interactive television services would transfer power from producers to viewers concealed a carefully stage-managed exercise in corporate control. Surveying American experiments combining computers and cable television for electronic polling in the early 1970s, he argued that the "claim that it can produce participatory programming, which permits the viewer/receiver to react to and – reformulate the context" in which she or he engages with what is shown on the screen begs the central question of "who will control the questions" on which people are encouraged to vote and "how and in [sic] whose behalf the answers will be used" (Schiller 1973, pp. 181–182). He saw this commercial impetus as the direct antithesis of the "popular participation in initiating messages and discussion as well as in responding" required by democratic communication (Schiller 1984, p. 113).

The recent expansion of interactive television has given his analysis a new urgency. It is now clear that the most heavily promoted forms of interactivity are primarily designed to generate new revenue streams for the companies involved, either through direct customer payments (as with gambling and home shopping) or through the charges viewers pay for the premium rate telephone calls they make to vote for contestants in hit shows such as *Pop Idol* and *Big Brother*. As Schiller argued, far from returning power to viewers, this system consolidates the power of producers. They compile the menu of choices on offer and gain access to an unparalleled array of personalized information they can employ to target promotional campaigns more effectively. This recognition led him to see "surveillance … and marketing as the near-certain outcomes of the utilization of new communications technologies" (Schiller 1984, p. 23).

Surveillance for Schiller was always a double process. Alongside the commercial panopticon operated by the polling, advertising and market research industries, which he analysed in detail from the outset, unusually for a cultural critic he also paid close attention to the ways communications facilities were deployed to support military and security agendas. Popular representations of the Cold War have privileged the figure of the spy or undercover agent, the pivot of human intelligence systems. He was more interested in how new technologies were being employed to compile consolidated data files on individual citizens, monitor domestic and global telecommunications traffic, and map the geographical distribution of strategic resources and potential threats. He was one of the first commentators to highlight the significance of remote sensing satellites, arguing that they confer "a critical advantage in global deployment of force and in gathering the intelligence necessary for intervention and military manoeuvre" (Schiller 1982, p. 119). He saw this system as part of a wider deployment of new information technologies "introduced to support business and enable a globe-girding military communication network to be prepared to be the ultimate enforcer" (Schiller 1984, p. 21).

He reached this conclusion half a decade before the collapse of the Soviet Union left the United States the world's sole superpower. Events since the 9/11 attacks on the Pentagon and the World Trade Center have again confirmed the prescience of his core analysis. We see an unprecedented extension and coordination of surveillance over civilian populations. We see the emphasis on adequate defence replaced by the promotion of pre-emptive strikes against possible threats. We see the network of US military bases and facilities being extended to confer global reach. But most of all we see the same "fabrication of fear" that "supported the edifice of the national security state" throughout the Cold War years (Schiller 1989, p. 155). Based on stark binary divisions between "us" and "them", "friends" and "enemies", and the conflation of the search for underlying causes with "fellow travelling" and collusion, this climate of suspicion militates against both the sustained interrogation of official accounts and the construction of more cosmopolitan and inclusive conceptions of citizenship.

These developments all too easily encourage pessimism about the prospects for fundamental change – a response that Schiller would certainly recognize. But he also drew attention to the instabilities in the present system, arguing that "despite its gigantic concentrations of capital, political power, and informational control, there are vulnerabilities ... that create or allow opportunities for popular expression" and that "for the first time in human development" these cracks "possess a global dimension, which may be expected to broaden and deepen" (Schiller 1984, p. 123).

Reconstructing the Cultural Commons

His vision of an alternative communications order was built around the "untold number of individuals and groups outside the mainstream working with tape recorders, cameras, video recorders, film, music, print, radio, graphics, and public art forms" who engaged in cultural creation "on their own initiative and out of their own desire to communicate", seeing this groundswell of non-commercial activity as the "strongest defence any society has against information control and mind management" (Schiller 1973, p. 189). At the same time, he acknowledged that there were also thousands of experienced and skilled media people working to provide alternative modes of expression "through independent papers and magazines and local cable-access and significant numbers of individuals in the commercial media" testing commercial boundaries on a daily basis and "attempting to carry out projects that may add something to human enlightenment and well being" (Schiller 1989, p. 167). His views were again shaped by personal experience.

On the acknowledgements page for *Culture Inc.*, he particularly thanks Dee Dee Hallack, his colleague at San Diego, for setting "the standard" for his "views on alternatives to commercially supported expression" through her work with radical video, cable and satellite initiatives (Schiller 1989, p. vii). As mentioned earlier, she produced and distributed the series that brought his own ideas to a wider audience. Lester Cole, the father of Michael Cole, a colleague in the San Diego department, was another important point of reference (Schiller 1989, p. 39). Cole, an activist and co-founder of the Screenwriter's Guild, was jailed for a year for refusing to answer questions on his political beliefs before Senator McCarthy's House Un-American Activities Committee. His unfinished script on the life of the Mexican revolutionary, Emiliano Zapata, was completed by John Steinbeck and released in 1952 as *Viva Zapata*, directed by Elia Kazan, who had cooperated with the Committee. Despite being blacklisted, however, Cole continued to work intermittently as a screenwriter under assumed names, including Lewis Copley and Gerald L. L. Copley.

There is, however, a fundamental tension in Schiller's position that has been shared by almost all proposals for democratizing cultural production up until recently. It centres on the potential clash between popular demands for participation and free access to cultural resources and professional cultural workers' legitimate desire to earn a reasonable living from their labour. He remained sceptical about the radical potential of the Internet, but the last four years or so have seen developments that might have given him cause for hope. Most obviously, there is the rapid growth of participatory and collaborative production. Notable examples include Wikipedia, the world's most comprehensive encyclopaedia, developed entirely from voluntary donations of knowledge and expertise; OhmyNews, the South Korean daily newspaper that mobilizes material submitted by a pool of over 26,000 registered citizen reporters; and the myriad personal testimonies, vernacular video footage and cellphone photographs of the Tsunami in the India Ocean in December 2004 and the London bomb blasts on 7 July 2005 posted on the World Wide Web, which, in the absence of eyewitness reports from professional reporters and camera crews, constitute the only first drafts we have of the history of two major contemporary events.

At the same time, we are also witnessing the revivification of public cultural institutions as libraries, museums, universities and public broadcasters move onto the Internet to make their holdings and expertise more readily accessible and to foster more open relations with their users, inviting contributions and comments, hosting message boards and accepting new creative contributions. Issues of copyright, which have traditionally limited secondary uses of professional produced materials, are being addressed by novel "creative commons" agreements that allow authors to grant free use of their work for specified non-commercial purposes while retaining the right to be compensated for other uses.

At the end of *Culture Inc.* Schiller called for a new "information-cultural politics" based on retaining as many symbolic resources as possible as "social and inexpensive good(s)", resisting their conversion into "saleable commodities" and "restoring public participation and accountability to media and cultural affairs". As he recognized, this would require "a massive expansion of the public sector" (Schiller 1989, p. 172). Given that his work had demonstrated with great force that in the postwar United States the meaning of "national policy" had "drastically narrowed from designation of the collective needs and rights of all Americans to a kind of code word expression of the concerns of the private sector" (Schiller 1989, p. 36), he not surprisingly saw little hope of securing the 180 degree turn needed.

Elsewhere, however, where the principle of free entry to museums and galleries has been retained (though not without a struggle) and public service broadcasting remains free of advertising and free at the point of use, there are, at least for the moment, arguably more promising arenas in which to pursue his vision of a cultural commons outside the orbit of corporate strategies and built around an alliance between public institutions funded out of taxation and creative initiatives grounded in an ethos of reciprocity (Murdock 2005). The basic building blocks are already to hand. The challenge is to work out how best to assemble them and defend the results against the encroachments of commercialism.

NOTE

1. Herbert Schiller left few autobiographical notes apart from the interview he gave to John Lent (1995) and the reflections on his life and career in his last book: *Living in the Number One Country* (Schiller 2000). I have supplemented these sources with information and insights gathered in the course of over a decade of conversation and intellectual argument with him conducted in many places, but most particularly in San Diego where I taught his class on political economy while he was on sabbatical leave working at home on his next book. This attempt to take stock of his legacy continues this dialogue.

REFERENCES

ADORNO, T. W. (1991) *The Culture Industry: Selected Essays on Mass Culture,* Routledge, London.
HORKHEIMER, M. & ADORNO, T. W. (1973) *Dialectic of Enlightenment,* Allen Lane, London.
KREISLER, H. (2002) *Activism, Anarchism and Power: Conversation with Noam Chomsky* [online], available at: http://globetrotter.berkeley.edu/people2/Chomsky/Chomsky-con1.html (accessed 10 September 2005).
LENT, J. A. (1995) 'Interview with Herbert I. Schiller', in *A Different Road Taken: Profiles in Critical Communication,* Westview Press, Boulder, CO, pp. 135–153
MILLS, C. W. (1959) *The Power Elite,* Oxford University Press, Oxford/Galaxy Books, New York.

MURDOCK, G. (2005) 'Building the digital commons: Public broadcasting in the age of the Internet', in *Cultural Dilemmas of Public Service Broadcasting,* eds P. Jauert & G. F. Lowe, NORDICOM, Goteborg University, Goteborg, pp. 213–230.

MURDOCK, G. (2006) 'Cosmopolitans and conquistadors: Empires, nations and networks', in *Communications Media, Globalization and Empire,* ed. O. B. Barrett, John Libbey Publishing, Eastleigh, pp. 17–32.

SCHILLER, H. I. (1969) *Mass Communications and American Empire,* Beacon Press, Boston, MA.

SCHILLER, H. I. (1973) *The Mind Managers,* Beacon Press, Boston, MA.

SCHILLER, H. I. (1976) *Communication and Cultural Domination,* M.E. Sharpe, New York.

SCHILLER, H. I. (1982) *Who Knows? Information in the Age of the Fortune 500,* Ablex, Norwood, NJ.

SCHILLER, H. I. (1984) *Information and the Crisis Economy,* Ablex, Norwood, NJ.

SCHILLER, H. I. (1989) *Culture Inc.: The Corporate Takeover of Public Expression,* Oxford University Press, New York.

SCHILLER, H. I. (2000) *Living in the Number One Country: Reflections from a Critic of American Empire,* Seven Stories Press, New York.

SMYTHE, D. (1994) *Counterclockwise: Perspectives on Communication,* Westview Press, Boulder, CO.

SOCIAL SECURITY ONLINE (2006) *Upton Sinclair* [online], available at: http://www.ssa.gov/history/Sinclair.html (accessed 14 February 2006).

WILLIAMS, R. (1974) *Television: Technology and Cultural Form,* Fontana Books, London.

YALE LAW SCHOOL (2005) *The Avalon Papers at Yale Law School* [online], available at: http://www.yale.edu/lawweb/avalon.presiden/speeches/eisenhower001.htm (accessed 7 September 2005).

THE UNACKNOWLEDGED LEGACY
Plato, the *Republic* and cultural policy

Eleonora Belfiore

Introduction: Why Plato?

The Greek philosopher Plato (427–347 BC) was born in Athens and grew up during the Peloponnesian war (431–404), which concluded with the victory of Athens' long-time rival Sparta. Towards the end of the fourth century BC, Plato joined the circle of Socrates' disciples. Socrates proved a most powerful influence on the young Plato, who went on to re-elaborate some of the central ideas of Socratic thought into what can be arguably described as the most influential philosophical system in Western civilization.[1] Although the influence of Plato's teachings has been undisputedly far-reaching and persistent over time, his ideas have never, to my knowledge, been discussed with a view of assessing the extent to which recent and old discourses of cultural policy are indebted to the Athenian philosopher. This paper therefore aims to fill this gap and show that, as a matter of fact, many of the ideas and beliefs that can be seen at work in European cultural policy from its very inception are profoundly indebted to Plato's ideas on art and poetry, and to his elaboration of the role of the arts in education and political life.

In particular, the present discussion will demonstrate that Plato's infamous attack on poetry and his banning of the poets from his ideal city – and the philosophical justifications for such a rejection of the arts – have given birth to a very lively and articulated intellectual tradition purporting that the arts, because of their corrupting potential, are dangerous to the individual and society as a whole and must therefore be regulated and censored by the state. Naddaff (2002, p. xi), indeed, contends that "Plato is the founding father of Western literary censorship". And yet, at the same time, the opposite (but only apparently contradictory) notion of the educational and formative function of the arts has equally found in Plato an ardent proponent.

Indeed, precisely in this respect, this paper advances an understanding of the Platonic legacy that counters the prevalent interpretation that sees the Platonic view of poetry and art as mainly negative and diametrically opposed to the more positive and optimistic Aristotelian conception of art. Aristotle was one of Plato's own disciples and, according to a very commonly held view, in his *Poetics* is credited with having "rescued the theory of poetry as mimetic form from the Platonic consequences, whilst in principle accepting all the major distinctions Plato had made" (Schaper 1968, p. 55). Aristotle indeed developed his aesthetic theory around the same central issues that were first introduced by Plato. With regards to poetry and drama in particular,[2] Aristotle agrees with Plato that art is mimetic and that it has a deep emotional impact. However, whereas – as we will see – Plato felt that the passions and human dilemmas witnessed by an audience at a tragic performance could have seriously damaging effects on their character, Aristotle believed that the "pity and fear" experienced though the stage could have a cathartic (and therefore beneficial) effect on the spectator. In other words, "Aristotle takes the view that the emotionality of poetry cleanses instead of corrupts" (Asmis 1992, p. 357). Hence, as Nettleship (1962, p. 343) maintains, Plato's treatment of art "presents us with the reverse side of the picture of art given by Aristotle in the *Poetics*".

However, this paper will attempt to show that Plato's theory of poetry and its effects on the individual and society is by far more complex than this interpretation would lead us to believe. Therefore, I will attempt to show that the traditional contraposition between Platonic and Aristotelian views, and thus between a view of the arts and poetry as corrupting or purifying, is rather less clear-cut than such a simplistic juxtaposition would lead to assume.

In order to achieve this, the paper will trace the influence of Platonic thought over time. In particular, it will attempt to show how, through a Greek-Roman mediation (represented by personalities such as Tertullian and Augustine), Platonic ideas have continued to exert a clear influence over Western civilization. More specifically, they have instigated, at certain particular historical times, very clear and focussed strategies of cultural polemic aiming at introducing changes in cultural policy. The discussion will ultimately demonstrate that what is effectively behind a number of instances of "negative cultural policy" – culminating, for instance, in the Puritan attack on the stage and the consequent ban of theatre in England in 1642 – can essentially be brought back to the fundamental criticisms moved by Plato against the arts, albeit in the new and modified guises that they assumed in the course of time.

I will also argue that, far from being limited to what I refer here as "negative cultural policy"[3] and to the justification of state censorship of the arts, Plato's influence on the cultural policy discourse is much more penetrating and subtle than it is currently given credit for. As this paper will show, the more "positive" Platonic ideas and values – especially the belief in the educational, formative and, in fact, transformative power of poetry and the stage – can be seen as operational in today's cultural policy making and in particular in the recent trend towards what has been described as "instrumental cultural policy". This is a label that refers to the growing popularity of policies for the cultural sector that conceive the arts not as the end of policy, but rather as a means towards the fulfilment of other, not artistic, policy objectives (Vestheim 1994; Belfiore 2002).

Plato the Prophet?

Having referred above to the broad-ranging influence of Plato's thought over Western civilization, it is useful to begin the present discussion with a brief review of the Platonic legacy, which will provide the background for the more specific discussion of Plato's criticism of the arts that will follow. Unsurprisingly, Plato has been credited with being the "inventor" of philosophy, so much so that A. N. Whitehead once remarked that the entire European philosophical tradition could be characterized as "a series of footnotes to Plato" (quoted in Murray 1996, p. 1). As Nightingale (1995, p. 10) explains, Plato shared in a culture that had witnessed the flourishing of various kinds of abstract and analytical thinking at the hands of pre-Socratic thinkers, mathematicians (and, more generally, scientists) and the sophists. However, before Plato came onto the Athenian intellectual scene, these various types of intellectuals, as well as poets, lawgivers and wise men in general, all belonged to a broad and un-specified category of "*sophoi*" and "*sophistai*".[4] Nightingale (1995, pp. 10, 60) shows that the word φιλοσοφεῖν (which can be translated as "to philosophise") and the other terms deriving from the same root-word, only occur rarely before the fifth century BC, and even then they were used to indicate intellectual cultivation in the broadest sense. The term only took the specialized and technical meaning that we attribute to it today once Plato appropriated it to describe his own intellectual enterprise and the ethical model of the good life that follows from it.

Much of Plato's work can indeed be described as the attempt to propose a narrower and more specific definition of the term φιλοσοφεῖν, an exercise that, as Richard Kraut (1992, p. 1) argues, eventually resulted in the creation of the discipline of philosophy as we know it. As we will see, this is just one of the numerous and diverse claims landed at Plato's door. It has been argued that many aspects of Platonic thought anticipated much later theoretical positions and developments in a number of different spheres (Cohn 2000, p. 34). Murray (1996, pp. 2–3), for instance, argues that: "Plato has been hailed as the originator of the Renaissance conception of the divinity of poetry, and of the romantic myth of the artist". Indeed, ever since Plato formulated his theory of poetical inspiration, the figure of the "mad poet", possessed by the creative "demon", has entered the Western imagination, having a remarkable and long-lasting impact on the Western understanding of poetry (Weineck 1998, p. 19). One might also argue that the modern practice of subsidizing artists and artistic production through public resources is built upon acknowledgement of the "special nature" of the artist and the recognition of the contribution that his or her talent (or, indeed, "gift") brings to the public sphere.

It is precisely on the basis of the vivid descriptions of poetic inspiration that can be found scattered in numerous Platonic writings (namely *Ion*, *Phaedrus*, *Apology* and *Laws*), which is of a nature clearly different from the kind of inspiration that Homer and Hesiod traditionally ascribed to the Muses, that commentators have found the evidence to claim that, in many ways, Plato prefigures psychoanalytical theories of poetical inspiration. According to Konstan (2004, p. 1; emphasis added) "it is a *commonplace* that the account of the soul that Plato develops in the *Phaedrus* and *Republic* is in certain respects analogous to the model or models elaborated by Freud and other theorists of modern psychoanalysis". Micaela Janan (1994, p. 7), for instance, claims that Plato's theory of the tripartite soul prefigures the tripartite psyche as mapped by both Freud and Lacan, and adds that all three thinkers "explicitly theorize a connection between desire and creative art".

Plato's alleged preludes of future theoretical developments do not end here. None other than Nietzsche (2000, p. 78), in his *The Birth of Tragedy*, attributes to Plato the invention of the modern literary genre *par excellence* – the novel – which he sees as the modern articulation of the Platonic dialogue. Cohn (2000, p. 39) goes one step further and, on the premise that Plato's writing on literature places great emphasis on "solitude as a state that presents a particular attraction for literature", suggests the possibility that Plato might have prophetically adumbrated the development of the realist and stream-of-consciousness novel of the nineteenth and twentieth centuries. Whether we accept this possibility as realistic or too farfetched, the fact remains that very few personalities in Western civilization have exercised the same degree of fascination over later generations, or have enjoyed equal levels of interest and engagement with their thought as Plato has done. Indeed, this brief review of the reflections engendered by the Platonic *opus*, while by no means exhaustive, is nevertheless representative of the enduring enthralment of Western scholars with the Athenian philosopher.

The extent of Plato's influence, spanning over two and a half millennia, is all the more remarkable when one considers that unlike Aristotle (the other great philosopher of classical Greece), Plato never wrote anything especially devoted to the discussion of the arts and literature. His aesthetic ideas, thus, can only be reconstructed from references and digressions that are scattered throughout the *corpus* of his writings (Murray 19967, p. 2). An obvious consequence of this is that his discussions of the arts always take place in the broader context of discussions of matters ethical, metaphysical and political. The reason behind this state of affairs is that, in ancient Greece, art was not something that could be conceived of as independent from the ethical (and hence the political) dimension. Plato does not accord an autonomous value to the aesthetic sphere. In his view, it is only the rational faculties of man that can, via the means provided by philosophical reasoning, capture and comprehend the metaphysical and ethical order of the world. For any positive value to be ascribed to the arts, they must faithfully represent this order or incite us towards the necessary process of philosophical enquiry; otherwise, they must be altogether rejected. In Plato's (1993, pp. 361, 607a) own words:

> You should concede that Homer is a supreme poet and the original tragedian, but you should also recognise that the only poems we can admit into our community are hymns to the gods and eulogies of virtuous men. If you admit the entertaining Muse of lyric and epic poetry, then instead of law and the shared acceptance of reason as the best guide, the kings of your community will be pleasure and pain.

As Iris Murdoch (1977, pp. 6–7) explains: "[T]he Greek lacked what Bosanquet calls the 'distinctively aesthetic standpoint', as presumably everyone did with apparent impunity until 1750, and this being so their attitude to art tended to be rather more moralistic than formalistic, and this is also true of Aristotle". Hence she concludes (1977, p. 12) that for Plato "the aesthetic is the moral since it is of interest only in so far as it can provide therapy for the soul". The watershed that Murdoch hints to here is the publication, in 1750, of Alexander Baumgarten's *Aesthetica*, which first introduced the term, as well as the concept, of "aesthetics" (now intended as an independent sphere of enquiry) into the philosophical debate. As Tolstoy (1930, p. 91) put it in his *What is Art?*: "[T]he ancients had not that conception of beauty separated from goodness which forms the basis and aim of aesthetics in our time". The close interrelationship of the aesthetic and the moral is indeed something that we must take into account when considering the articulations of Platonic aesthetic thought.

Of all the Platonic dialogues, the *Republic* is arguably the most accomplished (Abbagnano & Fornero 1986, p. 133) and the one that the present discussion will mainly focus on. The justification for this decision lies in the fact that this is the dialogue where Plato's evaluation of art appears clearest and his rejection of poetry and drama sharpest. Furthermore, since the aim of the *Republic* is to answer the question "What is justice?" through the depiction of an ideally just city, this is the dialogue from which we can best reconstruct the role of the arts in society as envisaged by Plato. The *Republic* is indeed the dialogue that expresses Plato's ideal cultural and educational policies, and it thus is the most relevant text for our discussion of the influence of Platonic philosophy over cultural policy.

Plato's Attack on Poetry

As we have seen, Platonic thought has attracted, over time, sustained interest and response. However, there is little doubt that one of the most controversial aspects of Plato's thought is the fierce and relentless criticism that he moves against the arts[5] (painting and dramatic poetry in particular) in Books 2 and 3, and culminating in the outright ostracism of poetry in Book 10. It is precisely the discussion of Platonic aesthetics in the *Republic* that prompted Nietzsche to refer to Plato as "the greatest enemy of art Europe has yet produced" (from *Genealogy of Morals*, quoted in Janaway 1995, p. 190). More recently, Arthur C. Danto (1986, pp. 1–13) has argued that the entire history of the philosophical understanding of art (through aesthetics) is the history of the attempt to suppress it, which he sees as being rooted in Plato's thought and resulting in what he calls the "philosophical disenfranchisement of art".

As noted above, the attack upon the arts, however, is by no means the central topic of the discussion presented in the dialogue, for the *Republic* deals with the issue of justice. The philosophical discussion here takes the shape of a dialogue between Socrates, his friend Glaucon and a number of other characters that they encounter during a visit to a friend's house. Here Glaucon and Adeimantus ask Socrates to answer the question "What is justice?" and to clarify how to distinguish what really *is* just from what merely appears to be so. Socrates provides an answer in the form of the discussion of an ideal just city, inhabited by equally just citizens. In the course of his discussion of the ideals that guide the just person and the just city, Plato, through the dramatic character of Socrates,[6] discusses epistemological, ethical and political issues (as well as what we would call "aesthetic" questions).

The *Republic* thus presents Plato's theories of knowledge and education as well as Plato's metaphysics and his political ideals, which culminate in the suggestion that the ideal state should be run by the "Philosopher-kings" – the only people within the city who possess the means to attain true knowledge of the eternal Forms. These are, according to Plato, perfect and immutable entities that exist independently of our world and constitute a sphere of being distinguished and separated from the human (Abbagnano & Fornero 1986, pp. 123–124). This "theory of Forms (or Ideas)" is at the very heart of Plato's philosophy. As we will see, ultimately his conception of knowledge, psychology, his ethical theory, his ideal city as well as his condemnation of art are all dependant on the notion of Forms.

The arguments on which Plato builds his attack of poetry evolve around the concept of artistic *mimesis* ("imitation"). Although Plato's discussion of the theory of imitation builds upon the example of the painter, and despite the fact that it is evident from his reasoning that painting is also a case of mimesis, it soon becomes clear that the true target of Plato's uncompromising condemnation is, as a matter of fact, poetry alone. Although admittedly a case of *mimesis*, Socrates never suggests that either the activity of painting or painters ought to be banned from the ideal city. This would seem to suggest that being imitative is not, in itself, reason enough to call for an outright ban (Nehamas 1982, p. 47). The reasons for the ban of poetry are therefore to be found beyond (but in relation to) its mimetic nature. Plato's principal arguments against poetry can be grouped under three headings:

- *Metaphysical argument*: art is a flawed imitation of reality, which itself is but a poor imitation of the Forms. Artistic representation is therefore two times removed from the true essence of things.
- *Epistemological argument*: Poets describe things that they do not necessarily understand or know. Hence, we would be highly misguided if we were to follow their teachings.
- *Psychological argument*: The arts appeal to man's emotional and irrational nature. They are therefore dangerous in that they destroy the moral fibre of the audience.

The Metaphysical Argument

The metaphysical criticism of art contained in Book 10 is based on Plato's theory of the mimetic nature of art. His theory of imitation has a metaphysical foundation, being based on the theory of Forms (or Ideas) and the related conception of a hierarchical structure of reality. According to Plato, the three levels into which reality is divided are: ideal forms, visible objects and images. This hierarchy in turn is reflected in Plato's distinction of three different grades of making (ποίησις), to which correspond three different makers. At the top of the hierarchy is God, who has full access to the Forms and creates all that which is in the order of nature. Objects that we use in everyday life are products of the craftsman or artisan, who looks at the Forms for inspiration in his process of creation. Finally comes the artist, whose creation is limited to the production of images of reality in a process that is akin to the holding up of a mirror before an object.[7] Artistic and poetic images are therefore two times removed from the truthful Form of the things represented.

The postulate of such argument is crucial: the production of images on the part of the artist does not require any genuine knowledge of the real things of which he or she is making an image. Hence the rhetorical question posed by Plato (1993, p. 352, 600e): "So shall we classify all poets, from Homer onwards, as representers of images of goodness (and of everything else that occurs in their poetry), and claim that they don't have any contact with the truth?" Socrates' ensuing remarks leave no doubt as to Plato's position on the topic: "An image-maker, a representer, understands only appearance, while reality is beyond him". Crucially, this argument is also extended to the theatre (Plato 1993, p. 348, 597e): "The same goes for tragic playwrights, then, since they're representers: they're two generations away from the throne of truth, and so are all other representers".

Besides being twice removed from the truth, dramatic poetry is also dubious on the grounds that to enact a dramatic scene (by making oneself interpret the part of a character in a play) entails that one becomes in real life the same kind of person as the character impersonated:

> The point is, my dear Adeimantus, that if the young men of our community hear this kind of thing [poetry depicting gods behaving untowardly] and take it seriously, rather than regarding it as despicable and absurd, they're hardly going to regard such behaviour as despicable in human beings like themselves and feel remorse when they also find themselves saying or doing these or similar things. Instead, they won't find it at all degrading to be constantly chanting laments and dirges for trivial incidents, and they won't resist doing so. (Plato 1993, p. 82, 388d)

As a result, the Guardians (the leaders of the ideal city envisaged in the *Republic*) should limit their involvement in all forms of mimesis, and restrict themselves to the enactment of wise and ethically sound characters, thus assimilating themselves with the sort of virtuous individual that ought to populate the ideal state:

> Any representational roles they [the Guardians] do take on must, from childhood onwards, be appropriate ones. They should represent people who are courageous, self-disciplined, just, and generous and should play only those kinds of parts; but they should neither do nor be good at representing anything mean-spirited or otherwise contemptible, in case the harvest they reap from representation is reality. I mean, haven't you noticed how if repeated representation continues much past childhood, it becomes habitual and ingrained and has an effect on a person's body, voice, and mind? (Plato 1993, p. 91, 395c–d)

This leaves no doubt as to the fact that poetry does not represent, for Plato, a value in itself, but only insofar as its suggestive powers are employed for good ends (in this case, the construction of the just society). Moreover, in Plato's view, the simple enjoyment of the image of something enacted in a dramatic narrative produces in us an increased disposition to emulate that behaviour in real life. This might seem a somewhat bizarre claim; and yet this would be one of the Platonic themes that, in the Middle Ages, Christian philosophers enthusiastically borrowed from Plato. As the last section of this paper will show, we will see this theory reappear in Christian attacks upon the stage and become one of the foundations of what Jonas Barish (1981) famously called the "antitheatrical prejudice".

The Epistemological Argument

The claims that poetic image-making is not based on genuine knowledge and therefore cannot be the source of truth and authentic understanding is of crucial importance in Plato's thought. This is because he is aware that many people actually look up to literature as a source of enlightenment. This is what Socrates has to say about the followers of the "teachings" of poetry:

> I think the important thing to bear in mind about causes like this, Glaucon, is that when people tell us they've met someone who's mastered every craft, and is the world's leading expert in absolutely every branch of human knowledge, we should reply that they're being rather silly. They seem to have met the kind of illusionist who's expert at representation and, thank to their own inability to evaluate knowledge, ignorance, and representation, to have been so thoroughly taken in as to believe in his omniscience. (Plato 1993, p. 349, 598d)

According to Plato (1993, p. 349, 598e), the root of this "silliness" is a deep-seated one: "It is said that a good poet must understand the issues he writes about, if his writing is to be successful, and that if he didn't understand them, he wouldn't be able to write about them". By redefining poetry as mere image-making, Plato declares its compatibility with the poet's ignorance about what is real and what is true (Janaway 2001, p. 6). Furthermore, mimetic poetry is dangerous to the intelligence of those of its listeners who do not have the privilege of being aware of the illusive nature of poetry (i.e., to the non-philosophers). Philosophers are safe from the intellectual corruption of mimetic poetry for they can see how poetry is twice removed from the true nature of things. But other men, especially young ones, have no protection from the deception of poetry and this is why, in the best interest of the citizens, poets and their art must be banned from the state or, at best, the object of careful state censorship:

> We'll implore Homer and the rest of the poets not to get cross if we strike these and similar lines [misleading depictions of the gods and Hades] from their works. We'll explain that it's

not because the lines are not good poetry and don't give pleasure to most people; on the contrary, the better poetry they are, the more they are to be kept from the ears of children and men who are to be autonomous and to be more afraid of losing this freedom than of death. (Plato 1993, pp. 80–81, 387b)

In order to fully understand the import of Plato's criticism of the arts we must remember that classical Greece conceived poetry as a medium for the communication of ethical values and teachings. Poets were often cited as authorities on ethical matters since, as Naussbaum (1986, p. 123) explains, "before Plato's time there was no distinction between 'philosophical' and 'literary' discussion of human practical problems. The whole idea of distinguishing between texts that seriously pursue a search for truth and another group of text that exist primarily for entertainment would be foreign in this culture". The radical nature of Plato's aesthetic thought cannot be fully grasped without understanding the authority of poetry in the civic discourse of Athens.

Like written laws that guaranteed constitutional rights for all citizens, the poetry of Homer and tragedy was the shared intellectual and moral patrimony of the entire *dēmos*, and provided standards against which behaviour could be assessed (Dué 2003, p. 4). Besides, the Greeks also regarded poets as reliable sources of all sorts of practical information; they would isolate from their context quotations from their most loved works of poetry and then turn them into general maxims and fragments of wisdom (Verdenius 1971, p. 262). In this sense, one could argue the Plato's rejection of the status of poetry as a source of true knowledge and understanding equated, in fact, to the wholesale rejection of one the principles of Athenian democracy itself.[8]

The Psychological Argument

In Plato's (1993, p. 359, 605c) own view, "the most serious allegation against representational poetry" was still to be made. For poetry "has a terrifying capacity for deforming even good people. Only a very few escape". The means by which poetry has the power to corrupt even a decent person is its capacity to affect the emotional and irrational part of the human soul. The nobler part of the soul is guided by rational thinking and concerns itself with the achievement of the overall good, but the images of mimetic poetry appeal to a distinct "inferior" part, which is childish, wild and emotional. Under the influence of his irrational side, man reacts in an unmeasured manner to events in real life and in fiction. The artistic context in which we encounter the material of dramatic poetry has a distancing effect that allows us to respond a-critically, if not even favourably, to actions and feelings that we would not normally condone in real life. In other words, the lure of poetry and the stage leads the irrational component of our soul to overrule and take over our rational selves.

What makes poetry dangerous is precisely the fact that, as a result of the powerful hold it has over its audiences, poetry surges to the role of competitor to the truly moral (and thus just) way of life (Annas 1981, p. 11). In Plato's (1993, p. 360, 606d) own words:

> And the same goes for sex, anger, and all the desires and feelings of pleasure and distress which we're saying, accompany everything we do: poetic representation has the same effect in all these cases too. It irrigates and tends to these things when they should be left to wither, and it makes them our rulers when they should be our subjects, because otherwise we won't live better and happier lives, but quite the opposite.

The attack that Plato builds on the accusations discussed above points towards the necessary conclusion that while alluring the audience with its promises of cognitive gain, poetry in fact only delivers serious psychological and ethical damage (Janaway 2001, p. 5). It is on the basis of these charges that Socrates logically reaches the conclusion that the poets are best banned from the ideal city: "[G]iven its nature, we had good grounds for banishing [poetry] earlier from our community. No rational person could have done any different" (Plato 1993, p. 361, 607b).

As the following section of this paper will show, Plato's psychological discussion of the emotional impacts of poetry and drama will give rise to two very different yet equally influential notions that have dominated cultural debate and cultural policy discourse ever since their development in Plato's thought: the idea that the arts have a crucial role to play in the education of just and mature citizens, and the seemingly opposite belief in the corrupting and dangerous effects of the arts upon the individual and thus society as a whole.

In the light of the arguments presented so far, we will now explore the legacy of Platonic thought and the ways it has filtered through into modern and contemporary cultural policy discourse. In particular the discussion will focus on what are arguably the two Platonic themes which, though apparently contradictory, have proven most influential in the sphere of cultural policy: the belief in the educational potential of the arts, on the one hand, and, on the other, the notion of the negative impacts (and consequently the dangerous nature) of the arts.

It would probably be over-ambitious and ultimately impossible to ascribe a Platonic origin to any specific policy programme. However, I will attempt to show that many arguments on a number of themes recurring time and time again in past and present cultural policy debates have a distinctively Platonic flavour, as further confirmed by those cases in which Plato's thought has been explicitly acknowledged as a source of inspiration. As John Gingell (2000, p. 71) argues: "[I]f we take Plato's implied message, that is, that art is to be judged on its contributions to our moral and intellectual life, then the history of thought about the arts abounds with thinkers and institutions who pay covert tribute to Plato".

Plato's Legacy: the Didactic Function of the Arts

Despite the defence of the decision to ban the poets from the ideal state, Plato (1993, p. 71, 377b–c) in the *Republic* still proposes to maintain within the ideal state some forms of poetry of a strongly didactic nature:

> So our first job, apparently, is to oversee the work of the story-writers, and to accept any good story they write, but reject the others. We'll let nurses and mothers tell their children the acceptable ones, and we'll have them devote themselves far more to using these stories to form their children's minds than they do to using their hands to form their bodies.[9]

As Plato's words make clear, the one redeeming feature of poetry is represented by the educational potential that comes with poetry's hold over the human soul:

> "Now, Glaucon", I said, "isn't the prime importance of cultural education due to the fact that rhythm and harmony sink more deeply into the mind than anything else and affect it more powerfully than anything else and bring grace in their train? For someone who is given a correct education, their product is grace ..."

The role of the arts and poetry in the "correct education" of the youth in the ideal city is expounded in detail by Plato in Books 2 and 3 of the *Republic*. Commentators have pointed out that Plato's attitude to poetry in this initial treatment seems very different from the stern attack that will follow in Book 10. Some (e.g., Annas 1981) have even suggested an inconsistency between these earlier discussions of poetry and the fierce attack of Book 10. However, I would rather suggest that the educational powers of poetry and the theatre are but the flipside of the transformative powers of the arts that make Plato ultimately suspicious of them.

When discussing the place of poetry and the theatre in the education of the young generations in the ideal polity, Plato argues for the need for the rulers of the ideal city to supervise epic and dramatic poetry by censoring both their form and content:

> The point is that a young person can't tell when something is allegorical and when it isn't, and any idea admitted by a person of that [young] age tends to become almost ineradicable and permanent. All things considered, then, that is why a great deal of importance should be placed upon ensuring that the first stories they hear are best adapted for their moral improvement. (Plato 1993, p. 73, 378d)

It is not hard to see how such a view of the potential of the arts to forge the ideal citizens to live in the just state could arguably be said to be the harbinger (or even the legitimization) of the promotion of an official state culture as put in place in ex-Soviet states. Stalin once defined writers as "engineers of the soul" (quoted in Debreczeny 1997) and it is hard to imagine that Plato would have found much to contend with in such a statement. Indeed, Annas (1981, pp. 15ff) puts forward a fascinating parallel between Plato and the literary critic Chernyvshevsky, whom she credits as the actual, if largely unacknowledged, source of the principles of social realism. Like Plato, Chernyvshevsky believed that art is not intrinsically valuable. Rather, in his view, the only point of the arts – and literature above all of them – is to reproduce and explain reality in a way "encouraging the good progressive elements in life, and bringing about improvement of character in the reader".

The ideal state that Plato constructs in the Republic is obviously not a democracy and, in that respect, the parallel with ideological views of the role of literature in society propounded by Soviet totalitarianism might not necessarily appear surprising. However, I think one could argue that the Platonic notion of the equation of the value of the arts with their educational and formative power can be seen as operational in current cultural policy discourses in a much more subtle way. Indeed I will try to show how the rhetoric that accompanies today's so-called "instrumental cultural policies" (Belfiore 2002, 2004) is in many ways resonant of the Platonic perspective. The suggestion that Plato's faith in the arts as *paideia* presupposes "art as sheer instrumentality" has been already put forward by Janaway (1995, pp. 185–186), who writes:

> Art, we might say, has its place because it is socially useful, politically powerful, it trains us as good citizens or as correctly class-conscious opponents of the society we inhabit. Of course art has always had such uses, but if its very *value* is going to be of this order, then we flow once again into a Platonic stream. Nobody much likes Plato's political ends, but if we say that art's value is as a political or social means, we shall not be disagreeing with him fundamentally *about art*. (emphasis in original)

Janaway only concerns himself with the theoretical aspects of such instrumentality so that the cultural policy implications of his observations are left unexplored. However, if we look at certain recent key cultural policy developments, we can rightfully conclude that an instrumentality of the nature described by Janaway is presently operational in the British context (and arguably other countries' too).

This is one of the main objectives of the Arts Council England as stated in the organization's latest manifesto, entitled *Ambitions for the Arts*, published in February 2003:

> We will argue that being involved with the arts can have a lasting and transforming effect on many aspects of people's lives. This is true not just for individuals, but also for neighbourhoods, communities, regions and entire generations, whose sense of identity and purpose can be changed through art.

The persistence, thus, in the Western world, of the Platonic idea that the worth of culture lies in its capacity to educate the citizen and therefore bring about all sorts of beneficial social and political impacts is proved by the fact that the social impacts of the arts (as well as the arts' alleged potential to foster local economic development) have become increasingly important rationales for public investment in the cultural sector over the last two decades. Even more significant is the fact that the growing trend towards instrumentality has not been slowed down by the obvious lack of evidence of the existence of such impacts (Selwood 2002). Despite the lack of evidence, the rhetoric of instrumentalism is still popular, though recently many attempts have been made on the part of arts organizations, politicians and policy makers to find alternative (and possibly non-instrumental) ways to articulate the value of the arts to society.

The current debate seems to be, therefore, caught in a deadlock. The recent essay by the UK Secretary of State for Culture, Tessa Jowell, entitled *Government and the Value of Culture* (2004), is a typical example of this *impasse*. Despite having been hailed as a welcome and overdue appeal for the reinstatement of "arts for arts' sake" arguments in the current debate, the essay is in fact fraught with internal contradictions and is in truth far from being a repudiation of instrumentalism in cultural funding and policy. For example, Jowell argues for a change of language among all parties involved in cultural policy making and arts administration in order to find ways to express the intrinsic value of the arts. Yet, Jowell herself cannot seem to avoid the reliance on many of the usual "instrumental" arguments for arts advocacy. On the one hand, she openly admits:

> We lack convincing language and political arguments for how culture lies at the heart of a healthy society. ... Too often politicians have been forced to debate culture only in terms of its instrumental benefits to other agendas – education, the reduction of crime, improvements in well-being – explaining – or in some instances almost apologising for – our investment in culture only in terms of something else. In political and public discourse in this country we have avoided the more difficult approach of investigating, questioning and celebrating what culture actually does in and of itself. (Jowell 2004, p. 8)

On the other hand, however, Jowell (2004, p. 3) also claims that one of the main tasks of government in today's society is to eliminate "the poverty of aspiration which compromises all our attempts to lift people out of physical poverty. Engagement with culture can help alleviate this poverty of aspiration". On page 15 she adds: "Addressing poverty of aspiration is also necessary to build a society of fairness and opportunities". I would suggest that this final statement brings us back full circle, for if the arts can and should address poverty of aspiration (as ostensibly Jewell is arguing), and addressing poverty of aspiration can bring about a just society, then the arts are entrusted with the task of bringing about the conditions for such a "society of fairness ad opportunities" to exist. Not only are we back to valuing the arts for the benefits they accrue to society, but we are also in front of a political programme very much alike that of Plato's *Republic*, whereby the transformative powers of the arts can and *should* be harnessed towards the achievement of a "just" polity.

Plato's Legacy: The Corrupting Effects of the Theatre and the Need for Censorship

Plato's legacy, however, can also be traced in the eclectic and diverse intellectual tradition that sees the arts as dangerous and potentially corrupting. This is a view of the arts that spans millennia and that has been applied to the most diverse array of cultural activities and products. I will therefore, of necessity, only cover the most illustrious examples and look in particular at how Platonic ideas have fuelled over time the so-called "antitheatrical prejudice" (Barish 1981). The interesting thing is that this "negative" tradition can be traced back to the very same discussion of the role of dramatic poetry in education that appears in the *Republic* as the foundation of the opposite view of the arts as promoter of beneficial social change that we have just discussed.

In the *Republic*, as we have seen, Plato expresses his belief that the enjoyment of theatrical performances brings with it a heightened disposition to imitate in real life what happens on the stage. This belief was embraced by Christian philosophers of greater and lesser significant intellectual standing starting with Tatian (c. 60 AD) through Tertullian and St Cyprian of Carthage (second-third century AD) to St Augustin (fourth century AD), to name but a few, and the other Middle Ages writers of Patristic philosophy.[10] Despite the different levels of sophistication displayed by the various thinkers involved in the Christian attack on the stage, the arguments they put forward tend to be always the same and often the influence of Plato's writing is explicitly acknowledged (Barish 1981). I will therefore quote from Tatian (first century AD), who is the author of the earliest example of Christian antitheatrical writing but already displays the signature vehemence and the stock accusations of the genre.

The target of Tatian's rage is the actor who "outwardly counterfeits what he is not" and whom he accuses of being "the epitome of superstition, a vituperator of heroic deeds, and actor of murders, a chronicler of adultery, a storehouse of madness" (quoted in Barish 1981, p. 44). It is, however, Tertullian who, in his *De Spectaculis*, first gives a Christian spin to many of Plato's arguments against theatre (especially the epistemological and the psychological arguments) reaching a conclusion that was to become a deep-rooted conviction throughout the Middle Ages: that creative literature excites the emotions *more* than actual life and is therefore extremely dangerous – to the extent that reading about or watching a crime take place on the stage soon becomes equated with committing the crime itself (Barish 1981, Chapter 2)!

The polemical and highly aggressive tone of Tatian was adopted by the Puritan writers in Elizabethan England who, on the basis of now well-worn yet still popular arguments, also strived to have the stage outlawed. Indeed, on this account, they proved more successful than their predecessors. Thus, the proclamation of 16 May 1559 forbids the handling of religious and political themes on the stage; and the statute of 1572 imposed heavy penalties for all those actors who were not formally employed by a nobleman (Ward & Waller 1932, p. 380). Fuelled by the work of the Puritan pamphleteers, the antitheatrical polemic progressively grew more intense, culminating in the closing of the theatres in 1642 (Barish 1981, p. 88). It might be wrong, however, to assume that suspicion around the corrupting power of theatre was only rife at times where religious belief played a crucial role in the public sphere. After all, Britain had a system of strict theatrical censorship in place until 1969!

Moreover, scepticism over the civilizing and humanizing powers of the arts is far from eradicated even in our more tolerant present postmodern culture. Nor can such scepticism be imputed to philistinism when it comes from personalities of the intellectual standing of George Steiner who, in his *Language and Silence* (1967, p. 86), wrote:

> We do not know whether the study of the humanities, of the noblest that has been said and thought, can do very much to humanize. We do not know; and surely there is something rather terrible in our doubt whether the study and delight a man takes in Shakespeare makes him any less capable of organizing a concentration camp.

Furthermore, the Platonic belief that fictional events might well lead to emulation has indeed proved a resilient one in Western civilization and can be seen, for instance, at the root of the so-called "Werther effect" (Phillips 1985). This label derives from the name of the main character in Goethe's novel, published in 1774, *The Sorrows of Young Werther*, which concludes with the suicide of Werther over a case of "impossible" love for the young Lotte, already engaged to his close friend Albert. This soon became an extremely popular novel, generating what has been referred to as a "cult following" (Bokey & Walter 2002, p. 397). Following an alleged spate of suicides among young readers of the book, however, the novel was banned in many European countries on account of its being a negative influence on young and impressionable minds. Interestingly, the idea behind the notion of "Werther effect" has been gaining an increasing amount of attention on the part of clinicians and media scholars preoccupied with the "copycat effect" that might be engendered by depictions of suicide and violence in the popular media – pornography being a case in point (see, e.g., Bokey & Walter 2002; Adams 2000; Seto *et al.* 2001; Shope 2004; Bondora & Goodwin 2005).

What are we to make, then, of the fact that such apparently contradictory views of the arts – as a formative and educational experience central to the creation of the just citizen on the one hand, and as a dangerous poison of the mind on the other – have been developed from the thought of a single influential thinker?

I would suggest that the complexity of Plato's theories of the transformative powers of the arts merely reflect the complexity of some questions that are central to the cultural, and hence the cultural policy, discourses. Such questions concern the nature of art, the cognitive and psychological mechanisms of artistic reception and the role of the arts in society and their relationship to the state, just to mention a few. Eva Schaper (1968, p. 40) has put forward a similar point:

> Whenever the art of emotional infection is attacked as detrimental to the moral life or defended as beneficial in some vaguely religious respect, Plato's problem appears in new guises. Whenever moral Puritans join forces to accuse the artist of undermining the serious business of living by emotional appeal, and whenever they are countered by defenders of the deeper sources of our humanity on equally moral grounds, Plato's dilemma is not far away.

Herein lies, I would argue, the enduring relevance of Platonic thought and its continuing influence over subsequent cultural policy debates.

ACKNOWLEDGEMENTS

This paper has been researched in the context of a Fellowship in Arts Impacts Assessment co-funded by the Arts and Humanities Research Council (AHRC) and the Arts

Council England (ACE). The author would like to thank two anonymous referees, the participants of the "Intellectuals and Cultural Policy" conference, Anna Upchurch and Dr Jane Woddis for their useful comments on an earlier draft.

NOTES

1. Plato's profound scepticism about the democratic form of political organization is also linked to his admiration for Socrates. Socrates was condemned to death in 399 by the newly restored democratic regime following the oligarchic reign of the Thirty that seized power after Athens' defeat in the Peloponnesian war in 404.
2. Poetry in classical Greece was transmitted orally, mainly via the performances of the rhapsodes. The distinction that we make between poetry and drama would therefore not have made sense to the Greek sensibility.
3. The expression "negative cultural policy" as used here does not imply a negative value judgement, but rather it refers to non-proactive cultural policies. I use this label to indicate policies that, rather than promote certain types of artistic form or cultural activity, aim to discourage or forbid them. Bennett (1995, p. 202) in his review of cultural policy rationales identifies what we are calling "negative cultural policy" as a typical example of governments' first intervention in the cultural policy arena, whereby the aim is "to censor rather than support".
4. At this stage, the label of "sophist" still had not acquired the pejorative sense that it eventually did as a result of Socrates and Plato's contempt for the group of intellectuals who began to provide, for money, philosophical and rhetorical tutoring to the Greek youth in the fifth and fourth centuries BC.
5. There is no word in the ancient Greek language whose meaning corresponds to our "art" or "arts". The closest approximation is represented by the word *techne* which covers, however, a much broader array of meanings ranging from poetry, painting and sculpture (i.e., our notion of "art") to shipbuilding, carpentry and other activities based on craftsmanship. This is because the distinction (both linguistic and conceptual) between the "fine arts" and crafts, which is at the very basis of our modern understanding of art, simply did not exist in antiquity (Murray 1996, p. 1).
6. Plato's writings are all in dialogue form: his philosophical concepts are proposed, discussed and criticized in the imaginative framework of a conversation involving two or more participants. Socrates appears as main character in many of them (including the *Republic*) and it is generally understood that his point of view coincides with Plato's. See Cohn (2001) for an account of the rejection of the so-called "mouthpiece theory".
7. Asmis (1992, p. 352) observes that: "Plato's mirror simile has had an overwhelming influence on the interpretation of his aesthetics and on aesthetic theory in general".
8. Plato's misgivings for Athenian democracy are very well documented (see, e.g., Stone 1989, p. 162).
9. Plato refers here to the Greek custom of massaging young children to strengthen and shape their bodies.
10. For a more detailed discussion of the arguments put forward by each of these authors against the theatre, see Barish (1981), Bruch (2004) and Spingarn (1908).

REFERENCES

ABBAGNANO, N. & FORNERO, G. (1986) *Filosofi e Filosofie nella Storia,* vol. 1, Paravia, Turin.

ARTS COUNCIL ENGLAND (2003) *Ambitions for the Arts, 2003–2006,* Arts Council England, London.
ADAMS, D. (2000) 'Can pornography cause rape?', *Journal of Social Philosophy,* vol. 31, no. 1, pp. 1–43.
ANNAS, J. (1981) *An Introduction to Plato's Republic,* Oxford University Press, Oxford.
ASMIS, E. (1992) 'Plato on poetic creativity', in *The Cambridge Companion to Plato,* ed. R. Kraut, Cambridge University Press, Cambridge, pp. 338–364.
BARISH, J. (1981) *The Antitheatrical Prejudice,* University of California Press, Berkeley, CA.
BELFIORE, E. (2002) 'Art as a means towards alleviating social exclusion: Does it really work? A critique of instrumental cultural policies and social impact studies in the UK', *International Journal of Cultural Policy,* vol. 8, no. 1, pp. 91–106.
BELFIORE, E. (2004) 'Auditing culture: The subsidised cultural sector in the new public management', *International Journal of Cultural Policy,* vol. 10, no. 2, pp. 183–202.
BENNETT, O. (1995) 'Cultural policy in the United Kingdom: Collapsing rationales and the end of a tradition', *European Journal of Cultural Policy,* vol. 1, no. 2, pp. 199–216.
BOKEY, K. & WALTER, G. (2002) 'Literature and psychiatry: The case for a close liaison', *Australasian Psychiatry,* vol. 10, no. 4, pp. 393–399.
BONDORA, J. T. & GOODWIN, J. L. (2005) 'The impact of suicidal content in popular media on the attitudes and behaviours of adolescents', *Praxis,* vol. 5, pp. 5–12.
BRUCH, D. (2004) 'The prejudice against theatre', *Journal of Religion and Theatre,* vol. 3, no. 1, pp. 1–18.
COHN, D. (2000) 'The poetics of Plato's *Republic*: A modern perspective', *Philosophy and Literature,* vol. 24, no. 1, pp. 34–48.
COHN, D. (2001) 'Does Socrates speak for Plato? Reflections on an open question', *New Literary History,* vol. 32, pp. 485–500.
DANTO, A. C. (1986) *The Philosophical Disenfranchisement of Art,* Columbia University Press, New York.
DEBRECZENY, P. (1997) *Social Functions of Literature: Alexander Pushkin and Russian Culture,* Stanford University Press, Stanford, CA.
DUÉ, C. (2003) 'Poetry and the Demos: State regulation of a civic possession', *The Stoa: A Consortium for Electronic Publication in the Humanities* [online], available at: http://www.stoa.org.
GINGELL, J. (2000) 'Plato's ghost: How not to justify the arts', *Westminster Studies in Education,* vol. 23, pp. 71–79.
JANAN, M. (1994) *When the Lamp is Shattered: Desire and Narrative in Catullus,* Southern Illinois University Press, Carbondale, IL.
JANAWAY, C. (1995) *Images of Excellence: Plato's Critique of the Arts,* Clarendon Press, Oxford.
JANAWAY, C. (2001) 'Plato', in *The Routledge Companion to Aesthetics,* eds B. Gaut & D. McIver Lopes, Routledge, London.
JOWELL, T. (2004) *Government and the Value of Culture,* Department for Culture, Media and Sport, London.
KONSTAN, D. (2004) *Plato's* Ion *and the Psychoanalytical Theory of Art,* paper presented at the 2004 annual meeting of the American Philological Association, San Francisco, 2–5 January.
KRAUT, R. (1992) 'Introduction to the study of Plato', in *The Cambridge Companion to Plato,* Cambridge University Press, Cambridge, pp. 1–50.
MURDOCH, I. (1977) *The Fire and the Sun: Why Plato Banished the Artists,* Oxford University Press, Oxford.
MURRAY, P. (ed.) (1996) *Plato on Poetry,* Cambridge University Press, Cambridge.
NADDAFF, R. A. (2002) *Exiling the Poets: The Production of Censorship in Plato's* Republic, University of Chicago Press, Chicago, IL.

NAUSSBAUM, M. C. (1986) *The Fragility of Goodness: Luck and Ethics in Greek Tragedy and Philosophy*, Cambridge University Press, Cambridge.
NEHAMAS, A. (1982) 'Plato on imitation and poetry in *Republic* 10', in *Plato on Beauty, Wisdom and the Arts*, eds J. Moravcsik & P. Temko, Rowman & Littlefield, Totowa, pp. 47–48.
NETTLESHIP, R. L. (1962) *Lectures on the Republic of Plato*, Macmillan, London.
NIETZSCHE, F. (2000) *The Birth of Tragedy*, Oxford University Press, Oxford.
NIGHTINGALE, A. (1995) *Genres in Dialogue: Plato and the Construct of Philosophy*, Cambridge University Press, Cambridge.
PHILLIPS, D. P. (1985) 'The *Werther effect*: Suicide and other forms of violence are contagious', *The Sciences*, vol. 7/8, pp. 32–39.
PLATO (1993) *Republic*, trans. R. Waterfield, Oxford University Press, Oxford.
SCHAPER, E. (1968) *Prelude to Aesthetics*, George Allen & Unwin, London.
SELWOOD, S. (2002) *Beyond Statistics? The Politics of Data Collection in the English Cultural Sector*, paper delivered at the International Symposium on Culture Statistics, Montreal, 21–23 October.
SETO, M. C., MARIC, A. & BARBAREE, H. E. (2001) 'The role of pornography in the etiology of sexual aggression', *Aggression and Violent Behaviour*, vol. 6, pp. 35–53.
SHOPE, J. H. (2004) 'When words are not enough: The search for the effect of pornography on abused women', *Violence against Women*, vol. 10, no. 1, pp. 56–72.
SPINGARN, J. E. (1908) *A History of Literary Criticism in the Renaissance*, Columbia University Press, New York.
STEINER, G. (1967) *Language and Silence: Essays, 1959–1966*, Faber, London.
STONE, I. F. (1989) *The Trial of Socrates*, Anchor Books, New York.
TOLSTOY, L. (1930) *What is Art?*, trans. A. Maude, Oxford University Press, Oxford.
VERDENIUS, W. J. (1971) 'Plato's doctrine of artistic imitation', in *Plato: A Collection of Critical Essays*, ed. G. Vlastos, Anchor Books, New York, pp. 259–273.
VESTHEIM, G. (1994) 'Instrumental cultural policy in Scandinavian countries: A critical historical perspective', *International Journal of Cultural Policy*, vol. 1, no. 1, pp. 57–71.
WARD, A. W. & WALLER, A. R. (1932) *The Cambridge History of English Literature*, Cambridge University Press, Cambridge.
WEINECK, S. (1998) 'Talking about Homer: Poetic madness, philosophy and the birth of criticism in Plato's *Ion*', *Arethusa*, vol. 31, pp. 19–42.

KRUPSKAYA, PROLETKUL'T AND THE ORIGINS OF SOVIET CULTURAL POLICY

Christopher Read

Bolshevism as a Cultural Project

It is often insufficiently recognized that, above all, Bolshevism was a cultural project. Beneath its vast institutional, social and economic aspirations was a fundamental guiding thread involving no less than a re-structuring of the human personality. The "New Soviet Person" of Stalinist times was not an aberration but a primary aim. In particular, Bolshevism was a struggle over values. In the long term the fate of the Soviet project was more the result of failure to "win over" the population to communist values, the failure to, in a more Leninist term, "raise consciousness" in key groups, than of any other factor. As a result it was eventually overwhelmed by a tide of "traditional" and "petty-bourgeois" values which continue to reign in post-Soviet Russia.

However, having pointed out the importance of culture and values to Bolshevism, it has to be said that Bolsheviks themselves were unable to define exactly what the values were to be or how they might best be transmitted. The task of "cultural revolution" was a site of major disputes within the movement. Before the revolution only A. A. Bogdanov (1873–1928) and his friends and admirers, notably his brother-in-law Anatoly Lunacharsky (1875–1933), the future minister of education, and the best-known and best-selling novelist of the time, Maxim Gorky (1868–1936), took cultural questions seriously. At the heart of Bogdanov's philosophy was the perception that, for centuries before it came to power, the bourgeoisie had been preparing its ultimately liberal, individualist, market-oriented and competitive values. It followed, he said, that in order to challenge the hegemony of bourgeois values the proletariat had to develop its own culture in order to establish its intellectual and ideological hegemony. He proposed among other things, a Proletarian University and, modelled on Diderot's project, a Proletarian Encyclopaedia. Under Gorky's patronage, he set up a party school in Capri in 1909 to teach and explore those values with workers from Russia who would return to the labour movement there after completing their course.

These efforts came to little not least because Lenin, who had been closely allied with Bogdanov from 1904 to 1907, began to suspect him of factionalism. In response, Lenin even set up a rival party school in Longjumeau, Paris. Lenin was much more conservative in tone. In Lenin's mind it was imperative to "raise consciousness" among key groups in Russia, mainly the working class and its supposed allies among agricultural labourers and poor peasants. Starting from the premise that Russia was backward in every sense and that the vast majority of workers themselves were backward, he said that at first the revolution should be content with teaching "real bourgeois culture".[1] Although this quote comes from later in Lenin's life it was true of his outlook earlier on. By comparison, Bogdanov believed it was necessary to be more radical and allow workers, rather than interfering intellectuals, to take the initiative in developing their own, new culture. He inspired the Proletarian Cultural-Educational Association that flourished in the years from 1917 to 1921, though because of Lenin's continuing enmity he took a back seat. Proletkul't, as it became known, focused its activities on trying to develop a distinctive proletarian culture. Neither before nor after the revolution would Lenin have any truck with these ideas. He ridiculed them as nonsensical and maintained his conservative line throughout.[2]

Differences of ideas were not the only problem in the early years of the revolution. Economically and socially Russia had been on a downward spiral that started in 1914 and finished in 1921. The country was brought to ruin by war, revolution and civil war. How does one prioritize the various demands on cultural policy? In the conditions of the time this was a zero sum game with very scarce material resources to play with. Main areas of demand included political education and propaganda; conventional schooling and/or the experimental "unified labour school"; middle and higher education; scientific research; developing key skills; adult education and literacy campaigns; and, not least, high culture and artistic life.

All these had to be presented within an acceptable class and Marxist wrapper. That required committed and "conscious" cadres. In reality there were very few and they were stretched very thinly across the demanding fields of political construction; civil war leadership; economic reconstruction as well as culture. The outcome was twin evils of bureaucratism, in which a handful of qualified cadres tried to keep tabs on ever-increasing numbers of less qualified people in crucial jobs, and productionism, maximizing economic output as a prerequisite to solving all other problems, which is mentioned below. To liquidate both required a massive effort to build up the core of conscious Bolsheviks as a priority, in itself a complex cultural task.[3]

Cultural policy was neither self-evident nor straightforward. No pre-revolutionary blueprint existed. Indeed, before the revolution, when acquisition of real power seemed a long way off – even in January 1917 Lenin said he did not expect to live long enough to see the decisive battles of the coming revolution – cultural policy seemed unimportant except as a means to raise consciousness. Once in power, however, it became crucial. The Bolsheviks had no more prepared for it before October than they had for economic or social transition. It was a party that had got where it was by brilliant demolition skills. Could they also construct? Many people were involved in trying to prove that they could and no outcome was pre-destined to prevail over the others. From this perspective the rest of this article is devoted to examining the role of one important constructor of cultural policy, Nadezhda Krupskaya.

Krupskaya Before the Revolution

Nadezhda Krupskaya (1869–1939) was one of many young, educated Russian women who were drawn into the revolutionary movement in the closing decades of the nineteenth century. In common with most of the others, a foundation of populism – mainly in the form of a desire, a duty even, to "serve the people" – was her prime motivation. In the claustrophobic atmosphere of autocracy noble aspirations of this kind could soon lead to illegality. Kruskaya had not yet reached this point when, in 1894, she underwent the experience that changed her life – meeting Vladimir Ulianov (1870–1924), the 23-year-old son of a provincial school inspector, a young man at that time in the throes of turning himself into Lenin, the name and persona by which he is known to history.

In standard historiography, Krupskaya is not only overshadowed by Lenin but her role is often reduced to that of a handmaid. In this view she is celebrated as the ever-loyal assistant to her husband. Indeed, throughout his life, Lenin did rely on a small, largely female, circle made up of Krupskaya, who played the key role, actual relatives including his sisters Maria and Anna and his mother, who was also Maria, plus his brother Dmitrii and his wife. In addition there was an intimate circle of close friends, at one time the Martovs, later Inessa Armand and the Zinovievs and Kamenevs. But Krupskaya was always more than Lenin's helper. She had her own, independent interests in the revolutionary movement which she continued to pursue in exile as well as during the couple's brief return to Russia in 1905–1907 and again after their permanent return in April 1917. In particular, worker education and the organization of women workers were central to her revolutionary career. From 1917 she was a prominent member of the Soviet government and a significant figure in Soviet politics especially after her husband's death in January 1924. She held posts at various times in the Education Ministry (from November 1917), the Komsomol (Communist Youth Organization) and the Soviet Central Executive Committee. In 1927 she became a member of the Central Committee of the Communist Party. She also became a member of the Socialist Academy (1918) and later of the Soviet Academy of Sciences (1931). Up until her own death in 1939 she remained a pillar of the Soviet establishment. In particular she had five somewhat intertwined roles. She was, of course, Lenin's assistant, especially in the pre-war years. She also became secondly, a memoirist/historian of Lenin's life and of the party and thirdly a key official interpreter of Lenin's intellectual legacy. A fourth area of her activity was in the Bolshevik women's movement and finally, the fifth role, the one which mainly concerns us here, was a lifelong commitment to worker education and cultural development.

Despite her importance, Krupskaya has attracted little attention from historians. There is a pioneering biography by Robert McNeal, unpromisingly entitled *Bride of the Revolution: Krupskaia and Lenin* (1973), a few Soviet-era hagiographies and a handful of post-Soviet studies in Russian which are more intrigued by the Krupskaya–Lenin–Armand triangle than by her ideas or work. The aim of the present paper is to look at some of the key points in Krupskaya's views on education and culture from 1917 to the time of her death in 1939.

Even before her momentous meeting with Lenin, Krupskaya was thoroughly convinced of the crucial value of education as a tool for liberating workers. Indeed, it was this interest which had brought them together. Krupskaya's account of their first meeting in

February 1894 is well known but remains very evocative. The occasion was a Shrovetide political gathering disguised as a pancake party.

> I remember one moment particularly well. ... Someone was saying that what was very important was to work for the Committee for Illiteracy. Vladimir Ilyich laughed, and somehow his laughter sounded quite laconic. I never heard him laugh that way on any subsequent occasion. "Well" he said, "If anyone wants to save the fatherland in the Committee for Illiteracy, we won't hinder them." (Krupskaya 1967, p. 16)

As Krupskaya tells the tale, the key difference between her and Lenin was apparent. For Krupskaya, education was, in itself, a much more powerful revolutionary tool than Lenin himself was prepared to accept. While the importance of "raising consciousness" developed greatly in Lenin's outlook, it was life experience and revolutionary propaganda rather than formal education that were the instruments. Initially, these issues were reflected on in the context of revolutionary overthrow – the "destructive" side of revolution. Rapid and largely unforeseen success in 1917 thrust them into a new context, that of revolutionary, socialist construction. Problems of transition – how one got to socialism from the actual conditions of the day on which the revolution took place – had played little part in Bolshevik thinking. The unlikeliness of revolution and the overwhelming problems of the destructive stage had occupied the full attention of most radicals.

From Destruction to Construction

The essence of Krupskaya's approach to cultural issues at the time of the revolution can be found in an article she wrote published in the *Education Ministry Journal* in its January 1918 issue.[4] The article, which focused on the principles upon which the socialist school should be constructed, was a kind of manifesto representing the hopes and ambitions of the rosy dawn of the revolution. Uncontroversially, at least in Bolshevik terms, Krupskaya started from a class-based analysis of education, attributing the nature of the school in bourgeois society to the interests of the ruling class rather than to the teachers. Less predictably, Krupskaya argued that the chief objective of the socialist school, indeed "its sole objective" was "the complete, all-round development of the pupil". It should "not stifle individuality but only help its formation" (Krupskaya 1988, p. 56). Of course, there was a strong element of social obligation and integration with labour involved, Krupskaya was not preaching unbridled egoism here, but even so there is an unmistakable "liberal" dimension to her ideas which is not to be found in Lenin.

Krupskaya was also more open to learning from experiments in the capitalist world. While, on the whole, education in capitalist society induced a spirit of enslavement in pupils, she argued, here and there individual schools did devote themselves to the development of the individual rather than the propagation of bourgeois values. The problem was, she continued, that once they left such schools, immersion in the society outside "very quickly deprived them of almost all the fruits of their education" (Krupskaya 1988, p. 57). Favourable references to experimental schools in the capitalist world are not surprising because Krupskaya, like socialists in many countries, had looked at them and saw some of them as guides to future socialist practice. Krupskaya was also indebted to John Dewey for many ideas and even argued that what she called democratized schools in post-civil war America were a step beyond traditional bourgeois schools. As for socialist education, Krupskaya concluded with a grand vision of a renewed individuality developing alongside a totally new type of division of labour. The gap between mental and physical labour would be bridged. In her words, physical labour would become imbued with the spirit and mental labour would take on flesh.[5] Each person's work would bear the stamp of their own individuality. Work would cease to resemble forced labour and, instead, become voluntary. It would not be narrow and boring but multi-dimensional. In these respects she was echoing Marx's famous dictum about being hunter, cook and critic. However, Krupskaya was not unaware of the difficulties of making progress in this direction, especially in such an "uncultured" (*nekul'turnyi*) country like Russia with such a low level of general education. Society could only be transformed through the emergence of a new generation educated under quite different circumstances. "It is to the socialist school that the task of educating this new generation falls" (Krupskaya 1988, p. 59).

These few words are very rich in potential for exploring the mentality of the new revolutionary leaders. There are some obvious points. Like many liberal and socialist educationalists they assume that the key to social transformation lies in the school, that labour can be transformed from wretched duty to a source of personal self-fulfilment for all and that individual and social development go hand-in-hand. But in addition there is also the tantalizing awareness of Russia's "backwardness", a key element in Menshevik criticism of the Bolshevik project and in Krupskaya's assumption that it would take a generation educated "under quite different circumstances" to bring about significant change. The practical difficulties associated with this last point were legion. Was Russia already under the "different circumstances" which would enable a start to be made on building the new generation? Or, given there were pitifully few socialist teachers or teaching materials, or indeed, educational resources of any kind, how long would it take to get to the point where "circumstances" were sufficiently "different" for serious progress to be made?

Productionism and Its Discontents

Comparable problems were plaguing the whole Bolshevik enterprise at the time Krupskaya was writing her article and the overall solution, which is not always sufficiently recognized as being crucial, had emerged with startling suddenness in early 1918. For the first few months after October sheer survival had been uppermost in Bolshevik thoughts. However, by spring 1918, once power had been secured and peace acquired through the immensely costly Treaty of Brest-Litovsk, reconstruction and social engineering rose to the top of the Bolshevik agenda. It should be remembered here that for the time being the civil war, which, as we know, had not yet really got going, was thought by the Bolshevik leadership to have been by-and-large won. It was only later in the year and mainly in 1919 that it began to flare up again and began to figure in the forefront of government thinking and strategy. Prior to that, the exigencies of socialist transition were dominant. However, the intractable reality of the situation quickly drove the revolution in unexpected and undesirable directions. Productionism – meaning the need to maximize the growth and modernization of the economy as the prerequisite for all other changes – began to establish itself as the bedrock of the Soviet system. Its heavy hand began to fall not only over the economy but also over educational and, increasingly, broader cultural policy

Productionism had emerged very quickly. The main steps towards it began as early as spring 1918 when, in a key article on 'The Immediate Tasks of the Soviet Government" (reprinted in Lenin 1967, vol. 2, pp. 643–680) Lenin outlined the importance of the entire workforce of the country working in harmonious discipline with one another. Like so many aspects of the emergence of the Soviet system, a reasonable assumption – the need for economic growth and organization – led to unexpected and often counter-productive extremes. Within the eminently sensible and practical imperatives of economic growth the would-be totalitarian juggernaut of Stalinism was already emerging. Productionism quickly established itself at the heart of the system and remained there until the fateful days of Mikhail Gorbachev.[6]

Conventionally, the adoption of the New Economic Policy (NEP) in 1921 is interpreted as a turn away from centralization towards a more "liberal", freer atmosphere. In some ways this is true, however it should be recognized that the adoption of NEP not only restored partial market relations in town and country but also sent a shock wave through Russia's public institutions and extensive public sector. War Communism (1918–1921) had created a barter economy and a vast black market of massive proportions. Public goods – including cultural ones such as cinema, theatre, publishing – were very cheap, even free. Under NEP, however, a cold shower of profitability doused expectations. Strict profit and loss accounting was introduced. Needs had to be adapted to measured resources. Resources were extremely scarce. Education and culture were not only no exception. As a high-spending area of crucial importance to the success of the revolution, which was trying to balance limitless needs and expectations, it was a particularly difficult area. It was in conflict with areas of more basic needs – food, jobs, infrastructure and, increasingly, defence. Competition between sectors for barely existent resources was fierce.

In the wider scheme of things it is hardly surprising that economic development should be a priority. In 1920–1921 not only the economy but Soviet society was in ruins. Up to 10 million people had died in the civil war, mostly from disease. State services were almost non-existent. The social and economic infrastructure was destroyed. Industrial production was somewhere between 10 and 20 per cent of pre-1914 levels. It was the peasant who pulled Russia through the crisis. The very backwardness of the rural economy helped recovery in that each, near-self-sufficient commune could restore its own strength, support its and an increasing number of the local population without being held back by lack of machinery, spare parts, chemicals or a full division of labour which would have been dependent on transport to facilitate exchange. In other words, the localism and under-mechanization of the rural economy were, for once, the country's saviour. In the longer term the near collapse of the working class (if there was no industrial production there were no jobs so workers returned to the village) was disastrous for the Bolshevik project which, of course, focused on exactly the opposite – the strengthening of the working class and the obliteration of the peasantry. At the end of the 1920s the state rewarded the peasantry by visiting the holocaust of collectivization on it. Alongside this there was a much-vaunted cultural revolution.[7] However, for our purposes, examination of Krupskaya's role indicates that underlying the familiar periodization of Russian social, economic and cultural life into revolution (1917); civil war (1917–1921); New Economic Policy (1921–1928); Stalin revolution (1928–1932) and "Great Retreat" (1932–1941) there was a degree of continuity, based on productionism, which has been widely underestimated. As was the case with other supposedly "temporary" pillars of the Soviet system such as the secret police, not only did productionism become permanent, it even transformed the Soviet system in its own likeness.

It was not, however, the only shaping influence that had come into existence in the early years. A major theme of early Soviet cultural life was the gradual emergence of a party policy on culture and a growing network of institutions gradually tightening party discipline and supervision of the cultural world. This involved two related processes. First, within the party, efforts had to be made to define what cultural policy should be. In the early stages there was little agreement on this. Second, party policy, however defined, gradually (and later not so gradually) encroached on wider and wider areas of Soviet cultural life, notably the arts, education and religion. Ensuing cultural debates have attracted considerable scholarly attention. Without reproducing all this discussion we need to note some key points.

First of all it should be recognized that in both theory and practice intellectuals were a thorny issue not only for Bolsheviks but for all Marxists. They did not fit neatly into the main Marxist class categories (aristocracy, peasantry, bourgeoisie, proletariat) and many different viewpoints existed. In Russia, in addition, the populist tradition, which left a mark on Lenin and the Bolsheviks despite their theoretical differences, emphasized the intellectual as "mind, honour and conscience" of society. In Lenin's *What is to be Done?* (1902, reprinted in Lenin 1967, vol. 1, pp. 97–256) intellectuals are assigned a modified version of the populist-defined role. Rapidly, however, Lenin became more workerist, probably through his first encounter with Bogdanov in 1904. In *One Step Forward, Two Steps Back* (1904, reprinted in Lenin 1967, vol. 1, pp. 257–449), Lenin's critique of lack of implementation of decisions taken at the crucial Second Congress (1903) at which the party is said to have "split", there is a more hostile tone about the role of intellectuals. From then on, though the reality of the party throughout Lenin's life was that the leading core was dominated by intellectuals, he played down their role in theory. Workerist discourse dominated his writings on the issue. Most intellectuals were consigned to the catch-all dumping ground of the (usually vacillating) petty-bourgeoisie. After the October revolution, despite the fact that Krupskaya, Lenin himself and his closest associates were all intellectuals, he continued to deny their importance.

The problem was compounded by another key question. After October the party was desperately short of personnel in all areas and was forced to turn to the despised "petty-bourgeois intelligentsia" as mangers, administrators, army officers, teachers, professors, doctors and so on. Such "specialists" who were prepared to work in industry were to be rewarded, extremely controversially, by higher pay. As early as spring 1918 Lenin turned to this policy. So scarce were party resources that for a decade even those teaching party doctrine in secondary schools and higher education were not all Marxists or party members. In December 1918 40 per cent of political commissars in the Red Army were non-party, though by May 1919 this had fallen, by instant incorporation, to 11.2 per cent (Read 1996, p. 210). Mass institutions like schools and universities were almost entirely denuded of party members in the early years. The crucial Leninist endeavour of "raising consciousness" was not dissimilar from the efforts of Baron Munchausen to pull himself out of a swamp by his own bootlaces. Krupskaya was in the frontline of this battle to produce a "new teacher" appropriate to Bolshevik conditions. It was only in 1928 with Stalin's "Second Revolution" that the leadership took a decisive turn against specialists who, henceforth, were to be controlled rather than "won over", which had been the aspiration of the party right in the 1920s. However, the practicalities of pursuing this extremely absorbing question lies beyond the scope of the present study which concentrates on the evolution of policy rather than the myriad practical problems of its implementation.[8]

One of the starting points of the discussion was what role should the party have in the field of culture? This question had been at the heart of one of the decisive decisions of the era – the decree on Proletkul't drafted by Lenin and promulgated by the Central Committee in December 1920 which emasculated the organization even though it continued to exist until 1932. There were numerous strands to this decision. Ostensibly, Proletkul't was criticized for being under the control of so-called futurists who supposedly wanted to destroy the cultures of the past in order to create a *tabula rasa* on which to construct a totally new, untrammelled, unpolluted, pure culture for the new proletarian and industrial age. Indeed, there were people who advocated this. The poet Mayakovsky argued for the closing of the Bolshoi Theatre on such grounds. Another poet urged "the burning of Raphael in the name of tomorrow" (Read 1990, p. 150). Neither of these, however, was closely involved in Proletkul't. Some members of Proletkul't did hold such views but they were as likely to be found elsewhere in the cultural bureaucracy – especially the Education Ministry itself, headed by Lunacharsky who had Nietzschean and futurist aspects to his own work – as in Proletkul't. Proletkul't's official line was that the "treasure-house of human culture" should be preserved so that the new proletarian culture could take what it needed from the cultures of the past.

Rather than the rather marginal issue of futurism, the real reason for restricting Proletkul't was to undermine the organization's claim to cultural autonomy. It saw itself as the experimental, pioneering, cultural wing of the revolution, setting up what it called "laboratories of proletarian culture" on its own initiative, beyond the tutelage of the party. According to Proletku'lt theory, out of the laboratories an as yet imperceptible but absolutely necessary proletarian culture would emerge. Lenin, whose whole distinctiveness as a party thinker, polemicist and strategist, had, since 1902, emphasized the crucial importance of party discipline, was not about to tolerate any areas of autonomy. Even worse, though he kept out of the limelight, the inspirational theorist behind Proletkul't was Alexander Bogdanov, an important party rival of Lenin since 1907.

While her emphases on issues often differed from those of Lenin, there can be no doubt that Krupskaya fully supported the need for party discipline. She had worked with Proletkul't since 1918, writing in its journal and attending some of its conferences but she was fully supportive of the need for it to be firmly under party control. Once the 1920 decree and the purge of personnel which followed had taken place, Krupskaya continued to maintain limited contact with Proletkul't which was no longer a cutting-edge experimental body but a more conventional worker education organization of the type Krupskaya had been involved with since the early 1890s.

There are, however, grounds for thinking that Krupskaya was not reconciled to the permanent domination of productionism over educational and cultural affairs. After all, she had already insisted that communist culture should not be simply utilitarian.[9] While it was clear to Krupskaya, later observers have not always recognized that, in essence, communism was a cultural project. While it obviously aimed to change fundamental social and economic institutions – the market; class; the family, to name a few – its ultimate fate was dependent on the degree to which it could change values. In this sense it was a kind of secular religion as much as it was a political movement and Krupskaya was a leading devotee.

The NEP Years

The *relative* freedom of NEP allowed the introduction and development of policies close to Krupskaya's heart like the mobilization of women and a campaign to eradicate mass adult literacy. However, in the early NEP years Krupskaya began to change her earlier priority by putting the major emphasis on society's claim on the individual. One way to measure the change is to examine Krupskaya's return to the theme of her 1918 article in 1921 in a way which sounded different, more world-weary and less idealistic. The title itself, "Problems of

Communist Education", was a warning. A very different tone predominated. Starting from the new imperative – that communism was based on planned, rational, organization of production in which "not a single force, not a single talent should be lost" – the new priority was "preparation of the younger generation for communist production."[10] To this end the so-called unified labour school was the centrepiece of education. It was unified in that the country had one education system for all. It was a labour school in that education, upbringing and work, were closely intertwined. Krupskaya emphasized that such schools should be polytechnical. By this she meant that a wide range of work skills should be available related to all the main economic sectors, notably agriculture, metal working, textiles and chemicals. It is not our place here to go into either the fierce arguments about the implementation of these principles or the practical difficulties of delivering them. For us the point is to note the new ideological/cultural/propaganda emphases that were emerging. No longer was there a proud assertion of developing the all-round abilities of every individual, instead there was a more specific aim – "the polytechnical school is a preparation for work" (Krupskaya 1988, p. 80). However, social rather than individual imperatives were uppermost even in Krupskaya's relatively liberal mind. It was not, she argued, sufficient to teach individual labour skills, learning how to organize labour collectively was also critical. The "interests of communist society" demanded that this should be done not at the level of "separate factories and workshops but for the whole country" (Krupskaya 1988, p. 80). The final peroration of her article contrasted vividly with the earlier one. Now it was "the requirement for economic growth" which demanded the "best preparation of living, creative, productive power". The unified labour school "responds to the working classes most acute need at the current historical moment; it facilitates the conversion of the working class into the owner and collective organizer of production" (Krupskaya 1988, p. 80).

These words are as rich in their implications as those at the conclusion of the earlier article. The new themes were based on the exigencies of "the current historical moment", leaving the door open for a return to a more person-oriented approach once the crisis was over and, indeed, Krupskaya's ideas oscillated between these two poles for the rest of her life. None the less, the fact that Krupskaya's words were written in 1921, as the supposedly more "liberal" economic and social policies associated with NEP were being introduced, reminds us that, at its heart, even NEP was productionist in concept.

In a 1922 article on Communist education of youth she stressed that a communist was, first and foremost, a social person[11] whose "personal life was subordinate to communist interests" (Krupskaya 1988, p. 103).[12] By 1927, however, Krupskaya was once again ready to re-assert, at least in part, her belief in all-round development of the individual. In an article ostensibly on Lenin's views on education and what were known as "people's teachers" (*narodnyi uchiteli*) she combined his conservative line on culture with her stress on all-round educational development. The aim of cultural policy was not so much to create a proletarian culture as Proletkul't had wanted but to achieve a classless culture involving taking culture out of the hands of the ruling class and using it as a weapon in the struggle for liberation of the labourers and the exploited.[13] The socialist school was the only tool for the full development of the individual. While she continued to put great weight on links between education and the working environment she also, in a way she had not done five years earlier, accompanied it with the assertion that the "upbringing of a collectivist" could only be achieved through the "education of a developed, multi-faceted, internally disciplined person [*chelovek*] capable of deep feeling, clear thought and organized action" (Krupskaya 1988, p. 180).

From NEP to Cultural Revolution

Not surprisingly, the massive leap forward in production and productionism in the form of the "Second Revolution" of 1928-1932, brought productionist themes to the fore in Krupskaya's writings. In her not very poetically entitled article "On Polytechnism" she put work and the need to overcome backwardness as the first educational/cultural priority. However, even in an overwhelmingly productionist article she maintained some of the broader aims. "Polytechnism" had to be distinguished from trade or professional modes of schooling because its objective was not simply to pass on know-how but to make work "meaningful" and to imbue workers with the ability to link theory and practice in their work.[14] Teachers should not just pass on facts but "they should be seduced by the romance of modern technology" (Krupskaya 1988, p. 196).

In 1932, as the apparently "radical" wave of 1928/1929 gave way to the so-called "Great Retreat" which was replacing the utopian gestures of four years earlier, Krupskaya wrote about the importance of the classics of Russian and world culture as guides to life. This apparently "conservative" line, was, however, also consistent with Krupskaya's more "liberal" tendencies in that classics – Tolstoy's novels, the opera, ballet and music of the Mighty Handful and of Tchaikovsky and others plus great world figures such as Goethe, Balzac, Dickens, Beethoven – became a sacrosanct arena of less crudely ideological values and intellectual discussion even in the deepest days of Stalinist utilitarianism and productionism. For the next few years Krupskaya, ageing and ailing, maintained her perhaps ambiguous position on current developments. In many ways she simply appeared to toe the party line in her public proclamations. In 1933 she pointed out Marx and Engels' dictum that the freedom of each individual depends on the freedom of all used the word freedom in a non-bourgeois sense. However, rather than use this to justify growing Soviet unfreedom, as many propagandists were doing, the article was a remarkable return to the writings of Marx and Engels, and also to the example of Marx's own intellectual life, to show that narrow productionism was not adequate. To implement Marx's call for freedom involved "a flourishing of scientific knowledge, knowledge of the laws of nature and of human development" which " would guarantee to each person the fullest, all-round development".[15] Under the grey prose Krupskaya's vision of an intellectual paradise was still present.

Touchingly one of her last major articles, written in 1938, brought together the two key themes of productionism and the fullest personal development. Once again she brought forward extensive Marxist texts, including the key ones from the 1933 article, to point out that a key feature of communist as opposed to bourgeois labour was that it was supposed to be "conscious". It should be imbued with the creativity of the worker, not just her or his mechanical, slave-like labour as required by capitalist industry. Towards the end of this, one of her last major articles, she concluded that Marx had argued that the key difference between capitalist and communist society was that under capitalism the worker existed to serve the system of production whereas under socialism the production system existed to serve the worker.[16] In the face of a continuing tidal wave of productionism, which resulted in an even greater subjection of individual to system than was the case under capitalism, we can only speculate on the degree of ironic protest concealed in Krupskaya's words.

NOTES

1. "Better fewer but better" (Lenin 1967, vol. 3, p. 774). Although this is Lenin's last work it does reflect a consistent line in his ideas about class and culture.

2. On early conflicts between Bogdanov and Lenin see Read (1979, pp. 40–57). On the revolutionary period see Read (1990).
3. For a fuller account see Read (1997).
4. "K voprosu o sotsialisticheskoi shkole" 1918 (On the question of the socialist school), in Krupskaya (1988, pp. 51–59).
5. "Iz knigi 'Narodnoe obrazovannie i demokratiia'" 1915 (From the book *Popular Education and Democracy*) in Krupskaya (1988, p. 34).
6. For an interpretation of the rise and fall of Soviet communism which gives prominence to the role of productionism and of cultural revolution in these processes see Read (2001).
7. See Fitzpatrick (1978).
8. See Read (1979, 1990) for a fuller discussion of these issues.
9. "Glavpolitprosvet i iskusstvo" 1921 (The political education department and art), in Krupskaya (1988, p. 76).
10. "Problema kommunisticheskogo vospitaniia" 1921 (Problems of communist education), in Krupskaya (1988, p. 79).
11. "K voprosu o kommunisticheskom vospitanii molodezhi" 1922 (On the question of the communist education of youth), in Krupskaya (1988, p. 101).
12. Note the use of term "interests" rather than "principles" or "morality".
13. "Lenin o prosveshchenii i narodnom uchitele" 1927 (Lenin on education and people's teachers), in Krupskaya (1988, p. 179).
14. "O politekhnizme" 1929 (On polytechnism), in Krupskaya (1988, p. 198).
15. "Marks o kommunisticheskom vospitanii podrastaiushchego pokoleniia" 1933 (Marx on the communist upbringing of the rising generation), in Krupskaya (1988, p. 316).
16. "Uchenie Marksa dliia sovetskogo pedagoga – rukovodstvo k deistviiu" 1938 (The teaching of Marx for the Soviet pedagogue – putting leadership into action), in Krupskaya (1988, p. 399).

REFERENCES

FITZPATRICK, S. (1978) *Cultural Revolution in Russia 1928–31*, Indiana UP, Bloomington and London.
KRUPSKAYA, N. (1967) *Memories of Lenin*, Panther, London.
KRUPSKAYA, N. (1988) *Izbrannye proizvedeniia (Selected Works)*, Politizdat, Moscow.
LENIN, V. I. (1967) *Selected Works*, 3 vols Progress, Moscow.
MCNEAL, R. (1973) *Bride of the Revolution: Krupskaia and Lenin*, Pall Mall, London.
READ, C. (1979) *Religion, Revolution and the Russian Intelligentsia 1900–1912: The 'Vekhi' Debate and its Intellectual Background*, Macmillan, London and New York.
READ, C. (1990) *Culture and Power in Revolutionary Russia: The Intelligentsia and the Transition from Tsarism to Communism*, Macmillan, London and New York.
READ, C. (1996) *From Tsar to Soviets: The Russian People and Their Revolution*, UCL Press, London.
READ, C. (1997) 'Bolshevik cultural policy', in *A Critical Companion to the Russian Revolution*, eds E. Acton, V. Cherniaev & W. Rosenberg, Arnold, London, pp. 490–498.
READ, C. (2001) *The Making and Breaking of the Soviet System*, Palgrave, Basingstoke and New York.

GEORG LUKÁCS
Cultural policy, Stalinism and the Communist International

W. John Morgan

Introduction

Georg Lukács has been claimed as a founder of Western Marxism, the basis of an anti-Stalinist New Left. This was due politically to his participation in the reform communist government in Hungary overthrown by Soviet armed forces in 1956. Intellectually it was due to growing awareness of Lukács through the publication of his work in English. *History and Class Consciousness* (1971) with its sophisticated exposition of an Hegelian Marxism, provided sustenance to an intellectually famished socialist movement, which was returning to ideological sources. Lukács, became an intellectual inspiration to this New Left. His focus on culture was attractive, with its emphasis on humanist ethical values. However, the enthusiasm for Lukács' Hegelian Marxism meant that few Western intellectuals considered the implications of Lukács' life-long membership of the Communist Party or those of his relationship with Stalinism. Yet both had an effect on how he perceived the responsibilities of intellectuals and the purposes of cultural policy. This is illustrated during the Communist International's Popular Front period. This article examines these issues through an analysis of Lukács' career in the Communist Party and concludes with a brief assessment of his continuing relevance for those interested in cultural policy today.

From Idealism to Bolshevism

Lukács was born in 1885 into an ennobled Jewish Hungarian banking family. He studied at Heidelberg where he became acquainted with Max Weber, Georg Simmel and

Ernst Bloch. On returning to Hungary, he became the leading figure in a "Sunday Circle", of bourgeois intellectuals, including Arnold Hauser, Karl Mannheim and Karl Polanyi. In 1917 Lukács took part in the Free School of the Humanities organized by Béla Balázs; its purpose was to consider "the gospel of idealism" through public lectures, seminars and discussions. It espoused ethical, utopian socialism, with Lukács described by Joszef Lengyel as a "Tolstoyan ethical socialist" (Morgan 2003, p. 86). However, in a move that for suddenness and completeness was likened to the conversion of St Paul, Lukács joined the Hungarian Communist Party in December 1918. Lukács, German in intellectual orientation, was familiar with Marx, with Kautsky and Bernstein and the pressures of war and of the October Revolution caused him to consider the possibilities of revolution. "Bolshevism as an ethical problem" shows him weighing up the options (Lukács 1995). Bolshevism, he says: "rests on the metaphysical assumption that good can issue from evil … This writer cannot share this faith and therefore sees at the root of Bolshevism an insoluble ethical dilemma" (Lukács 1995, p. 220). He believed that the proletarian struggle had an ultimate value: "the end of all class struggle and the creation of a new social order. … At this moment [December 1918] it is seductively within our reach to realize this goal" (Lukács 1995, p. 218). This meant dictatorship, terror and class oppression, justified by the belief that proletarian rule will wither away and with it all class rule. He committed himself to this Bolshevik ethic, believing it was no longer possible to wait: "until humanity's own conscience will give birth to what its conscious members have already known for a long time as the only possible solution" (Lukács 1995, p. 219).

He admitted later that:

> The World and the Russian Revolution of 1917 brought about a crisis in my whole worldview, and my Syndicalist tendencies intensified under the personal influence of Ervin Szabó, who was the most important representative of Syndicalism in Hungary. Thus, when I joined the Communist Party of Hungary in 1918, my views were Syndicalistic and Idealistic. Notwithstanding my experiences of the revolution in Hungary, I let myself be led by an ultra left-wing opposition to [the] Comintern line (1920–1921). (Sziklai 1992, pp. 199–200)

Lenin agreed, identifying Lukács with the "infantile disorder of left-wing communism", criticizing his views as "left-wing and very poor" and describing his Marxism as "purely verbal" (Lenin 1966, p. 165).

During the Hungarian Commune of 1919 Lukács was deputy People's Commissar for Education and Culture.[1] He was motivated by: "an abstract utopianism in the realm of cultural politics" (Lukács 1971, p. xii). He aimed to establish communism as a moral and cultural force. This meant an end to the élitism in education and culture of which he was such a classic product. Instead, he began a debate, in *Red News*, on intellectuals and art in the proletarian revolution, coining the slogan "Art is the end and politics is the means" (Kadarkay 1991, pp. 216–217). Lukács believed that cultural revolution was the fundamental aim, but his campaign of decrees, such as for the confiscation of private libraries and art collections, and exhortation failed. Workers and peasants regarded the Commissariat of Education and Culture as patronizing and lacking in a sense of political pragmatism. The Hungarian Commune lasted six months. Lukács escaped from Hungary and, apart from some brief clandestine visits on party missions, spent the next twenty-six years in exile in Austria, Germany and Russia.

History and Class Consciousness

Throughout the 1920s Lukács was in political struggle with opponents in the Hungarian Communist Party, notably with the former leader of the Commune, Béla Kun and his allies in the Communist (Third) International or Comintern (founded in Moscow in 1919 to coordinate Communist Party campaigns for world revolution). Lukács' writings during this period were both theoretical and pragmatic. The former included *History and Class Consciousness* (1923) and *Lenin: A Study on the Unity of His Thought* (1924). The latter focused on political strategy for the communist movement and the most important of these were the *Blum Theses* of 1928 (Lukács 1978).

History and Class Consciousness has acquired a considerable reputation and is regarded, with Karl Korsch's *Marxism and Philosophy*[2] and Antonio Gramsci's *Prison Notebooks*,[3] as a seminal work of "Western Marxism". Lukács' intention was to make clear the fundamental revolutionary meaning of Marx's work, focusing on the section on "the fetishism of commodities" in the first volume of *Capital* and on the *Theses on Feuerbach*. Lukács attempts nothing less than a philosophical diagnosis of the cultural crisis of his world. It relies on Hegelian logic, but is also influenced by the activist spirit of Feuerbach and especially of Marx (Berki 1972, p. 55). The problem is that human relationships under capitalism are treated as commodity exchanges. This obscures the exploitative social relationships involved and results in the false consciousness and reification that are fundamental characteristics of capitalism. But Lukács goes further and explains "the entire development of modern rationalist philosophy in terms of reification" (Berki 1972, p. 54). Although they are obviously related, Lukács was only able to consider the concept of alienation later, on reading Marx's *Economic and Philosophical Manuscripts* (Marx 1977) in 1930. Lukács points out, following Marx and anticipating Gramsci, that the bourgeoisie: "really does attempt to organize the whole of society in its own interests (and in this it has had some success). To achieve this it was forced to develop a coherent theory of economics, politics and society" (Lukács 1971, p. 65). But such a theory could never achieve more than a class-biased understanding of the world. The way forward was through a proletarian revolution leading to a classless society, humane in an authentic rather than an illusory way. Lukács ascribed, as Marx had done, universal significance to this analysis of capitalist society. He also believed that capitalism might adapt and continue, threatening the ultimate destruction of civilization. The proletariat, which was far from homogenous, might adjust itself to the hegemony of bourgeois culture and to the demands of capitalist political economy. He stated: "In view of the great distance that the proletariat has to travel ideologically, it would be disastrous to foster any illusions" (Lukács 1971, p. 80).

By a proletarian class-consciousness in opposition to that of the bourgeoisie, Lukács did not mean anything that the working classes might *actually* think and feel. He drew the Leninist conclusion that the proletariat had to acquire class consciousness "through the leadership of intellectuals, who by theoretical understanding have learnt what the class-consciousness of the proletariat ought to be" (Borkenau 1962, p. 172). He was aware of the dangers, arguing that the vanguard party had to gain and merit the support of the proletarian masses. In "The Marxism of Rosa Luxemburg" Lukács emphasized:

> The true strength of the party is moral: it is fed by the trust of the spontaneously revolutionary masses whom economic conditions have forced into revolt. ... Only when the party has fought for this trust and earned it can it become the leader of the revolution. For only then will the masses spontaneously and instinctively press forward with all their energies towards the party and towards their own self-consciousness. (Lukács 1971, p. 42)

Lukács believed the vanguard party should be educative, leading by moral example, a culturally hegemonic alternative to bourgeois capitalism. In his pamphlet on Lenin he argued that the vanguard party: "pre-supposes the fact – the actuality – of the revolution" (Lukács 1977, p. 26).

History and Class Consciousness is: "an impressive exercise in Hegelian logic to the end of drawing out the full implications of Lenin's doctrine of the vanguard" (Lichtheim 1965, p. 370n). The objective was proletarian rather than bourgeois hegemony. This would wither and die as commodity relationships gave way to a humane and classless society. The totalitarianism was noted by Nicholas Berdyaev in *The Origin of Russian Communism*. He observed: "Lukatch [sic] … a Hungarian, and the most interesting and philosophically cultured of communist writers, who writes in German and displays great acuteness of mind, makes an original, and, in my opinion, a true judgement about revolution" (Berdyaev 1948, p. 105). Berdyaev meant that Lukács recognized that, for the revolutionary: "there are no *separate* spheres; he tolerates no division of life into parts, nor will he admit any autonomy of thought in relation to action or autonomy of action in relation to thought" (Berdyaev 1948, p. 105). In short, a revolutionary has an integrated world-view in which theory and practice organically coalesce. This is the meaning of Leninism. Lukács understood and accepted Bolshevism as the "only orthodox i.e. totalitarian integral Marxism, which refused to tolerate the breaking up of the Marxist world-view into fragments and the adoption of separate parts of it" (Berdyaev 1948, pp. 105–106). Lukács was committed to this as his political history demonstrates.

Ironically for Lukács, the publication of *History and Class Consciousness* coincided with the campaign of the Communist International to "bolshevize" its "national sections", that is, bring them directly under Soviet control. This meant the purging of communist deviationists (Bates 1976). Lukács' book was symbolic of intellectual unorthodoxy and political dissidence. The Communist International could not tolerate the implication that there was a cultural difference between the prospects of communism in Europe and that of Russian bolshevism. To do so would undermine its authority, a view shared by Béla Kun who, in *Kommunistische Internationale*, attacked: "attempts undertaken in German literature to revise dialectical materialism or, to put it more accurately, to emasculate [it] by expunging materialism" (Watnick 1958, p. 52). Lukács' work was criticized also by Soviet philosophers, such as A. M. Deborin, "for its Hegelian influences, utopian idealism "and deviation from the tenets of Marxism-Leninism" (Watnick 1958, p. 52).

Lukács was not the only West European communist censured for ideological deviation. He was joined by Karl Korsch and Antonio Gradiazei.[4] Korsch had held a post as a Commissar for Education during the period of communist control in Thuringia during the German Revolution of 1919, while his *Marxism and Philosophy* had come to the same conclusions as those of *History and Class Consciousness*. There was also the Italian economist Antonio Graziadei who published *Price and Surplus Price in the Capitalist Economy: A critique of Marx's theory of value*, in 1923 (Graziadei 1923) Official censure was pronounced at the Fifth Congress of the Communist International in 1924. Gregori Zinoviev, its President, emphasized the ideological significance, stating: "This theoretical revisionism cannot be allowed to pass with impunity. Comrade Graziadei is a professor; Korsch is a professor. (Interruption: "Lukács is also a professor!") If we get a few more of these professors spinning out their Marxist theories, we shall be lost. We cannot tolerate … theoretical revisionism of this kind in our Communist International" (Watnick 1958, p. 53).

By 1928, after bitter struggles, Korsch and Graziadei were expelled from the Communist Party, but Lukács survived. Unlike the others, he accepted censure and kept his membership. As Lukács stated in his 1967 Preface to History and Class Consciousness, "the Third (Communist) International correctly defined the position of the capitalist world as one of relative stability. These facts meant that I had to re-think my theoretical position. In the debates of the Russian Party I agreed with Stalin about the necessity for socialism in one country and this shows very clearly the start of a new epoch in my thought" (Lukács 1967, p. xxvii). Lukács was not guilty of a failure of nerve; rather the contrary. Instead he preferred, from a powerful sense of party discipline, to follow the logic of his own arguments in *History and Class Consciousness*. These identified the Communist Party as "the institutionalized will and expression of proletarian class-consciousness and thereby endowed it with a superior view of 'total' reality" (Watnick 1958, p. 53). Nothing more was required of him than silent acquiesence in the decisions of the party. Lukács, despite his intellectual sophistication, was prepared to accept this.

The *Blum Theses*

Lukács continued to live in Vienna and in Berlin, but spent a year in Moscow in 1930–1931. There he worked under David Ryazonoff, Director of the Marx-Lenin Institute,[5] which gave him the opportunity of studying Marx's *Economic and Philosophical Manuscripts*. Lukács remained active in the Hungarian Communist Party, but was realistic about the prospects for proletarian revolution in Western Europe. This was shaped by his experience of the 1919 Commune, his cultural assessment of Hungary and Europe and of developments in the Soviet Union, where he observed that, ideologically, the proletarian movement had a long way to travel. This cultural realism led Lukács to prepare a political statement debated internally by the Hungarian Communist Party and by the Communist International. This was a re-evaluation of the political possibilities in Hungary that became known as the *Blum Theses* (Blum was then Lukács' party name).

The *Theses Concerning the Political and Economic Situation in Hungary and the Tasks of the Hungarian Communist Party* were prepared by Lukács in 1928 and debated by the party the following year. They were the outcome of an alliance between Lukács and the communist railway worker and trade unionist Jenö Landler. Together they developed a gradualist programme with the aim of establishing a bourgeois democracy in Hungary creating a climate in which the Communist Party might operate. This led to the formation of a Hungarian Social Democratic Party linked with the illegal Communist Party in Vienna. Béla Kun, the official leader of the Hungarian Communist Party, with the support of the Communist International, criticized this as opportunistic right wing deviationism.

Lukács argued for a democratic dictatorship, by which he meant a republic governed by workers and peasants. It was necessary for communists to understand the difference: "between a democracy where the bourgeois is the politically dominant class and one where – although it maintains its economic exploitation – it has ceded at least part of its power to the broad masses of the workers" (Lukács 1972, p. 243). The point was that: "the struggle for bourgeois liberties must be connected with the everyday needs of the workers" (Lukács 1972, p. 249).

Lukács developed this strategy throughout the 1920s and it is argued that: "There is a consistent line in his essays on this subject from 'Organization and Revolutionary Initiative' (1921) and 'The Politics of Illusion-Yet Again' (1922) right up to the *Blum Theses*" (Lukács 1972, xix). This influenced his thought on communist educational and cultural work. The significance of the *Blum Theses* was that they anticipated the Popular Front strategy adopted by the Comintern in 1935. In 1928 and 1929 they were anathema to a Communist International committed to a sectarian policy of struggle against so-called "social fascism". Lukács realized that a formal self-criticism was necessary to avoid expulsion from the party; this was published in the Hungarian Communist Party journal in 1929. It anticipated his censure by the Executive Committee of the Communist International in an *Open Letter* to the Hungarian Communist Party. As Comrade Blum, he was accused of seeing the chief task of the party "not in the struggle against bourgeois illusions, but in the struggle against the Nihilism confronting bourgeois democracy. When he proposes that the Communist Party should proclaim to the workers that bourgeois democracy is the 'best battle-ground', he really puts himself in the position of social democracy." The statement ended ominously: "These theses have nothing in common with Bolshevism" (Lukács 1972, p. xx).

Lukács' retraction of his views was a tactical matter of political survival within the party. In practice, it has been observed that the defeat of the *Theses*: "marked the *beginning* of his career as a realistic [party] ideologist and led to the 'revolutionary' change in his whole philosophy, strengthening Marxism in both its content and method. [However] [t]he theses had only opened a *crack* in sectarianism, instead of breaking through along a *wide* front, as the Seventh Congress of the Comintern was to do. That was their historical weakness" (Sziklai 1992, p. 56). Lukács noted: "None of us recognized that, in Europe, it was not Socialism versus Capitalism that was in the forefront, but the mobilization of all the anti-Fascist forces against Fascism. *No one* recognized that, at that time in Europe, including the author of the 'Blum Theses' … In view of this, it cannot be declared that [the] 'Blum Theses' had made the turn in strategy and tactics that was to come only later" (Sziklai 1992, p. 56).

Cultural Communism

Isaiah Berlin places disputes "on the cultural front" within the context of disagreements within the Russian Communist Party about foreign policy and policy towards communists and communist parties outside the Soviet Union. As he says: "A good deal of experiment, sometimes bold and interesting, at other times merely eccentric and worthless, occurred at this time in the Soviet Union [1920s] in the guise of cultural warfare against the encircling capitalist world" (Berlin 2004, p. 137). Lenin and Trotsky were scornful of "proletarian" art and culture. Lenin "disliked all forms of modernism intensely; his attitude to radical artistic experiment was bourgeois in the extreme" (Berlin 2004, p. 138). He criticized the *Prolet'cult* severely, stating it mistaken to think one could: "become a Communist without assimilating the wealth of knowledge amassed by mankind" (Lenin 1970, p. 127), bringing it under the control of the vanguard Communist Party as early as 1920 (Morgan 2003, pp. 131–135). In the preface to *Literature and Revolution* (1924) Trotsky made it clear that he was of the same opinion. He wrote: "It is fundamentally incorrect to contrast bourgeois culture and bourgeois art with proletarian culture and proletarian art. The latter will never exist, because the proletarian regime is temporary and transient" (Trotsky 1960 [1924], p. 14).

The debate about "Cultural Bolshevism" continued throughout the 1920s. As Berlin states:

> The advocates of "proletarian" culture were divided on whether it was produced by individuals of talent who distilled within themselves the aspirations of the proletarian masses, actual and potential, acting as it were, as their mouthpieces or rather megaphones; or whether, as the extremer ideologists proclaimed, individuals as such had no part at all to

play in the new order, for the art of the new collectivist society must itself be collective. (Berlin 2004, p. 138)

Others believed that the artist's political task consisted in documentary reportage of the building of the new society – the advent of socialist realism. As Lev Averbakh, of the Russian Association of Proletarian Writers (RAPP) stated: "The issue is not the making of national culture accessible to the workers. It is the class struggle that defines the content and direction of culture" (Kadarkay 1991, p. 342). Communists elsewhere echoed this. For instance, the French communist Paul Nizan, in a 1930 review of Emmanuel Berl's book *The Death of Bourgeois Values*, wrote: "Between culture ... and the proletariat ... there cannot be any reconciliation. This is because culture is a system of values erected against the proletariat ... One must have the courage to say: bourgeois culture is a barrier" (Guiat 2003, p. 58).

Cultural Bolshevism, "against which Communist policy later so sternly set its face" (Berlin 2004, p. 137), was popular in Germany; as Ernst Toller, Erwin Piscator and Bertold Brecht indicate; there was also a long history of social-democratic cultural activity that continued during the Weimar republic (van der Will & Burns 1985). The Institute for Social Research, or "Frankfurt School", was also part of the debate. Lukács, was concerned with the critical analysis and appropriation of bourgeois culture, like Max Horkheimer, Theodore Adorno and others of the Frankfurt School, but Lukács was convinced that the "critical realism" of say the Mann brothers, overcame their subjective tendencies and made them superior to works which had a progressive tendency, but which were superficial in execution. This led him to look for equally effective works of "socialist realism". This theory of art was rejected by Adorno and by the other members of the Frankfurt School as essentially conservative culturally, and "alien to the nature of art" (Slater 1977, p. 128), though they were themselves élitist and remote from working-class life. Lukács' party affiliation and discipline was the fundamental difference that for him decided his course of action (or inaction).

The "cultural front" was crucial for the Comintern in dealing with its "national sections", individual communists, with socialist parties and with those who became known as "fellow-travellers" (Caute 1973; Hollander 1981). After 1928 the Comintern was intransigent in dealing with deviations from Soviet policy and Lukács played a part in this. In 1926 he declared himself sceptical of the revolutionary contribution of "proletarian" culture, publishing an article on "Art for Art's Sake and Proletarian Poetry" in the magazine *Die Tat* (The Deed) (Kadarkay 1991, p. 283). He drew upon Trotsky's *Literature and Revolution* in his criticisms of *Tendenzkunst* or propaganda art, developed by people such as Ernst Toller (1934), calling it "an abstract and romantic utopianism" (Löwy 1979, p. 194). This encourages an interpretation of Lukács' article as a self-criticism of his utopian hopes of 1919. He believed that the workers' revolution would provide conditions that would revitalize art, but warned: "It is wrong for a proletarian revolutionary, for a Marxist, to overestimate in a utopian way the real existing possibilities" (Sziklai 1992, p. 130). The question of cultural policy and the proletarian revolution needed rethinking and this included the bourgeois cultural heritage.

Lukács did this through literary and cultural criticism, book reviews and journalism, in party journals and magazines such as *Die Linkscurve* (Left Turn) and, from the early 1930s, *Moskauer Rundschau* (Moscow Review). After the defeat of the *Blum Theses*, Lukács survived Communist Party censure, although he withdrew from active participation in the policy debates of the Hungarian Communist Party and was registered formally with the Communist Party of Germany. Apart from his year at the Marx-Lenin Institute in Moscow in 1930–1931, Lukács remained in Berlin. There, with the party name of Dr Hans Keller, he worked as a party functionary and led the communists within the Association of German Writers. "In this capacity", said Lukács, "I succeeded in organizing a United-Front movement involving left-wing bourgeois. Social Democratic and Communist writers." This accomplished, Lukács was elected vice-chairman to the social democrat Heinz Pol. "These successes encouraged the Party to send me to other organizations of intellectuals as a leading official" (Sziklai 1992, p. 160).

Lukács was now delegated to assist László Radványi, a Hungarian communist and also a member of the "Sunday Circle". Radványi, whose party name was Johan-Lorenz Schmidt, was responsible for the party's Marxist Workers' Schools in Germany. Lukács gave lectures at the Berlin School about six times a week His lectures dealt with trends in modern bourgeois literature, the literature of the French Revolution, Marxist literary criticism and on aesthetics. He focused on the intellectual origins of Fascism and gave lectures on the literary theory of National Socialism, the literary crisis of contemporary Fascism and the Fascist falsification of Hegel (Congdon 1989, pp. 509–519; Sziklai 1992, p. 164). Motivated against sectarianism, he advocated the merits of realism in literature in lectures and literary articles, although the term "socialist realism" was not yet in use.[6] Lukács remained in Germany until 1933, when Hitler and the Nazis saw him seek refuge in the Soviet Union.

Cultural Policy and the Popular Front

Between 1928 and 1934 the national communist parties followed the Comintern line of "class against class". This endorsed a proletarian class war in cultural policy. However, in April 1932, a decree of the Central Committee of the Russian Communist Party disbanded the RAPP; a consequence of Stalin's mistrust of the cultural revolutionary, even ultra-leftist tendencies of its leadership. This was followed by the emergence of "socialist realism", devised essentially by Maxim Gorky with the approval of Stalin. It attempted to distinguish between "social" and "critical" realism, emphasizing that artistic work must be assessed in its philosophical and social context. This coincided with Lukács' return to the Soviet Union. There he contributed to Moscow journals, such as *Internationale Literatur* and "more precisely, above all – for the Russian language *Literaturny Kritik*" (Sziklai 1992, p. 44). The policy of the journal was to consider the contribution of bourgeois literature to the development of Marxism. In 1934, the First Congress of the Union of Soviet Writers (replacing RAPP) endorsed this trend. It emphasized "cultural continuity" in literature and art; a return to the original positions of Lenin (and of Trotsky). Lukács was admitted to the Union, following his lecture to the Philosophical Institute of the Communist Academy on 24 June 1934. In this he made a self-criticism, reviewing past errors; especially those in *History and Class Consciousness*. This was not merely a tactical move by Lukács to ensure his position in the party and in practical terms in Moscow. The lecture also signalled the concerns that were to absorb him throughout his years in the Soviet Union, notably a critique of German philosophy and its part in the evolution of Fascism, together with a search for potential intellectual allies in the struggle against it. As Sziklai points out: "He had recognized the changes in the world-historical situation and was familiar with conditions in the Soviet Union" (Sziklai 1992, p. 198).

Lukács contributed 25 articles to *Literaturny Kritik* between 1934 and 1940. These focused on the importance of continuity, even of tradition, in the development of literature and "appropriated 'classical' values on behalf of a proletarian state in need of socialist mass-culture" (Kadarkay 1991, p. 344). In a sense Lukács complemented the efforts of that very different communist Maxim Gorky and his scheme for *World Literature* (Morgan 2003,

167–186). In the articles, later to become books, such as *The Historical Novel* (1962) and *The Young Hegel* (1975), Lukács expounded bourgeois culture to the culturally influential readership of *Literaturny Kritik*. His article on "The Novel as Bourgeois Epic" argued that the function of the artist is to find the spirit of the people and the mode of artistic expression corresponding to it. The socialist novel was a "transitory epic", in the same way as the great classical novels of the bourgeois epoch, and incorporates them and eventually transcends them (Kadarkay 1991, p. 344). Criticized for Hegelianism, Lukács had raised the crucial political issue of "what to retain and what to discard from bourgeois culture?" (Kadarkay 1991, p. 344). This he considered in "Grand Hotel Abyss" (1933), a satire on intellectuals he saw accommodating Fascism. However, for Lukács the role of bourgeois intellectuals and of bourgeois philosophy in the development of Fascism was not primarily one for moral condemnation. In "Die deutsche Intelligenz und der Faschismus", he comments: "The immense sociological, legal, philosophical, etc. literature produced about the crisis of the state, the party, parliamentarism and democracy all but blazed the trail for the ideology of Fascism" (Sziklai 1992, p. 177).

This was the beginning of a theoretical explanation of the role of intellectuals in the development of Fascism. He had no sympathy with intellectuals "floating above social strata", as advocated by yet another member of the "Sunday Circle", Karl Mannheim (Mannheim 1936). Lukács' view was that bourgeois intellectuals opposed to Fascism should affirm this by affiliation to the workers' movement, for which they needed opportunity. That was why sectarianism should be replaced by anti-Fascist unity. This analysis had, for Lukács, an urgent political purpose. It required him to balance the objectives of ideologist and of intellectual; an intensely difficult task aggravated by the political climate in which he lived as an émigré communist in Stalin's Russia. Lukács' views were expressed chiefly through his literary work, but also through journalism. He commented: "that outstanding journalistic achievements could be produced only when and where partisanship remained free from narrow sectarianism, the Communist Party literature adjusted itself to the whole of the left-wing movement, and Communist ideas came to be articulated as questions with a universal appeal" (Sziklai 1992, p. 44). Gramscian in tone, this was a commitment to the political and cultural principles of the Popular Front. For the moment at least, Lukács' literary views were "backed by political power", requiring an assessment of who and what might be regarded as "progressive" (Kadarkay 1991, pp. 344–345). The articles in *Literaturny Kritik* demonstrate this, even though the regular publication of literary magazines in Soviet Russia was, to say the least, uncertain.

The Comintern showed this change of policy. Since 1928 it had followed a "class against class line" which had proved disastrous, especially in Germany. This was abandoned in favour of the anti-Fascist alliance known as the Popular Front. The extinction of the German Communist Party and of the German labour movement by Hitler convinced Stalin that the Russian Communist Party and the Comintern had to change direction. This began with the Franco–Soviet Mutual Assistance Treaty in 2 May 1935, announced at the Seventh Congress of the Communist International, held in Moscow in July and August. The main address was by the Chairman of the Comintern, the Bulgarian Georgi Dimitrov. He explained the change in line, declaring Fascism to be: "the most vicious enemy of the working class and of all working people". Its threat made it essential to build "unity of action by all sections of the working class, irrespective of the party or organization to which they belong"; with anti-Fascism being the only criterion for collaboration. He emphasized that: "the formation of a wide anti-fascist People's Front on the basis of the proletarian united front was a particularly important task" (Drachkovitch & Lazitch 1966, pp. 189–190).

The new line was a return to and an extension of the United Front established at the Fourth Congress of the Comintern in 1924. The difference was that the Popular Front was generated by Fascism's advance; soon to be aggravated by the war in Spain. These, coupled with the apparent successes of Soviet planning compared with the apparent failures of capitalism, increased the appeal of the Stalin cult and of the Soviet Union. It also rescued the Comintern, albeit temporarily and superficially from intellectual sterility. The new line had clear implications for the debate on cultural policy. This included not only art and literature, but also education, science, media, leisure activities and physical culture. In fact, the entire range of activities and associations that come under the heading of civil society, as well as those provided formally by the state. In cultural terms, this meant a campaign to recruit and to propagandize for the anti-Fascist cause on as broad a basis as possible. This gave plenty of scope for the "front" organizations promoted by the extraordinary Willi Muenzenberg, such as the International Congress of Writers for the Defence of Culture, held in Paris in 1935 (Caute 1973, pp. 132–137).

Lukács' contribution was, in the long term, more influential. He had not had a direct part in the Comintern's Seventh Congress, as he remained excluded from the Hungarian delegation. Yet its decisions allowed Lukács to express cultural views with political confidence and to take advantage, as he put it, "of the extension of the field of conflict". There were Popular Front tendencies in the Moscow literary circles to which he had access, while explorations of the potential for ideological resistance to Fascism were welcome politically (Lukács 1983, pp. 164–166; Sziklai 1992, p. 14). Lukács attacked the barbarism of Fascism, emphasizing the importance of cultural continuity in uniting progressive forces for Democracy (and Socialism). After 1935, Lukács recruited the work of bourgeois humanistic writers such as Anatole France, Romain Rolland, Heinrich and Thomas Mann and Bernard Shaw in opposition to Fascism. His 1936 article on Thomas Mann in *Internationale Literatur* has been identified as the decisive beginning of this new position (Sziklai 1992, p. 185). Lukács' attempts to find common cause with such writers were the cultural equivalent of the Popular Front's tactic of establishing political coalitions that ignored class positions (Löwy 1979, p. 202). Thomas and Heinrich Mann epitomized for Lukács the rationalism and critical realism of bourgeois humanism, in opposition to the irrationalism of Fascism.

This may be contrasted with Lukács' attitude to Bertold Brecht. They had first encountered each other during Brecht's attempt, probably in 1931, to organize a journal *Krisis und Kritik* to encourage debate between communists and leftist intellectuals. The attempt failed and, in a draft letter to Lukács found in his notebook, Brecht complains of condescension and of Lukács' abstract definition of "intellectuals". Brecht complains that: "A manifestly preachy attitude and the stress on our superiority are not sensible now, even if we are aware that, due to their deteriorating economic position, the intellectuals would be willing to come to terms with us over certain issues" (Brecht 1983, pp. 145–146; Sziklai 1992, p. 161). Brecht, who despised the bourgeoisie and was radical artistically, appeared to Lukács a caricaturist when compared with the sophisticated Mann brothers. But Brecht aimed to represent artistically a different Germany and his view was that the circumstances of the proletarian class struggle should recognize this difference; a concept of realism: "that provided Brecht with the key to the artistic avant-garde" (Slater 1977, p. 130).

Lukács also considered Fascism's open ideologists such as Arthur Rosenberg and their treatment of intellectuals such as Schopenhauer, Nietzsche, Simmel, Weber and Spengler. He also brought his re-evaluation of bourgeois classics into line with the Popular Front's cultural policy. "Lukács asserted – ... all the more trenchant for its expressing a deep conviction – that the "great" writers can instruct the socialist writers about the human potential of the peoples who suffer under the "yoke of fascism" (Kadarkay 1991, p. 334). He regarded the work of anti-Fascist bourgeois humanist writers, such as Romain Rolland, Thomas and Heinrich Mann and Arnold Zweig, "as the main *political* support of the Popular Front" (Sziklai 1992, p. 221). He went further, identifying in their work an anti-capitalist content that exposed, if unconsciously, the irrationality of bourgeois society. He considered that: "Here is the clear voice of the newly awakened revolutionary democracy of Germany. Words like these in the writing of the German emigration spring from the soul of the fighting German people" (Lukács 1962, p. 269).

Towards the end of *The Historical Novel*, Lukács declares that the new historical novel

> born of the popular and democratic spirit of our time, will indeed *contrast* with the classical historical novel. ... [I]t is clear that this new perspective exists not only for the writers of the Soviet Union, but also for the humanists of the anti-Fascist popular front; although of course, these tendencies are inevitably more distinct and developed in the Soviet Union. But the struggle for the democracy of a new type, the realization that the problems of this democracy are connected with the economic and cultural liberation of the exploited – something we have seen especially vividly in the writings of Heinrich Mann – show that this perspective is also a reality for the fighters of the popular front. Thus it can also become a reality for their literature. (Lukács 1963, p. 347)

He had in mind Heinrich Mann's novel *Henri Quatre*, published in two parts in 1933 and 1938, in which the sixteenth-century wars of religion were intended as a mirror to Hitler's Europe. In this novel Mann attempted to "move from abstract humanism to political realism, historicity and active sympathy for violent political struggle against class tyranny" (Caute 1973, p. 237). Lukács praised him as "the most progressive and determined leader of anti-Fascist writing" (Lukács 1963, p. 269).

For many years, Lukács' work was available chiefly in journals and in Russian or German editions. This meant that his influence at the time of the Popular Front was greatest amongst communists in Europe. It was inevitably less so in the English-speaking world, though his influence on Christopher Caudwell's *Studies in a Dying Culture* and *Illusion and Reality*, on Ralph Fox's *The Novel and the People* and on John Strachey's *The Coming Struggle for Power*, has been noted (Mosse 1963, p. 388). He was also mentioned in Karl Mannheim's influential *Ideology and Utopia* (Mannheim 1936). To this might be added the political and cultural thinking that lay behind the Left Book Club launched by the socialist and publisher Victor Gollancz, with the editorial assistance of John Strachey and of Harold Laski in May 1936 (Lewis 1970). Such influences may repay further investigation. As Isaac Deutscher stated: "He [Lukács] elevated the Popular Front from the level of tactics to that of ideology; he projected its principle into philosophy, literary history and aesthetic criticism" (Deutscher 1971, pp. 291–292). Years later, justifying his actions by what he perceived as their historical and political necessity, Lukács confirmed this. He stated: "I consider it the central task of my life to employ correctly the Marxist-Leninist ideology in the areas of my competence. Inasmuch, as my activity coincided with the world historical significance of socialism in one country, and the struggle for its interest, it is natural that all my concerns, including those of my work, were subordinate to this consideration" (Kadarkay 1991, p. 326). Lukács' aim was to contribute to a left-wing programme, under the leadership of the Communist Party that would be effective internationally.

Lukács and Stalinism

The Communist International came under Stalinist direction with the Sixth Congress of 1928 that met after the defeat of Trotsky. This meant that, as political circumstances changed, so did the Comintern line. The Popular Front was the classic example of such a switch, coming to an end with the signing of the Nazi–Soviet Non-Aggression Pact of 23 August 1939. This was motivated by Stalin's need to defend the Soviet Union and "socialism in one country". Party discipline required of communists the "necessary lie", as Maxim Gorky had described it in 1929, when he described his hatred for "that truth which is an abomination and a lie for ninety nine per cent of the people" (Wolfe 1967, p. 59). This was also Lukács' justification of his party loyalty and support for Stalin. Lukács' desire for and acceptance of "totality" in revolution, as identified by Nicholas Berdyaev, explains this. It was also a pragmatic act of survival in the conditions of Soviet Russia; In the 1967 Preface to *History and Class Consciousness* Lukács claimed that he had been "on Stalin's side on the central issue of Russia", but was deeply repelled by the attitude to the United Front in 1928; when Stalin had "described the Social Democrats as the 'twin brothers' of the Fascists" (Lukács 1971, pp. xxviii).

This meant balancing the development of theory, the acceptance of party commissions and periods of silence. In Russia he engaged in what he claimed was a covert criticism of the Stalinist sectarian line. He commented later: "For that reason I had to wage a guerilla war in order to advocate my ideas. I had to secure publication of my works by including some appropriate quotations from Stalin. By following this method I could explicate my dissenting views with the required caution ... Naturally, there were times when it dictated *silence*" (Lukács 1967, p. 647; Sziklai 1992, p. 41). Lukács accepted the change of line in 1939, because to do otherwise could have been fatal, but also from communist discipline. When his own assessment of political strategy differed from that of the party, he bowed to the party, in public at least. After the *Blum Theses*, this occurred when Stalinism failed to align itself with Western democracy and culture in common cause against Fascism.

The difficulty of maintaining such a position is shown between 1939 and 1941. As the line began to change to reflect Stalinist policy towards Fascism and the bourgeois democracies, *Literaturny Kritik*, Lukács' chief vehicle for publication, was closed in 1940. He was accused of right-opportunism by the Hungarian Party and by the Comintern and in 1941 the NKVD arrested him. This was almost certainly because he was identified as a potential opponent of Stalinist accommodation with Nazi Germany, although he took care to obscure this in the autobiographical statement he wrote preparatory to his interrogation. He was released shortly after the German invasion of Russia, following the intervention of Georgi Dimitrov. The objectives of the Popular Front returned with the alliance against Nazi Germany and "his intellectual services to anti-fascism became useful once more" (Löwy 1979, p. 204).

Lukács' *Curriculum Vitae* states: "Since the day of my discharge I have been working on war propaganda, my primary concern being the ideological fight against Fascism" (Sziklai 1992, p. 207). Evacuated to Central Asia in October 1941, Lukács' work ranged from journalism for English and American newspapers through the Soviet Information Bureau, articles for *Internationale Literatur*, propaganda radio broadcasts, to the political re-education of German and Hungarian prisoners of war. Lukács' appointment in 1942 to the Institute of Philosophy of the Academy of Sciences allowed him to work on the history of philosophy. In short, he continued the "duality of roles between the scholar and the publicist, the philosopher and the propagandist, the aesthete and the staff-member of editorial boards" (Sziklai 1992, p. 208).

Conclusion: The Legacy

Lukács returned to Hungary in 1945 and became engaged in political and cultural affairs, as a member of the now ruling Hungarian Communist Party and as a university professor. He based his position on a 1944 publication in Hungarian on the responsibility of writers. In 1948 he broadened this into a general statement of the responsibility of intellectuals in the post-war world. The question was would they, "like the intellectuals of France in the 18th century or those in Russia in the 19th century, become path-breakers and champions of a progressive turn in world history; or, like the German intellectuals of the first half of the 20th century [would they] become helpless victims, witless helpers of a barbaric reaction?" (Lukács 1969, p. 131). Lukács was in conflict, on Marxist tactical grounds, with the Stalinists of the Hungarian Communist Party. In 1956, at an open meeting of the *Petöfi Circle* of communist intellectuals critical of the leadership, he complained of: "the bankruptcy of Marxism in Hungary" (Braunthal 1980, p. 414). In the same year he joined the national communist government of Nagy, ironically once more as Minister of Culture. He was removed from office by the Soviet suppression of Nagy's government, but managed to survive execution and was re-admitted to membership of the Hungarian Communist Party.

After 1956 and up to and beyond his death in 1971, Lukács' reputation grew as he was claimed as a founder of Western Marxism. This was enhanced by the surge of the New Left in the late 1960s, accompanied by the English translation and publication of his work, especially *History and Class Consciousness* (which Lukács himself continued to reject). His attitude to Stalinism remained ambiguous. In the 1957 preface to the German edition of *The Meaning of Contemporary Realism*, he referred to events which demand a rethinking of certain problems connected with Stalin's legacy. Only then "as with Rosa Luxemburg's complex legacy, can Stalin's positive achievements be seen in perspective" (Lukács 1963, p. 10). In the preface to the English edition in 1962, he went further, stating: "Nevertheless, the effort to rid the movement of the disastrous legacy of Stalinism – and to recover the creative teaching of Marx, Engels and Lenin – remains our most urgent task" (Lukács 1963, p. 7).

Lukács' political importance declined with the failures of the orthodox communist movement and of the New Left that aspired to replace it. He was a man of great learning and intellectual power and his work, notably *History and Class Consciousness* and *The Historical Novel*, retains considerable importance for those interested in the relationship between the communist movement and cultural policy. However, as Deutscher has pointed out, one has to be wary of Lukács' erudite sophistication (Deutscher 1971, pp. 292–293). At best, Lukács struggled to maintain an ambiguity between the European culture with which he was imbued and the totality of the communist movement to which he had given himself. At worst, he adopted a "notoriously Stalinist standpoint", with his writings on Heinrich Mann "a pendant to the Stalinist 'struggle for allies'" (Deutscher 1971, pp. 291–292). Kolakowski makes a similar point when he observes that Lukács' critique of Stalinism "did not step outside its fundamental bases" (Kolakowski 1978, p. 307). Instead, Lukács saw only Stalinism's tactical errors and sectarian basis and did not attempt any fundamental assessment of its moral direction, remaining to the end what he had been since 1919: a committed Communist Party ideologist. The implications for Lukács' continuing relevance as a cultural theorist are profound. His work should be read in historical context and only applied to the development of a new anti-capitalist cultural politics in the light of an understanding of Lukács' original motivation and perspective.

NOTES

1. His nominal superior was Zsigmond Kunfi, a member of the Socialist Party and an authority on education.
2. Originally published in Leipzig in 1923.
3. A number of editions of the *Notebooks* are now available.
4. Graziadei was an Italian count and so, like Lukács, had an aristocratic title.
5. Later a victim of Stalinism.
6. He continued to sign literary articles with his own name.

REFERENCES

BATES, T. R. (1976) 'Antonio Gramsci and the bolshevization of the PCI', *Journal of Contemporary History*, vol. 11, nos 2–3, pp. 115–132.

BERDYAEV, N. (1948) *The Origin of Russian Communism*, Geoffrey Bles, London.

BERKI, R. N. (1972) 'Georg Lukács in retrospect: Evolution of a Marxist thinker', *Problems of Communism*, November–December, pp. 52–71.

BERLIN, I. (2004) *The Soviet Mind: Russian Culture under Communism*, ed. H. Hardy, Brookings Institution Press, Washington, DC.

BORKENAU, F. (1962) *World Communism: A History of the Communist International*, University of Michigan Press, Ann Arbor, MI.

BRAUNTHAL, J. (1980) *The History of the International 1943–1968*, Gollancz, London.

BRECHT, B. (1983) *Briefe 1913–1956*, vol. 1, Aufbau Verlag, Berlin and Weimar.

CAUTE, D. (1973) *The Fellow Travellers*, Weidenfeld and Nicholson, London and New York.

CONGDON, L. (1989) 'Lukács, Radvanyi und die Marxistische Arbeiterschule', in *Lukács – Aktuell*, ed. L. Sziklai, Akademiai Kiado, Budapest, pp. 509–519.

DEUTSCHER, I. (1971) *Marxism in Our Time*, ed. T. Deutscher, The Ramparts Press, Berkeley, CA.

DRACHKOVITCH, M. M. & LAZITCH, B. (1966) 'The Communist International', in *The Revolutionary Internationals, 1864–1943*, ed. M. M. Drachkovitch, Stanford University Press, Stanford, CA and Oxford University Press, London, pp. 161–202.

GRAMSCI, A. (1971) *Selections from the Prison Notebooks*, eds Q. Hoare & G. Nowell Smith, Lawrence and Wishart, London.

GRAZIADEI, A. (1923) *Price and Surplus Price in Capitalist Economy: A Critique of Marx's Theory of Value*, Edizioni Avanti, Milan.

GUIAT, C. (2003) *The French and Italian Communist Parties: Comrades and Culture*, FRANK CASS, London and Portland, OR.

HOLLANDER, P. (1981) *Political Pilgrims: Travels of Western Intellectuals to the Soviet Union, China and Cuba*, Oxford University Press, New York and Oxford.

KADARKAY, A. (1991) *Georg Lukács: Life, Thought and Politics*, Blackwell, Oxford, UK and Cambridge, USA.

KOLAKOWSKI, L. (1978) *Main Currents of Marxism: Its Origin, Growth and Dissolution*, 3 vols, trans. P. S. Falla, Oxford University Press, Oxford.

KORSCH, K. (1970) *Marxism and Philosophy*, New Left Books, London.

LENIN, V. I. (1966) *Collected Works*, vol. 31, Progress Publishers, Moscow.

LENIN, V. I. (1970) *On Culture and Cultural Revolution*, Progress Publishers, Moscow.

LEWIS, J. (1970) *The Left Book Club: An Historical Record*, Gollancz, London.

LICHTHEIM, G. (1965) *Marxism: A Historical and Critical Study*, Routledge and Kegan Paul, London.

LÖWY, M. (1979) *Georg Lukács: From Romanticism to Bolshevism*, New Left Books, London.

LUKÁCS, G. (1926) 'Art for art's sake and proletarian poetry', *Die Tat,* June, pp. 104–188.
LUKÁCS, G. (1962) *The Historical Novel,* Merlin Press, London.
LUKÁCS, G. (1963) *The Meaning of Contemporary Realism,* Merlin Press, London.
LUKÁCS, G. (1967) *Schriften zur Ideologie und Politik,* Luchterhand Verlag, Neuwied.
LUKÁCS, G. (1969) 'On the responsibility of the intellectuals', *Telos,* vol. 2, no. 1, pp. 123–131.
LUKÁCS, G. (1971) *History and Class Consciousness: Studies in Marxist Dialectics,* Merlin Press, London.
LUKÁCS, G. (1972) *Political Writings 1919–1929: The Question of Parliamentarism and Other Essays,* ed. R. Livingstone, New Left Books, London.
LUKÁCS, G. (1975) *The Young Hegel: Studies in the Relations between Dialectics and Economics,* translated by R. Livingstone, Merlin Press, London.
LUKÁCS, G. (1977) *Lenin: A Study on the Unity of His Thought,* New Left Books, London.
LUKÁCS, G. (1983) *Record of a Life,* Verso, London.
LUKÁCS, G. (1995), 'Bolshevism as an ethical problem', in *The Lukács Reader,* ed. A. Kadarkay, Basil Blackwell, Oxford, UK and Cambridge, USA, pp. 216–221.
MANNHEIM, K. (1936) *Ideology and Utopia,* Routledge and Kegan Paul, London and Henley.
MARX, K. (1977) *Economic and Philosophical Manuscripts of 1844,* 5th rev. edn, Lawrence and Wishart, London and Progress Publishers, Moscow.
MORGAN, W. J. (2003) *Communists on Education and Culture 1848–1948,* Palgrave Macmillan, Basingstoke and New York.
MOSSE, G. L. (1963) *The Culture of Western Europe: The 19th and 20th Centuries,* John Murray, London.
SLATER, P. (1977) *Origin and Significance of the Frankfurt School: A Marxist Perspective,* Routledge and Kegan Paul, London, Boston and Henley.
SZIKLAI, L. (1992) *After the Proletarian Revolution: Georg Lukács's Marxist Development. 1933–1945,* Akademiai Kiado, Budapest.
TOLLER, E. (1934) *I was a German,* John Lane, The Bodley Head, London,
TROTSKY, L. (1960 [1924]) *Literature and Revolution,* University of Michigan Press, Ann Arbor, MI.
VAN DER WILL, W. & BURNS, R. (1985) 'The politics of cultural struggle: Intellectuals and the labour movement', in *The Weimar Dilemma: Intellectuals in the Weimar Republic,* ed. A. Phelan, Manchester University Press, Manchester and Dover, NH, pp. 162–201.
WATNICK, M. (1958) 'Georg Lukács: An intellectual biography, II, sensibility and alienation', *Soviet Survey: A Quarterly Review of Cultural Trends,* no. 24 (April–June), pp. 51–57.
WOLFE, B. D. (1967) *The Bridge and the Abyss: The Troubled Friendship of Maxim Gorky and V. I. Lenin,* Pall Mall Press, London.

THE URGE TO JUDGE
Intellectuals and communism in postwar Poland, past and present

Laurie Koloski

Popular narratives of modern Polish history privilege the Poles' heroic struggle against foreign occupation and domination, and they often put intellectuals at centre stage. After all, these narratives affirm, it was philosophers who drafted the 1791 constitution that sought to rescue Poland from internal stagnation and external partition; poets who inspired insurgents to take up arms against tsarist rule; painters and novelists who stoked nationalist aspirations with their inspired renderings of victorious battles; historians who spearheaded a dissident movement that eventually helped bring down communist rule; and a Catholic publicist who became premier of the country's first post-communist government.[1] There are good historical reasons for intellectuals' pre-eminence in such national narratives: in a country stripped of sovereignty in the late eighteenth century, and from a gentry class deprived of political and even economic influence (the partitioning powers could easily dispossess troublesome nobles), the *intelligentsia* had emerged to carry the banner of the stateless nation (Gella 1989, pp. 132–134, 139–144).[2] As Jerzy Jedlicki has noted, they did so not by "awakening" a new nation, but by extolling the traditions of the old one. "It was precisely the preservation of tradition, the enrichment of the content of the symbols uniting the nation, and the imbuing of them with an almost religious significance which became the principal imperative of literature and art", Jedlicki writes. With words and images as their tools, the intelligentsia sought to "nourish, organize and … extend to all, even to the still indifferent social classes, the feeling of nationhood and the desire for independence" (Jedlicki 1990, p. 43). Thus the intelligentsia saw itself, and has been seen retrospectively, as a decisive factor in the persistence of a Polish nation and the re-emergence of a Polish state. Acting out of a sense of moral obligation, intellectuals earned recognition as a force of moral authority.

In recent years, however, Poland's intellectuals have come in for something of a rhetorical and moral drubbing, not because they are no longer expected to serve as moral authorities, but because, their accusers claim, they failed to do so at a crucial historical moment. The issue here is intellectuals' behaviour and choices during the communist years. In debates on "intellectuals and communism" that surfaced soon after communism's collapse in 1989, critics have drawn attention to Poland's "dishonourable" intellectuals, who embraced communism after 1945 and even assisted in its imposition on an unwilling populace. Undeniably, some Polish intellectuals were open supporters of the communist regime and worked closely with it, though others just as openly opposed it. Far more straddled a middle ground, struggling to balance the pressures of state-imposed constraints with their own political, intellectual and moral agendas. Yet critics have cast their judgmental net widely, suggesting that except for a very few honourable exceptions, all intellectuals are guilty. As Jedlicki points out, "the debate about the intelligentsia restarts at every turn of history", raising questions about what intellectuals are and should be, whether they are necessary, and whether they should be held to higher moral standards than other groups in society. What is really at issue, in Jedlicki's view, is "identify[ing] the sources of moral authority in the transition period" (Jedlicki 1995, pp. 31, 35).

Debates over intellectuals' responsibility for communism are part of a larger effort in post-1989 Poland to assign blame for a system now widely considered misguided (at best) in theory and coercive in practice. As elsewhere in the post-Soviet bloc, Polish legislators have passed "lustration" laws aimed at unmasking public officials who collaborated with the communist-era regime – and as elsewhere, Poles have come up against the difficulties of assigning and assessing blame.[3] For years, political candidates have used the lustration laws to undercut opponents, accusing them of lying about past links to the communist regime and demanding investigations. In the presidential election of 2000, both Lech Wałęsea – "Mr Solidarity" himself – and Aleksander Kwaśniewski, a former communist official, found themselves under investigation by the lustration court (both were cleared of any wrong-doing). Since lustration laws apply only to candidates for public office, most intellectuals have not been subjected to public censure of this type. But occasionally efforts to officially sanction collaborators seep beyond the halls of political power, as in July 2005, when a secret policeman's handwritten note listing people who had informed for him in the late 1980s was used against historian Andrzej Przewoźnik, a candidate for director of the Institute for National Memory (Instytut Pamięci Narodowej, IPN; a state-sponsored historical research centre which holds and investigates secret police archives).[4] From the start, there had been questions about the document's authenticity, and the lustration court eventually ruled there was no evidence to show Przewoźnik had collaborated. By then, however, parliament had approved another candidate as IPN director.[5]

What can such debates (and debacles) tell us about intellectuals and cultural policy? Whether intellectuals have the right to claim moral authority today, they suggest, depends in part on how they positioned themselves within a system that sought to make them the objects of its cultural policy. From the very beginning, communist leaders had sought to reshape cultural values and endeavours and to engage intellectuals in their efforts to do so. How did intellectuals respond? Did they help to impose this system, and if so, does that disqualify them as national and moral leaders? Once they found themselves within the communist system, how did they behave? Did they fall in line or resist? Were they driven by honour or by fear? In debating intellectuals' post-1945 actions, critics have held them to a standard which relies on an idealized image of intellectuals as the nation's defenders – consistently and heroically resisting that which might harm the nation – and on categorical notions of good and bad. That there could be divergent visions of what the nation needs, that heroism might imply not only resistance, or that "good" and "bad" could overlap, seem beyond the realm of possibility. Intellectuals should have known communism was evil, and should have opposed it at every turn.

In the pages that follow, I explore the debate over intellectuals' complicity with and responsibility for communism, presenting an overview of its claims, supporters, and detractors.[6] My emphasis here is on what I call the "urge to judge", which permeates not only supporters' views, but even many detractors'. I also draw on an example from my work on Poland's early post-World War II period to argue that such efforts to judge will almost certainly falter at the level of individual historical experience and action. Condemnatory narratives of intellectuals' responsibility for communism are highly selective, and seek to promote specific imperatives for what intellectuals are and should be. They have far more to do with current political and moral agendas than with the complexities of the past being invoked. As we will see, there were divergent visions of the best path to take and "good" and "bad" could overlap, as some intellectuals simultaneously implemented and undermined the policies of the communist state. It may well make political or moral sense to select out certain aspects of this story for public consumption and even to promote specific policies in response to them. But it makes no historical sense at all.

National Heroes – Or Traitors? Debating Intellectuals' Postwar Choices

When Soviet-backed Polish communists claimed power from behind Red Army lines in the summer of 1944, among them were a handful of prominent intellectuals, primarily writers. Months before the liberation of Warsaw and other major Polish cities, these men – Julian Przyboś, Adam Ważyk, Mieczysław Jastruń, Jerzy Putrament, Jerzy Borejsza, to name but a few – began creating the institutions that would dominate postwar Poland's cultural sphere, including the Ministry for Culture and the Arts, the writers' union (Związek Zawodowy Literatów Polskich, ZZLP), the major cultural journal *Rebirth* (*Odrodzenie*), and the state publishing house Czytelnik (Fik 1989, pp. 12–20). Were these intellectuals the heroic restorers of Polish statehood, culture and identity? Or were they the handmaidens of Soviet leaders determined to deprive Poland of its political, cultural, and spiritual future (and past as well)? Today, more than fifteen years after the collapse of communism in east central Europe, debates continue over essentially these same questions: "Why did intellectuals support communism?" and "To what extent should we hold them responsible for helping to impose and/or perpetuate a system we now agree was coercive and corrupt?"

Even before 1989, public interest in intellectuals' (and others') responsibility for communism was high.[7] Czesław Miłosz was among the first to raise the issue in his 1951 publication *The Captive Mind*, which sought to explain to Western readers why writers like him had embraced the "New Faith" of Soviet-supervised state socialism. He wrote of the void intellectuals felt in the absence of an overarching explanatory system (which had been supplied by religion in the pre-modern period); of the need to feel accepted by the masses and to play an active part in History's (with a capital "H") inexorable march forward; of the fears of being on the wrong side of History and of being relegated to the country's literary sidelines; of the horrors of the occupation and the resulting collapse of moral authority; of fatalism in the face of the "East's" geopolitical power and disappointment with the complacency and "tawdry" consumerism of the "West" (Miłosz 1990 [1951], pp. 3–53). Though fully aware of "Russia's" and "the Method's" shortcomings, Miłosz, like many of his colleagues, saw no viable alternative. "I agreed to serve", he writes in the preface to *The Captive Mind*, "not for material reasons, but through conviction" (Miłosz 1990 [1951], p. ix). It didn't take long for Miłosz, who was literally serving the Polish government as a diplomat in Washington and Paris, to realize that the costs were too high, and in early 1951, he gave up his Polish citizenship and, for all he knew at the time, his ability to reach a Polish audience with his poetry. (In fact, he was able to reach probably tens of thousands through underground publications before his work was published officially in Poland in 1981, the first time since the early 1950s.) *The Captive Mind* is a warning and an accusation, but Miłosz judges the system far more harshly than the individuals caught up in it. "It is not my place to judge", he writes of the author Jerzy Andrzejewski (dubbed "Alpha" in the book). "I myself traveled the same road of seeming inevitability" (Miłosz 1990 [1951], p. 109).

Throughout his long life, Miłosz earned praise from Western critics for his poetry and his uncompromising opposition to communist rule, but some of his exiled compatriots criticized *The Captive Mind* and its emphasis on communism's ideological appeal as exculpatory. Most vociferous among them was writer and Soviet gulag survivor Gustaw Herling-Grudziński, who insisted that intellectuals' own "fears, stupidity, and depravity" rather than any sort of "Hegelian bite", as Miłosz had put it, were to blame (Herling-Grudziński 1990, p. 192; cited in Słabek 1997, p. 10). By implication, intellectuals with moral integrity were those who refused to cooperate with Poland's communist authorities on any level, whether from exile or inside the country. Far better to make one's living by repairing shoes, one exiled writer wrote in his journal, than to accept a part in Poland's official cultural sphere (Lechoń 1992, p. 288; cited in Słabek 1997, p. 10).[8]

Jacek Trznadel, one of the earliest and most cited voices in the post-1989 debates on intellectuals and communism, echoed Herling-Grudziński's condemnatory tone. Trznadel published a series of interviews with writers – some former communists, some not – titled *A Domestic Disgrace*, which left little room for doubt about his determination to pass judgment. (Trznadel's book had been circulating underground since 1986, but it was reissued in 1990 and quickly became a central reference point in the debates.[9]) When speaking with his subjects, Trznadel's tone is relatively neutral, and the interviews reveal a range of motivations, from fear to naive optimism, the lack of clear alternatives (particularly among young intellectuals), the lure of ideology and self-deception. But in a lengthy introduction, and in an afterword published in the mid-1990s, Trznadel shifts from interlocutor to judge. In articulating his central question – "Why did so many of Poland's literary elite, at a particular moment, embrace an intellectual position that was false, a disgrace, and [aimed at] the annihilation of [our] literature?" – he dismisses communist ideology as not just deceptive or illusory, but worthless and wrong (Trznadel 1994, p. 7). Not surprisingly, then, he has little but contempt for those who succumbed to it. Collaborating with official institutions and state structures was often a necessity, he acknowledges, but "accepting this new ideology, believing the lies, and supporting them [the lies]" was a disgrace (Trznadel 1994, p. 27).

In Trznadel's view, Miłosz had overemphasized communist ideology's mobilizing power and sidestepped the necessity to "morally judge" and assign "blame" to the individuals who succumbed (Trznadel 1994, p. 293). Trznadel even includes himself, once a young man who had embraced communism as a way to "save the world" – among those to be blamed.[10] Individuals' discomfort, he insists, must take a back seat to "society's historical awareness" and "our obligation to young people" (Trznadel 1994, p. 29). Uncompromising to the end, Trznadel writes that "the historian in me" (he is a literary scholar by training) "does not shrink from revealing names, and my historical philosophy is not free of strong moral judgments". Painful though it is, he insists, societies need to "settle their accounts" with the past (Trznadel 1994, p. 29).[11]

Many other contributors to the debate have followed Trznadel's lead, and even efforts to present nuanced assessments have stumbled over the perceived necessity to morally condemn. One example is a 1999 edition of the Catholic monthly *Znak* (*The Sign*) subtitled "Intellectuals and Communism", which offers a relatively recent overview of the debate. The brief editorial note that opens the volume effectively illustrates the draw, and the drawbacks, of moral condemnation:

> Nearly 10 years have passed since the collapse of communism. Nonetheless, discussions of it – of what the system really was, of its sources, of where to uncover its poisonous legacies and how to defend ourselves against them – have not faded. To the contrary, it seems that only now that the emotions and pain have eased and the political situation has stabilized can rational analysis and neutral assessment prevail.
>
> In taking up the problem of intellectuals' responsibility for communism – or, more broadly, for totalitarianism – we do not aim to vet (*lustrować*) individual life histories or throw around accusations. Passing moral judgment on the intellectuals ["people of culture"] who supported communism in one period or another is an activity that belongs only to these individuals and their consciences. … But taking up the topic "intellectuals and communism" is necessary if we are to build a community of values, culture, and memory. Without this community, the moral foundation of democracy will always be in danger. In asking about intellectuals' entanglement with totalitarianism, then, we are less concerned with the past than with the future … (Turowicz *et al.* 1999, p. 3)

As with so many entries in this debate, the tone here is didactic and the emphasis is on participants' obligation to the future. In spite of insisting that they do *not* intend to judge, moreover, the volume's editors suggest that this is precisely what they have asked contributors to do. That a volume on "intellectuals and communism" might focus on aspects other than intellectuals' *responsibility* for engaging with (and presumably helping impose and perpetuate) communism seems out of the question. That communist Poland was totalitarian (the subject of another post-1989 debate inside Poland) is presumed, and the implication here is that only by understanding totalitarianism's "poison" (past or present) can Polish society move toward a secure democratic future. This amounts, of course, to passing moral judgment on the system. To insist, then, that the individuals who became "entangled" with the system are not being morally judged is disingenuous. In emphasizing both "intellectuals' responsibility for communism" – a system now judged reprehensible in moral as well as practical terms – and their own decision *not* to judge, the editors seem to want to have it both ways.

That moral judgment is the goal here is bolstered by the volume's lead article, in which philosopher Ryszard Legutko sets a sharp tone. It was intellectuals' faith in humanism's power to topple the status quo combined with their fascination (and need) for radical change and revolution, Legutko writes, which led to "a certain kind of blindness" and "allowed them to ignore the evils of the new system" (Legutko 1999, pp. 6–10). Though they cannot be blamed for *not opposing* communism and not being heroes – that accusation could be levelled against all members of society – they can and should be blamed for their "public and long-standing approbation". Intellectuals "should have been able to see more clearly and accurately than others", he writes, and "there's something puzzling in the fact" that they so easily "surrendered to such compromising illusions" (Legutko 1999, p. 5). That intellectuals believed they were building a genuinely humanist system is no excuse, Legutko insists, because in the process they convinced so many others to follow their lead. Official propaganda was much easier to ignore than that linked to a well known artist, writer or academic (Legutko 1999, pp. 17, 18).[12]

Of the eight *Znak* contributors who follow Legutko, four concur with his approach and moral judgments, adding their own views on the "why intellectuals supported communism" question. One focuses on intellectuals' desire for prestige and their "infatuation with communism as a 'prime mover'" (Roszkowski 1999); others consider the metaphysical aspects of communist ideology and their attraction (Bieńkowska 1999), intellectuals' perceptions of the socio-economic and cultural limitations of liberal capitalism (Prokop 1999), and the potent mixture of "radicalized Enlightenment" and anti-rightist views (Gawin 1999). A fifth author (Życiński 1999) criticizes what he sees as efforts to *avoid* passing judgment, particularly academics' efforts to "banalize evil". In their insistence that Poland's communist past is too complex to distinguish the "sheep" from the "goats" and that different "levels of responsibility" must be applied, he writes, these scholars seek to "neutralize uncomfortable ethical questions and present a 'sheep-goat' hybrid as the greatest zoological achievement of the communist period" (Życiński 1999, pp. 91, 92).[13] Two-thirds of the entries in the *Znak* volume, then, echo Trznadel's early calls for condemnation.

There have been dissenting voices, among them Henryk Słabek, who insists that intellectuals should be judged favourably rather than condemned. In a 1997 book titled *Intellectuals in Their Own Words*, Słabek drew on journals, memoirs and letters to remind his audience that many intellectuals had good reasons for doing what they did after 1945, at least in their own minds (Słabek 1997).[14] He cites their frustrations with rightist governments and nationalists in the interwar period, agonized reactions to the Warsaw uprising of August 1944, and optimism at the war's end. He also lists by name the dozens of writers who supported socialist parties and agendas before the war, as well as those who returned to Poland from exile in London, and he includes several passages in which writers muse on the extent to which social justice is fundamental to both communism and Catholicism (Słabek 1997, p. 61).[15] Surely these intellectuals, he suggests, cannot be categorized as communist stooges and moral cowards.

Though Słabek is clearly criticizing the Trznadel "school" of moral condemnation, he is just as eager to judge his subjects. Writers, he insists, and "especially eminent ones, have an inalienable right to carry out their profession as they see fit", and they should be judged not just according to their political relations with the state or authorities, but on the cultural merits of their work ((Słabek 1997, p. 98). At the very end of the book, Słabek draws a parallel between the intellectuals he discusses and late nineteenth-century intellectuals in Russian Poland, who eschewed armed insurrection in favour of "organic work" and cooperation with the Russian authorities. "What are we to do with our home-grown 'collaborators' and 'lice' [a reference to a 1979 underground publication critical of cooperative intellectuals]", he asks? "Perhaps we should simply recognize them as positive 'organic' activists (*pozytywnych organiczników*)? After all, did they betray the noble ethos of the intelligentsia? They struggled to make it reality, helping in the process to develop the country between 1945 and

1989" (Słabek 1997, p. 209). Rather than dismissing intellectuals as cowards, Słabek is arguing, Poles should add them to their pantheon of national heroes. Perhaps because Słabek stands so far to the "anti-condemnatory" end of the spectrum, or perhaps because his book can be read as unapologetically "pro-communist", it is rarely invoked in the debates.

There have also been proponents of a middle ground approach to the intellectuals-and-communism debate. Hanna Świda-Ziemba's (1989) "Stalinism and Polish Society" is perhaps the best early example. Like Trznadel's work, Świda-Ziemba's appeared before communism's collapse, but it quickly became a reference point in the debates about intellectuals and communism (though her analysis concerns Polish society as a whole rather than just intellectuals). Her emphasis is on the complex pressures that pushed Poles toward accepting communism (fear, destruction of social ties, war fatigue, early postwar optimism, the struggle for material well-being), as well as the mechanisms that enabled them to survive it with their "identity and dignity" intact (demarcating limits on conformism, focusing inward on family and friends, establishing links with those who were "party members but decent people" (*partyjni ale porządni*).[16] Though lumping intellectuals with opportunists, prewar leftist radicals, and those looking for social advancement as the system's "creators", she nonetheless attempts to dispel the "myth" that all intellectuals supported Stalinism, insisting that "primarily writers and a portion of young intellectuals" were at fault (Świda-Ziemba 1989, pp. 24, 26).[17] Before we can condemn, Świda-Ziemba is arguing, we need to know exactly who supported communism, why they did so and whether they remained "decent" in the process.

This is not to suggest Świda-Ziemba does not want to judge. "I am not letting go of the category of *responsibility*", she writes; "Every creator of the system, including those at the rank-and-file level, is at fault and is *deeply* responsible to society" (Świda-Ziemba 1989, p. 93). Yet she qualifies this accusation, reserving her harshest judgment for those who "*accepted an ideology* that sanctions violence against society" and believed they had the right to impose it. Toward the "party members but decent people", she is even ready to show "a certain tolerance". Given their "false consciousness", she explains, these individuals "accepted the ideology of force as a 'historical necessity'", but "in their actions, they treated it as an *evil* that needed to be moderated (*łagodzić*)" (Świda-Ziemba 1989, pp. 94, 95).[18] Not all of communism's "creators", Świda-Ziemba concludes, can be treated, or judged, equally.

More recently, a small handful of scholars have looked beyond the complexities of judging intellectuals' past engagement with communism to question the very act of judging and the selective narratives it produces. Most vocal among them has been historian and sociologist Jerzy Szacki, who, in a gesture tinged with weariness and dismissal, titled his contribution to the 1999 *Znak* volume "It's Those Horrible Intellectuals Again" (Szacki 1999).[19] What, he wonders in this piece, are critics like Legutko and Trznadel really after? Is the goal to delineate the societal and ethical parameters within which all intellectuals should work, insisting that they rise above the "dirty" realms of ideology and politics? Or is it to chastise intellectuals for making the wrong political choice? "In condemning them", he asks, "are we saying that there are certain things intellectuals should never do, or are we simply saying that it's a mistake to have anything to do with communism?" (Szacki 1999, p. 24). Szacki questions not just debate participants' motives, but also the extent to which their judgments are historically tenable, and here he shares the concerns of historian Marcin Kula and the well known theologian, philosopher, and priest Józef Tischner (Kula 1999; Tischner 1999).

Collectively, these scholars point to the difficulties of generalizing, the limitations of anachronistic approaches, and a misplaced emphasis on where individuals have gone wrong rather than on what they have accomplished. Communism was just one of three major ideologies in play in 1945, Tischner writes, alongside nationalist-independence and Catholic-religious ones. Divisions between and among proponents of these ideologies posed genuine dilemmas at the time, as one group's (or faction's) hero became another's villain. "What was more heroic", Tischner asks: "to believe in war and take to the forests to prepare for victory", as did part of the armed nationalist underground, or to follow the lead of others in the movement and "believe in the 'bolsheviks'' democratic intentions, working with the new government to rebuild the country?" (Tischner 1999, p. 43). Both were bona fide choices for individuals at the time, Tischner argues, and to anachronistically insist that only a single position was the "correct" one makes little sense. Tischner also stresses, along with Szacki, that intellectuals' accomplishments as well as mistakes must be acknowledged. In coming to terms with communism, he writes, we must recognize individuals' "gradual maturation" toward "freedom from communism":

> It's really not interesting that someone who has barely reached adulthood has written a poem about Stalin. What's interesting is that this individual never wrote another poem like it. How did it happen that after an initial period of enslavement, freedom took hold? Today's anti-communist, who demands that we fix our gaze on various "domestic disgraces", is not so different from the communist who in precisely the same manner demanded we focus on the "reactionary deviations" of [authors like] Zygmunt Krasiński, Stefan Żeromski, or Henryk Sienkiewicz. (Tischner 1999, p. 51; see also Szacki 1999, p. 29)

As Tischner and Szacki see it, some critics' urge to judge intellectuals' worst has led them not only to ignore the past's multilayered reality, but to fall into the trap of dogmatism – much as they accuse intellectuals of doing.

The *Znak* volume's "dissenters" also highlight the difficulties of judging intellectuals who were *simultaneously* "good" and "bad". Most people, as Szacki puts it, cannot be tagged with a "single, ready-made label" (Szacki 1991, p. 404). Kula also notes that while it is always possible to find "out-and-out bastards", it is much harder to judge those who "straddled both sides, lighting candles for the good Lord and cigarette butts for the devil". Like it or not, Kula claims, these people were "us": "I didn't like them – but a huge proportion of society (which means all of us) acted more or less in this fashion for years. And moreover, regardless of whether I liked them or not, thanks to them – to the conscious among them who worked inside the system's orbit – Poland ended up in better shape than, say, Bulgaria." Reminding readers that the generation which led to the events of 1989 was educated by such "straddlers", Kula concludes that "the results of their [straddlers'] actions were not the worst, in the end" (Kula 1999, p. 83).

Concerns like these have hardly put an end to the debate on Poland's intellectuals and communism, and it is unlikely that they will, given continuing efforts to politicize and morally judge the past.[20] Debates will continue, and the questions "why did they do it?" and "how do we judge them?" will no doubt remain central. But as these scholars point out, perhaps there are two other questions every participant should have to answer as well: "*why* do we judge as we do?" and "*can* we judge at all?"

Beyond Moral Dichotomies: The Good–Bad Intellectual

My own work on visual artists in early postwar Kraków raises these same questions, and highlights the retrospective quandary of assessing intellectuals who were simultaneously "good" and "bad". I would like to share a case study that reveals the fine and often-crossed line between collaborating with the communist regime and resisting it. It concerns the painter Jonasz Stern (1904–1988), an avant-garde artist who believed passionately that a communist political and social system and abstractionism in art were good for postwar Poland. When it became clear in the late 1940s that the two could not easily coexist, his convictions did not change. What did change was the tension between his priorities as an engaged communist and those of a committed artist. As we will see, he fought to articulate and protect both.

Stern's story raises two important questions that cannot be considered here in depth but that nonetheless deserve mention. The first of these is the division between "political" and "cultural" intellectuals (a distinction Słabek raises in his discussion of writers). As described by Jerzy Szacki, the political intellectual is embodied by the "professor, writer or artist, who signs appeals, protests and manifestos, speaks his mind in public on every more or less important occasion, participates in congresses, expresses his concern for the fate of humanity, goes on 'political pilgrimage', etc." (1990, p. 232). By contrast, the cultural intellectual need not play a public political role. Instead, "[t]he quality of being an intellectual is ascribed ... because of what he does as a writer, philosopher, scholar or artist. If any question of leadership is involved, his right to it is based on this 'normal' activity and not public acts of another kind" (Szacki 1990, p. 243). A critical factor here, as Szacki explains, is the different assumptions about the intellectual's responsibility:

> In the one case responsibility is essentially identical with *political involvement*, with coming out of "laboratories and libraries", and in the second it consists primarily in absolutely loyalty to oneself and to values that determine the identity of literature, science, art, philosophy, etc. The political intellectual feels responsible for the entire world; the cultural intellectual feels responsible for his own field, dealing with other fields only in so far as they have direct consequences in the sphere of culture values. (Szacki 1990, 235)[21]

Szacki focuses his attention on the increasing politicization of culture in the twentieth century, noting that totalitarian regimes in particular have deprived intellectuals of their ability to refrain from political engagement: "Either one accepts the imposed ideological norms and, under pressure of circumstances, adopts the career of political intellectual" – losing one's intellectual autonomy in the process – "or one sticks heroically to one's opinions and thereby moves into some form of political opposition in spite of oneself" (Szacki 1990, p. 244). Stern never shied from his role as a political intellectual. At the same time, however, he defended his own aesthetic agenda and the intellectual autonomy of artists, much as a "cultural" intellectual would. His story highlights the growing politicization of art – but also the limits to which such politicization could go.

An additional question raised by Stern's story is the extent to which the vocation of the intellectual, and debates about intellectuals' responsibilities, include visual artists. There can be no doubt that artists served alongside writers as national standard bearers in the nineteenth century: the painter Jan Matejko (alluded to in the first paragraph), who used his enormous historical canvases to fan Polish nationalist fires far beyond the confines of gallery walls, is but one example.[22] Nor can there be any question that Stern felt the same sense of mission that writers did in the twentieth century, or that he sought to act on it. As a group, writers were the first and most eager to embrace communist rule after 1945, and it was writers like Miłosz and Herling-Grudziński who were quickest to condemn them. Post-1989 debates have also focused on, and been charted by, writers. Yet these facts say more about artistic media (after all, writers live to write and to disseminate their words as widely as possible) and the audiences for them (it is much easier to read an article than parse abstract paintings in a gallery) than about the nature or endeavours of the archetypal "intellectual". Stern certainly saw himself as an engaged intellectual, and so did his contemporaries. We should see him the same way.

Visual artists in postwar Poland had more room for manoeuvre than writers, given the less "literal" nature of the language they employed, and particularly in the realm of the visual arts, a "communist" agenda for art emerged slowly and haltingly. Nonetheless, by the late 1940s, it was increasingly difficult for Polish artists to side-step politics or the policies enacted by state officials. For years before 1949, some artists had publicly debated the merits, or lack thereof, of "tangible" and "engaged" realism, but from June 1949, the debate was cut short. That month, state officials arrived at the artist union's annual conference with a list of socialist realist guidelines. Art now had to be

> first: realistic – offering a typical view of reality. Second: comprehensible – presenting reality which is compatible with common sense and the laws of physics. Third: creative – presenting a complete picture of life in keeping with the artist's creative vision, a vision which is based on society's labors; it thus cannot be [merely] a lifeless photograph of reality. Fourth: social – serving society, mobilizing its consciousness [with regard] to the struggle and to work. (cited in Fijałkowska 1985, p. 113)

As envisioned and implemented by Polish state and communist party officials, of course, socialist realism was both an exhortation (to harness one's skills and ambitions to the "socialization" of art) and a warning (of what would happen to those who did not fall in line). It was art-as-mandate, a programme in which artists were to serve actively the building of socialism and a socialist society.

State officials' socialist realist expectations could not easily penetrate the private world of artists' studios, but they had a lock on public art life – at least in theory. Yet as the story which follows reveals, theory and practice were quite different things. Artists had no choice but to follow policy guidelines, and some – including Stern – even helped implement these policies. At the same time, they found surprising ways to manoeuvre and even resist aesthetic norms such policies demanded. Their experiences on both sides of the collaboration–resistance spectrum confirm that categorical efforts to judge are doomed, if not to failure, then to inaccuracy.

When Stern came to Kraków in 1928 to study art from his home in an east Galician *shtetl*, he brought his sympathies for communism with him. He helped create the interwar *Grupa Krakowska*, an avant-garde artistic group, and participated actively in the city's left-leaning political life until the outbreak of World War II. Narrowly escaping death at Nazi hands in Lwów in 1943, he found temporary refuge in Hungary, and returned to Kraków in 1945. In the artistic realm, Stern soon joined the ranks of Kraków's postwar avant-garde, as one of only two members of the *Grupa Młodych* (Group of Young [Artists]) old enough to have exhibited before the war.[23] Drawing on the rich traditions of interwar avant-garde movements in Poland and abroad, these artists devoted the early postwar years to ridiculing prominent post-impressionists' "sterile academicism"[24] and formulating an abstraction-based vision of what art and artists should be.[25] As Grupa Młodych artists saw it, art was not about celebrating beauty or even enjoying recognition, but about struggling for what was right and teaching viewers to see and to appreciate all that was most "modern".

For Stern, this aesthetic vision melded perfectly with his commitment to political activism. He had been a member of the Polish Communist Party (Polska Partia Robotnicza, PPR) in the interwar period, but after 1945 he redoubled his efforts. He helped form a PPR-sponsored local "artists' circle" in late 1945, and was also a member of an "Artists' Subcommittee" affiliated with the party's Central Committee in Warsaw. In the local circle, he and other members challenged union rules on the distribution of relief packages and countryside retreats, wrote exhibit reviews for local newspapers (and demanded byline credit for the PPR group in exchange), volunteered to serve on election commissions, helped plan a national gathering of leftist artists, and agreed to act as an intermediary and arrange a meeting between local union officials and premier Edward Osóbka-Morawski in an effort to increase state subsidies for artists.[26]

In the late 1940s, the artistic and political possibilities for artist-activists like Stern seemed endless, and he found time for both, producing cubist and abstract works as well as "metaphorical" drawings that suggest movement and an almost musical cacophony of lines and forms. When a new member of the local PPR artists' circle wondered aloud whether his party activities might not interfere with his art, Stern reassured him that "working 'for ourselves' artistically, we are also working for the party … one can perfectly well reconcile, and even connect, political work within the [PPR] circle with one's own artistic work" (cited in Świca 1991).[27] Stern's political convictions and his commitment to public involvement in artists' institutions remained firm even after socialist realist dictates in mid-1949. From early 1951, he served on the artists' union board, as secretary of the "basic party organization".[28] In addition, he became the manager of the union's "artistic club" in August 1951, played a central role in the union's "ideological training" programme, and from September 1952 lectured at the art academy in the set design division (he took on the position of assistant rector [prorektor] in September 1954).[29]

Perhaps surprisingly, given Stern's unwavering commitment to official political life after 1949, he refused to embrace or support the *aesthetic* requirements of the period. Indeed, he virtually disappeared from public artistic life between 1949 and 1956. He participated only at the third of the four all-Poland exhibits (December 1952–February 1953), where he exhibited two monotypes titled "The Construction Site" (*budowa*). The first of these (Figure 1) offers a relatively standard view of a building site, with a pile of logs in the foreground opening to reveal a view of a cityscape-in-process. In the distance but at the centre of the canvas, a huge crane towers over the still-incomplete buildings. There are people at work in this image – in the foreground, a small man off to one side pushes several upright logs (suspended by a crane which we cannot see) into place, and tiny figures move about in the middle plane as well – but they are nearly stick-like in their simplicity and come into view only slowly, after the viewer has digested the more complexly rendered logs, buildings and crane.

If this seems a relatively standard rendition of a construction site, the second of Stern's all-Poland prints (Figure 2) is anything but.[30] Here, the logs have become a staircase that leads up to a platform, on which a tall, totem-like form stands. The context and long-distance perspective of the first image are gone, and except for wood grain on some of the surrounding supports and the upper portion of a ladder in the background, this could be an up-close rendering of a temple rather than a construction site. The tall form at the centre of the image echoes the vertical logs of the previous image, caught by a crescent-moon shaped hook and in the process of being hoisted by the invisible crane, but this shared construction site iconography only further highlights the differences between the prints. Without the first image as a point of reference, the centrepiece of the second one is virtually unrecognizable.

FIGURE 1
Jonasz Stern, "The Construction Site" ("Budowa"), 1952. With permission of Muzeum Narodowe, Warsaw.

Rather than a hook, pulleys and cables, the viewer sees a geometric abstraction which draws the eyes up toward an ethereal sky and seems to promise an experience more mystical than concrete.

Stern's second image echoes the atmosphere and even some of the shapes of a "metaphorical" work he had produced two years earlier (Figure 3; note the cube-topped tower and the sharp swooping forms), this one combining his earlier upswing of movement with what look like the metal booms of a crane. But even if both images contain (disembodied) parts from industrial equipment, neither comes close to canonical socialist realism. That Stern's first construction site print seems to be the only "realistic" image he displayed during these years suggests both that he had chosen to resist socialist realist aesthetics and that he had largely succeeded in doing so.[31] Did this make him a persona non grata? Apparently not, as in May 1953, he won "state recognition" (*odznaczenie panstwowe*) for his work, and a month later he received a state prize from the Ministry of Culture and the Arts. The ministry's award recognized both Stern's "artistic" and "social" activities, which in light of his "outsider" status as an artist at the time seems rather odd. Given Stern's political activities and sacrifices on behalf of the communist cause, however, it was perhaps fairly easy to gloss over potential problems. Though supporting documents note that Stern had helped

FIGURE 2
Jonasz Stern, "The Construction Site" ("Budowa"), 1952. Reproduced in Chrobak and Świca (1999, p. 266). With permission of Barbara Jaroszyńska-Stern.

create the prewar Grupa Krakowska, they say nothing about the kind of art this group produced. As for Stern's artistic activities after 1945, the documents say only that "since 1945, he has taken part in exhibits, and at the Third All-Poland Exhibit received an honorable mention".[32] Stern's decision to publicly display two works titled "The Construction Site" – even if one looked nothing like it was supposed to – was perhaps the best party officials could hope for.

From the post-1989 vantage point, compromise – "straddling both sides" – can easily seem the equivalent of selling out. Stern, however, seems to have viewed compromise as a way to *avoid* selling out and to retain at least part of what mattered most. His story illuminates the extent to which even intellectuals who took clear positions at one end of the political spectrum could end up at the opposite end of the cultural one, as well as the complexities and fluid boundaries of intellectuals' everyday life during the Stalinist years.

Stern worked closely with state and party officials, helping to implement the political and cultural policies they decreed. At the same time, he stretched the boundaries of and

FIGURE 3
Jonasz Stern, Untitled, about 1950. Reproduced in Chrobak and Świca (1999, p. 267). With permission of Barbara Jaroszyńska-Stern.

even defied those policies, in an effort to protect his aesthetic and intellectual autonomy. Did he "collaborate" with the communist system? Clearly yes. Did he "resist" it? Just as clearly, yes. What does this mean in terms of the "urge to judge"? Are we to condemn artists like Stern because they helped *im*pose coercive policies or praise them for their efforts to *op*pose them? And where are we left if the answer to both questions is "yes"?

NOTES

1. I am thinking in particular of philosopher and educational reformer Hugo Kołłątaj (1750–1812), poet Adam Mickiewicz (1798–1855), novelist Henryk Sienkiewicz (1846–1916), painter Jan Matejko (1838–1893), historians Jacek Kuroń (1934–2004) and Adam Michnik (born 1946), and dissident publicist Tadeusz Mazowiecki (born 1927).
2. On the difference between "intellectuals" and "the intelligentsia", which Aleksander Gella sees as a distinct and historically constructed "social formation", see Gella (1976, pp. 19–23). Since I consider the post-1945 intellectuals I am discussing in this article closely linked to the nineteenth-century intelligentsia in terms of their sense of national/universal mission, I use the terms interchangeably.
3. Poland's lustration law was passed only in 1997 after more than a decade of heated debate. It stipulates that candidates for public office must publicly acknowledge whether or not they collaborated with the communist-era secret police. There is no sanction if they did, but if a candidate is found to have lied, s/he may be removed from office. For an overview of Poland's lustration tribulations, see Grzelak (2005).
4. IPN's full name is Instytut Pamięci Narodowej – Komisja Ścigania Zbrodni przeciwko Narodowi Polskiemu, or Institute for National Memory: Committee for the Prosecution of Crimes against the Polish Nation. It was created by an act of parliament in December 1998. See www.ipn.gov.pl.

5. See Subotić and Stankiewicz (2005). The IPN's own statute noted that if secret police or other archival materials showed that an individual had collaborated with communist-era secret police, s/he could not be appointed as director. But the document in question had not come from the secret police archives: it was a former secret policeman's 1990 description of the work he had done in early 1989, which he submitted to a verification commission with his application for employment in a post-communist security organization. The verification commission's documentation then found its way into the IPN archives in 2001. IPN director Leon Kieres and other prominent members argued that this meant Przewoźnik could be approved as director, but the head of the IPN's judicial committee (kolegium) disagreed and refused to accept Przewoźnik as a formal candidate. The position of IPN director was not one covered by the lustration law, but Przewoźnik was eager to clear his name and appealed to the lustration court to hear his case. It did, and ruled in his favour on 28 November 2005. See Czuchnowski's articles (2005a, 2005b, 2005c).
6. Since it would be virtually impossible to assess (or even uncover) every published entry in the debate, I have focused on a handful of the most discussed books and a 1999 special edition of the Catholic journal *The Sign* (*Znak*), which provides a particularly illuminating overview of the key issues. For reprints of representative press articles published between 1989 and 1999, see Śpiewak (2000).
7. See Torańska (1987) for a series of 1981 interviews with communist party functionaries that is scathing in its tone. It is a good example of the Solidarity generation's eagerness to condemn previous generations' engagement with the communist state.
8. See Słabek (1997, pp. 9–16) for a brief overview of London emigré writers' critiques and of the less categorical position adopted by exiled writers in Paris, grouped around Jerzy Giedroyć's publication *Kultura*.
9. The first above-ground Polish edition was published in Lublin by Test (1990).
10. See the autobiographical section of his introduction (Trznadel 1994, pp. 11–21). Curiously, Trznadel's reliance on third-person and impersonal grammatical forms suggests he's not entirely willing to shoulder the blame. "They" shouldn't have done what they did, Trznadel says again and again, but he refrains from saying "we".
11. He presents "the Germans" as the model of a society which has accounted for its past, and "the Russians" as the archetype for one which has not (see Trznadel 1994, pp. 28, 29, 295).
12. Legutko also dismisses both Miłosz's and Herling-Grudziński's analyses. If "intellectual mistakes" were responsible for intellectuals' engagement, he writes of *The Captive Mind*, then "it would be natural to expect the correction of these mistakes", that is, a serious attempt at reflection on the part of most intellectuals (p. 19). "That this has not happened, one can surmise, means that Polish intellectuals either do not agree" with Miłosz's thesis "or have not yet understood the nature of their mistakes" (p. 19). Herling-Grudziński's hypothesis of fear and character flaws, on the other hand, seems to Legutko to inaccurately minimize the intellectual elements involved (p. 20).
13. Życiński is referring in particular to Andrzej Walicki, whose "sheep and goat" argument he cites earlier; see Walicki (1997).
14. Słabek uses sources from more than eighty intellectuals, and aims for a representative sample of writers, critics and scholars who had been in their twenties and thirties in the late 1940s. About half had been members of the Polish United Workers' Party (PZPR, Polska Zjednoczona Partia Robotnicza) in the 1940s and 1950s, though most left its ranks after 1956. Most were critical toward socialist realism, which state officials sought to impose in 1949; more than a third had spent time in the USSR, most as wartime

deportees and labour camp prisoners; some 70 per cent were well known writers. See Słabek (1997, pp. 5–8).

15. See chapters II, "Refleksja czasów klęski", and III, "Nowa wiara", for more on writers' pre- and early post-1945 positions (Słabek 1997).

16. Świda-Ziemba (1989) discusses pressures on pages 26–43 and coping mechanisms on pages 57–66.

17. Regrettably, Świda-Ziemba offers neither evidence for nor a discussion of this claim. Perhaps because she is a sociologist, her approach to evidence differs from that employed by most historians. As she notes in the first few pages, she draws on her own personal experiences, comments made by people she knows and students she has taught, the observations she has done in schools, factories and worker housing developments, and "chance conversations". She does not comment on any difficulties that her role in producing and/or mediating such evidence might raise.

18. Świda-Ziemba seems to be using "false consciousness" (*zafałszowanej świadomości*) in a purely descriptive way rather than in reference to Marx; she does not use quotation marks, and I see no touch of irony in her phrasing.

19. See also Szacki (1990, 1991).

20. Such efforts are visible in many realms of everyday life. To cite but one small example, a recently published book on the communist period aimed at a popular audience carries the following title: *Communism in Poland: Betrayal, Crime, Lie, Enslavement.* The entire narrative revolves around the communists' repression of the Poles, and ends with a chapter devoted to the "post-communists" of the 1990s. The last page features a photograph of Polish president Aleksander Kwaśniewski (president from 1995 to 2005) warmly embracing Russian president Vladimir Putin. As the book jacket notes, the book was clearly "written with passion" – perhaps too much. See Bernacki *et al.* (2005).

21. Here Szacki refers readers to T. S. Eliot's essay "The Man of Letters and the Future of Europe", in Huszar (1960, pp. 256–260).

22. Matejko aimed his 1883 painting of King Sobieski's 1683 victory over the Ottoman Turks at Vienna at an international audience. Exhibiting the painting first in Vienna, Matejko then donated it to Pope Leo XII, on behalf of the Polish nation. See Dabrowski (2004, pp. 59, 60, 70–72). Dabrowski also chronicles the impact of a musician-intellectual in the early twentieth century, the great pianist Ignacy Paderewski (2004, pp. 165–173).

23. For more on Stern, see the catalogues from two retrospectives (Świca 1997; Nowaczyk 2005).

24. Kraków's post-impressionists were the Kapists, so named because of their prewar experiences in Paris (Kapist is derived from Komitet Paryski, or Paris Committee). They controlled the postwar artists' union, a major artistic monthly and Kraków's art academy.

25. For more on the Grupa Młodych, see Chrobak and Świca (1999, 2000). See also Czerni, based on interviews with the Grupa Młodych's theoretician, Mieczysław Porębski (Czerni & Porębski 1992). The Grupa Młodych held its last exhibit in December 1948–January 1949, but it was revived in 1957 as the Grupa Krakowska (II), an informal artistic alliance which continues to exist today.

26. These activities are described in a number of Artists' Circle protocols that are reproduced in Świca (1991). Józef Chrobak received the originals years ago from group members and holds them in the Grupa Krakowska's archive. There is no trace of Artists' Circle documents in the regional party or city archives, or in the Warsaw archival holdings on the PPR artists' committee.

27. The document in question is "Protokół z posiedzenia koła Plastyków PPR 23 XI 1946 r", reproduced in Świca (1991).

28. Stern joined the board in February 1951; see Archiwum Państwowe w Krakowie (APKr), Związek Polskich Artystów Plastycznych (ZPAP), folder 33: "Posiedzenie Zarządu 20 II 1951". The basic party organizations (Podstawowa Organizacja Partyjna, POP) were the lowest-ranking organizational "cells" in the party-state system. They were nearly ubiquitous in the 1950s, attached not just to factory workshops and service professions, but to theatres, universities, and, as this case reveals, professional unions.
29. See APKr, ZPAP, folder 33: "Protokól z Walnego Zebrania Okręgu Związku P.A.P. w Krakowie z dnia 6. V. 1950 r"; APKr, ZPAP, folder 33: "Posiedzenie Zarządu, 19 I 1950"; APKr, ZPAP, folder 34: "Posiedzenie prezydium w dn. 8 kwietnia br. [1953]".
30. Special thanks to Barbara Jaroszyńska-Stern, Jonasz Stern's widow, for permission to reproduce the images here as Figures 2 and 3.
31. In a 1988 interview, shortly before he died, Stern looked back on the early 1950s only reluctantly, saying the period belonged to the past and he preferred not to return to it. He also claimed that "I never broke down and I never painted tractor drivers or labor heroes." Though correct on this count (he had not mentioned construction sites), Stern also insisted he had been able to work at the art academy only after Stalin's death, which was not accurate. See Stern (1988, p. 41; cited in Chrobak & Świca 2000, p. 262).
32. See the documents in Stern's union personnel file, APKr, ZPAP, folder: Akta Personalne 2.

REFERENCES

ARCHIWUM PAŃSTWOWE W KRAKOWIE (APKr), Związek Polskich Artystów Plastycznych (ZPAP), folders 33, 34, Akta Personalne 2.

BERNACKI, W., GŁĘBOCKI, H., KORKUĆ, M., MUSIAL, F., SZAREK, J. & ZBLEWSKI, Z. (2005) *Komunizm w Polsce: zrada, zbrodnia, zaklamanie, zniewolenie*, Wydawnictwo Kluszczyński, Kraków.

BIEŃKOWSKA, E. (1999) 'Cienie w pieczarze', *Znak*, vol. 51, no. 2/525, pp. 30–37.

CHROBAK, J. & ŚWICA, M. (1999) *I Wystawa Sztuki Nowoczesnej: Pięćdźiesiąt lat pózniej*, Gallery Starmach, Kraków.

CHROBAK, J. & ŚWICA, M. (2000) *Nowocześni a socrealizm*, Gallery Starmach, Kraków.

CZERNI, K. & PORĘBSKI, M. (1992) *Nie tylko o sztuce. Rozmowy z profesorem Mieczysławem Porębskim*, Wydawnictwo DolnoŚląskie, Wrocław.

CZUCHNOWSKI, W. (2005a) 'Kapral Kosiba donosi na Przewoznika', *Gazeta Wyborcza*, 6 July, p. 5.

CZUCHNOWSKI, W. (2005b) 'Przewoznik nie był agentem SB', *Gazeta Wyborcza*, 30 November, p. 4.

CZUCHNOWSKI, W. (2005c) 'Utrącenie Przewoznika', *Gazeta Wyborcza*, 7 July, p. 3.

DABROWSKI, P. (2004) *Commemorations and the Shaping of Modern Poland*, Indiana University Press, Bloomington/Indianapolis.

FIJALKOWSKA, B. (1985) *Polityka i twórcy, 1948–1959*, Wydawnictwo Naukowe, Warszawa.

FIK, M. (1989) *Kultura polska po Jalcie*, Polonia, London.

GAWIN, D. (1999) 'Obsesje rozumu', *Znak*, vol. 51, no. 2/525, pp. 68–80.

GELLA, A. (1976) 'An introduction to the sociology of the intelligentsia', in *The Intelligentsia and the Intellectuals: Theory, Method and Case Study*, ed. A. Gella, Sage Publications Inc., Beverly Hills, CA, pp. 9–34.

GELLA, A. (1989) *Development of Class Structure in Eastern Europe: Poland & Her Southern Neighbors*, State University of New York Press, Albany.

GIEDROYĆ, J., ed. *Kultura*, Instytut Literacki, Paris (published 1947–2000).

GRZELAK, P. (2005) *Wojna o lustrację*, Trio, Warszawa.

HERLING-GRUDZIŃSKI, G. (1990) *Dziennik pisany nocą 1973–1979*, Respublica, Warszawa.

HUSZAR, G. B. DE (ed.) (1960) *The Intellectuals: A Controversial Portrait*, Allen & Unwin, London.

INSTYTUT PAMIĘCI NARODOWEJ – KOMISJA ŚCIGANIA ZBRODNI PRZECIWKO NARODOWI POLSKIEMU, http://www.ipn.gov.pl/ (accessed 1 March 2006).

JEDLICKI, J. (1990) 'Holy ideals and prosaic life, or the devil's alternatives', in *Polish Paradoxes,* eds S. Gomułka & A. Polonsky, Routledge, London and New York, pp. 40–61.

JEDLICKI, J. (1995) 'The Polish intelligentsia at the turn of history', in 'Intelligentsia in the interim: Recent experiences from central and eastern Europe', ed. F Björling, *Slavica Lundensia,* vol. 14, pp. 31–42.

KULA, M. (1999) 'Trudny orzech do zgryzienia', *Znak,* vol. 51, no. 2/525, pp. 81–88.

LECHOŃ, J. (1992) *Dziennik,* t. 2, Państwowy Instytut Wydawniczy, Warszawa.

LEGUTKO, R. (1999) 'Intelektualiści i komunizm', *Znak,* vol. 51, no. 2/525, pp. 4–22.

MIŁOSZ, C. (1990 [1951]) *The Captive Mind,* Vintage Books, New York.

NOWACZYK, W. (2005) *Stulecie: Prace Jonasza Sterna (1904–1988) z lat 30.–80.,* Państwowa Galeria Sztuki, Sopot.

PROKOP, J. (1999) 'Klerk i diabeł', *Znak,* vol. 51, no. 2/525, pp. 59–67.

ROSZKOWSKI, W. (1999) '"Półwiedza" i emocje', *Znak,* vol. 51, no. 2/525, pp. 53–58.

SLABEK, H. (1997) *Intelektualistów obraz własny 1944–1989,* Książka i Wiedza, Warszawa.

STERN, J. (1988) 'Rozmowa *Sztuki*: Jonasz Stern', *Sztuka,* 2 excerpted in Chrobak, J. & Świca, M. (2000) *Nowocześni a socrealizm,* Gallery Starmach, Kraków, p. 262.

SUBOTIĆ, M. & STANKIEWICZ, A. (2005) 'Inspektor SB obciąża Przewoźnika', *Rzeczpospolita,* 5 July.

SZACKI, J. (1990) 'Intellectuals between politics and culture', in *The Political Responsibility of Intellectuals,* eds I. MacLean, A. Montefiore & P. Winch, Cambridge University Press, Cambridge/New York, pp. 229–246.

SZACKI, J. (1991) 'Wokół polskiej "zdrady klerków"', in *Dylematy historiografii idei oraz inne szkice i studia,* Wydawnictwo Naukowe PWN, Warszawa, pp. 402–418.

SZACKI, J. (1999) 'Jeszcze raz ci okropni intelektualiści', *Znak,* vol. 51, no. 2/525, pp. 23–29.

ŚPIEWAK, P. (ed.) (2000) *Spór o Polskę 1989–1999. Wybór tekstów prasowych,* Wydawnictwo Naukowe PWN SA, Warszawa.

ŚWICA, M. (1991) *Wybrane problemy z życia środowiska artystycznego Krakowa w latach 1945–1949,* MA thesis, Uniwersytet Jagielloński, Instytut Historii Sztuki, Kraków.

ŚWICA, M. (ed.) (1997), *Jonasz Stern, 1904–1988,* Galeria Starmach, Kraków.

ŚWIDA-ZIEMBA, H. (1989) 'Stalinizm i społeczeństwo polskie', in *Stalinizm,* ed. J. Kurczewski, Instytut Profilaktyki Społecznej i Resocjalizacji UW, Warszawa, pp. 15–95.

TISCHNER, J. (1999) 'Niebiańskie ideały i ziemskie złudzenia', *Znak,* vol. 51, no. 2/525, pp. 38–52.

TORAŃSKA, T. (1987) *Them: Stalin's Polish Puppets,* Harper & Row, New York.

TRZNADEL, J. (1994) *Hańba domowa. Rozmowy z pisarzami,* Agencja Wydawnicz Morex, Warszawa.

TUROWICZ, J. (editor-in-chief) (1999) 'Od redakcji', *Znak,* vol. 51, no. 2/525, p. 3.

WALICKI, A. (1997) 'Moralność polityczna liberalizmu, narodowa moralistyka i idee', *Znak,* vol. 49, 7/506, pp. 21–37.

ŻYCIŃSKI, J. (1999) 'Amnezja czy salonowe tabu?', *Znak,* vol. 51, no. 2/525, pp. 89–95.

INTELLECTUALS AS CULTURAL AGENDA-SETTERS IN THE FEDERAL REPUBLIC?

Rob Burns and **Wilfried van der Will**

The Historical and Theoretical Background to the Role of the Intellectual

Origin, Context and Uses of the Word Intellektueller *in Germany until 1945*

Our basic proposal[1] here is that the role which critical intellectuals fulfil in contemporary society, and the gravity attaching to it, are fundamentally determined by the positions they take up in public life, the discourses they engage in and the agendas they promote. The extent to which they can become agenda-setters either within the political culture or in cultural policy decisively depends on the degree of resonance and respect they command from the general public. In the Anglo-American world it has become customary to designate such figures as "public intellectuals". While in England there are attempts to enhance the role of these, at least within the universities, by making them into objects of institutional study,[2] there have been concerned musings in the United States[3] about the decline of the "public intellectual" in the face of other communicators taking centre-stage: utopian proselytizers, sellers of religious redemption and rapture, fundamentalist ayatollahs, crusaders against evil empires, party ideologues, pseudo-scientific campaigners or dot.com messiahs. It is also argued, however, that now, more than ever, the "public intellectual" is needed, "to puncture the myth-makers ... whether it's those who promise that utopia is just around the corner if we see the total victory of free markets worldwide, or communism worldwide or positive genetic enhancement worldwide, or mouse-manoeuvring democracy worldwide, or any other run-amok enthusiasm" (Elshtain 2001). Within the context of continental European cultures, and in particular that of Germany, the notion of the intellectual often implicitly refers to a figure of such distinct critical status that it renders the epithet "public" redundant. Indeed, during periods of lesser prominence the intelligentsia's "silence" immediately becomes a matter for alarm in the Federal Republic.[4] Intellectuals in a quite specific sense have come to be understood as those who, while enjoying a prominent reputation in their own areas of specialization, have demonstrated the ability to communicate ideas and influence debate outside of it, usually by dissenting or provocative intervention in matters of public concern.

It is therefore not surprising, perhaps, that when the noun *Intellektueller* first entered the German language at the end of the nineteenth century in the wake of the Dreyfus Affair it carried a distinctly defamatory charge. This was due in part to its connotations at the time in the original French, but in the process whereby the word became accepted as a lexical fixture in German it was above all party-political rhetoric which served to reinforce its negative associations. At its annual party conference in Dresden in 1903 the SPD (Social-Democratic Party of Germany) engaged in a three-day debate on the question of academics, in the course of which the party chairman, August Bebel, elicited ecstatic applause when he exhorted the assembled delegates "to take a careful look at every party comrade, but in the case of an academic or an intellectual, don't just look once but twice or three times".[5] Even before this indictment another leading Social Democrat, Karl Kautsky, had likened the intelligentsia's social position to that of the petty bourgeoisie and thus branded intellectuals "fickle and unreliable"[6] in their ideological allegiance, an assessment echoed somewhat more acerbically eleven years later, in 1910, by Karl Liebknecht when he averred that the intellectuals' "remoteness from the great political struggles" made them the "will-o-the-wisps of politics".[7]

In the 1920s such denunciations proliferated to the extent that at one level of usage the word "intellectual" became merely a term of convenience denoting some alleged political deficiency such as "opportunism", "indecision" or "lack of discipline". That on occasion it could even be extended to encompass diametrically opposed "disorders" – revisionism, on the one hand, and left sectarianism, on the other – illustrates the degree to which the word gradually became shorn of any specific connotations and was collapsed into an omnibus term of vilification. Paradoxically, in parallel to this process there developed an increasing awareness of the need to win over to socialism the "progressive" sections of the intelligentsia. For not least in the field of cultural politics the SPD and the German Communist Party were highly dependent on the active collaboration of intellectuals. This was indeed forthcoming, from prominent theorists of modern culture such as Gustav Radbruch, Anna Siemsen and the contributors to *Die Linkskurve* to writers, poets and dramatists such as Ernst Toller and Bert Brecht.[8] There were, of course, other intellectuals like those associated with what became known as the "conservative revolution" who helped prepare the ideological climate that issued in National Socialism. Nevertheless, it was largely the left-wing intelligentsia which, battered constantly by Nazi rhetoric, was pilloried to the point where the very word *Intellektueller* gained currency as a term of censure and abuse. In the most extreme sense intellectuals could be portrayed as deficient human beings, dangerously divorced from the people. This is illustrated by the entry in a "people's encyclopedia" of 1941. The intellectual is here defined as epitomizing the opposite of a true German: "– onesidedly intellectual person in whom character and soul have regressed and who lacks any deeper connections with the culture of the ordinary German people" (*Volks-Brockhaus* 1941).

Theories of Intellectuals in a Situation of Cultural, Ideological and Class Warfare

The political situation and the occupational shifts in German and other European societies in the 1920s and 1930s called for major ideological and sociological reassessments. On the political left many theories seeking to define the position of intellectuals were elaborated during the inter-war years. The most interesting and subsequently the most influential of these appeared in Antonio Gramsci's *Prison Notebooks*.[9] The historical terrain in which Gramsci's thoughts were developed was that of an actual or envisaged class warfare and his theory sought to assign to all educated and professional people a status in this struggle. He considered that for the maintenance of its hegemony any class had to evolve so-called "organic" intellectuals, that is to say, an elite of persons from its own ranks who had to take on organizing activities of a general social and explicitly political nature to suffuse the entire society with ideas that projected the class interest as a general interest. In so doing the dominant class made use of the traditional estates of intellectuals (the clergy, the judiciary, teachers, writers and publishers, etc.), just as it was assumed to be the aim of the subaltern classes trying to overcome the established hegemony to generate an organic intelligentsia of its own which would recruit to its cause representatives from the professional classes. The prerequisite for this was the establishment of a mass party, without which social hegemony and political government could not be exercised (Gramsci 1971, p. 12). Gramsci's scheme dispensed with the somewhat unsophisticated view of intellectuals amongst socialists in the early twentieth century that regarded them as uncertain, forever wavering allies, all too independent individualists or simply as lackeys of the bourgeoisie. He resisted the temptation of labelling the intellectuals summarily as a petty bourgeoisie, allegedly located firmly within neither the one nor the other of the opposing classes of capitalist society. Instead, he stressed that all human beings were endowed with intellectual capacities, although some exercised these as specialist professional functions. He therefore regarded the mass party essentially as a mass of intellectuals forging an organic social synthesis of class interests.

While for most analysts at that time the trajectory of politics in Europe was unthinkable without a background of class warfare it neither necessarily took the form desired by Gramsci nor did intellectuals inevitably have to be marked out as instruments of revolutionary agency. Different theses that were implicitly dismissed by Gramsci and other committed socialists, therefore, also merit some examination in this context, not least because they commanded attention in Germany at the time. Tutored by the situation of internal ideological strife in the Weimar Republic a number of social theorists gained prominence, including Karl Mannheim with his remarkable book *Ideologie und Utopie*, which first appeared in 1929. In it he developed further Alfred Weber's ideas[10] and provided an analysis of intellectuals as only partially determined by the social class of their origin and hence ideologically "free floating" (*freischwebende Intelligenz*). The reference here is in the first instance to a particular social stratum that cannot satisfactorily be defined in terms of its socio-economic background, typically the stratum of rentiers or the liberal professions. The intelligentsia is considered to be ideologically too heterogeneous to be seen as determined simply by its bourgeois or petty-bourgeois provenance. Rather, intellectuals are viewed in the first instance as fulfilling certain vital functions in modern society on account of their education: "Although they are too differentiated to be regarded as a single class, there is, however, one unifying sociological bond between all groups of intellectuals, namely, education, which binds them together in a striking way" (Mannheim 1972, p. 138). Mannheim, who is both troubled and challenged by the ideological and class warfare he sees being waged all around him, is essentially seeking a way out of an impasse. This, he believes, is embedded in the ever growing antagonism between political parties that foreshadows a scenario of civil war without any hope of pacification. To this end he is looking to the intelligentsia who, while a living replica of a modern secular society riven by ideological divisions, nevertheless is united by the homogenizing medium of education and, above all, by its facility for reflection on this ideological pluralism: "This acquired educational heritage subjects him [the intellectual] to the influence of opposing tendencies in social reality, while the person who is not oriented toward the whole through his education, but rather participates directly in the social process of production, merely tends to absorb the *Weltanschauung* of that particular group and to act exclusively under the influence of the conditions imposed by his immediate social situation" (Mannheim 1972, pp. 138–139). In other words, the process of higher education can so broaden the individual's perceptual horizons that it helps to burst the limiting determinative fetters of his or her generic social position. Accordingly, Mannheim invests the expanding educated stratum with an enormous hope on account of its utopian capabilities, namely that its members "might play the part of watchmen in what otherwise would be a pitch-black night" (Mannheim 1972, p. 143). Still a relatively small grouping in the 1920s, the intelligentsia is nevertheless said to be capable of perceiving that it is called upon to fulfil an important "mission", the development of a "synthetic perspective" (Mannheim 1972, p. 143) for the whole of society overriding the constraining and hence antagonistic interests of class.

The Intellectual as Part of the Political and Cultural Landscape in the Federal Republic

Although a critical intelligentsia was able to establish itself in Germany after the Second World War, no such optimism regarding the role of intellectuals appeared to be warranted at this stage. On the contrary, with democratic government restored at least in West Germany, the term *Intellektueller* retained its negative polemical charge. When famously on one occasion in the Federal Parliament Konrad Adenauer was out to denigrate a Social Democrat opponent, he simply called him "the most intellectual of all intellectuals".[11] Although often referred to in the ostracizing vocabulary of some conservatives as "knockers of their country", "unpatriotic vagabonds", "rats and blowflies" and "self-important little pipsqueaks", those who developed a critical presence post-1945 as essayists, fictional authors, film-makers, artists and broadcasters became part of a vibrant and public discursive process. Even before the Federal Republic was formally founded in 1949 a number of critical intellectual groupings had formed, centring initially on cultural and political journals like *Der Ruf*, *Die Wandlung* and *Frankfurter Hefte* and developing a potent public presence in the shape of *Gruppe 47*.[12] Despite their differences they were so distinctly left-of-centre that an authoritative German encyclopedia could offer the following entry on intellectuals in 1970: "Criticism of institutions is felt by them to be a necessary role. The kind of argumentation which, particularly in recent times, tends to be deployed reveals that politically this grouping is to be located on the 'left'."[13] It must be noted here that although the lexical item being defined (*Intellektueller*) was in the singular the encyclopedia authors felt compelled to refer to the grouped existence of such individuals. In the context of post-1945 Germany, there did indeed arise an ideological consanguinity which came to be shared by many prominent thinkers, writers, film-makers and artists like Alfred Andersch, Heinrich Böll, Günter Grass, Peter Weiss, Martin Walser, Hans Magnus Enzensberger, Erich Fried, Eugen Kogon, Walter Dirks, Dolf Sternberger, Karl Jaspers,

Theodor W. Adorno, Jürgen Habermas, Joseph Beuys, and by younger ones like Peter Schneider, Peter Handke, Georg Baselitz, A. R. Penck, Rainer Werner Fassbinder, Volker Schlöndorff, Alexander Kluge, Wim Wenders, Margarethe von Trotta and Peter Sloterdijk. For all their differences they could be seen as articulating a broadly similar message, inveighing against Germany's reluctance to acknowledge the deep break with civilization committed by the Hitler regime and against the apparently oblivious attitude to the reinstatement of old Nazis in positions of power. Committed to democratic and human rights as constitutionally enshrined in the Basic Law (*Grundgesetz*) they repeatedly exposed the lack of concern for any violation of such fundamental rights. In a historical situation where fascism was entirely discredited and communism disavowed they were in thrall to no particular political lobby, social class or ideology and could be regarded as intellectual non-conformists who spoke in their own right as prominent advocates of a pluralist culture. While some of the intellectuals, notably Heinrich Böll and Hans Magnus Enzensberger, at times felt like emigrating from a state and society which seemed set in a backward-looking, authoritarian mould, they did in fact stay, were not alienated in hatred like the intellectuals of the Weimar Republic from the established form of democracy and effectively contributed to a gradual, long-term shift towards a more liberal and tolerant political culture. Eventually they were simply accepted as part of the discursive landscape and to this extent one may speak of an "institutionalisation of the intellectual's role" in the Federal Republic (Habermas 1987a, p. 47). Plainly, they had vitally contributed to the historical process of re-inventing Germany as a protagonist of democratic structures, human rights and international law.

This development was accompanied by both admiring comment and dismissive polemics. On the one hand, intellectuals, particularly those associated with *Gruppe 47*, were frequently dubbed "the conscience of the nation", a term intensely disliked by most of the intellectuals themselves. It was notably Böll who rejected it because it implied a delegation of conscience by the general public to an elite group who was assumed to have that special competence. He feared that his compatriots, instead of actively exploring practical forms of critical citizenship, might be lulled into complacency by the belief that a vociferous intelligentsia in itself sufficed to guarantee the well-being of democracy. There was also the related danger that intellectuals, reduced to a media image, might be used by society as a fig-leaf for its democratic deficiencies and by the state as an advertisement of its democratic culture. On the other hand, the hold that intellectuals appeared to have on public opinion motivated the conservative sociologist Helmut Schelsky in 1975 to engage in a sustained attack. In stark contrast to Horkheimer and Adorno, who had assigned critical intellectuals a position of impotence,[14] Schelsky identified them as a priest caste disseminating meanings through the media which amounted to a massive undermining of the work ethic. He saw them as an institutionalized alliance between freelance opinion-makers and a sympathetic corps of opinion-disseminators. Heinrich Böll was cited as the most prominent example of the former and Rudolf Augstein, then editor of the weekly political magazine *Der Spiegel*, as a model of the latter. Böll's reaction was expressed in a mixture of satire, astonishment and qualified acceptance: to be sure, he had an influential voice, but no-one had officially appointed him "cardinal" of a new religion of social redemption; consequently, he lacked the apparatus of power that went with such a position, his only weapons being a typewriter and a telephone. He deplored the fact that the real reason why writers like himself had become moral authorities had not been analyzed. With some plausibility Böll insisted that his prominent position in public life was not something he had actively sought, but was merely a symptom of the vacuity of public morals (Böll & Linder 1975, pp. 104–106).

In engaging in the debates that shaped the political culture of post-war (West) Germany intellectuals were indeed privileged by the extensive exposure they received. Apart from becoming polemical targets in the process this also meant that they could seize opportunities for critical reflection within sections of the media that might otherwise have been foreclosed by the workings of the culture industry. For these intellectuals writing, addressing audiences and broadcasting were different ways of subverting widely accepted versions of reality to the extent that they could in the 1990s be seen by a younger generation of writers as proponents of an overbearing public morality and advocates of a new political correctness.[15] In other words, Schelsky was mistaken only in the polemical hyperbole of his attack. Intellectuals were to a moderate extent capable of manipulating the instruments of manipulation for the purposes of fostering a broad, critically informed awareness, thereby sustaining a role devolving on them as public prosecutors in matters of fundamental democratic concern. They had become part of the communicatory structures in which public opinion was formed, were agenda-setters within the political culture and, together with their opponents in the political establishment, were a contributing force in the re-invention of Germany as a Western democracy.

The Notion of Intellectuals as Public Protagonists in Critical Debates

The notion of the critical intellectual as a public protagonist clearly feeds off the polemical charge with which the word *Intellektueller* was endowed from the outset. Meanwhile the term, in Germany as much as in other countries, may in its most frequent usage now refer neutrally to the member of a sociologically identifiable group, stratum or class. This was evident already in Karl Mannheim's writings, however much they retained an ambiguity between the intellectual understood in this sociological sense and the figure conceived as a holistic social critic. In the post-fascist years and, in an accelerated way, in the Cold-War era and thereafter all modern and modernizing societies have witnessed a huge expansion of education and the knowledge industries. Hence the ranks of the professional classes or the "traditional" intelligentsia, those whom in the broadest sense one might call intellectuals, have swelled immensely. This secular process continues, so that the ordinary encyclopedia definition now tends to say that an intellectual is a person who uses his or her mind to earn a living or is a member of a group who occupies a prominent social position because of his or her qualifications and intellectual occupation.[16] The preferred definition in the former German Democratic Republic before the fall of the Wall is strikingly similar. Leaving aside dissidents who furnished some public criticism of the old *Stasi* regime, the "intelligentsia" was here understood in a quite anodyne fashion as a "social stratum whose members were engaged in predominantly intellectual labour, demanding advanced qualifications".[17] There can be little doubt that the significant expansion of both the professional classes and the functionalist intelligentsias in the public services and private corporations has helped defuse the antagonism between the social classes, at least as far as the Western world is concerned. Relatively high levels of consumption, the embourgeoisement of the working class and voter de-alignment have made the notion of entrenched ideological and class struggles appear anachronistic. In most contemporary European societies individuals tend to define themselves in one or more sub-cultural contexts with attendant mentality-shaping milieux and distinct life-styles, thus having to cope to some extent with multiple identities. With regard to Germany since the middle of the last century, this restructuring of society primarily into diverse publics has been most marked in the redefinition of the political parties. All attempts at harnessing their appeal to some kind of class awareness have been abandoned in favour of projecting social and political issues that cut across generic class constituencies: for example, the problems of creating and maintaining a healthy environment and a desirable quality of life; the rejection or exploration of forms of participation in public life; the preservation or development of ethnic, regional, national and transnational identities and the fostering of a praxis for intercultural tolerance.

The danger of certain groups becoming marginalized or forming parallel universes, as it were, that are divorced from mainstream society, with the latter palpably riven by conflicts of all kinds, constantly calls for analysis. This unleashes an immense discursive process in which a large number of variously positioned intellectuals, a "reflexive elite" (Schelsky's *Reflexionselite*) with more or less distinct conceptual and professional briefs, take part: journalists in both the print and electronic media, university academics, think-tank experts, church dignitaries and, last but not least, politicians. However, none of these individuals and groups are central to our present analysis, because the focus here is specifically on those within the public discourse who, sometimes against and despite all specialist knowledge, provide both theoretical reflection and critical comment of a more strategic nature. It seems they are passionately preoccupied with a pressing epistemological question about the nature of contemporary society and the direction of its social, political and cultural development, but without treating this question purely academically. On the contrary, they see the need to argue for particular values from an engagé position, not beholden to narrowly ideological points of view. They may be trying to make sense of things, and are therefore "mediators of meaning" (Schelsky's *Sinnvermittler*), but they neither offer ideological edifices nor constitute a priest-caste since they lack reverence and are consecrated by no-one. Their gaining a public profile is intrinsically bound up with a struggle for the channelling of the intellectual's voice. As figures who in the first instance are dependent on wielding the reasoning, assertive and appellative power of the spoken and written word, critical intellectuals, given conditions of a free society, will use a great variety of media spaces. They stand apart from intellectuals as a sociological stratum for they gain their status primarily in the process of communicating with and being recognized by an informed general public open to the reception of critical thinking. These intellectuals are thus inherently "public" both because they address their ideas to the public at large and because that public in turn affords them a special recognition. In other words, it is that public which, polemically or admiringly, confers on them the title of intellectuals.

Within an analysis of intellectuals in relation to cultural policy in Germany it is important to explore, first, the wider discursive context in which this field of activity is embedded and, second, the particular ways in which that activity is conceptualized. Without attempting any kind of comprehensive answer to these questions we have selected two outstanding figures, Jürgen Habermas and Hilmar Hoffmann, whose work is discussed here for the purpose of illustrating the extent to which they have become cultural agenda-setters as critical intellectuals. They have been chosen as case studies because they exemplify both the close interrelationship and the distinctions between two areas of cultural practice: cultural politics as the exploration by theory and discursive intervention of a changing terrain of institutions, values, orientations and mentalities within the trajectory of an ambivalent modernity (Habermas) and cultural policy as a defined field of professional administration, policy-making and theoretical reflection (Hoffmann). Between them, these two figures aptly illustrate the two meanings of the German term *Kulturpolitik*, which indeed embraces both cultural politics and cultural policy. The similarities these two intellectuals reveal in their basic epistemological approach cannot, however, serve to gloss over the fact that they differ in the respective primary audiences they address. Hoffmann has for most of his career as a prominent cultural administrator been associated with a commitment to the Social-Democratic Party of Germany (SPD), while Habermas, for all that he too may be located on the "left of centre", could not be classified as an allegiant of any particular political organization. Rather, he acquired international distinction as a critical theoretician rooted in academia, but with an audience gradually extending deep into the general educated public. Both figures can boast eminence in their respective fields and both would openly claim partisanship in the fundamental positions they advocate, without such partisanship ever entailing the unquestioned subordination of their thinking to the demands of party discipline or ideological dogma. On the contrary, the projection of their intellectual profile beyond any party-political or dogmatic boundaries into wider constituencies of the informed public depends on them being seen as individuals who are entirely unimpeded by constraining apparatuses or organizations. At the same time they are clad – unlike, for example, writers such as Günter Grass or Hans Magnus Enzensberger – in the garb of academic and civil-servant professionalism. Without this status delimiting the range of their influence it has given them a certain respectability, has made it less possible to attack them as irresponsible mavericks and hence contributed to their and other intellectuals' critical voice becoming accepted as part of the political culture that now exists in Germany. They may still be touched by the stigma or the aura of being "gadflies", "fowlers of the nest", "watchmen in the dark" or the "conscience of the nation", yet they have helped bring about a profound change in the cultural climate such that intellectuals are no longer regarded as alien, alienated and ostracized.

Jürgen Habermas: The Optimism of the Intellectual as Theoretician of Cultural Politics

The Theoretician, the Intellectual and his Relevance to Cultural Politics

That Habermas is a philosopher is proved by his philosophical publications. That he is a social scientist is attested to by his work on social theory. That he might be credited with some standing as an international public intellectual has recently been affirmed, although without much academic authority, by the widely discussed list of the top 100 intellectuals in the world, where he came seventh.[18] As far as the contemporary cultural context in Germany is concerned he can, of course, be placed within that broad left-liberal group of intellectuals who saw the need to raise their voice at critical moments in the Federal Republic's development in order to ensure that Germany face up to its past and remain firmly committed to democracy and international law. In his own reflections on the "role of the intellectual in Germany" Habermas, as a "partisan contemporary", does not hesitate to associate himself with this grouping whose overriding concerns in the early history of the Federal Republic were the democratic legitimacy of politics and the development of a participative political culture (Habermas 1987a, pp. 25–54). However, the proposition that Jürgen Habermas should belong in a discussion on cultural politics is at first sight more than a little problematical, for this thinker does not hold office as a policy-maker on any local, regional, national or international stage. He also is not, unlike some party-political figures and prominent commentators, in the frontline of media protagonists that constantly make their presence felt in public debates and television round tables, of which there is no shortage on German channels. Yet he has an immense influence both as a philosophical author and as an intellectual, comfortable with that designation, whose thought has an interventionist quality, as his supporters and also some of his detractors would readily agree. Counter to some fashionable declarations on both sides of the Atlantic that the time for intellectuals is now no more,[19] a figure like Habermas is proof of the contrary, namely that the critical intellectual, far from having physically or mentally departed the contemporary stage, is able to exploit to the full the existing culture of public argumentation. As a theoretician he can lay the measure of his ideas upon the dissonances of published opinions to outline a theoretical framework for discourse and urge the possibility for a lived consensus. Habermas is fundamentally concerned with a vital precondition of all policy-making, and in particular of the framing of cultural policy, namely with the broad discursive processes on which it is based. This entails for him the elaboration of analyses and theories capable of explaining the way in which contemporary society may realize a social synthesis against a background of party-political, ideological, ethnic, cultural and class divisions. Habermas's thought is pervaded by the incorrigible optimism of one who believes in the self-corrective power of the public argumentative process.

It is clear that as a public figure of national and, since the 1970s, increasingly of international and indeed global standing he has a double presence. In the first place he gained authority as a distinguished theoretician on the basis of a number of demanding books, which are incisively informed by analyses of both culture and social practice. In *Strukturwandel der Öffentlichkeit* (1962; *The Structural Transformation of the Public Sphere*) he dealt with the fundamental change of the modern public which originally gained self-confidence as a culturally reasoning bourgeoisie in the literary societies of the late eighteenth and early nineteenth centuries, only to be transmuted in the twentieth century into a diversity of publics more or less passively consuming the products of cultural industries. The next major study, *Theorie und Praxis: Sozialphilosophische Studien* (1963; *Theory and Practice, Studies in Social Philosophy*), appeared a year later. In it Habermas considered methodological questions in the social sciences as well as the framework of science and the foundations of contemporary society. It is evident from the start that Habermas reworks two European legacies, that of the Enlightenment and that of German philosophical idealism, in his quest to enter into and promote a type of thinking capable of shaping the mental environment required for both democratic politics in general and the parameters of cultural policy in particular. Just as the formation of modern bourgeois subjectivity – the prerequisite of politics as a discursive process between free beings – is for him unthinkable without the cultural ratiocination that characterized the early gatherings of citizens in a private sphere pervaded by communication about literature, so the relationship between the world of ideas and that of social action is repeatedly made an explicit object of analysis, notably with reference to Kant, Hegel and Marx.

Perhaps it is not surprising, then, that there is a second side to Habermas's existence as a figure within the cultural landscape, a terrain which he would view as extending into that of the political discourse and predetermining it. If his university lectures, seminars and theory-laden books are reflections conceived with intervention in political practice in mind, then this is even truer – in the immediate sense of affecting important issues in the democratic discourse – of his public speeches, newspaper articles, interviews and essays. In this latter activity he becomes recognizable as a critical intellectual in the continental sense as defined earlier on, namely as someone who, while enjoying a prominent reputation in his or her own area of specialization, has demonstrated the ability to communicate ideas and influence debate outside of it, usually by dissenting or provocative intervention in matters of topical concern. As an intellectual Habermas commands a second mode of accessing audiences that far exceed the circles of his basically professional clientele tuned solely into readings of philosophical and social-theoretical tracts. In other words, Habermas, although sometimes accused by old-style socialists of having withdrawn into accommodation with the powers that be, is not satisfied with the existence of a recluse who develops his ideas with his back to the shrill world of metropolitan life. On the contrary, he has embraced the "guardianship of public criticism",[20] continuing this role from his earliest beginnings in the review pages of earnest journals and broadsheets through to the present day.

This is easily illustrated with reference to recent events: some weeks before France voted on the EU constitutional treaty Habermas, in an article in *Le Monde* entitled "A nos amis français", anxiously asked the question: "Do the majority of French people really wish to hide away in the bunker common to the nationalists of the right and the left?" (Habermas 2005a). This would surely amount to a betrayal of reason by the land that had given Europe the Enlightenment, he surmised in anticipated disbelief. A few days later he fired another warning shot at the French left with his cogitations on "Le non illusoire de la gauche" in *Le Nouvel Observateur* (Habermas 2005c). In between he gave an interview to the German daily *Die Welt*, in which he sketched out his position on a number of topical issues like the aftermath of the illegal war in Iraq, the political and mental split into "old" Europe and "new" Europe, the miserable state of affairs in matters of mutual trust between European countries, their want of a common constitutional identity and, lastly, the relationship of democracy, religious faiths and the Catholic church (Habermas 2005b). A month later, after the referenda in France and the Netherlands had taken place and, as Habermas had feared, returned a resounding "non" or "nee" to the proposed constitutional treaty, he lambasted the way that political elites had lost touch with the people and stated in resignatory mood: "The EU has been steamrollered over the heads of ordinary Europeans" (Habermas 2005d). While he agreed with the then President of the European Union, Jean-Claude Juncker, that the EU in its current form was unloved by its citizens and had killed their dreams of an ever closer union, he also argued that this treaty crucially did not capture the imagination for the simple reason that it regurgitated the tedious detail of international agreements without providing a transparent structure of basic constitutional norms and a convincing reason for the necessity of a constitution. His fear was what he termed "the most likely scenario" to follow, namely an economically united but politically fragmented Europe being sucked into the maelstrom of the hegemonic hyperpower. This left him with but one suggestion, more desperate than hopeful: that there should be politicians in Europe who under articles 43 and 44 of the Nice Treaty might form a core of countries with closely aligned policies in fiscal, economic, environmental and social matters in order to prevent the relatively small scale of national politics from being marginalized by the power of large, globally operating corporations. However, he could not really identify any European leaders who might expedite such a bold move, particularly since Schroeder and Chirac were embarked on their swansong, while he considered Baroso, Merkel and Sarkozy as too infected by neo-liberal ideas. Given their ideological make-up he could not see them insisting that Europe should lead the way in fashioning the type of desirable society which incorporated a balance of cultural, social and economic advantages accessible to all citizens. Schröder and Fischer could, albeit as a parting gift, still engage in an important symbolic act by urging on their successors the legacy for such a policy. Whether Habermas had thought through the budgetary implications for such policies must remain open to question.

It is clear from this sketch of Habermas's newspaper publications over a period of one month that a partisan commitment to an intellectual mission, including an engagement with fundamental issues of European and world politics, if necessary with the full deployment of polemical invective, constitutes the discursive existence in the public sphere of this perceptive thinker. But his relevance within the framework of a discussion on cultural politics and perhaps of politics as culture must rest on a critical exploration of his own proposition that it is substantially a cultural struggle in which intellectuals are, and necessarily must be, involved. Clearly, it is itself a cultural struggle, whereby intellectuals formulate and expose their individual perceptions of modern life and bring them into dialogue with wider audiences. They can but gain public legitimacy by constantly participating in and offering contributions to a discourse about orientations of culture as the way in which individuals define the nature and quality of their lives and elaborate an understanding of themselves within social environments. Hence, when he discusses the prospects of European politics in the context of an American-controlled process of globalization he feels prompted to state that "taking up a position within the cultural struggle that divides the blue and the red America today" (Habermas 2005d) is inevitable. What might appear to most people as a typical issue of political or ideological choice is regarded by Habermas as a matter which can only be settled in a discursive battle that is a cultural struggle over the values and orientations of modern societies. Unencumbered by party line and parliamentary whip the intellectual exploits the existence of informed, independently critical publics in which he or she can presume to elicit resonance. His or her function, as defined by Habermas, is prominently to participate in articulating the "civilizing role of a democratically enlightened common sense, which carves out a path for itself as a third party between science and religion within the cacophony of the cultural struggle" (Habermas 2003, p. 251).

Culture as Discourse and the Interventions of the Intellectual

Accordingly, culture is understood by Habermas not merely as a repository of artefacts to be preserved and admired through the generations but as a primary terrain, at times a battleground, in which interested parties advance their interpretation of reality and experience the dynamics of their lifeworlds. Historically culture is the enabling base for the development of modern politics which even today remains moored in a myriad of ethical, religious, aesthetic, behavioural, linguistic – in short, cultural – assumptions. The most important structural aspect of this primary terrain, inaugurated by the European bourgeoisies since the late eighteenth century, is a public sphere that allows and in principle enables all citizens to raise their voice, trusting in the idealist premise that there is persuasive power in reasoned argument. Max Weber's influence on Habermas is apparent in a number of precepts that govern his thinking, not least his proposition that discourse can be analyzed as an ideal-typical form of communication, that systematically undistorted communication can be conceived and ideal speech acts can be analyzed in their many different functions. A number of language philosophers are also referenced routinely (for example, Ludwig Wittgenstein, John L. Austin and John R. Searle). This yielded his most extensive, two-volume analytical exposition, *Theorie des kommunikativen Handelns* (1981; *Theory of Communicative Action*). Consensus-driven communication constitutes at once the speculative practical norm and the ultimate target and, even where not explicitly pushed into the foreground of argumentation in the rest of Habermas's theoretical work, it remains the indispensable matrix within which discourses are thought to be anchored and to which they must implicitly aspire. Habermas passionately believes in the "unity of reason within the multiplicity of voices".[21] It is a fundamental prerequisite of democratic culture and hence both the object of analysis as well as its practical objective. The inspiration of reflection is, therefore, the entire cultural orbit within which Habermas is located as a German, as a European, as a Westerner and as a world citizen. He makes it his task both as a theoretician and as an intellectual to subject these roles to critical scrutiny, define and redefine them and thus search for his own identity in a public sphere whose cognitive and political agendas he moves by interpreting them. The more one immerses oneself in Habermas's writings, the more it becomes plain that the transcendental deity is here philosophically reduced to a secular notion, that of the actively democratic public and its discourses as ultimate arbiters of all aspects of life. This type of public is sharply distinguished from manipulated media audiences rendered passive by the presentation and self-enactment of people purely for the augmentation of their prominence (Habermas 2005e, p. 15). Committed to the idea that rational communication is necessary in order to uphold political and ethical standards and the freedom of the public sphere itself, the intellectual feels challenged at all times to subject society to his critical gaze and to interpret the changing meanings and problems of its contemporaneity. In so doing he has to choose suitable weapons of verbal intervention in order to argue centrally for such public understandings – interpersonal, international and intercultural – that by the standards of a universal pragmatics are deemed threatened or underfulfilled. In so doing the analyst, both as interventionist intellectual and as academic theoretician, has not only to probe constantly the meanings of modernity and its social, political and cultural agendas, but he also has to scrutinize himself as a learning discussant, prepared to revise his own positions. It is particularly through the prefaces to a number of his books that Habermas gives testimony to his self-awareness as a learner and it is evident that this further augments the respect he enjoys. Over the years the weight of his public presence has become such that some fellow intellectuals, like Peter Sloterdijk, indignantly and jealously want to wrest from him the *"Deutungsmonol"*, meaning that Habermas in the eyes of many has become endowed with an interpretative or diagnostic primacy in contemporary Germany.

Unlike political, legal, economic, social and cultural institutions, the public sphere in modern societies does not itself appoint its guardians. Its continued existence is the result of ever renewed efforts and struggles by individuals and groups which have established it in the first instance. The political culture that is engendered by it does, of course, have institutions and structures, classically a legislature, an executive and a judiciary, that have been installed to underpin it. However, this institutional structure is crucially dependent on other, less formalized activities and organizations pre-dating or running concurrent with them, like commodity production, commodity and service markets and public platforms for ideas that range from literary circles to political parties, from books and newspapers to electronic media. The public sphere, made up of a changing cluster of spontaneous and formal agencies, renders society as an arena in which values are both preserved and contested and where intellectuals are able by virtue of their appeal to smaller or larger audiences to map out for themselves important positions of critical reflection that feed into and influence the private and the public discourse. There is no institutional security about their critical presence, be they "tenured radicals" or freelance writers. The seemingly self-appointed status of critical intellectuals is wholly dependent on the vibrancy, plausibility and authority of their verbal presence infused by the conceptual power and rational persuasiveness of their language. Only the critical echo they are able to elicit from within the public realm legitimates them. Despite the relatively distinctive compartmentalization of the public discourse into professionally specialized spheres (political, religious, organizational, scientific, technological, economic, budgetary, etc.), these must be understood as not hermetically sealed from each other. Within the compartments of the discourse professionals have an important say but without being exclusively in control. The intellectual's calling arises from the voids that they leave open and the desire of the public for specialized knowledge to be placed in a wider context of contemporary experience.

The themes which preoccupy Habermas, therefore, arise as much from significant events as from existing discourses, debates and dialogues in which contestants, amongst them the politicians seeking to legitimate their power, strike up their argumentational stances. Concern about the necessity for a European constitution is certainly among them and has made itself felt since the mid-1990s. His "politically engaged analytical thinking" – as he calls it himself (Habermas 1987b, pp. 104–107) – embraces gene-technology and eugenics as well as ethics generally, also the umbilical connections between a state founded in law and democracy, the break with totalitarian pasts and the possibilities for a commitment on the part of global society to international law. All these are seen as embedded in the overarching and intermeshed realities of culture and politics. A comparison of the dates when these issues arose with their occurrence in Habermas's writings reveals that he by no means necessarily always acts as their originator. Plainly, the agenda is sometimes already set prior to any intervention by Habermas. Take the question of the European constitution which Habermas addresses in a public lecture on the invitation of the Hamburg Senate and the weekly *Die Zeit* in June 2001. He explicitly here tunes into a debate amongst leading European politicians, initiated in the late 1990s by Joschka Fischer, the then German Foreign Secretary, and pursued by other politicians like Jacques Chirac, Romano Prodi, Johannes Rau, Gerhard Schröder and Lionel Jospin.

Habermas clearly acts in this context as a free agent and articulate participative citizen who takes up an existing agenda and makes a contribution to a debate that already has a Europe-wide audience. He therefore appears not so much as an agenda-setter than as someone who, in pursuing an established agenda, invests it with new prominence and gives it stronger cognitive import, ultimately by networking it into the larger theoretical context within which all the themes he takes up are linked by a single agenda: the foundation and defence of a culture of intersubjective communication whose rationality is constantly tested by the plausibility, persuasiveness and the transnational reach of its propositions. Thus, when he tackles the question of the European constitution he does so not merely as a pragmatic political thinker but by locating it in a historical narrative. The generic roots of such a constitution were to be sought first of all in a negation of antagonisms which, after the World Wars, drove Europeans into the conception of a joint future. He also insisted on general precepts that should principally govern such a constitution. With recourse to Immanuel Kant he pointed to the necessity of a universal constitution for which a European one should ideally be but a pilot project. It is easy to see that the topics that move him and the themes that are tossed into his hermeneutical grip by the ongoing public discourse are interconnected: opposition to any tendencies to re-couple present-day society with the dictatorial and repressive past, revealing the ambivalence of modernity as both a development towards greater individual liberty and the loss of valuable cultural traditions and sensibilities, opening up visions of participative political citizenship, transnationalism and the rule of international law adhered to world-wide and necessitating in the last resort what he terms a *"Weltinnenpolitik"*, a global interior politics. There can be little doubt that Habermas is hermeneutically driven by cultural utopianism. Inviting his audiences to stretch themselves beyond the boundaries of their natively acquired limitations, Habermas nevertheless allows for the significance of their particularity as a foreshadowing of what by intellectual projection might become visible as a desirable state of affairs globally. His persistent dialogical challenge in the public sphere is the preparation of politics for the broad steer by a citizenry that is informed by a culture of enlightened self-reflection, critical of all dogmatic limitations, be they inherited by historical or social background or acquired by prejudice or blind ideological choice.

This undertaking entails great interpretative burdens which sometimes have to be carried forward against scholarly specialists as, for example, when he insists on an adequate understanding of historical totalitarianisms and the fate of nation states. Engaging in the so-called "battle of the historians" in the 1980s, he famously opposed as an intolerable revisionism Ernst Nolte's interpretation of Soviet Socialism and National Socialism as mutually imitative systems, with Hitler believing himself to be merely involved in an attempt to stop the westward march of Stalinism. On another occasion, in the face of the concern expressed by other public figures, Habermas affirmed as a meaningful act the opening of a monument site close to the Brandenburg Gate in remembrance of the Holocaust, initiated, as it was, not by the political class but by German citizens. In these and other interventions he was pursuing the same broadly based stratagem, namely that of arguing for a framework of culture which was open to ever greater critical self-reflection on the part of nations, which ensured anamnetic solidarity with the victims of past brutalities – whether committed in the name of nation states, hegemonic ethnicities or totalitarian ideologies – and which, above all, kept alive a democratic discourse that would pave the way for more tolerance and greater participation in material and cultural wealth. Habermas sees his own role as substantially to contribute to and influence, but by no means to govern, the public discourse. Still forcefully defending the traditions of a self-critical enlightenment against renewed tendencies to the contrary in Germany, he nevertheless could by the late 1980s begin to acknowledge a decisive shift in the overall mentality that now characterized contemporary culture. Without being self-congratulatory about this process, of which he had clearly been an important part, he felt encouraged that through the critical discourse since 1945 a politically alert public, driven on by new social movements, had actually reshaped the cultural orientations of the population at large (Habermas 1990, p. 17). It is this achievement of *Kulturnation*, the cultural nation and its maintenance, that in the eyes of Habermas is the most significant initial project. Nevertheless, with reference to Germany as his most pressing historical case study, he registers advances so cautiously that he is too severe both on the past philosophical traditions since Kant and on the emancipative forces at work in some of the political parties since the nineteenth century. He states:

> The cultural nation of the Germans has only through and after Auschwitz absorbed convictions anchored in universalist constitutional principles – by a long delayed public reflection on this last and until then unimaginable destination in a process that was openly engaged right from the earliest days of the Nazi regime, in a process of exclusion and expatriation of the Jews and the communists, of the aliens and the weak, of citizens steeped in different thinking and different life-styles, of "internal enemies" as defined by the state. (Habermas 1999)

However, far from being obsessed with Auschwitz and allowing it to paralyse the critical memory of the past, Habermas understands it as a spur for advocating plural life-styles and the togetherness of different ethnicities which, by following the universal pragmatics of their communicational competence, can enter into multicultural exchange and create cultural hybridity.

It lies in their nature that the large-scale discursive currents involved in the relevant policy processes,[22] while capable of theoretical description, transcend the control even of the most ambitious intellect. Hence Habermas defines the critical agency of the intellectual not just as an individual task but as the struggle of an intellectual vanguard for public discursive spaces and agendas. This is exemplified most clearly by the way in which he sought to support the case for a European constitution. In coordination with a number of other prominent intellectual figures writing for seven quality newspapers in Europe – Umberto Eco in *La Repubblica*, Gianni Vattimo in *La Stampa*, Adolf Muschg in the *Neue Zürcher Zeitung*, Richard Rorty in the *Süddeutsche Zeitung* and Fernando Savater in *El País* – he resorted not merely to penning letters to newspapers, issuing essays and giving talks but also to composing a kind of manifesto that appeared under his name and that of Jacques Derrida in the *Frankfurter Allgemeine Zeitung* and in *La Libération* on 31 May 2003 (Habermas & Derrida 2003a). True, he had in the 1980s crossed swords with Derrida over the problem of reason in modernity and the cabalistic obscurity of Derrida's grammatology (Habermas 1988, pp. 191–218). But they had subsequently found common platforms of debate and had been thrown together as virtual joint authors in a book on terrorism (Habermas & Derrida 2003b). In the course of separate interviews on the phenomenon considerable similarities in their shared commitment to European traditions of criticism and self-criticism had emerged. Consequently, it was now no longer so far-fetched that Derrida, in a brief prefatory note to the joint manifesto, could state that while Habermas had authored it he fully identified with the text.

The manifesto rides on a number of claims which evince both the clarity of the European intellectuals' projections and the succinct nature of their self-conceived role while, at the same time, revealing the precariousness of the task they face. To what extent the manifesto points to a hoped-for future is signalled in its title: "Our Renewal. After the War: The Rebirth of Europe". First of all Habermas, and with him Derrida, state that, given the mass protests in London, Rome, Madrid, Barcelona, Berlin and Paris, the makings of a distinct European public united in a common feeling against the illegitimacy of war in Iraq had shown itself. While the whole world had become irritated with US unilateralism it was Europe that had been most deeply concerned with the flagrant breech of international law. This called into question the meaning of the old alliances of the West, the relevance of international law for the world community and the role of the UN. The emerging rifts were not simply between the hyperpower on the one hand and its traditional allies on the other, but they occurred between the governments of what came to be called "old" and "new" Europe. They were equally in evidence in the counsels preparing a European constitution, notably between those nations which were prepared to cede certain state powers to the EU and others which, facilitating the exercise of US hegemony, wished to freeze the present situation of intergovernmental arrangements. The way out was to be sought in the formation of a core-Europe which would not be an inward-looking alignment of states but by its attractiveness and openness gradually absorb the rest of the EU into closer integration. Internationally, Europe was to form a counterbalance against the "hegemonic unilateralism of the United States" and press for the design of a global interior politics in the institutions of the World Trade Organization, the World Bank and the International Monetary Fund. As far as European integration itself was concerned a new stage had been reached which went beyond the "functional imperatives" of achieving a common trade and monetary zone. Majority decisions on matters of a common foreign and defence policy were acceptable by minorities only on the basis of a perceived common identity. The national publics had to build another dimension, a European one, into their identity. Their abstract civic solidarity had to acquire a transnational extension. An "attractive, infectious vision" of a future Europe had to be evolved out of the confusion, torment and helplessness governing the present situation. Crucially, intellectuals could either fulfil or fail to fulfil a vital function at this juncture. "If the theme [of a common European vision] has so far not even reached the public agenda, then we have failed as intellectuals", Habermas states self-critically but also implicitly exhorting the vanguard to which he belongs (Habermas & Derrida 2003a). The conscious evolution of a common European identity again characterizes the central task of the intellectuals' agenda-setting activity, the projection of a peace-loving, co-operative, dialogue-seeking culture that is open to other cultures and able to offer models of government beyond the restrictive confines of the nation state and of wealth-creation combined with social justice. The destructive histories of class warfare, rival nationalisms, totalitarianism and mass killings and the chequered history of modernity as a trajectory of secular disenchantment with traditional institutions of authority establishing the ideological neutrality of the state contain exemplary lessons not only for the Europeans themselves but also for nations and regions beyond Europe. In being prepared to curtail their own sovereignties and build partnerships founded in mutually recognized legal frameworks Europeans might provide designs for a new cosmopolitan understanding amongst peoples. The intellectual here puts forward a vision that measures what is against what could be, the merely given against a desired state of affairs. Culture as a dialogical enabling terrain for politics is to be invested with a utopian tension that is informed not by the sheer force of power but by the force of persuasive reason permanently tested by the dynamics of free communication.

Critical Annotations

As a thinker it is Habermas's overarching purpose to expound political, legal, social and cultural action and truth-finding itself as grounded in discursive practice. Criticism is invited and the opposition to dogmatism and ideological totalitarianism is implicit, without a rampant relativism being given centre-stage. Habermas's efforts to inaugurate ethics as anchored in discourse is both enlightening and revealing. Discourse is understood as an arbiter of the ethical, legal or cultural validity of arguments because it is based on "idealising presuppositions" (*idealisierende Unterstellungen*; Habermas 1991, p. 14), such as, for example, the notion that all participants are free and equal and that they are engaged in a co-operative process of truth-finding. With reference to ethical self-reflection Habermas avers: "Just as an individual is capable of reflecting on himself and his life as a whole, in order to become clear about what sort of person he is and wants to be, so the members of a collective can trustingly come together in public counsel, in order solely by the coercion-free compulsion of the better argument to arrive at an understanding of their shared way of life and their identity" (Habermas 1991, p. 123). A critical annotation is inevitable here, for Habermas's trust in the capabilities of public discourse and his hopes for the convincing force of rational argument in the public sphere seem boundless. In the light of this it is tempting to judge the intellectual's interventions and the philosopher's hefty theories as elaborations of an idealist utopian. To cite the case of another incorrigible optimist, might not Habermas, like Gottfried Leibnitz, be excused, *pace* Voltaire, for teaching that we live in the best of all possible worlds? Crucially, however, Leibnitz's assertion was primarily an ontological one referring to a god-created universe, while in Habermas's case we are squarely in the realm of human society which frequently flouts all principles of consensus by verbal communication, daily producing evidence of lawless and brutal practices. Is one, then, not left with an essentially idealistic framework of thought that is predicated on the utopian ideal of rational communication supposedly free from all interpersonal or systemic violence, where participants, straining for agreement, are guided solely by the discursive ethics of always acknowledging the best, that is, the most generally convincing, argument? The idealism of this war-free scenario of truth-seeking brings to mind Raphael's famous fresco in the Vatican, *The School of Athens*, where, counter to the known history of lethal misunderstandings between their peoples, the best representatives of Middle-Eastern, ancient Greek, Italian and Egyptian philosophers are gathered in animated conversation, clustered in open tutorial groups on the steps and coffered vaults of an expansive classical building. This painting may be interpreted as presaging a time of peaceful discourse between plural truth-claims which, as European history has shown, subsequently took hundreds of years of violence eventually to evolve into co-existing systems of modern democracy. The internal tensions suffered by modern polities, however, hardly make them into regions of blissful tolerance even when, with the exception perhaps of the marginalized losers of modernization, individuals or groups may mostly desist from resorting to violence and full-scale internal warfare. In his Paulskirche lecture of 2001 entitled "Faith and Knowledge" Habermas himself spells out the difficulties of tolerating cultural pluralism:

> As soon as an existentially relevant question arrives on the political agenda, citizens – whether they be believers or non-believers – and their ideologically impregnated convictions clash with each other and, while labouring under the shrill dissonances of quarrelling public opinions, are confronted with the offensive fact of ideological pluralism. (Habermas 2003, p. 252)

Raphael, too, by the idealized depiction of philosophical and multicultural inclusiveness, implicitly points to the historical disjuncture of the West with the rest of the world, to the cleavage obtaining between the renaissance of a knowledge-based society and that immersed in an authority-guarded faith. The same contrast applies to democratic modernity and pre-modern communitarianism, which has so far prevented the freely discursive model of uncoerced argument from becoming universal as a global norm.

The greatest threat to Habermas's vision of a society suffused by ideal speech acts predicated on consensus is constituted by both the speechless brutality of terrorist violence and the blind force of global markets squeezing mankind for private corporate profit. These twin threats keep catapulting the philosopher from his professional contemplations into the public responses of the intellectual confronting the topicality of world-changing events. As to the former, Habermas was uncertain in an interview in New York whether the destruction of the twin towers of the World Trade Centre on 11 September 2001 could be classed as a world-historical caesura, similar in its far-reaching importance to the outbreak of the First World War. But he considered that the "fanatically hardened mentality" of fundamentalists arose from their repression of a modernizing social reality characterized by cognitive dissonances (Habermas & Derrida 2004, p. 56). Islamic fundamentalism and the hunt for witches in medieval and early modern Europe had in common a "defensive reaction to fears of a violent uprooting of traditional forms of life" (Habermas & Derrida 2004, p. 57). In view of these dangers, which, even in twentieth-century Europe, contributed to the embrace of fascism by social milieux that felt all traditional certainties to be under threat, Habermas has engaged in an effort to reconnect with the wisdoms of religious faith, not in order to reinstate them in their unquestionable authority but in an attempt at recalibrating modern society with a set of positive values in secular translation. He obviously believes that individuals cannot be so de-emotionalized as to be left purely with the necessary, but abstract, frameworks of rights and obligations formally guaranteed by the democratic state. Within the forensic practice with which Habermas defends his position he repeatedly points to a fundamental aspect that governs speech acts and, he believes, separates his thinking from all reality-divorced idealism. When questioned about the validity of his philosophical edifice in view of the rise of global terrorism with its suspension of consensual dialogue, Habermas pointed to the pragmatics of everyday communication, which, he insists, is predicated on a primary anthropological assumption, namely that intersubjective understanding can be achieved and that consensus must therefore be possible.

Hence his constant battle for the reinstatement of politics as a universal conversion to verbal communication with the potential for consensus, "jaw-jaw not war-war", a cultural project directed against the weight of unfettered economic coercion. The dumb expansion of global corporate powers without effective political sanctions reduces the human being to a tongue in the head of the profit-seeking commodity (Marx 1972, p. 110). All discourse in this realm is merely manipulative and language simply a subaltern instrument of the market, strategically blind to its inherent capacities for global destruction: "Hence we need a politics designed to strengthen the political capability for action by containing and tempering the economic dynamic which has gone wild" (Habermas 2001, p. 180). Habermas finds himself at one with Derrida in demanding that Europe not be reduced simply to a supra-political firm for commodity transfer: "Economism, monetarism, adaptation to competitiveness on the world market ... it seems to me that we must answer all this with a decidedly political project" (Derrida 1998). Here again it is the utopian power of a European heritage, trust in the culture of the public discourse and the civilizing power of the state that fires his optimism in the face of the brutal ravages of a rampant market economy. Without setting out to detail specific cultural policies Habermas is clearly set on a course to help inaugurate such policies, to infuse all policy-making with a cultural dimension and to reinvigorate with a political discourse areas which have ostensibly become immunized against it.

Hilmar Hoffmann: The Utopianism of the Intellectual as Practitioner of Cultural Policy

Hilmar Hoffmann's formidable career as a practitioner of cultural policy is quite simply without parallel in the history of the Federal Republic. In 1951, at the age of twenty-six, he became the Director of the Oberhausen Institute of Adult Education (the youngest person in Germany to hold such a position). Two years later he founded the International West German Short Film Festival in Oberhausen, over which he presided until 1970 (an event which could be seen as the birth-place of the New German Cinema in that it helped launch the careers of such distinguished directors as Rainer Werner Fassbinder, Volker Schlöndorff and Alexander Kluge). In 1965 Hoffmann became the Head of the Department of Culture in Oberhausen and five years later he assumed the same role in the city of Frankfurt, a post he filled for fully twenty years. Between 1990 and 1993 he acted as the General Secretary for the Stiftung Lesen (a foundation dedicated to the promotion of reading skills) and in 1992 he was nominated by the city of Berlin as Cultural Commissioner for the Olympic Games that were planned for the year 2000. The following year, 1993, Hoffmann became President of the Goethe-Institute and as such was responsible for the cultural policy of the German Foreign Office, a post he held until 2002.

Hoffmann's standing as an acclaimed academic intellectual is attested to by the numerous Visiting or Honorary Professorships in Media Studies that have been conferred on him (by the universities of Bochum, Frankfurt, Tel Aviv, Jerusalem, Marburg and the Frankfurt Hochschule für Musik und Darstellende Künste). Additionally, his prodigious publication record, which includes twelve edited volumes and thirteen monographs, has given him a remarkable public position as a critical intellectual. The centrepiece of those publications is his trilogy on cultural policy, *Kultur für alle* (1979), *Kultur für morgen* (1985) and *Kultur als Lebensform* (1990a), the first of which influenced a readership extending far beyond the narrow circle of cultural administrators for whom the book quickly attained a quasi-biblical status. In a recent interview looking back over his long career Hoffmann was reminded of his characterization of the ideal cultural policy-maker as someone possessing "a wealth of education, imagination, oppositional spirit and intellectual irony". He replied that whereas the current generation of cultural administrators, for ever under pressure to defend their shrinking budgets, scarcely had the time or opportunity to write articles setting out their own visions of the future, he himself would have been able to achieve little during his period of office in Frankfurt without the books in which he had sought to do precisely that.[23] It is, of course, above all this ability to generate and put in the public domain new ideas that distinguishes the intellectual politician from the "mere" practitioner of politics. Since Hoffmann himself lays great store by the theory-praxis-nexus, it seems appropriate to begin a discussion of his role as cultural agenda-setter by considering his many reflections on the place of culture in contemporary society.

Hoffmann as Cultural Theorist and the Inclusive Concept of Culture

These in turn were shaped in the first instance by his reaction to two particular moments – one positive, the other negative – in the history of the cultural sphere in Germany. Born in 1925, Hoffmann could experience first-hand the consequences of a deformed cultural policy in which all artistic and cultural activity was subject to rigorous ideological control and manipulation. In place of its participation in the process of cultural production the state exercised under National Socialism a total "custodianship legalized if necessary by coercion and terror" and resulting in the complete "abdication of the free intellect" (Hoffmann 1990a, p. 16). The lesson Nazism taught Hoffmann was that "the moment culture loses its autonomy, the open society is in jeopardy" and, correlatively, "the task of cultural policy is not to produce culture but to open up the spaces necessary for it to thrive".[24]

The second formative influence on his thinking Hoffmann locates generally in the history of the German labour movement, which – he notes correctly – "conceived of itself from the very beginning primarily as a cultural movement", and in particular in the tradition of cultural socialism epitomized by the Social Democrat Gustav Radbruch (Hoffmann 1990a, pp. 60 and 164).[25] Radbruch was typical of a large group of oppositional intellectuals in the Weimar Republic whose working environment was constituted by the organizations of the working class. For them the problems of reconciling individuality and collectivity, workers and intellectuals, resolved themselves through the continuity of lived experience within the terrain of cultural struggle that had begun long before the 1920s. They were in no doubt that if there was to be any advance towards greater humanity and creative freedom, then such an advance would have to be pressed and fought for by socialist organizations of the working class. In other words, they believed that in terms of its potential for effecting cultural progress the bourgeois class was a spent force and that, on the contrary, it would generate more chauvinism, more intensive exploitation of labour and a marketed mass culture apt to accentuate rather than dissolve existing patterns of prejudice and unequal participation in cultural activity. Hence a concerted effort based on the organizational talent of the proletariat had to be made lest Germany fall into the hands of the same forces that had been responsible for the spiritual devastation and material destruction of the First World War. Even before 1914 there existed a number of organizations more or less openly attached to the SPD – such as the Worker Sports and Gymnastic League, the Worker Singers' Association, the Worker Theatre Association – which began to express the cultural aspirations of the organized proletariat. In the Weimar Republic a sense of urgency asserted itself within sections of the working class in respect of the need to establish a cultural identity for the proletariat as a creative force and a counter-cultural space challenging the existing culture. By the mid-1920s a notion had developed amongst socialists that the attack on capitalist society had to advance in three columns: "The working-class movement", the leading educationalist Valtin Hartig argued in 1926, "is a political, economic and cultural one. Alongside party and trade union there stands as a further column the workers' cultural movement" (Hartig 1926, p. 97). This provided a fertile terrain where intellectuals could deploy their creative talents in the service of socialism and at the same time forge innovative and harmonious modes of collaboration with the organized working class. For the later socialist intellectual Hilmar Hoffmann the worker culture movement, in which millions of individuals were involved, exemplified one of the two main trends in the theory of the labour movement with regard to culture: "One of these sees in culture a compulsory task which subjects the public to a certain extent to an 'enforced state of happiness', while another trend would like to elevate the right to pleasure and personal development for everyone to the status of a political programme" (Hoffmann 1990a, pp. 60–61). It is, of course, the latter project of providing "culture for everyone" that Hoffmann was resolved to sustain in the Federal Republic.

Although this was first given programmatic expression in 1979 in *Kultur für alle*,[26] the conception of culture elaborated in that pioneering work has continued to inform both his subsequent writings and his administrative practice. Essentially, Hoffmann subscribes to the view of culture that was propounded paradigmatically within the discipline of cultural studies by Raymond Williams,[27] namely the broad, anthropological and extended sociological use of the term to indicate a "whole way of life", the entire mental and material habitat of a distinct people or other social group. Accordingly, for Hoffmann culture is to be understood as embracing "that extensive realm of human activity within which the arts are only one part, albeit a particularly important one …; culture also includes our dealings with our selves and with our fellow human beings, with nature and history" (Hoffmann 1990a, p. 19). Decisively wrenched from its exclusive anchorage in "high culture" and its elitist institutions and freed from its restrictive equation with the privileged sphere of artistic production and aesthetic appreciation, culture is to be aligned with broader practices in the media, social action and cognitive behaviour. For Hoffmann the ultimate goal of culture, now conceived as a network of communicative practices, is to generate emancipated citizens empowered to think critically about themselves and their position in the contemporary world. By the same token, that objective can only be attained if access to culture is enjoyed by everyone:

> Every citizen must basically be enabled to appreciate what is available in all branches [of education and culture], no matter how complex and demanding the personal investment of time and money may be. No barriers are to be erected on the basis of income. Neither

money nor unfavourable working hours, neither family and children nor the lack of private transport can be allowed to form obstacles which, in the long term, make it impossible to avail oneself of cultural choices and corresponding activities. ... The range of culture available should neither entrench existing privileges nor erect new ones that are insuperable. ... On the one hand, culture conceived in this fashion is naturally there for everyone because basically everyone contributes through their labour to its fulfilment and the participation in culture is a form of meaningful consumption of social wealth. On the other hand, culture is there for everyone because it is of great significance for the process of discourse and development taking place in society as a whole. Thus conceived, culture is of long-term importance both for society and individuals, if not indeed absolutely essential. (Hoffmann 1979, pp. 11–12)

Predictably, in the light of this, Hoffmann has no qualms in embracing the notion of Germany as a cultural state (*Kulturstaat*). Following the example of Friedrich Schiller in his *On the Aesthetic Education of Man* and long before nationhood assumed political form through the founding of the Second Empire under Bismarck in 1871, it was commonplace to conceive of Germany as a cultural nation (*Kulturnation*). When Hoffmann insists that, as enshrined in the articles of the Basic Law (*Grundgesetz*), the Federal Republic is constitutionally defined as a cultural state, his aim is not, however, the political promotion of national identity on the basis of cultural tradition. Rather, he is arguing that the state (and the municipalities) have a constitutional duty to guarantee the basic provision of, and general access to, culture and to that extent his cherished project of "culture for everyone" can lay claim to constitutional legitimation.[28] This is far from being a plea for greater centralization, however, as is evident from his insistence that "it is only at the grassroots that the Federal Republic can realize itself as a cultural state" (Hoffmann 1979, p. 20). Ideally those grassroots will be constituted by the burgeoning ranks of "cultural citizens" (*Kulturbürger*), a neologism coined by Hoffmann as a positive alternative to the negative associations attaching to the terms *Bildungsbürger* (member of the educated classes) and *Wohlstandsbürger* (affluent citizen).[29]

The emphasis placed on facilitating access to culture in Hoffmann's writings should not prompt the conclusion that he is solely concerned with promoting the (passive) consumption of cultural artefacts. For he frequently quotes with approval the slogan popularized by the sculptor Joseph Beuys, "Everyone is an artist" (*Jeder Mensch ist ein Künstler*; Hoffmann 1979, p. 242; 1990a, pp. 33, 154–155), partly to counter the view that artistic performance by amateurs is synonymous with amateurish practice and to encourage a radical re-reading of "culture for everyone" as the potential programme of "culture by everyone". More substantially, though, Hoffmann wishes to endorse the philosophical premise underpinning Beuys's maxim: for Beuys creativity, imagination and the capacity for dream are the most human of all capabilities and it was less important to him that these be channelled into art than that they be seen as a challenge to everyone to bring about change in themselves in the course of their everyday activity. Interpreted politically, then, Beuys's slogan was meant to imply that "everyone should – as otherwise only the artist in our society can – lay claim to the right to free, self-determined labour" (Hoffmann 1997, p. 242). Utopian though Hoffmann deems this to be, it nevertheless accords with another of his own idealist projects, the humanization of labour, namely his efforts "to define labour in such a way that it is not the case that the one half of society works itself to death and the other half bores itself to death. This is a cultural task of the first order, for it is culture that first mediates the images of how our life could be or, indeed, should be".[30]

This last sentence, of course, could have been articulated by any number of German idealist philosophers (and, indeed, by two contemporaries of Hoffmann whose affinities with the city of Frankfurt are as profound as his own, Theodor W. Adorno and Jürgen Habermas). Certainly, Hoffmann is not embarrassed by the unashamedly idealist nature of his thinking, for "culture is not simply *how* we live but also how we *wish* to live" and consequently "utopias are essential components of culture" (Hoffmann 1990a, pp. 160 and 115). Undoubtedly, however, his most explicit commitment to utopian thought is represented by the following statement, not least because, either in part or whole, it has appeared in three different essays of his:

> Culture and the arts can help design the utopia of a humane future that is constructed on ethical foundations. This utopia lies not in some other place and some far-off time. The time of the utopia is now – and its place is here. (Hoffmann 1990a, p. 36; 1990b, p. 84; 2001, p. 267)

Although Hoffmann very slightly modifies them – albeit, strangely, without acknowledging the original source – the final two sentences were actually uttered by another distinguished German proponent of utopian thinking, Ernst Bloch, the title of whose most influential work, *Prinzip Hoffnung* (The Principle of Hope), could just as easily have emanated from Hilmar Hoffmann himself.

Hoffmann as Cultural Practitioner

In his capacity as practitioner of cultural policy Hoffmann has been described variously as "a practical visionary of civic culture" (Roth 2000 [1990], p. 87) and "the greatest cadger of our cultural republic" (Lunkewitz 2000 [1990], p. 130). Certainly, his period of office as Head of the Department of Culture and Leisure in Frankfurt illustrates perfectly these twin sides of his character, for it is inconceivable that he could have fulfilled his vision of "transforming the city of banks into the city of culture" (Hoffmann 1999b) without the extraordinarily lavish funding he was able to extract from the public purse. At its peak this amounted to some 11 per cent of the annual municipal budget while other towns in Germany had to be satisfied with less than half that sum. To put this figure into further perspective, it can be noted that in 1990 Hoffmann disposed over a budget of almost DM 400 million, a sum half as big again as that made available to him by the end of the decade when he was running the Goethe-Institute with its 150 branches and 4000 employees world-wide! Armed with such munificent financial support Hoffmann was able to reconfigure completely Frankfurt's cultural landscape: the city's historic market square underwent reconstruction and the old opera house was restored; fifteen museums and galleries were built either on new premises or in converted town houses (including the Film Museum, the Architecture Museum, the Jewish Museum and the Schirn Hall of Art); resisting the expansionist desires of the financial services industry (whose imposing buildings are now glorified at night by a newly designed "architecture of light") Hoffmann succeeded in reserving for the cultural projection of Frankfurt a long stretch of the banks of the river Main on which ten of the city's museums and exhibition centres were housed as an integral part of the conceptionally all-embracing programme of the *Frankfurter Museumsufer*. Thus, as demonstrated by the three million visitors drawn annually by this magnificent range of exhibits, under Hoffmann's stewardship the sphere of high culture flourished in Frankfurt as never before. However, impressive though such statistics may be, the clarion call of "culture for everyone" was clearly meant to resonate beyond the traditional institutions of the arts. Hence as a long-standing proponent of adult education Hoffmann could be equally proud of the twenty-three civic community centres and the thirty public libraries that the city boasted as part of his development of its education programme. Similarly, Hoffmann's love of film sustained him, in the face of considerable resistance in the courts from the major commercial cinema chains, in his ambition in the early 1970s to found the first Municipal Cinema in the Federal Republic, an innovation that was to be much imitated throughout the country. Moreover, when Hoffmann first took office he quickly became aware of a lively alternative theatre scene in Frankfurt which, unlike the subsidized private theatres, received no support from the city. This omission he quickly remedied both through the provision of financial subsidies and the development of civic centres where these groups could perform. Most notably, he helped found the *Mousonturm*, the prototype of the multi-media centre that facilitates interaction between professional and alternative culture. This and other activities such as multicultural street parties and festivals were all given generous support "because we wanted to enhance the status of this alternative scene and because the cultural infrastructure of a town is just as important as the 'noble and majestic' municipal theatre".[31]

Hoffmann's commitment to multiculturalism – in a city where some 30 per cent of its inhabitants are not of German nationality, the highest percentage figure in the country – was above all evident in his tenure as President of the Goethe-Institute. Echoing the rhetoric commonly deployed by socialists in the Weimar Republic, and specifically by Willy Brandt in 1967, Hoffmann positions cultural policy, alongside politics and the economy, as the "third pillar" (Hoffmann 1999a; 1999b; 2005, p. 58) of Germany's foreign relations, the primary aim of which is the furtherance of peace and international understanding by means of an intensive but open dialogue between the cultures. In tandem with Foreign Minister Joschka Fischer, Hoffmann could oversee a paradigm change in foreign cultural policy based on their shared conviction that globalization had opened up new opportunities for the Goethe-Institute in addition to those deriving from its status as "an early warning system for political and social change" (Hoffmann 1997, p. 19):

> In the light of increasingly rapid technological cycles our modern economies are based more than ever on our citizens' creativity and freedoms. Freedom is, it is true, an invisible commodity, but nowadays a decisive factor of production. Successful modernization and sustained development require individual rights to freedom. Such a comprehensive "culture of freedom", which is based on the respect for human rights, on the state founded on the rule of law and the separation of powers, is a challenge to the future foreign cultural policy of our democracy … [which], if successful, is then in the very best sense a policy of peace. (Fischer 2000, pp. 194–195)

Hoffmann as Cultural Agenda-Setter

While Hoffmann's many achievements as head of the Goethe-Institute have been heralded by various figures prominent in the political and cultural life of the Federal Republic – including Helmut Kohl, Hans-Dietrich Genscher, Gerhard Schröder, Joschka Fischer, Rita Süßmuth and Alexander Kluge[32] – his claim to the status of cultural agenda-setter rests squarely on the impact his ideas had on the public sphere in the 1970s and 1980s. In the first instance, of course, that influence was most apparent within Hoffmann's own specialist field of cultural policy, which underwent a sea-change in the course of the 1970s. Prior to that, and particularly in the immediate aftermath of the Third Reich, the main objective of cultural policy in the Federal Republic had been to reconnect with, and firmly build on, the cultural traditions of the West. From this early phase onwards the municipalities, wary of any relapse into the fatal error of allowing culture to become streamlined in the service of a loudly proclaimed ideology – as was, indeed, occurring in the German Democratic Republic – took on an elaborate set of activities in the cultural field in their role as self-styled "custodians and nurturers of German culture" (Heinrichs 1997, p. 24). Clearly, the bureaucrats in charge of cultural policy at this time felt obliged to demonstrate that culture was capable of playing an important part in rescuing Germany from the moral pariah status that Nazism had bequeathed it, but they thereby committed themselves almost entirely to a bourgeois concept of culture. Consequently, the main focus of their activity was the mediation of the German and European traditions of high culture in music, drama, literature and art, with popular and mass culture left to look after themselves and little consideration given to more inclusive notions of culture. Precisely the latter concern brought together a group of progressive cultural administrators in the early 1970s who were inspired by the ideal of "culture for everyone" and pledged themselves to the premise that "cultural policy is social policy" (Scheytt 2000, p. 296). In 1976 they formed the Society for Cultural Policy (*Kulturpolitische Gesellschaft*), whose first statement of basic principles included the following:

> It is also increasingly recognized that culture is not mere superstructure, pure decoration of the everyday and ideological idealization of life-contexts through the invoking of the good, the true and the beautiful; rather, it can itself be a productive element of social circumstances. … In Dortmund in 1973 "culture for everyone" has quite rightly been proclaimed by the Council of German Cities and Towns as a communal task of the municipalities: "Cultural work must serve the development of the social, communicative and aesthetic possibilities and needs of all citizens". (Scheytt 2000, p. 296)

Such deliberations also gave rise to what in the 1970s and 1980s became one of the dominant concepts in the discourse of cultural policy, socio-culture. *Sozio-Kultur*, defined abstractly by Hoffmann as "the social use-value of art and culture and its emancipatory quality" (Hoffmann 1990a, p. 327), was construed as a network of communicative practices by his fellow cultural administrator (in Nuremberg) and self-styled "propagandist of the niche", Hermann Glaser:

> Socio-culture is the attempt to conceive of art as a medium of communication: as one very important possibility of providing an additional communicative level within a pluralist society which is dissected into diverse individual interests and conflicts and shot through with specific barriers to understanding. Culture (art) thereby becomes less of a mediator for the content of communication (although it continues to do this) than the originator of new communicative structures. (Glaser 1974, p. 49)

As Dubois and Laborier point out, the new strategic orientations in cultural policy in the early 1970s and the institutional launch of socio-culture were largely initiated by a group of critical intellectuals affiliated to, or aligned with, the SPD (Dubois & Laborier 2003, p. 200). This group, in which Hilmar Hoffmann was a central figure, exerted an influence on their party that went far beyond the sphere of municipal politics and made itself felt in the broad ideological sweep of the party programme. At a time when all the established political parties in Germany were setting out their vision of the Federal Republic as a *Kulturstaat* (cultural state), it was the Social Democrats who advanced the most sophisticated and comprehensive elaboration of the concept of the "culture society" (*Kulturgesellschaft*). Their deliberations, initially formulated in 1986, culminated in the SPD's new Basic Programme of 1989, with its centrepiece, Section IV, pleading for a "new culture of mutual toleration and collaboration" (SPD 1989, p. 20). The projected "culture society" was to engage in responsible interaction with nature, enhance the quality of labour and evolve a political culture which thrived on adversarial debate (*Streitkultur*) rooted in a basic social consensus. Culture, once thought of by socialists as part of an ideological superstructure that was subject to economic determinations, now became defined as the basic social environment which channelled, and gave meaning to, economic activity. In other words, the *Kulturgesellschaft* was clearly seen by the SPD as a project in which society was to be endowed with its cohesion and purpose through the transformative impetus of culture. Although he was not a member of the working party that drew up the SPD's Basic Programme,[33] such thinking bears the unmistakable hallmark of Hilmar Hoffmann. Moreover, the recommendation in that Programme of a thirty-hour working week, while part of an overall strategy for achieving full employment, was also conceived in the spirit of Hilmar Hoffmann as a means of increasing the individual's leisure time, thus affording him/her greater opportunity for participation in cultural activity. Even if this particular vision of the "culture society" had quietly lapsed by the time the SPD was finally re-elected to federal government in 1998, the special status now attaching to culture was recognized in Chancellor Gerhard Schröder's decision to establish what effectively amounted to a federal ministry of culture by creating the new post of Federal Commissioner for Culture and the Media (*Bundesbeauftragter der Bundesregierung für Angelegenheiten der Kultur und der Medien*). Furthermore, Hans Eichel, who for all but the first six months of Schröder's Red-Green government occupied the position of Finance Minister, could still state in the year 2000 that he fully endorsed the postulate of a "culture for everyone" and that "it is an important task of cultural policy to open up unlimited access to culture – and, indeed, in the sense defined by Hilmar Hoffmann" (Eichel 2000, p. 290).

For all that he is clearly cherished by his own party, Hoffmann nevertheless regards cultural policy as too important for it to be the exclusive property of any particular political organization: "As Head of the Department of Culture I am not there in the first instance to carry out a party programme but rather to react to the wishes and needs of the population. Cultural policy is not party politics."[34] This view was reciprocated in 1977 when the SPD lost power on the Frankfurt city council and the new Christian-Democrat Mayor, Walter Wallmann, nevertheless retained Hoffmann in his post as Head of the Department of Culture. Perhaps it is Hoffmann's integrity as a politician *and* intellectual that accounts for the respect in which he is held regardless of political party, for as former Federal President Richard von Weiszäcker has put it: "Hilmar Hoffman is a man of culture who is a political being in the comprehensive and best sense of the word" (von Weizsäcker 2000 [1996], p. 484).

Although Hoffmann insists that the project of "culture for everyone" is today as relevant as ever,[35] it remains to be seen whether the conceptual and practical policy framework he has so ably elaborated and argued for will survive an era where the cultural budgets of the municipalities in Germany are subject to ever greater erosion. Needless to say, this is scarcely a danger to which he is oblivious, for although his writings are infused with an essential optimism bordering at times on the utopian, Hoffman remains constantly alert to what he has termed the "destruction of culture" (*Kulturzerstörung*).[36] Budgetary cuts pose one such threat: "economizing on culture to the point where it is budgeted into the ground is in the long term tantamount to nothing less than the demolition of culture" (Hoffmann 1983, p. 13) given the inevitable social repercussions of such a policy. If, for instance, public libraries are denied the means for new acquisitions, then not only will fewer books come on the market but this will also "hamper both the development of the reading culture and the right to public information" (Hoffmann 1983, p. 13). Similarly, when cultural institutions with high fixed labour costs, such as theatres and opera houses, are subjected to drastic cuts, this entails not only a loss of quality in performance and repertoire but also the destruction of jobs. Moreover, high unemployment is positively detrimental to culture since for most people such "enforced leisure time" will have a demotivating effect rather than opening up real opportunities for cultural participation and access to education (Hoffmann 1983, p. 19). Nor do radical policies predicated on the primacy of market forces and privatization, the frequently touted alternative to financial cuts, gain Hoffmann's approval since "the total subjection of the cultural sphere to the laws of supply and demand would scarcely be less destructive of culture than its subordination to the political demands of the moment" (Hoffmann 1983, p. 13).

Finally, one further aspect of "the destruction of culture" merits discussion here, both because it is singled out by Hoffmann as being especially pernicious and because it returns us to the starting-point of our deliberations. Hoffmann deems culture to be particularly under threat whenever a social atmosphere prevails that is conducive to the wholesale castigation of intellectuals. Such a moment in German history is epitomized for Hoffmann by the burning of the books in May 1933. The most shocking aspect of this anti-intellectual orgy was not so much the participation of students and reputable university professors but the fact that so patent an act of cultural barbarism could be both welcomed and applauded by substantial sections of the German population. The groundwork for this, Hoffmann argues, was laid in the Weimar Republic by the authoritarian treatment meted out to the arts and the critical sciences (Hoffmann 1983, p. 24). Surveying the cultural climate in the Federal Republic exactly fifty years later, Hoffmann could detect an analogous mood fuelled by the thesis that the country was rapidly becoming ungovernable. According to the latter argument the stability and prosperity of Germany as a modern industrial state was being undermined by perpetually carping intellectuals and defeatist artists who, unsolicited, call into question established social bonds and traditions, classical values and virtues (Hoffmann 1983, p. 25). For Hoffmann this negative attitude to intellectuals has its ideological roots in an endemic tradition of cultural pessimism:

> The distorting vocabulary for the disparagement of intellectuals is derived ... from the "glossary of inhumanity". The defamation of intellectuals and artists who by their moral rigour rock the boat, coupled with the unthinking invocation of tradition, prepares the way for a climate in which the disparagement of intellectuals can again be sustained. Are intelligence and creativity, when they cannot be affirmative, only to be despised as destructive elements? (Hoffmann 1983, p. 25)

By contrast, Hoffmann advocates precisely this "critical and, perhaps, even destructive task of art and artists" (Hoffmann 1983, p. 25) while accusing the cultural pessimists of confusing cause and effect. Citing Jürgen Habermas he insists that "the real trouble spots in society have not been created by the spectre of a subversively exuberant culture that allegedly transforms or destroys the patterns of motivation and identity in the lifeworld" (Hoffmann

1983, p. 26). Rather, as Habermas argues, "they owe their existence to economic and administrative imperatives that monetarize and bureaucratize ever more areas of life" (Habermas 1982, p. 1056). By referencing the most prominent social theoretician in Germany the country's foremost intellectual in the field of cultural policy is thus underlining once again the close interrelatedness of culture, theory and politics.

NOTES

1. This essay has been authored in close collaboration, with Wilfried van der Will being mainly responsible for the section on Jürgen Habermas and Rob Burns being mainly responsible for the section on Hilmar Hoffmann.
2. See Saunders (2004).
3. See Posner (2002) and Jennings (2002).
4. See Lohmann (1981) and Lepenies (1992).
5. See *Parteitagsprotokolle SPD 1903: Protokoll über die Verhandlungen des Parteitages der Sozialdemokratischen Partei Deutschlands, abgehalten zu Dresden vom 13.–20. September 1903*, Berlin, p. 225 (cited in Bering 1978, p. 73).
6. See Kautsky (1899, p. 133, cited in Bering 1978, p. 178).
7. See Liebknecht (1958, pp. 166–167, cited in Bering 1978, p. 245).
8. See van der Will and Burns (1982, 1985).
9. These were written by Gramsci between 1929 and 1935 and first published in Italy in six volumes between 1948 and 1951. The section on intellectuals appeared in 1949 (Gramsci 1971, pp. 5–23).
10. See Weber (1923, 1927).
11. This was a reference by the then Federal Chancellor, Konrad Adenauer, to the SPD's law expert, Adolf Arndt (Burns & van der Will 1988, p. 18).
12. See Parkes (1999, pp. 270–271); also Burns and van der Will (1988, pp. 19–52).
13. *Brockhaus Enzyklopädie* (1970, p. 164).
14. See the section on "The Culture Industry: Enlightenment as Mass Deception", in *Dialectic of Enlightenment* (Adorno & Horkheimer 1973, pp. 120–167).
15. See for example the controversial essay by Botho Strauss, "Anschwellender Bockgesang" (Strauss 1994, pp. 19–40).
16. See, respectively, *The Chambers Dictionary* (1997) and *Meyers großes Taschenlexikon* (Mannheim 2001).
17. See *Kulturpolitisches Wörterbuch* (1970, pp. 302–303) and Langenbucher, Rytlewski and Weyergraf (1983, pp. 280–282).
18. This list, put forward jointly by *Prospect* magazine (October and November 2005) and the American journal *Foreign Policy*, received much attention in the British media, principally from *The Guardian* and the BBC "Today Programme".
19. See Lohmann (1981), Lepenies (1992), Posner (2002) and Jennings (2002).
20. This telling phrase (*die Wächterschaft der öffentlichen Kritik*) occurs in Habermas's review of Martin Heidegger's lectures of 1935, *Einführung in die Metaphysik* (Habermas 1953).
21. "Die Einheit der Vernunft in der Vielfalt ihrer Stimmen", originally the title of a lecture at the Fourteenth German Congress for Philosophy in 1987, now in Jürgen Habermas (1992).
22. For example: defining the framework for the media of public opinion and the status of culture as an indispensable asset for a lived European identity; determining the changing levels of legitimation needed for the exercise of power in the modern democratic state;

finding adequate institutional presentation of the nation's attitude to its past; arriving at the right administrative and constitutional expression of European states bound by the Rome and Mastricht treaties, *et al*.

23. "Interview des Monats: Hilmar Hoffmann" (conducted by Bernd Hesse, 11 May 2001), LAKS Hessen (Landesarbeitsgemeinschaft der Kulturinitiativen und soziokulturellen Zentren in Hessen e.V.), 2002 (http://www.laks.de/public/aktiv/interv-hoffmann.htm, accessed 9 February 2004).
24. Quoted in Genscher (2000, p. 17).
25. For a discussion of the workers' cultural movement in the Weimar Republic and of Radbruch's contribution to the development of the SPD's cultural politics, see van der Will and Burns (1982).
26. This was, of course, a conscious echo of a slogan coined by the architect of West Germany's post-war "economic miracle", Ludwig Erhard, namely "affluence for everyone" (*Wohlstand für alle*), which was used very effectively in a election poster in 1957 and as the title of a book by Erhard.
27. This debt to Williams's work is implicitly acknowledged in the very title of the third part of Hoffmann's trilogy, *Kultur als Lebensform* (Culture as a Way of Life), and is made explicit in the text itself (1990a, pp. 98–99).
28. This argumentation is set out in detail in the section "Verfassung und Kulturpolitik", in *Kultur für alle* (Hoffmann 1979, pp. 21–34).
29. The term *Bildungsbürger* acquired negative connotations in that it indicated a social type lacking in political awareness that was produced in great numbers by the nineteenth- and early twentieth-century German grammar school system. Similarly, the term *Wohlstandsbürger* evokes the – for Hoffmann – negative image of a person who equates their quality of life solely with their material standard of living. For the positive attributes evinced by the ideal-typical *Kulturbürger*, see Hoffmann (1990a, pp. 114–115).
30. Quoted in von Weizsäcker (2000 [1996], p. 478).
31. "Interview des Monats: Hilmar Hoffmann", LAKS Hessen (see note 23).
32. See their contributions in Wapnewski and Mucher (2000, pp. 224–225; 186–192; 285–288; 193–195; 214–223; 256–257 respectively).
33. See Burns (1995, pp. 258–261). Inspired by the idealism of Willy Brandt, Hoffmann joined the SPD in 1966 and has remained a member since then (see Hoffmann 2003, pp. 48–50). Between 1983 and 1990 he was Federal Chairman of the party committee Cultural Forum of Social Democracy (*Kulturforum der Sozialdemokratie*).
34. Quoted in Unseld (2000, p. 135). Compare also the following statement: "The politician amongst cultural workers cannot be bound by party policy in the narrower sense. He should be acting on behalf of all sections of the population and therefore he cannot accept the imperative mandate of a party. If need be, he must also go against his own parliamentary group should he consider this necessary" (Hoffmann 1979, p. 19).
35. Cf. "The motto 'culture for everyone' is nowhere near over and done with", "Interview des Monats: Hilmar Hoffmann", LAKS Hessen (see note 23).
36. *Kulturzerstörung* is a key concept in Hoffmann's theoretical armoury. In 1983 he edited a book with this title with invited contributions from, amongst others, Ivan Illich, Eric Hobsbaum, Erich Fried, Melvin J. Lasky and the then Chancellor of Austria, Fred Sinowatz. Hoffmann's introductory essay to this volume was republished in 1990 as a section entitled "Kulturpolitik und Kulturzerstörung" in *Kultur als Lebensform* (Hoffmann 1990a, pp. 119–135).

REFERENCES

ADORNO, TH. W. & HORKHEIMER, M. (1973) *Dialectic of Enlightenment*, Verso, London.

BERING, D. (1978) *Die Intellektuellen: Geschichte eines Schimpfwortes*, Klett-Cotta, Stuttgart.

BÖLL, H. & LINDER, C. (1975) *Drei Tage im März: Ein Gespräch*, Kiepenheuer & Witsch, Cologne.

BROCKHAUS ENZYKLOPÄDIE (1970) vol. 9, Brockhaus Verlag, Wiesbaden.

BURNS, R. (ed.) (1995) *German Cultural Studies: An Introduction*, Oxford University Press, Oxford and New York.

BURNS, R. & VAN DER WILL, W. (1988) *Protest and Democracy: Extra-Parliamentary Opposition and the Democratic Agenda*, Macmillan, Basingstoke.

THE CHAMBERS DICTIONARY (1997) Chambers Harrap Publishers Ltd, Edinburgh.

DERRIDA, J. (1998) 'Interview mit Jacques Derrida. Von Thomas Assheuer', *Die Zeit*, 25 February.

DUBOIS, V. & LABORIER, P. (2003) 'The "social" in the institutionalisation of local cultural policies in France and Germany', *The International Journal of Cultural Policy*, vol. 9, no. 2, pp. 195–206.

EICHEL, H. (2000) 'Kultur in Zeiten knapper Kassen', in *Realitäten und Visionen: Hilmar Hoffmann zu ehren*, eds P. Wapnewski & C. Mücher, DuMont, Cologne, pp. 289–294.

ELSHTAIN, J. B. (2001) *The Nation*, 25 January, p. 3, [online], available at: nation.com/doc.mhtml?i=20010212&c=3&s=forum (accessed 10 January 2004).

FISCHER, J. (2000) 'Ein Glücksfall für Goethe', in *Realitäten und Visionen: Hilmar Hoffmann zu ehren*, eds P. Wapnewski & C. Mucher, DuMont, Cologne, pp. 193–195.

GENSCHER, H.-D. (2000) 'Der Glücksfall Hilmar Hoffmann – Teil 1', in *Realitäten und Visionen: Hilmar Hoffmann zu ehren*, eds P. Wapnewski & C. Mucher, DuMont, Cologne, pp. 17–22.

GLASER, H. (1974) 'Das Unbehagen an der Kulturpolitik', in *Plädoyers für eine neue Kulturpolitik*, eds O. Schwenke, K. H. Revemann & A. Spielhoff, Hanser, Munich, pp. 47–65.

GRAMSCI, A. (1971) *Selections from the Prison Notebooks*, Lawrence & Wishart, London.

HABERMAS, J. (1953) 'Mit Heidegger gegen Heidegger denken: Zur Veröffentlichung von Vorlesungen aus dem Jahre 1935', *Frankfurter Allgemeine Zeitung*, 25 July.

HABERMAS, J. (1962) *Strukturwandel der Öffentlichkeit*, Hermann Luchterhand Verlag, Neuwied and Berlin.

HABERMAS, J. (1963) *Theorie und Praxis: Sozialphilosophische Studien*, Hermann Luchterhand Verlag, Neuwied and Berlin.

HABERMAS, J. (1981) *Theorie des kommunikativen Handelns*, Suhrkamp, Frankfurt/Main.

HABERMAS, J. (1982) 'Die Kulturkritik der Neokonservativen in den USA und in der Bundesrepublik', *Merkur*, vol. 11, pp. 1047–1061.

HABERMAS, J. (1987a) *Eine Art Schadensabwicklung: Kleine Politische Schriften VI*, Suhrkamp, Frankfurt/Main.

HABERMAS, J. (1987b) 'Parteinehmendes analytisches Denken – Ein Brief', in *Befreiung zum Widerstand*, eds K. Brede, H. Fehlhaber, H.-M. Lohmann & M. Mitscherlich, Suhrkamp, Frankfurt/Main pp. 104–107.

HABERMAS, J. (1988) *Der Philosophische Diskurs der Moderne. Zwölf Vorlesungen*, Suhrkamp, Frankfurt/Main.

HABERMAS, J. (1990) *Die nachholende Revolution: Kleine Politische Schriften VII*, Suhrkamp, Frankfurt/Main.

HABERMAS, J. (1991) *Erläuterungen zur Diskursethik*, Suhrkamp, Frankfurt/Main.

HABERMAS, J. (1992) *Nachmetaphysisches Denken: Philosophische Aufsätze*, Suhrkamp, Frankfurt/Main.

HABERMAS, J. (1999) 'Der Zeigefinger. Die Deutschen und ihr Denkmal', *Die Zeit,* archiv, 14 [online] available at: http://zeus.zeit.de/text/archiv/1999/14/199914.denkmal.2_.xml (accessed 12 May 2004).
HABERMAS, J. (2001) *Zeit der Übergänge: Kleine Politische Schriften IX,* Suhrkamp, Frankfurt/Main.
HABERMAS, J. (2003) *Zeitdiagnosen: Zwölf Essays,* Suhrkamp, Frankfurt/Main.
HABERMAS, J. (2005a) 'À nos amis français', *Le Monde,* 3 May.
HABERMAS, J. (2005b) 'Europa ist heute in einem miserablen Zustand', *Die Welt,* 4 May.
HABERMAS, J. (2005c) 'Le non illusoire de la gauche', *Le Nouvel Observateur,* 5 May.
HABERMAS, J. (2005d) 'Europa ist uns über die Köpfe hinweggerollt', *Die Welt,* 6 June.
HABERMAS, J. (2005e) *Zwischen Naturalismus und Religion: Philosophische Aufsätze,* Suhrkamp, Frankfurt/Main.
HABERMAS, J. & DERRIDA, J. (2003a) 'Unsere Erneuerung. Nach dem Krieg: Die Wiedergeburt Europas', *Frankfurter Allgemeine Zeitung,* 31 May.
HABERMAS, J. & DERRIDA, J. (2003b) *Philosophy in a Time of Terror: Dialogues with Jürgen Habermas and Jacques Derrida,* University of Chicago Press, Chicago, IL.
HABERMAS, J. & DERRIDA, J. (2004) *Philosophie in Zeiten des Terrors: Zwei Gespräche, geführt, eingeleitet und kommentiert von Giovanna Borradori,* philo Verlag, Berlin and Vienna.
HARTIG, V. (1926) 'Vom Bildungs- und Kulturproblem der Zeit', *Kulturwille, Monatsblätter für Kultur und Arbeiterschaft,* vol. 3, no. 4, pp. 92–102.
HEINRICHS, W. (1997) *Kulturpolitik und Kulturfinanzierung,* C.H. Beck, Munich.
HOFFMANN, H. (1979) *Kultur für alle: Perspektiven und Modelle,* S. Fischer Verlag, Frankfurt/Main.
HOFFMANN, H. (ed.) (1983) *Kultur-Zerstörung? 10 Römerberggespräche in Frankfurt Am Main,* Athenäum Verlag, Frankfurt/Main.
HOFFMANN, H. (1985) *Kultur für morgen: Ein Beitrag zur Lösung der Zukunftsprobleme,* Fischer Verlag, Frankfurt/Main.
HOFFMANN, H. (1990a) *Kultur als Lebensform: Aufsätze zur Kulturpolitik,* Fischer Verlag, Frankfurt/Main.
HOFFMANN, H. (1990b) *Die Aktualität von Kultur – Probleme mit dem Kulturboom,* Picus-Verlag, Vienna.
HOFFMANN, H. (1997) '"Wir wollen jetzt ein Moratorium". Interview mit dem Präsidenten des Goethe-Instituts Hilmar Hoffmann', *Die Zeit,* 28 November.
HOFFMANN, H. (1999a) 'Basteln an der dritten Säule. Die Aufgaben der auswärtigen Kulturpolitik und die Bedeutung der Goethe-Institute', *Frankfurter Allgemeine Zeitung,* 23 January.
HOFFMANN, H. (1999b) 'Ich war eine Art Überzeugungstäter', *Die Welt,* 10 September.
HOFFMANN, H. (ed.) (2001) *Kultur und Wirtschaft,* DuMont, Cologne.
HOFFMANN, H. (2003) *Erinnerungen: 'Ihr naht Euch wieder, schwankende Gestalten',* Suhrkamp, Frankfurt/Main.
HOFFMANN, H. (2005) 'Ein Minister für Kultur und Medien: Über notwendige Umstrukturierungen der Bundeskulturpolitik', *Kulturpolitische Mitteilungen,* vol. 3, pp. 57–58.
'INTERVIEW DES MONATS: HILMAR HOFFMANN' (2002) 11 May 2001, LAKS Hessen (Landesarbeitsgemeinschaft der Kulturinitiativen und Soziokulturellen Zentren in Hessen e.V.), [online], available at: http://www.laks.de/public/aktiv/interv-hoffmann.htm (accessed 9 February 2004).
JENNINGS, J. (2002) 'Deaths of the intellectual: A comparative autopsy', in *The Public Intellectual,* ed. H. Small, Blackwell, Oxford, pp. 110–129.
KAUTSKY, K. (1899) *Bernstein und das sozialdemokratische Programm,* J. H. Dietz Nachf, Stuttgart.
KULTURPOLITISCHES WÖRTERBUCH (1970) Dietz Verlag, Berlin.

LANGENBUCHER, W. R., RYTLEWSKI, R. & WEYERGRAF, B. (eds) (1983) *Kulturpolitisches Wörterbuch: Bundesrepublik Deutschland/DDR im Vergleich,* J.B. Metzlersche Verlagsbuchhandlung, Stuttgart.

LEPENIES, W. (1992) *Aufstieg und Fall der Intellektuellen in Europa,* Campus Verlag, Frankfurt/Main and New York.

LIEBKNECHT, K. (1958) *Gesammelte Reden und Schriften, III,* Institut für Marxismus-Leninismus bei ZK der SED, Berlin.

LOHMANN, H.-M. (ed.) (1981) *Schweigen die deutschen Intellektuellen? Eine Debatte,* Medusa Verlag, Berlin.

LUNKEWITZ, B. F. (2000 [1990]) 'Hilmar, mein Teuerster!', in *Realitäten und Visionen: Hilmar Hoffmann zu ehren,* eds P. Wapnewski & C. Mucher, DuMont, Cologne, pp. 127–131.

MANNHEIM, K. (1929) *Ideologie und Utopie,* Cohen Verlag, Bonn.

MANNHEIM, K. (1972) *Ideology and Utopia: An Introduction to the Sociology of Knowledge,* Routledge and Kegan Paul, London.

MARX, K. (1972) *Das Kapital: Kritik der politischen Ökonomie,* vol. 1, Dietz Verlag, Berlin.

MEYERS GROSSES TASCHENLEXICON (2001) Bibliographisches Institut & F. A. Brockhaus AG, Mannheim.

PARKES, S. (1999) 'Gruppe 47', in *Encyclopedia of Contemporary German Culture,* ed. J. Sandford, Routledge, London and New York, pp. 269–270.

POSNER, R. A. (2002) *Public Intellectuals: A Study in Decline,* Harvard University Press, Cambridge, MA.

REVIEW (1953) of Martin Heidegger's lectures of 1935, *Einführung in die Metaphysik* (Tübingen, 1953) in *Frankfurter Allgemeine Zeitung,* 25 July.

ROTH, P. (2000 [1990]) 'Hilmar Hoffmann: ein praktischer Visionär der Stadtkultur', in *Realitäten und Visionen: Hilmar Hoffmann zu ehren,* eds P. Wapnewski & C. Mucher, DuMont, Cologne, pp. 87–91.

SAUNDERS, F. S. (2004) 'What have intellectuals ever done for the world?', *The Observer,* 28 November.

SCHEYTT, O. (2000) 'Kulturpolitik als Gesellschaftspolitik – Zum Begründungs-Zusammenhang kommunaler Kulturarbeit', in *Realitäten und Visionen: Hilmar Hoffmann zu ehren,* eds P. Wapnewski & C. Mücher, DuMont, Cologne, pp. 295–310.

SCHILLER, F. (1967) *On the Aesthetic Education of Man, in a Series of Letters,* Oxford University Press, Oxford.

SPD (1989) *Grundsatzprogramm der Sozialdemokratischen Partei Deutschlands: Beschlossen vom Programm-Parteitag der Sozialdemokratischen Partei Deutschlands am 20. Dezember 1989 in Berlin,* Vorstand der SPD, Referat Öffentlichungsarbeit, Bonn.

STRAUSS, B. (1994) 'Anschwellender Bockgesang', in *Die selbstbewußte Nation,* eds H. Schwilk & U. Schacht, Ullstein Verlag, Frankfurt/Main and Berlin, pp. 19–40.

UNSELD, S. (2000) 'Rede anlässlich der Verabschiedung von Kulturdezernent Hilmar Hoffmann', in *Realitäten und Visionen: Hilmar Hoffmann zu ehren,* eds P. Wapnewski & C. Mucher, DuMont, Cologne, pp. 132–141.

WAPNEWSKI, P. & MUCHER, C. (eds) (2000) *Realitäten und Visionen: Hilmar Hofmann zu ehren,* DuMont, Cologne.

WEBER, A. (1923) *Die Not der geistigen Arbeiter,* Duncker & Humblot, Leipzig and Munich.

WEBER, A. (1927) *Ideen zur Staats- und Kultursoziologie,* G. Braun Verlag, Karlsruhe.

VAN DER WILL, W. & BURNS, R. (1982) *Arbeiterkulturbewegung in der Weimarer Republik,* 2 vols, Ullstein Verlag, Frankfurt/Main and Berlin.

VAN DER WILL, W. & BURNS, R. (1985) 'The politics of cultural struggle: Intellectuals and the labour movement', in *The Weimar Dilemma: Intellectuals in the Weimar Republic,* ed. A. Phelan, Manchester University Press, Manchester, pp. 162–201.

VOLKS-BROCKHAUS (1941) 9th edn, Verlag Brockhaus, Leipzig.

VON WEIZSÄCKER, R. (2000 [1996]) 'Laudatio zur Verleihung des Wartburg-Preises an Hilmar Hoffmann am 9. November 1996', in *Realitäten und Visionen: Hilmar Hoffmann zu ehren,* eds P. Wapnewski & C. Mucher, DuMont, Cologne, pp. 478–484.

PUBLIC INTELLECTUALS AND CULTURAL POLICY IN FRANCE

Jeremy Ahearne

In an encyclopaedia entry on intellectuals and cultural policy in France, Rémy Rieffel argues that "state intervention in cultural matters has always provoked a certain mistrust on the part of French intellectuals, who are inclined to be individualist and anti-authoritarian. The figure of the intellectual as 'critic of power' has remained dominant throughout the Fifth Republic [i.e. since 1958], although one can observe the beginnings of a change in this posture with the accession of the Left to power in 1981" (Rieffel 2001, p. 342). It is certainly true that intellectuals in France over the Fifth Republic have tended to remain averse to the nuts and bolts of policy-making (cf. also Reader 1987, p. 22). I propose in this article, however, to nuance somewhat the picture painted by Rieffel: over the years of Gaullist and right-wing government between 1958 and 1981, one can observe interesting forms of participation in the policy process on the part of broadly left-leaning intellectuals; in the years after 1981, one is struck not simply by further instances of such participation, but also by a persistent reticence or hostility towards cultural policy on the part of both left and right-wing intellectuals. I shall look to probe further this aversion to the world of policy-making as such, asking why it might seem surprising to an outside observer; why nonetheless, on consideration of French intellectual history over the twentieth century, it can be seen as understandable; and how, indeed, it can in some senses be seen as all too understandable. I shall consider not just policy processes associated with the Ministry of Culture and Communication, as it is now called, but also certain policy developments issuing from the Ministry of Education, insofar as these have as much and often more bearing on the overall action that a regime directs towards culture (understood not just as aesthetic education, but also as historical memory, the vulgarization of science, and the diffusion of information within the contemporary media landscape).

Public Intellectuals and Public Policy: A Curious Divergence?

The figure of the public intellectual as it evolved in France over the twentieth century can be seen as representing a form of extra-governmental cultural-political action in its own right. This is not simply because, to take the inaugural case of Zola in the Dreyfus affair as analyzed by Bourdieu, the intellectual exploits symbolic capital accrued in the cultural field in order to achieve properly political effects (Bourdieu 1996 [1992], pp. 129–131). Nor is it just because the intellectual can be usefully defined, to adapt Ory and Sirenelli's terms, as a figure from the cultural world taking up a position in the political world.[1] Public intellectuals have not always used culture purely as a kind of external leveraging device to pursue political objectives. Instead, their interventions have frequently been characterized by a particular style and content, insofar as they can bring broader frames of reference to bear on given political problems and issues. They can take a "long view" of cardinal notions in public policy debate (laicity and religion; the cathartic or incitive effects of violent aesthetic spectacles; the purposes of education or the value of art; cultural democracy, etc.). Certainly, this long view can amount to little more than a vague view. However, where the operation is performed effectively, the broader frames of reference that constitute an intellectual "culture" as such are thereby given a political valency which they would not have if these problems and issues were the province purely of technical experts and politicians. As a persistent mode of engagement, running beneath the threshold of specific debates or interventions, this amounts to something like a "sub-liminal" form of cultural politics. As a course or style of action, the implicit message is repeatedly conveyed that a detour through the works of a cultural tradition (or counter-tradition) can give us a better understanding of the issues immediately facing us. I shall consider below how this message has found it increasingly more difficult to get a hearing amidst ambient interference and noise. Nonetheless, it provided for a long time for the French intellectual a forceful *raison d'être*.

In the light of this, it would seem logical that French intellectuals should look to position themselves in such a way that they can bring the demands of culture to bear upon the development of governmental public policy. There have been powerful precedents for this. The function of the intellectual clearly predates the invention of the name at the turn of the twentieth century, and one might cite the great *philosophe* and mathematician Condorcet presiding over the 1791–1792 Legislative Assembly's Committee for Public Instruction (often seen as drawing up the blueprint for the republican tradition in French education).[2] The *Cartel des Gauches* government of 1924 was famously described as the "Republic of the Professors" on account of the symbolic prominence within it of the products of the *Ecole Normale Supérieure*, the almost exclusive breeding ground of French intellectuals (Thibaudet 1927). Intellectuals and cultural organizations in general played a key role in the campaign and subsequent administration of the Popular Front government in 1936 (Ory & Sirenelli 1992 [1986], pp. 93–113).

At the same time, however, the relations between the "intellectual" and "political" fields (or between "spiritual" and "temporal" powers) have been marked by fundamental tensions. This is manifest in the theme of intellectual "treason" that runs at least since Charles Péguy (1959 [1907], p. 1116) like a leitmotif through the twentieth-century history of French intellectuals. For Julien Benda (1975 [1927], pp. 171, 177), intellectual "clerics" committed treason when they subordinated their responsibility for the "eternal and disinterested values" of justice and reason to the temporal "passions" of nation or political party. For thinkers such as Nizan (cf. 1960 [1932], p. 123), clerical detachment was in itself a betrayal insofar as the mission of intellectuals should be radically to challenge and practically to overturn an unjust political order. For both such tendencies, however, extended participation in "really existing" policy processes would, in one way or another, amount to a form of treason. The "mistrust" evoked above as regards intellectuals' public policy involvement during the Fifth Republic is not, therefore, without a tradition of its own.

The Surrender and Preservation of Intellectual Autonomy

If one considers French intellectual history over the mid-twentieth century, one will find further reasons why subsequent intellectuals might want to mark absolutely their distance with regard to political authorities. Like the occupying Nazi powers in the North, the collaborationist Vichy government in the South placed the cultural "renovation" of the country high on its agenda, and was able to enlist willing intellectuals to help it in its mission. Using the example of Paul Morand, Ory and Sirinelli show how Vichy could assign to its intellectuals the classic functions of an "organic intelligentsia": Morand could be used for purposes of symbolic "ostentation" (he had worked at the Foreign Office after the Munich concessions to Hitler in 1938, and was later named by Vichy as an ambassador at Bucharest and then Bern); he could be used as a "counsellor" in cultural affairs (he was given a place on Vichy's Book Council); and he could be deployed in the "management of cultural life" (via the all-powerful Commission for Control of Publishing Paper, and also the Commission for Film Censorship) (Ory & Sirinelli 1992 [1986], p. 127). After the war, as Paxton has noted, "those traditionalists [at Vichy] who had occupied policy-making positions came before the High Court of Justice", while "the fate of the overtly fascist intellectuals and party leaders in occupied Paris was even more final. Men of public platforms, their words condemned them to suffer at the Liberation" (Paxton 2001 [1972], pp. 344–345). Alongside such dramatic national stagings of intellectual complicity, there were also less clear-cut examples whose very ambiguity, nonetheless, may have exerted after the event a similarly dissuasive force on some. *Jeune France* and the leadership college at Uriage, paragovernmental organizations first promoted and then disavowed by Vichy, brought together a number of figures who would become prominent intellectuals after the war (Chabrol 1990).

The French Communist Party played a major part in the internal resistance to the Vichy regime, and this played no small part in the intellectual prestige (some speak of "hegemony") it enjoyed in the immediate post-war years. Many intellectuals saw in it not just an alternative to fascism and bourgeois liberal democracy, but also a means of combining theoretical sophistication, as they conceived it, and political efficacy. Indeed, the rallying of intellectuals was itself a key component of the French Communist Party's cultural policy (Caute 1964, pp. 11, 15–16). In an attempt to coin a self-fulfilling prophecy, Georges Cogniot described it in 1945 at its Tenth Conference as "The Party of French Intelligence", and the party leader Maurice Thorez proclaimed at the Twelfth Conference in 1950 that "to those intellectuals who are disorientated and lost in the labyrinth of their questions, we bring certainties and possibilities of unlimited development" (quoted in Ory & Sirinelli 1992 [1986], pp. 151, 160). The cultural policy apparatus of the Party was extensive, and offered the possibility of practical "orientation" to any number of minor and major intellectuals and fellow travellers, many of whom, David Caute argues, saw in communism and/or Marxism a continuation of the tradition of the Enlightenment (1964, p. 212). What is striking in retrospect is the readiness of intellectuals to suspend the legacy of the Enlightenment (Bayle's "droit de la conscience errante" – the right to a wandering/erring consciousness) in order to fall into line with the aesthetic and theoretical norms laid down by party apparatchiks. As Ory and Sirinelli note, the relations which these cultural apparatchiks, such as Laurent Casanova, entertained with regard to culture and intellectuals were purely "external" and "instrumental" (1992 [1986], pp. 159–160). For Caute, "the tragedy of French communism was not the intellectuals it seduced or those it lost, but rather those it maimed" (1964, p. 366). Interestingly, Jeannine Verdès-Leroux suggests that this intellectual abdication may be explained in terms of an inveterate malaise, a tendency of intellectuals themselves to doubt of that very culture that constitutes their identity and their *raison d'être*:

> If communist intellectuals during the Cold War bowed, humiliated, lowered and cretinised themselves so willingly on the orders of the Party, it is because intellectuals in some parts of the field entertain permanent doubts not only about intellectual work but also about the value of culture; these are sometimes expressed in scholarly, rationalised, or euphemised forms, but sometimes also in brutal forms. For Nizan, "Between culture as an inheritance and symbol of an inheritance, and the proletariat, the mass of non-inheritors, no reconciliation is possible." (Verdès-Leroux 1983, pp. 23–24)

Lest one pronounce judgement in undue haste, one can clearly not through a kind of contrary dictate prevent a critically disposed "wandering consciousness" from turning on itself and uncovering the socially overdetermined composition of culture. Strands in the thinking of figures such as Tolstoy, Sartre or Bourdieu all attest to the "brutal" irruption of such doubts. But it is clear in retrospect that these doubts – and perhaps a desire to eject them once and for all out of one's consciousness – led many intellectuals during the Cold War to become footsoldiers in what one might call an anti-cultural cultural policy.

In explaining the aversion of intellectuals over recent decades towards engagement in the nuts and bolts of the policy process, one can therefore invoke, as it were, a principle of the scalded cat (who, in French parlance, looks to learn from his experience by giving boiling water – organic adhesion to party politics – a wide berth). Certainly, a detailed analysis of the immediate aftermath of the war would introduce important nuances. Significant policy thinking had taken place within the institutional apparatuses of the Resistance. Even the most anti-authoritarian of thinkers (such as Sartre himself) were for a while prepared to take part in certain more or less official "nation-building" activities on behalf of the French State (Kelly 2004, pp. 95–99). Nonetheless, the very different records of intellectuals' policy collaboration with Vichy or the French Communist Party would, like dead stars, continue to project powerful and dissuasive historical after-images.

There is, however, also a more positive tradition in French intellectual history that looks to preserve the free unbounded inquiry seen as constitutive of the cultural realm from the instrumentalizing thrust of party political strategy. A powerful and perhaps formative statement of this can be found, paradoxically it might seem, in the educational policy reports of Condorcet. It is a statement of what I would call an anti-political cultural policy: anti-political not in the sense of a depoliticization, but in the sense of a politically conditioned resistance to the short-term demands of political expediency in the name of certain longer term demands associated with the cultural realm (what Condorcet in his political theory would call the sovereignty of truth). Condorcet was writing against the model of a "total" educational/cultural policy, and the concomitant "political religion" (1994 [1791], p. 93) espoused by the likes of Robespierre, Rabaut de Saint-Etienne, and other followers of Rousseau. Imagining they were following in the footsteps of Ancient Sparta, such figures argued for a "common education" whose function was to instil in future citizens a common set of beliefs, principles and character-traits that would ensure a cohesive, virtuous and virile republic. By contrast, Condorcet argued that the Republic should provide all citizens with "instruction" designed precisely to protect them from such indoctrination, and that active policy steps needed to be taken to institute and maintain school as a cultural apparatus set off from the political field as such in which an effective liberty of thought could be cultivated:

> The freedom of such opinions would only be illusory if society took hold of new generations to dictate to them what they must believe. The man who enters society with those opinions that his education has given him is not a free man; he is the slave of his masters, and his chains are all the more difficult to break because he himself does not feel them, and he thinks he is obeying his reason when he is only submitting to that of another. [...] The Ancients had no notion of this kind of freedom; indeed the only goal of their institutions seemed to be to destroy it. They would have wanted to leave men only those ideas and feelings that fitted in with the system of their legislator. (Condorcet 1994 [1791], pp. 85–86)

Condorcet was, of course, pioneering that most misunderstood of French political notions – laicity (*laïcité*). The term itself would not be coined until the nineteenth century, but its principal elements can be found in his reports: the wresting away of control over education and culture from all agents of dogmatic orthodoxy, whether ecclesiastical or political, in order to allow individual opinions and reason to develop in a non-clerical or "lay" environment. Significantly, the term would be strongly reasserted 150 years later, in another classic educational blueprint produced by two prominent intellectuals, Paul Langevin and Henri Wallon. In the immediate aftermath of the Second World War, and of the "streamlining" (*Gleichschaltung*) of the political and cultural spheres operated this time by the Nazis and associated collaborators, Langevin and Wallon were once again arguing for the institutionally guaranteed disjunction of the two:

> Public schooling, like the State itself, is, in the terms of the constitution, a lay institution ['laïque" – non-clerical would be an inadequate translation], which is to say that, open to all children, it cannot and must not offer any doctrinally, politically or religiously motivated teaching. (Langevin & Wallon 2004 [1946], p. 70)

This tradition of a distance between the State and culture that intellectuals call upon the State itself to institute and maintain was further developed by Bourdieu another 50 years later. In a conversation with the conceptual artist Hans Haacke, we see him developing it beyond the reference to *laïcité* and schooling (which undoubtedly represented the most significant cultural apparatus at the time of both Condorcet and the Langevin–Wallon report) to embrace the cultural policy field as a whole:

> There are a certain number of conditions regarding the existence of a critical culture that can only be assured by the State. In short, we [in the cultural field] must expect (and even demand) from the State the instruments through which we can acquire our liberty in relation to the powers-that-be – economic powers, but also political powers, i.e. as regards the State itself. (Bourdieu & Haacke 1995 [1994], pp. 71–72; trans. mod.)

There are thus good negative reasons as well as good positive reasons for French intellectuals to resist being drawn too closely into the party political policy process. Not only has twentieth-century history shown the price that can be paid for the abdication by intellectuals of their cultural autonomy, the protection of that autonomy from political control also represents an important political principle. The paradox is perhaps that this deliberate distantiation from political pressure – an "anti-political cultural policy" – could not be effectively maintained through a generalized abstention on the part of intellectuals from processes of policy formation.³

Intellectual Play and Prestige

There are other reasons one can adduce to explain the aversion of French intellectuals to meaningful engagement in the cultural policy-making process. One can perhaps best describe these not so much as understandable as all too understandable, insofar as they can be correlated with the dynamics of self-interest and symbolic capital accumulation as they function in the field of intellectual production. In a famously clamourous debate on the "silence of the intellectuals" that ran in the columns of Le Monde, the leading French intellectual newspaper, over the summer of 1983, much was made of the reluctance of most intellectuals to throw their weight behind the policies of the Socialist government (see Looseley 1995, pp. 84–87). This has been explained in terms of the difficulty for narcissistically or naively "radical" intellectuals in coming to terms with the compromises required by real politics (the economic U-turn of the Socialists took place in 1983). Ory and Sirnelli also suggest that intellectuals had not identified with Mitterand's government insofar as, when it became the first left-wing administration of the Fifth Republic in 1981, they had done little to secure its victory, having become prematurely fatalistic about the Socialist Party's chances after its electoral defeat in 1978 (1992 [1986], p. 234). I think that much could also be made, however, of an apparently flippant remark by Philippe Sollers, a famous ex-maoist, whom the arrival of the Socialist government had pushed to the political right: "Intellectuals are on the side of the opposition. By definition. In principle. Through physical necessity. As part of their game (*par jeu*)" (quoted by Ory & Sirnelli 1992 [1986], p. 234). Admittedly, my translation skews the text a little here. "Par jeu" also evokes the intellectual "free play of ideas" that one would certainly not wish to belittle. Nevertheless, the fundamental point stands. It is undoubtedly true that an oppositional stance did for a number of decades play well in the French intellectual field – a field described by Bourdieu as "the economic world reversed" (1993, pp. 29–73) – and one need not be entirely misanthropic to see the cultivation of oppositional credentials as a prudent device for self-advancement (among many other things, of course).

The same point can be made the other way round, as it were, by examining the fate of intellectuals who have become too closely tied to policy processes for their own good, at least insofar as their intellectual reputation is concerned. The educationalist Philippe Meirieu recounts how his sustained collaboration under Lionel Jospin's prime ministership with Socialist Ministers of Education Claude Allègre (1997–2000) and Jack Lang (2000–2002) sent his standing among his peers into freefall:

> My move into the political sphere has proved disastrous in more than one sense [...]. I have, for many people, gone from the status of an intellectual reference point to that of an ideologue, a polemicist, or even simply "Allègre's puppet".

I am convinced that the fact of having accepted institutional responsibilities has been the determining factor in this disaffection. Traditionally, teachers are distrustful of those who get engaged in and support the development of a policy; they find it easier to identify with those who opt for the side of resistance and opposition. They think that the proper academic posture is that of critical elevation, of distance with regard to decision-makers that allows one to exercise the function of impertinence that the French cherish so much. People generally think that you need a lot of courage to say no. [...] That's clearly true when you're facing up to pressure from the powers-that-be, to prejudices, fashions and, *a fortiori*, all forms of totalitarianism. But I believe that, for intellectuals and academics, you also need a certain amount of courage to say: "Yes ... yes, I'll sign up, that's what I support." It's even, in many ways, the height of nonconformism. (Meirieu & Le Bars 2001, pp. 35–36)

Meirieu recounts in the same book his doctrinal disagreements with Régis Debray (as an educationalist promoting a "socio-cultural" and pupil-centred approach to pedagogy, Meirieu was accused by some on the self-styled "republican" pole of educational debate of diluting cultural standards in education).[4] Nevertheless, one is struck in reading the passage above by the similarities between the experiences of Meirieu and those of Debray himself. Debray's political memoirs recount how his experience as full-time advisor to President Mitterand over much of the 1980s – notwithstanding his own ambivalence about this – was seldom seen as adding an extra dimension to his reflection, and was often seen as simply disqualifying that reflection (see e.g. Debray 1996). It was perhaps in part due to this experience that, when Debray and Meirieu met to discuss their differences, rather to Meirieu's surprise, Debray was prepared to listen and learn, rather than simply to assert and condemn (Meirieu & Le Bars 2001, pp. 72–74).

It goes without saying that intellectuals must get involved in politics. It sometimes seems to go without saying that intellectuals must not get too closely involved in the policy process. Why might this be? In a very different context, Ian Maclean (1993) has studied the shifts that made a notion like "policy" conceivable at all over the early modern period (from Machiavelli through Justus Lipsius to Hobbes). Prior to these shifts, a ruler's actions were seen as a direct emanation of his moral disposition, or "habitus" in the Aristotelian sense. The key attribute of this moral disposition was Prudence, insofar as, again for Aristotle, "Prudence is the only form of goodness which is peculiar to a ruler".[5] Policy in the modern sense could only be conceived when a course of action could, as it were, be detached from the moral disposition of the ruler, stated in neutral terms and thus assessed in its own right as an artifice selected from among other artifices designed to achieve defined objectives. Maclean argues that the direct association of political action with a moral disposition constituted an "obstacle" to the emergence of "policy" in its modern sense (1993, p. 18). Now one might contend, it seems to me, to follow a rather uncontrolled analogy, that the types of politics to which French intellectuals gravitated over the twentieth century were those that could be seen directly to express a certain moral disposition or habitus. Clearly, this disposition was seldom one of Aristotelian "Prudence", and was closer to the kind of a priori oppositionalism described above (Looseley speaks of an "instinctively oppositional mind-set": 1995, p. 85). Such political moves, while occasionally no doubt disastrous, could be seen as salutary and necessary insofar as they place on the political agenda through public controversy issues that a political class would rather ignore. However, they evinced an important limitation.

A classic example, to remain within the domain of cultural policy, would be Francis Jeanson's resonant denunciation in 1968 of Malraux's policy of cultural democratization and his evocation of the vast "non-public" represented by those whom it was unlikely ever to touch. This was an accurate diagnosis, and phrased in such a way that it could readily chime with the period's oft-affirmed "politics of desire" (hence its place in the famous "Villeurbanne declaration" of May 1968: Jeanson et al. 2002 [1968], p. 71). When it came to framing realistic policy measures to address the situation, however, it was difficult to retain the same resonance (Looseley describes the text of the declaration as a "curious hybrid": 1995, p. 44). Indeed the notion of a "policy of desire" seems, in English, rather more incongruous (the French "politique" allows the two notions to be run together and thus not to jar with each other). "Policy" as an intellectual object seems altogether less conducive to the untrammelled ostentation of high moral conscience. It is in this sense less gratifying for public intellectuals. It requires, as it were, a certain suspension of the immediately "expressive" inclinations of their disposition in order to be considered as a quasi-technical artifice statable in neutral terms and designed to take its place in a crowded field of other such policies and forces, with unpredictable side-effects or unintended consequences. Olivier Donnat, for example, a policy analyst at the Ministry of Culture, described in 1991 how well-meaning endeavours to attract fractions of a "non-public" to cultural institutions have often backfired in a number of ways. Attempts to bring in audiences from different social backgrounds are liable to have little impact on overall attendance figures as more established audiences are driven away (amongst other things, the mechanisms of social distinction analyzed by Bourdieu are obdurate and deep-seated in the cultural field). Attempts aimed at increasing overall attendances are liable to reinforce the preponderance of higher social classes among audiences, insofar as these constitute the densest pool of potential attenders in which to publicize performances (cf. Donnat 2002 [1991], pp. 142–143). None of this necessarily invalidates Jeanson's call to arms (indeed, Jeanson was one of the very rare intellectuals prepared to get involved not just in the framing but also in the very implementation of policy, by taking on from 1967 the directorship of the *House of Culture* at Chalon; Jeanson 2002 [1971]). It does suggest, however, what is involved in a move from a classic "tribune-based" function of the intellectual (pronouncing resonantly from a raised platform – cf. the Latin, *tribunal* – on issues of public relevance) to an involvement in the refractory and often perverse world of policy. It seems at least conceivable (and this is just a hypothesis) that the impatience of the public intellectual to (be seen to) pursue a moral mission and to declaim this in sonorous terms might constitute an "obstacle" in its turn to a more alienating and less gratifying engagement with the artifices of policy.

It is true that over the last two or three decades, the "purely" oppositional intellectual has become less exclusively dominant in France. The discredit of radical "leftism" and the international communist movement that so marked the late 1970s in France opened a space for a more assertive reformist and liberal seam of French intellectuals. Such figures have congregated notably around reviews like *Le Débat* and *Esprit*, or, on the right, around *Commentaire*. In a sense, they have projected themselves in opposition to the a priori oppositionalism described above, describing themselves less as radical critics than as "competent guides" in a context of "anti-totalitarianism" and "intellectual democracy" (Pierre Nora, in Lepape 1990). They have certainly not, as is sometimes suggested, simply effaced more systemically critical intellectuals from the scene (one might cite, among such figures who have worked on the interface between culture and politics, important thinkers like Pierre Bourdieu or Jacques Rancière). They have, however, inevitably spoken in a language that is less incompatible with reformist government. Gérard Noiriel has even categorized such figures as "intellectuals of government" (2005, pp. 103–199). This seems to me to be somewhat tendentious (indeed, the term oscillates in Noiriel's account between a useful analytic term and a term of denigration for intellectuals of whom he disapproves).[6] For simply to take up a reformist or liberal position within the intellectual field, or even to mix with certain political figures, is not in itself equivalent to participating in the process of government.

Intellectuals in the Policy Process

Nevertheless, as indicated above, a number of French public intellectuals have become more or less involved in policy processes affecting the cultural domain over the Fifth Republic. Whilst this may have represented for some a degree of nonconformism along the lines suggested by Meirieu, one should not necessarily think of this as some kind of abnegation. Kingdon distinguishes three incentives for "policy entrepreneurs" to become involved in the policy process: material and personal career incentives; "purposive" incentives (the promotion of values or an ideology in which one believes); and "solidary" incentives (attracting what Kingdon calls "policy groupies" who "simply like the game", and who "enjoy being at or near the seat of power [and] enjoy being part of the action") (2003, p. 123).[7] Material incentives seem a pertinent consideration in many respects for their absence in the present context (though this may well warrant closer inspection in some cases). "Purposive" incentives, as far as French public intellectuals are concerned, would seem to be a generally evident necessary condition of their involvement in the policy process. But it may be worth dwelling a little more on the notion of "solidary" interests. Ory and Sirinelli note how those communist intellectuals who had most difficulty severing their links with the party were those who had been most involved in the party apparatus (1992 [1986], p. 186). Their affective investment in this apparatus, which they had, so to speak, introjected so that it constituted the core of their self-conception, made their departure into an existential crisis rather than an intellectual decision. Other less intense examples also suggest that the apparatus of policy-making can be more subjectively involving, and indeed gratifying, than it may appear from the outside (whence it may look, in Matthew Arnold's phrase, like mere "machinery"). Laurent Gayme describes the Cultural Commission of the Sixth Plan (1969–1971) as a "veritable structure of sociability" (1995, p. 67), and this is confirmed by accounts of the informal socio-intellectual networks forming around the Ministry's research unit in the years following the Sixth Plan (see e.g. Dosse 2002, pp. 443–462). Certainly, such "solidary" incentives can cloud as well as invigorate judgement. Régis Debray evokes self-disparagingly his inveterate desire to be "dans le coup" (where the action is), and the self-dispersion to which this led him over the 1980s (1996).

A number of public intellectuals in France have thus become involved in the policy process despite the general censure that has often been attached to such moves, and they have done this for a range of complex reasons. Indeed, one of the most prominent and singular of French intellectuals, André Malraux, became France's first Minister for Culture, and played a major part in "inventing" the cultural policy that became institutionalized through the country's first Ministry for Cultural Affairs. However, Malraux's case is fairly well known even outside France, and so I will concentrate in what follows on other less familiar developments.[8]

Some intellectuals seem to have become enmeshed fairly unproblematically in the policy process. Vincent Dubois has described a period during the 1960s that was marked by a "planning utopia" (2003, p. 26), when the higher echelons of the State administration looked to develop public policies directly informed by "scientific" expertise. This was promoted particularly through the peculiarly French institution of "The Plan", a then powerful advisory body officially set off from government as such, but supposed to inform the policy of government and other institutions by indicating the means for its "rationalisation" and "modernisation". The fledgling Ministry of Culture looked to attach itself to this movement both in order to legitimate its as yet uncertain existence and to secure extra funding for its projects. In this way, principally through their participation in those commissions of the Fourth and Fifth Plans dedicated to cultural policy, a number of social scientists were drawn into the development of policy. Some of these could be described as public intellectuals. The prime example would probably be Joffre Dumazedier, the president of the popular education movement "Peuple et Culture" and generally seen at the time as the leading expert on the "sociology of leisure". Dumazedier's major discursive achievement was to pioneer and consolidate the acceptance of a broadly conceived notion of "cultural development" as an adjunct to the established categories of "economic" and "social" development, and as a proper object for governmental concern.[9] It is true that the notion ran counter to Malraux's insistence on a more restrictive understanding of culture, but the category would in due course be taken up not just by the French Ministry of Culture (it would become a guiding notion for the Duhamel administration between 1971 and 1973), but also internationally (notably via UNESCO).

The collaboration of academic social scientists would become an enduring component of the development of French cultural policy due in large part to the work of Augustin Girard. Having collaborated with researchers in his role as *rapporteur* for the Plan, Girard set up in 1963 a dedicated research unit at the Ministry of Culture, which he would subsequently direct for thirty years. I have suggested elsewhere how this unit (now called the *Département des Etudes, de la Prospective et des Statistiques* (DEPS)) became the prime mover in the fostering of a highly developed cultural policy research ecology in France. Antoine Hennion describes it as playing a "decisive" role in mobilizing researchers around particular themes or programmes, and gaining a position as a "privileged interlocutor" for academic researchers in their relations with "political powers and the State with regard to cultural questions" (1996, pp. 3, 5). It allowed, as Jean-Louis Fabiani has put it, researchers, administrators and cultural agents to "co-produce" over time a set of intellectual "tools" for the critical understanding of cultural policy issues (Fabiani et al. 2003, p. 310).[10] It has provided, as it were, a niche in which particularly acute forms of cultural policy expertise could develop (one might cite just a few names – Paul-Henry Chombart de Lauwe, Raymonde Moulin, Olivier Donnat, Pierre-Michel Menger, Antoine Hennion, Pierre Mayol, Jean-Louis Fabiani …). However, the focus of the present article is not cultural policy expertise as such. It is, rather, the role of the public intellectual within cultural policy processes. And the figure of the public intellectual cannot be subsumed under that of the expert. On the contrary, there is a basic difference, and not infrequently an antagonism between the two (with, of course, predictable strategies for mutual belittlement). For public intellectuals can be defined, for better and for worse, by a will to move beyond their range of expertise, to throw themselves about and, in Sartre's classic phrase, to "get involved in things that are none of their business" (Sartre 1972, p. 377). How have such figures been involved in policy processes?

The first point to be made is that the dividing line between the "expert" and the "public intellectual" is neither clear-cut nor stable. Particularly in such an elastic domain as the cultural field, where does expertise begin and end? Virtuosity in the statistical and sociological apprehension of the cultural field can co-exist with considerable naivety in the approach to cultural content – and vice-versa. Moreover, it is a peculiarity of French cultural policy debate that certain specialist products of the Ministry's research unit have themselves become the objects of a widespread debate that has transcended specialist interpretation (a statistical synthesis published in 1990 sold 11,000 copies: Dubois 2003, p. 28). Finally, the role of the Ministry's research unit is not best understood as that of a well-oiled supplier of up-to-the-minute evidence dovetailing neatly with the demands of government. It has tolerated and even nurtured – sometimes against the inclinations of government – considerably more refractory and contrary approaches to policy engagement.

I have studied some of these at considerable length elsewhere (Ahearne 2004), and so will just briefly evoke them here. The work for Pierre Bourdieu's classic study from 1966 uncovering the sociological determinants of art appreciation, *The Love of Art* (Bourdieu & Darbel 1991), was partially sponsored by Girard (Poirrier 1997, pp. 31–32). It seems that the research itself, at the time, met largely with bemusement and indifference on the part of policy-makers (Poirrier 1997, pp. 31–32), though its subsequent influence has been such that it has become a classic reference point in policy debate, and can even appear as mere "common sense". Interestingly, at the time, Bourdieu would omit any mention of his contacts at the Ministry when the book was published, while Girard himself was apparently obliged to conceal the publication from his superiors (Moulin 1993, p. 69). Although Bourdieu at the time was effectively a sociologist of culture rather than a public intellectual as such, this work clearly played a role in his accession to a more public stage. Similarly, Michel de Certeau was able to develop the groundwork for his classic 1980 study *The Practice of Everyday Life* through a succession of formal and semi-formal arrangements with Girard's unit over the 1970s, at a time when the prevailing neo-liberal government would have been hostile to his agenda of broadening cultural policy programmes to integrate a wider range of practices. Again, Certeau's studies have since become a classic reference point in cultural policy debate. The point I want to underline here is that engagement in public policy processes does not necessarily imply total absorption into a State conceived as a homogeneous entity. A point made by Kingdon in reference to American politics could equally well be applied to the research unit at the Ministry of Culture: "Civil servants in locations like planning and evaluation offices continue to work on proposals of various kinds, keeping them ready for the opportunity that will be provided by a receptive administration to push the idea into prominence" (2003, p. 32). In other words, the labyrinth of the modern liberal State can be seen as holding potential interstices, maintained by different kinds of agents, within which public intellectuals can on occasion access resources and pursue agendas that can contradict or at least unsettle official governmental agendas of the time.

At other times, public intellectuals have looked to take a more prominent role than that of working covertly within the interstices of the system within a more or less long-term horizon. In the wake of May 1968, one even sees an effort to impose an official forum for policy deliberation that would rival that of the Ministry itself. This began with the Cultural Commission for the Sixth Plan (1969–1971), which took on a much more critical stance with regard to the State than the equivalent commissions of the Fourth and Fifth Plans (designed to cover the periods 1962–1965 and 1966–1970). This was driven in particular by the "Long-Term Group" of the commission, with input from intellectuals such as Joffre Dumazedier, Jean-Marie Domenach, Michel de Certeau, Pierre Bourdieu and Edgar Morin. Laurent Gayme has argued that the Commission could even be seen as a kind of "counter-ministry" (1995, p. 72). Interestingly, the propositions of the commission were at first positively received by the incoming administration of Jacques Duhamel, who found their reports conveniently fresh on their desks precisely at the moment they came into office.[11] One of the propositions initially implemented was the creation of an advisory body called the Council for Cultural Development designed, as Gayme puts it, to perpetuate "the domination of intellectual and cultural networks" over policy (1995, p. 74) (the Council contained notably a lot of ex-members of the Cultural Commission for the Sixth Plan). Inevitably, however, relations between the Minister's cabinet and the claims of what they saw as an unelected and unpredictable rival policy-framing forum grew increasingly strained, and the Council eventually dissolved itself in 1973 when it became clear that the more hardline minister Maurice Druon was simply sidelining them. Since then, public intellectuals have not been given a comparable public platform within the policy process itself. The Plan itself has also diminished very substantially in importance due to changes in the conduct of politics as a whole, and thus the milieu that allowed the Cultural Commission of the Sixth Plan to assume such prominence subsequently faded away.

This has not prevented intellectuals from setting up in a more autonomous way their own collective platforms in order to push particular policy agendas. I have already evoked the classic example of the "Villeurbanne declaration" from 1968, when the directors of the Houses of Culture collectively expressed their lack of confidence in Malraux's resolutely top-down strategy for culture. More recently, Pierre Bourdieu looked over the 1990s self-consciously to institute federated platforms for intellectuals designed to promote forms of cultural "counter-policy", organized around themes such as autonomy in publishing or the reform of the university (see Ahearne 2004, pp. 67–68). The difficulties that have beset such enterprises in the long term derive from the individualism (or spirit of independence) that characterizes autonomous intellectuals as such (cf. Noiriel 2005, pp. 203, 234–241).

It is also worth bearing in mind here the capacity of the traditional "commission" assigned to an intellectual to function as a public platform in sometimes unpredictable ways. A minister or even a president may ask an intellectual to head up a particular commission charged with looking into a particular topic. Such a commission will gather evidence, canvas opinion and come to a view. Sometimes that view will be grist to the minister's mill, but sometimes the outcome will be less politically convenient. The commission may function a little bit like a "garbage can", in the sense memorably assigned to the term by Cohen, March and Olsen (1972). All sorts of issues, agendas, interests and sundry ideas may be thrown into the mix, and what finally comes out when the lid is lifted off may reconfigure the political agenda in unpredictable ways. Example of such commissions presided by intellectuals that would repay closer study are those charged with looking into the educational curriculum by Pierre Bourdieu and Frédéric Gros (2002 [1989]) and by Edgar Morin (cf. 1999, pp. 9–11); that charged in 2002 with investigating the relations between television and violence headed by Blandine Kriegel (2003); that charged in 2001 with considering the provision of non-religiously inspired religious education in State schools by Régis Debray (2002), as well as the Commission on *laïcité* set up in 2003 by President Chirac on which Debray among others sat (Debray 2004).

Such examples underline the fact that one should not, when trying to assess the input of French public intellectuals into public policies for culture, limit one's research to the domains administered by the Ministry of Culture as such. It should have become clear over this article that the domain of education constitutes a fundamentally important site for the articulation of policies affecting the culture that is transmitted to succeeding generations. Certainly, the Ministry of Education in France has its own experts and technicians, and Philippe Meirieu notes how the great majority of educational reports are produced via these "in-house" channels (Meirieu & Le Bars 2001, p. 144). Nevertheless, one is struck by the capacity of those reports written by public intellectuals whose authority transcends local expertise (Condorcet, Langevin and Wallon, Bourdieu and Gros …) to become enduring reference points in subsequent policy reflection (cf. also van Zanten 2004, p. 72). And insofar as these reports focus not just on specialized knowledge, but on what Langevin and Wallon call "general culture" (Langevin & Wallon 2004 [1946], pp. 20–21), they can be seen as important cultural policy statements.

Policy experts are prone to castigate the "generalities" contained in the reflection of public intellectuals on public policy. Intellectuals themselves seem perpetually frustrated by the reception of their work by politicians: their ideas are misunderstood, distorted, misleadingly packaged, binned, etc. They suffer perhaps from what Robert Damien calls a "Syracuse complex": like Plato in Syracuse, they want to derive directly from ideal principles a blueprint for an ideal republic (Damien suggests that the inductive empiricism of a Machiavelli or a Bacon provides a more modest starting point) (Damien 2003, p. 9). I think that both of the principles of dissatisfaction outlined above need to be reframed. Intellectuals' "generalities" should not necessarily be seen as vague notions that need to be firmed up by expert knowledge. One can just as legitimately see expert knowledge as sectorally bound information that needs to be integrated into a more general context for its implications and relative importance to become apparent, and one could see public intellectuals in their overhastily derided traditional role as those best equipped to do this. And while it is important to take account of the limitations of their influence on policy development, such influence as they do exert can best be appreciated in terms of a dispersed and long-term framework (rather than simply observing whether this or that report or proposition was accepted by this or that minister). There is not space to pursue these two notions in the present article.[12] It is enough simply to have indicated in this section the kinds of incentives and institutional channels through which public intellectuals have become involved in cultural policy development during the Fifth Republic.

Intellectuals as the Objects of Cultural Policy?

I have considered in this article French public intellectuals in their quasi-traditional role as external critics of State cultural policy (speaking truth to power – though I have suggested that other less noble considerations may also apply). I have also considered the ways in which some intellectuals have become involved in policy development of one kind or another, and the tensions and sometimes abdication that this can produce as regards intellectual autonomy. I will conclude with some brief remarks on intellectuals as a potential object of cultural policy. We have already seen a negative manifestation of this. A key objective of the French Communist Party's cultural policy was to rally intellectuals to its cause so that it could present itself as the "Party of French Intelligence". When the soon-to-be German Ambassador Otto Abetz arrived in Paris in 1940, he is reputed to have said that to take control of the *Nouvelle Revue Française* (a leading intellectual journal) would be as important as taking control of a Ministry (Ory & Sirinelli 1992 [1986], p. 134). Clearly, public intellectuals constitute a potentially influential though unruly element that politicians can look to bring under control through their cultural policies. But we can also conceive of public intellectuals (or at least the resources required for public intellectual debate) as potential objects of cultural policy in a rather different way. Régis Debray has noted how the current cultural climate, dominated by the demands of image, instantaneity, rapid response and limited attention span (he calls it the "videosphere"), is inhospitable to the public intellectual. In Debray's account, the public intellectual evolved in a climate where the dominant medium was print and the dominant institution the education system (the "graphosphere"). In such a milieu – and Debray is self-confessedly looking at this through a veil of nostalgia – complex chains of reasoning and broader frames of historical reference could more easily be unfolded in the public sphere (Debray 1991). Pierre Bourdieu argued in the 1990s that he found it virtually impossible to say anything worthwhile in the fora offered him by standard television channels (1998 [1996]). Are Bourdieu and Debray simply relics of a previous cultural technology, fish out of water condemned to mental asphyxia in the contemporary mediasphere? Or must we necessarily assume that technological progress equates with cultural progress? It seems eminently plausible that some kinds of technological progress, along with associated shifts in cultural and educational markets, facilitate as side-effects certain kinds of intellectual regression. It would seem an entirely appropriate objective for a cultural/educational policy to look to work against such side-effects. This has traditionally happened at the level of curriculum design, or in the public provision of dedicated media platforms for intellectual content of a kind that would be unfeasible in an unfettered cultural marketplace. By defending and building on such contested traditions in a policy environment that is, as Jim McGuigan puts it, "dominated by economic reason" (2004, p. 1), the kind of intellectual ecology can be sustained in which the interventions of public intellectuals can obtain an informed critical hearing. In this way, intellectuals would be not so much the direct objects of cultural policy (surely the kiss of death) as its indirect object.[13]

NOTES

1. Their definition in French runs as follows: "Dans notre ouvrage, l'intellectuel sera donc un homme du culturel, créateur ou médiateur, mis en situation d'homme du politique, producteur ou consommateur d'idéologie" (Ory & Sirinelli 1992 [1986], p. 10).
2. The committee's *Report on Public Instruction* was presented to the Assembly on 20 and 21 April 1792. A fuller exposition of Condorcet's educational policy thinking can be found in Condorcet (1994 [1791]).
3. It may be worth underlining that the principles I am isolating here combined in complex ways in the concrete existence of individual intellectuals. Both the psychologist Henri Wallon and the eminent physicist Paul Langevin were members of the French Communist Party. After many years of close association, Langevin had finally decided to join in 1944 (after, among other things, the execution of his son-in-law and the deportation to Auschwitz of his daughter, both communists) (Caute 1964, p. 156).
4. When one reads certain foundational texts of the "republican" tradition in French education, such as Condorcet (1994 [1791]), or Langevin and Wallon (2004 [1946]), one is struck by the somewhat artificial nature of recent divisions between "republicans" and "pedagogists" in French educational debates.
5. For Aristotle on "habitus", see *Nichomachean Ethics*, ii.4, 1105 b; and on the ruler's Prudence, *Politics*, iii.4.17–18, 1277 b (both cited by Maclean 1993, pp. 6, 10). I capitalize "Prudence" to distinguish it from its dominant sense of "caution" in contemporary English. The Greek term *phronesis* signifies "practical wisdom" or "common sense", and the term might also in such discussions carry the notion of foresight. Cf. *Nichomachean Ethics* (Aristotle 2004) notes at pages 150, 312. My thanks also to Ingrid de Smet for enlightenment.
6. For a discussion of such intellectuals in English, see e.g. Jennings (1997, pp. 75–79).

7. I engage much more fully with Kingdon's "multiple streams" model of the policy process in Ahearne (2006).
8. On Malraux's role in the "invention" of cultural policy, see Urfalino (2004 [1996], pp. 39–108). Urfalino also underlines the complementary and contrasting role of another intellectual, Malraux's friend Gaëtan Picon, in this process. For discussions of Malraux as minister in English, see Looseley (1995, pp. 33–48) and Lebovics (1999).
9. For an extended treatment of the relations between 1960s cultural policy and State planning (including the role of Dumazedier), see Dubois (1999, pp. 189–231). For Dumazedier's thinking on "cultural development", see e.g. Dumazedier and Ripert (2000 [1966]).
10. See also Ahearne (2004, pp. 10–11).
11. See the comments of Duhamel's cabinet director, Jacques Rigaud, in Duhamel (1993, p. 10).
12. For an extensive discussion of the two notions, see the reference in note 7 above.
13. For further indications regarding such an "ecology", see Ahearne (2004, p. 72).

REFERENCES

AHEARNE, J. (2004) *Between Cultural Theory and Policy: The Cultural Policy Thinking of Pierre Bourdieu, Michel de Certeau and Régis Debray,* Centre for Cultural Policy Studies, University of Warwick, Coventry.

AHEARNE, J. (2006) 'Public intellectuals within a "multiple streams" model of the cultural policy process: Notes from a French perspective', *International Journal of Cultural Policy,* vol. 12, no. 1, pp. 1–15.

ARISTOTLE (2004) *The Nichomachean Ethics,* trans. J.A.K. Thomson & H. Tredennick, Penguin, London.

BENDA, J. (1975 [1927]) *La Trahison des clercs,* Grasset, Paris.

BOURDIEU, P. (1993) *The Field of Cultural Production,* ed. R. Johnson, Polity, Cambridge.

BOURDIEU, P. (1996 [1992]) *The Rules of Art: Genesis and Structure of the Literary Field,* trans. S. Emmanuel, Polity, Cambridge.

BOURDIEU, P. (1998 [1996]) *On Television and Journalism,* trans. P. Parkhurst Ferguson, Pluto Press, London.

BOURDIEU, P. & DARBEL, A. (1991 [1966]) *The Love of Art: European Art Museums and their Public,* trans. C. Beattie & N. Merriman, Polity, Cambridge.

BOURDIEU, P. & GROS, F. (2002 [1989]) 'Principes pour une réflexion sur les contenus d'enseignement', in Bourdieu, P., *Interventions, 1961–2001: Science sociale et action politique,* eds F. Poupeau & T. Discepolo, Agone, Marseille, pp. 217–226.

BOURDIEU, P. & HAACKE, H. (1995 [1994]) *Free Exchange,* trans. R. Johnson & H. Haacke, Polity, Cambridge.

CAUTE, D. (1964) *Communism and the French Intellectuals 1914–1960,* André Deutsch, London.

CERTEAU, M. DE (1984 [1980]) *The Practice of Everyday Life,* trans. S. Rendall, University of California Press, Berkeley.

CHABROL, V. (1990) 'L'ambition de "Jeune France"', in *La Vie culturelle sous Vichy,* by J.-P. Rioux, Editions Complexe, Brussels, pp. 161–178.

COHEN, M., MARCH, J. & OLSEN, J. (1972) 'A garbage can model of organizational choice', *Administrative Science Quarterly,* vol. 17, pp. 1–25.

CONDORCET, J. A. N. DE CARITAT DE (1994 [1791]) *Cinq mémoires sur l'instruction publique,* eds C. Coutel & C. Kintzler, Flammarion, Paris.

DAMIEN, R. (2003) *Le Conseiller du Prince de Machiavel à nos jours,* PUF, Paris.

DEBRAY, R. (1991) *Cours de médiologie générale,* Gallimard, Paris.

DEBRAY, R. (1996) *Loués soient nos seigneurs. Une Education politique,* Gallimard, Paris.

DEBRAY, R. (2002) *L'Enseignement du fait religieux dans l'école laïque,* Odile Jacob, Paris.

DEBRAY, R. (2004) *Ce que nous voile le voile. La République et le sacré,* Gallimard, Paris.

DONNAT, O. (2002 [1991]) 'Cultural democratization: The end of a myth', in *French Cultural Policy Debates: A Reader,* ed. and trans. J. Ahearne, Routledge, London, pp. 135–147.

DOSSE, F. (2002) *Michel de Certeau: Le Marcheur blessé,* La Découverte, Paris.

DUBOIS, V. (1999) *La politique culturelle: Genèse d'une catégorie d'intervention publique,* Belin, np.

DUBOIS, V. (2003) 'La statistique culturelle au ministère de la Culture, de la croyance à la mauvaise conscience', in *Le(s) Public(s) de la culture: Politiques publiques et équipements culturels,* vol. 2 (on CD-ROM), eds O. Donnat & P. Tolila, Presses de Sciences Po, Paris, pp. 25–32.

DUHAMEL, J. (1993) *Jacques Duhamel, Ministre des Affaires culturelles 1971–1973: Discours et écrits,* La Documentation Française, Paris.

DUMAZEDIER, J. & RIPERT, A. (2002 [1966]) 'Leisure and culture', in *French Cultural Policy Debates: A Reader,* ed. and trans. J. Ahearne, Routledge, London, pp. 45–54.

FABIANI, J.-L., HENNION, A., HERPIN, N. & MENGER, P.-M. (2003) 'Eléments de synthèse', in *Le(s) Public(s) de la culture: Politiques publiques et équipements culturels,* vol. 2 (on CD-ROM), eds O. Donnat & P. Tolila, Presses de Sciences Po, Paris, pp. 309–323.

GAYME, L. (1995) 'La commission des affaires culturelles du vi^e plan (1969–1971)', in *Les Affaires culturelles au temps de Jacques Duhamel, 1971–1973,* eds G. Gentil & A. Girard, La Documentation Française, Paris, pp. 57–82.

HENNION, A. (1996) *Le grand écart entre la recherche et l'administration,* Ministère de la Culture et de la Communication, Département des Etudes et de la Prospective, Paris.

JEANSON, F. (2002 [1971]) 'Chalon: Four years of cultural action', in *French Cultural Policy Debates: A Reader,* ed. and trans. J. Ahearne, Routledge, London, pp. 79–82.

JEANSON, F. ET AL. [collective declaration] (2002 [1968]) 'The Villeurbanne declaration', in *French Cultural Policy Debates: A Reader,* ed. and trans. J. Ahearne, Routledge, London, pp. 70–75.

JENNINGS, J. (1997) '"Of treason, blindness and silence: Dilemmas of the intellectual in modern France', in *Intellectuals in Politics from the Dreyfus Affair to Salman Rushdie,* eds J. Jennings & A. Kemp-Welch, Routledge, London, pp. 65–85.

KELLY, M. (2004) *The Cultural and Intellectual Rebuilding of France after the Second World War,* Palgrave Macmillan, Basingstoke.

KINGDON, J. W. (2003) *Agendas, Alternatives, and Public Policies,* 2nd edn, Longman, New York.

KRIEGEL, B. (2003) *La Violence à la télévision: Rapport de la mission d'évaluation, d'analyse et de propositions relatives aux représentations violentes à la télévision présidée par Blandine Kriegel au ministre de la Culture,* PUF, Paris.

LANGEVIN, P. & WALLON, H. (2004 [1946]) *Le rapport Langevin-Wallon,* eds C. Allègre, F. Dubet & P. Meirieu, Mille et une nuits, Paris [original 1946 title: 'La réforme de l'enseignement. Projet soumis à M. le ministre de l'education nationale par la commission ministérielle d'étude'].

LEBOVICS, H. (1999) *Mona Lisa's Escort: André Malraux and the Reinvention of French Culture,* Cornell University Press, Ithaca and London.

LEPAPE, P. (1990) 'Un entretien avec Pierre Nora', *Le Monde,* 1 June.

LOOSELEY, D. (1995) *The Politics of Fun: Cultural Policy and Debate in Contemporary France,* Berg, Oxford.

MACLEAN, I. W. F. (1993) *From Prudence to Policy: Some Notes on the Prehistory of Policy Sciences,* Katholieke Universiteit Nijmegen, Nijmegen.

MCGUIGAN, J. (2004) *Rethinking Cultural Policy,* Open University Press, Maidenhead.

MEIRIEU, P. & LE BARS, S. (2001) *La Machine-école,* Gallimard, Paris.

MORIN, E. (1999) *La Tête bien faite: Repenser la réforme/Réformer la pensée,* Seuil, Paris.

MOULIN, R. (1993) 'Augustin Girard, acteur privilégié de la recherche sur la culture et les arts', in *Trente ans d'études au service de la vie culturelle, table ronde organisée à l'occasion du départ à la retraite d'Augustin Girard, chef du département des études et de la prospective du ministère de la culture de 1963 à 1993,* Ministère de la Culture et de la Communication, Paris, pp. 68–71.

NIZAN, P. (1960 [1932]) *Les Chiens de garde,* Maspéro, Paris.

NOIRIEL, G. (2005) *Les Fils maudits de la République. L'Avenir des intellectuels en France,* Fayard, Paris.

ORY, P. & SIRINELLI, J.-F. (1992 [1986]) *Les Intellectuels en France de l'Affaire Dreyfus à nos jours,* Armand Colin, Paris.

PAXTON, R. (2001 [1972]) *Vichy France: Old Guard and New Order, 1940–1944,* Columbia University Press, New York.

PÉGUY, C. (1959 [1907]) 'De la situation faite au parti intellectuel dans le monde moderne devant les accidents de la gloire temporelle', in Péguy, C., *Oeuvres en Proses 1898–1908,* Gallimard, Paris, pp. 1115–1214.

POIRRIER, P. (1997) 'Présentation', in *La Naissance des politiques culturelles et les Rencontres d'Avignon 1964–1970,* Ministère de la culture et de la communication, Comité d'histoire, Paris, pp. 15–52.

READER, K. (1987) *Intellectuals and the Left in France since 1968,* Macmillan, Houndmills.

RIEFFEL, R. (2001) 'Intellectuels et politique culturelle', in *Dictionnaires des politiques culturelles de la France depuis 1959,* De Waresquiel, Larousse/CNRS Editions, Paris, pp. 342–344.

SARTRE, J.-P. (1972) 'Plaidoyer pour les intellectuels', [lectures given in 1965] in Sartre, J.-P., *Situations VIII,* Gallimard, Paris, pp. 375–455.

THIBAUDET, A. (1927) *La République des Professeurs,* Grasset, Paris.

URFALINO, P. (2004 [1996]) *L'Invention de la politique culturelle,* Hachette, Paris.

VAN ZANTEN, A. (2004) *Les Politiques d'Éducation,* Presses Universitaires de France, Paris.

VERDÈS-LEROUX, J. (1983) *Au service du Parti: Le Parti communiste, les intellectuels et la culture (1944–1956),* Fayard/Minuit, Paris.

INTELLECTUALS AND CULTURAL POLICY IN FRANCE
Antoine Hennion and the sociology of music

David Looseley

Introduction

The French sociologist Antoine Hennion, member and former director of the influential Sociology of Innovation Centre based at the Écoles des Mines in Paris, may not seem an obvious choice for a case study of the relationship between intellectuals and cultural policy in France. An academic researcher in the sociology of music for over thirty years (he was born in 1952), he has engaged with cultural policy matters only occasionally and his status as a "French intellectual", in that iconic sense these inverted commas imply, is problematic. This is partly due to a long-standing uncertainty in France as to whether those in university employment deserve inclusion among a select group of freelance public thinkers like Sartre or Camus; and partly because Hennion's self-styled "pragmatic" sociology is, at one level at least, quite remote from the high abstraction associated with the French intellectual, coming closer to the Anglo-American empirical tradition. He himself occasionally displays a dry scepticism about some of the theory produced by his compatriots. "Theoretical work", he insists (Hennion 1981, p. 16), "is valuable by virtue of the limits that its coherence allows us to set, the contradictions that its concern with rationalisation brings out, not by virtue of its armour-plating. Perhaps one writes less with one's ideas than against them". Similarly, he demarcates himself from the intelligentsia's traditional disdain for mass culture. In a broadly sympathetic ethnography of French pop music (Hennion 1981), he is ironic about intellectuals who, because they are unable to make sense of a musical taste they do not share, assume that pop music is empty of meaning, rather than trying to understand the meanings it has for its fans.

Yet, despite all this, Hennion is something of a rising star in cultural theory. His work is regularly cited outside France, in the fields of sociology, musicology and cultural studies. Tia DeNora (2000), for example, in her ground-breaking study *Music in Everyday Life*, cites him as one of the theorists arguing for the interactive nature of what she calls the "music–society nexus". Simon Frith (1996), Richard Middleton (2003) and Keith Negus (1996) also allude to him in the context of popular music. Like Bourdieu, his analysis has an empirical starting point but reaches a level of interpretative generality that occasionally comes close to philosophy, ranging from the phenomenological description of the ways in which music is carried out, to the dense argumentation, sinuous syntax and customized lexis familiar in French cultural theory, though always with a determination not to lose sight of the "pragmatics" of cultural practice. At times, his professional and personal styles are also tinged with humour, particularly face to face, suggesting a readiness, unusual in French academic circles, not to take himself too seriously.

The first part of this article will explore Hennion's conceptualization of the music–society nexus. This analysis will necessarily be introductory and provisional, since his output is substantial and constantly growing, making it impossible to do it justice in a few pages. In the second part, I shall explore some of the policy implications of this conceptualization, implications which suggest themselves when we measure the distance that separates him from the social determinism associated (rightly or wrongly) with Bourdieu (Hennion 1996b, p. 5).

Towards a Musicology of Society

What gives Hennion's work its international stature is the empirical contribution he makes to a major theoretical debate in the sociology of culture: how do music and society interact? As DeNora maintains (2000, pp. 1–3), this debate was triggered by Adorno's intuition that music is formative of social and cultural behaviour. This intuition was exciting, DeNora contends, but little more than a grand speculative theory. Subsequently, the American production of culture perspective, exemplified by Howard Becker, Richard Peterson and Vera Zolberg, challenged Adorno's position by proposing an empirically demonstrable music–society nexus. This is broadly Hennion's ambition too, though he moves away from the production of culture perspective because, as DeNora also argues (2000, p. 5), it treats the aesthetic too deterministically, as if music were merely the hapless product of collective structures, rather than "an active and dynamic material in social life".

Despite this engagement with international thinking, Hennion's sociology actually takes off from a home-grown version of social determinism: that of Bourdieu – the Bourdieu of *The Love of Art* (Bourdieu & Darbel 1990 [1966]) and *Distinction* (1979). Both Bourdieu and Hennion use the empirically grounded sociology of cultural practice as a platform for social theory. But Hennion figures among a cluster of French social scientists who, while indebted to Bourdieu, are at pains to distance themselves from his "critical sociology" which, to their mind, accounts for cultural practice too rigidly in terms of social system and strategies of social distinction (Béra & Lamy 2003, pp. 172–173; Berthelot 2003, p. 254), determinants that only the shrewd, detached sociologist (Bourdieu himself) is capable of recognizing. Hennion acknowledges these determinants but is much more interested in their boundaries. What he posits instead is a constitutive relationship between music and society, which takes account of the work of art itself, the voluntarism of listening, and the active aesthetic experiences of the music user (Hennion *et al.* 2000, pp. 28–31).

In this respect, he comes closer to the conceptualization of cultural practice advanced by Michel de Certeau, by whom he was influenced in his formative years. Certeau does not see the social forces identified by Bourdieu as determining cultural practices in a monolithic way. Between the plurality of these forces, which for Bourdieu irresistibly *produce* cultures, Certeau locates gaps, cracks, flaws – a margin of play in the machine, in which cultures grow. For Certeau, a common element in all cultural activity, including consumption, is creativity, a creativity that springs up in the tiniest interstices of our public and private existences, and which is characterized by impermanence and perishability (Looseley 2003, pp. 97–98). Everyday creation is about acts, not objects: acts that are the result of what he calls "the genius, the practical thought and the wily intelligence of all those unknown authors" (quoted in Ahearne 2004, p. 104), namely, ordinary people.

This is broadly the point from which Hennion sets out: the cultural practitioner's margin of creative manoeuvre. Rather than being the unconscious victim of external determinants, the practitioner is fully aware of them as productive constraints, which s/he works with or against (Hennion 2005c). This margin makes Hennion, like Certeau, reject Adornian or Bourdieusian readings of popular culture as dominated, degraded and deluded about its subjection. What he has to say about the agency, creativity and pleasure of musical practice applies equally to all genres, including those disparaged as low culture. His first major work, *Les Professionnels du disque* (The Record Professionals; Hennion 1981), was in fact an ethnographic study of the production of commercial pop songs by the French record industry. One aim was to show the complexity and creativity of the "original mode of production" the industry has evolved (Hennion 1990, p. 186). For the meaning, the "expressive value" (Hennion 1990, p. 186) of a pop song does not lie in its musicological or lyrical content. Nor can this content explain why it is successful or otherwise. The final product is the result of negotiation between the various actors involved in its production, which entails "a fusion between musical objects and the needs of the public" (Hennion 1990, p. 186). As this argument hints, his work on record production prefigures a major though not exclusive preoccupation with consumption.

This preoccupation is loosely related to the extensive surveys of cultural practices in France produced periodically by the Ministry of Culture since the early 1970s, though Hennion considers that their undoubted value when it comes to quantifying tastes is limited by their recourse to a Bourdieusian sociology of taste (2003a, p. 287). The surveys in fact originated in the study of museum-going that the Ministry commissioned from Bourdieu, which subsequently became *The Love of Art* (Bourdieu & Darbel 1990 [1966]), though, in Hennion's view, they also spawned complementary research projects which have contributed to a much finer apprehension of cultural practices than Bourdieu ever achieved (Hennion 1996b, p. 13). Such studies have consistently shown up three features of music practice that are relevant here: an enormous increase in listening to recorded music, an equally substantial rise in amateur music-making, especially among the young, and the domination of French musical tastes by popular music (both French and Anglo-American). These findings point to what one might call a "musicalisation" of French society since the 1960s (Looseley 2003, pp. 3–4), a phenomenon not peculiar to France but one which nevertheless represents a major cultural shift for a nation that for years had assumed it was not musical but had defined itself by its print culture. It suggests therefore a significant change in France's cultural identity (Looseley 2003, pp. 203–213).

Although Hennion does not to my knowledge use the term "musicalisation" in this sense, his work on pop music, and then on what he calls the "passion" for music generally, may be regarded as teasing out the phenomenon's sociological nature and implications. His way of conceptualizing it is to speak of the need for not so much a sociology of music as a musicology of society, by which he means the study of the myriad ways in which people inventively use music today in their everyday social lives, which allows sociology to learn as much from music as vice versa (Hennion 2001, p. 3):

> If music has invaded the world, and is becoming the leading register of existence for a generation, it is perhaps because, without predetermining the issue of its task of self-definition, it gives an idea to those who seize upon it and those it takes hold of, of the ways to make a world. (Hennion 1999, p. 4)

However, he argues, in order properly to understand this "world building" (DeNora 2000, p. 44), the sociologist should not attempt to decode "the music itself", in isolation – as musicologists often do and as the sociology of culture began by doing. The meaning of a musical work is not locked within its form and content, a Sleeping Beauty waiting to be awoken by musicological analysis. Music is a doing, not a being:

> What does music do? And not, what is music? What does it make people do? And not, how is it made? ... An orientation such as this, which is a pragmatist one, avoids positing at the outset the existence of its object. It seeks not to define – i.e. to limit – music's properties but to mark its boundaries through its consequences, its effects, what it makes possible, what it makes happen. (Hennion 2005a, p. 121)

The term "pragmatist" here, used in its philosophical sense, is key, drawing attention to an overarching philosophical stance. Music is not a static aesthetic object but is always in situation. It is an "unpredictable event" in an ephemeral present, and therefore its definition and its effects are never immutable (Hennion 2001, p. 2). Unlike a sculpture or a painting, it has no existence other than as sound and therefore performance – whether live or recorded, given or listened to. It is in fact "performative", in that it changes those who use it, and those who use it change it by using it. It is a "co-production": music and society are constitutive of each other. Music cannot be defined outside the experience of those who listen to it, play it or otherwise appropriate it; that is to say, it is indistinguishable from its "mediations": "music is nothing without everything on which it can rely. Better still, it is everything on which it relies" (Hennion 2001, p. 6).

"Mediation" here, another key term in Hennion's work (though one he now tries not to use, to avoid confusion), does not simply signify the intervention of intermediaries. Whereas an intermediary is a self-contained third element between two elements which its intervention leaves intact, mediation is a co-formative relation between two elements, without which neither exists: "Worlds are not given, with their own sets of laws. There are only strategic relations, which define in one and the same process the terms of the relation and its modalities. Outside a mediation, there appears not an autonomous world but another mediation" (Hennion 1993, p. 224). This chain of mediations is ultimately infinite, but, where music is concerned, it most obviously includes the instrument, the concert venue or record, the engagement of the musician's or the listener's body, the sensations and emotions involved in the musical experience, and so on. Mediation also includes discourse in its various forms – the discourse of composers, musicians, critics, musicologists, cultural and educational intermediaries, and of the institutions that support music making or listening, from the music industry to training schools and the Ministry of Culture. These institutional mediations point directly to cultural policy, as we shall see.

But, more generally, what makes his work relevant to cultural policy is the emphasis he places on the formation of tastes.

This concern was already present in his early work, but became more direct with a new project in the late 1990s, involving what he calls the figures of the amateur (Hennion *et al.* 2000). His originality here lies in his freeing the amateur from associations with the second-rate (the embarrassing uncle who insists on murdering the tuba at family parties) by placing all forms of non-professional practice on an equal footing, both making and listening to music. The French language takes the first step for him, since the word *amateur* means both those who sing or play without payment and those who are music "lovers", a term usually connoting listeners with a degree of informed competence. But what primarily justifies the conflation of listener and amateur musician is the fact that the standard binary of passive/active, according to which the pop fan listening to their favourite hits on an iPod is passive, while the amateur musician playing in a string quartet or singing in a choir is admirably active, is false. For Hennion, there are no passive amateurs.

This leads him to posit a "pragmatics" of taste, or, as he increasingly puts it, "attachments". Taste – in the sense of a love of certain types of music – is not determined, not a biological or sociological given; nor is it pure subjectivity or a "natural", spontaneous response to the inbuilt aesthetic qualities of a piece of music. Just as much as the music itself, taste is a production, a performance; it is always in the making and in situation; always reflexive and under test conditions. It is also an ongoing co-production, of both a loved musical object and a body which is training itself to love it (Hennion 2003a, 2004). By cataloguing and analysing the ways in which the individual respondents in his survey on amateurs talked about how they like, make, and listen to music, Hennion identifies common patterns that allow the extrapolation of a new sociology of taste to challenge Bourdieu's. The pragmatics of taste does not begin with the assumption that taste is a social game. It begins with ethnographic description, taking respondents' statements about how they listen seriously and at face value, rather than as encoded signs of their victimization by the capitalist hegemony of the culture industry. What in fact struck Hennion in the study was how far a naturalized version of Bourdieu's class theory had made his respondents lose the ability to talk unselfconsciously about their tastes in terms of feelings, gestures, routines, how they form attachments to particular musics. But once their discourse was "desociologised" by specially devised methods of questioning, their tendency to apologize for their tastes was replaced by a remarkable enthusiasm and volubility.

To fully understand what these unchained interviewees revealed, it is important to realize that, for Hennion, listening too is mediated, not spontaneous: we have learnt to do it and we perform it. This implies that there is a history of listening, just as there is a history of composition: listening in the fullest sense is in fact a twentieth-century invention. The way in which a Beethoven symphony was heard by concert-goers in the nineteenth century differed from how it is heard today, as a result of what Hennion calls a "discomorphosis" of listening, that has produced "the listener turned customer" (Hennion 2001, p. 5). Phonograph technology and the corresponding rise of the media, record retail outlets, and so on, have transformed our ways of appropriating music. Whereas the nineteenth-century music lover might have heard the Beethoven symphony two or three times at most, today's audiences go to the concert with a multitude of previous listenings in their head and can compare different performances via various media. One might add that musical democratization in Western societies (music schools and conservatoires, concert venues, museums of music, etc.), has also played a part in "training" the concert-goer's ear. As a result, music lovers can now roam freely in a private garden of earthly delights, "internal spaces reconstructed by the music lover, where he [sic] navigates mentally when he chooses a track, buys a record, feels like listening to a particular interpretation, switches his radio on and off, plays a few notes on the piano, etc." (Hennion 1996a, p. 49). And yet, the intimacy of this experience does not prevent its being sociologically representative, "the most characteristic product of the modern discomorphosis of listening" (Hennion 2001, p. 6).

The music fan's listening practices, therefore, reveal an enthusiastic, and an increasingly skilled, voluntarism that Bourdieu's critical sociology does not account for. Irrespective of the genre of music in question, the listener of today engages in what Hennion calls ceremonies of pleasure: we may dim the lights in the living-room or listen late in the evening, when everybody else in the house is out or in bed; we may play our favourite record only once in a blue moon, with a glass of fine single malt, and so on. In such routines and rituals, we are meticulously stage-managing a set of conditions likely to conjure up listening pleasure, that elusive moment of helpless transportation that he calls musical passion. There is, of course, a paradox in these ceremonies, since we are actively seeking a moment of complete passivity, of surrender to the music, a *jouissance*. So, as with sexual ecstasy, this moment must not be too carefully engineered: surrender must be allowed to come about of its own accord and there will be times when it does not. But, as this very unpredictability reminds us, its coming about is not a causal result of aesthetic meanings written into the work itself, but of the ways the meanings sought by the composer are mediated, brought into being, by performance, recording, use.

Such rituals of listening, which often have an almost clandestine quality, are customized, self-aware and transgressive, in so far as the music lover happily composes a musical menu with little concern for musicological orthodoxies. They in fact resemble the "poaching" by which, according to Certeau, we "ruse" with the "texts" that society has mapped out for us. Music practices are strategies of identity formation in themselves and relate to other such strategies, as with youth music, which is indissociable from practices such as dance, styles of dress and self-presentation, drugs, festivals, sexual conduct, and so on (Le Guern 2003, pp. 17–18).

We need to be clear, however, that such "emotional procedures", as Hennion calls them, are not independent of the music itself, for his anti-essentialism is also an anti-dualism. If musicology is wrong to see the "work itself" as a self-contained aesthetic object, in which the social plays no intrinsic part, "sociologism" is equally at fault for accounting for musical tastes exclusively in terms of social forces, which makes the work disappear altogether (Hennion 1993, p. 225). Therefore, while certainly stressing that the meaning of a work is never immanent, Hennion wishes to restore the aesthetic as a legitimate concern of sociological enquiry. He does not, as the casual reader might think, diminish composition in favour of reception. On the contrary, in a discussion of Bach, for example, he stresses that it was largely the composer who redefined the love of music in the nineteenth century (Hennion 2003c, p. 86). It is rather that the creative process is shared between composer and user:

> a music is not an inert object but a live project, which already proposes its own interpretations, which calls for certain reactions; and often it is constructed and evolves as a genre by virtue of these reactions – this is why the history of a genre is part of the genre, it participates in the collective work which isolates the relevant features and characterises what one has to do. (Hennion 2005a, p. 132)

As this suggests, Hennion's pragmatic deconstruction of the music–society binary necessarily impacts on the notion of genre. A genre too is a co-production, involving, on the one hand, a style of music and its self-presentation, which actively solicit its users to interpret and use it in certain ways; and, on the other hand, those same users' reappropriations of this solicitation on their own terms, redefining the music's proposed meanings by the uses they put it to, the materials they bring to its use, the way they deploy and train their bodies in order to use it better, and the discourses they produce about it. The meaning and contours of a genre, therefore, are again dynamic.

Hennion's ambition, then, is to show that, just like the composer, music users are characterized by their creativity, built upon a reflexive and growing knowledge and competence, without which the music itself would be merely a collection of notes. Hence his recent interest in what he calls "the great amateur", who, he insists, must be revalorized in public discourse. This would require us to rethink the sterile binaries of creator and consumer, highbrow and lowbrow, art and leisure. In the process, we would also have to think differently about cultural policy.

Towards a Pragmatics of Cultural Policy

The development of French cultural policy since the creation of the Ministry of Cultural Affairs (now the Ministry of Culture and Communication) in 1959, under minister André Malraux, is well documented (see, for example, Looseley 1995) and need only be summarized here. It has explored much the same paths as in other Western European countries, albeit in a more centralized way, and it has seen much the same polarization about whether the Ministry's social mission should be restricted to the democratization of "works" or embrace a more radical interpretation of cultural democracy. This debate was rearticulated after May 1968 by cultural militants who contested Malraux's policies. The Ministry initially construed its democratic mission as simply to broaden public access to the great works of art and heritage, and it has continued to devote the lion's share of its budget to this endeavour ever since. But since 1968, it has also periodically responded to calls for a more comprehensive cultural democracy to be established, in which the state would look beyond artists and works alone by also concerning itself with the cultural lives of ordinary people, with citizenship, discrimination and exclusion.

In practice, however, this wider remit has for the most part been pursued half-heartedly and with few palpable outcomes, becoming a contributory factor in the urban unrest of November 2005. In the 1990s, there was even a return to democratization Malraux-style, though with a different construction of the cultural that included popular-cultural and audio-visual works alongside consecrated art forms. Indeed, the 1990s and 2000s have seen prolonged battles to further protect such works (film, television and music) from globalization, under the banner of the French cultural exception and now cultural diversity. This campaign continues, with the adoption in October 2005 of the UNESCO convention on the protection and promotion of the diversity of cultural expressions and the current minister's bill, presented unsuccessfully to the National Assembly in December 2005, to adapt copyright regulation to the Internet in response to the perceived menace of downloading. So, although the conception of the "work" has been altered in recognition of contemporary practices, the priority it receives prevails. And this is where Hennion's cultural sociology enters the frame.

Although relations in France between the sociology of culture and cultural policy have sometimes been tense (Hennion 1996b; Berthelot 2003, p. 252; Ahearne 2004, pp. 10–11), the two grew up together, at least to the extent that some of the key texts since the 1960s began as commissions from the Ministry's research department – including studies by Bourdieu, Certeau and Hennion (Hennion 1996b, 2002; 2003a; 2003b; Hennion et al. 2000). Hennion himself has so far only addressed cultural policy in fairly broad terms and in the specific context of music, though he has pointed out (2002) that the diversity of practices that music involves could make it a useful case study for the grounded analysis of policy issues generally. He has also recognized the need for sociologists to make the "effort of translation" from theory to policy that cultural agents are asking them for (Hennion 2003b, p. 315); and his own sociological pragmatism would certainly seem to suggest itself as a possible bridge between the two. My remarks in this section, therefore, combine two types of analysis: partly they draw on his occasional writings on policy and my recent interview and correspondence with him on the subject (Hennion 2005b, 2005c); but they are also in part deductive, deriving from what I perceive to be the implications of his pragmatism for policy agendas today. I am not seeking to argue, as one may easily do with Bourdieu or Certeau, that Hennion has influenced policy; rather that he belongs among the sociologists and policy-makers who, in eschewing the pessimistic conclusions associated with Bourdieu, make policy possible.

One area of common ground between his preoccupations and those of policy agents since the 1980s is popular music. The French Ministry of Culture started developing measures for popular music in 1982, under Jack Lang. Whereas policy for classical music has been conducted fairly consistently since the mid-1960s, the need to evolve a policy ex nihilo for popular practices, which are forever being renewed and which also represent a form of social production par excellence, has raised policy issues on which Hennion's reading of the music–society nexus casts significant light. As he points out, new forms like rap and techno are of special interest for the study of music as co-production, because they have not yet been hardened off into genres by the discourses of musical historiography. This was what initially attracted him to study commercial pop in the 1970s, for it represented a form that was not yet concerned with achieving the respectability of cultural legitimation (Hennion 1981, p. 21).

Clearly, one extrapolation from this work on popular music concerns the relativization of genre. As we have seen, examining music from the point of view of users undermines the accepted aesthetic hierarchy, since the strong element of agency in music use applies equally across the high-popular binary. This challenges both the morphological differences between them and the assumption that popular music is a degraded, dominated and passive practice:

> Forms of attachment to music which fit less snugly into the traditional mould of the connoisseur are no weaker or less indispensable or vital for those who value them, and warrant as much attention as the classic format of development of good taste in a cultured domain. (Hennion 2001, p. 2)

What connects this view to a potential policy position is an implied concern with cultural democracy, suggesting that a properly democratic music policy needs to abandon generic hierarchies and legitimate all forms of musical taste. Where France is concerned, it is a position that both has and has not been adopted. Policies for popular music have evolved considerably since 1982, but they remain relatively marginal in budgetary terms (even though this marginality is in inverse proportion to their rhetorical importance over the last twenty-five years: Looseley 2003) and they have tended to privilege "the works themselves".

However, Hennion's view that the work does not exist in isolation calls for a different form of legitimation, directed at users. One fault of French cultural policy that he identifies is its essentially elitist separation of production and consumption, activity and passivity. Effort and money have gone into contemporary creation and preservation on the one hand, and audience development on the other; but the effervescent world of amateur enthusiasts that falls between the two has gone virtually unnoticed. A further conclusion to be drawn, then, is the need to rethink policies for the amateur sector, particularly in relation to the excluded: often minority-ethnic young people living in the ghettoized neighbourhoods relegated to the periphery of big cities (the infamous *banlieues*), which were dramatically brought into the spotlight by the protests of November 2005.

But Hennion's analysis has more radical policy implications than simply the need for a welfare policy for suburban minorities. The *banlieues* today are associated with "urban", "emergent" or "street" arts, chiefly hip hop, which are one feature of a wider set of dynamic new cultural practices in the city. These include experiments in aesthetic cross-fertilization and the spaces in which they are being conducted – the "new territories of art" or *"friches"* (literally "wasteland") as the Ministry calls them: alternative sites for the production and reception of emergent forms, usually abandoned industrial facilities taken over by arts collectives (see Looseley 2004, 2005). Other such practices engage with the new technologies, from raves centred on electronic dance music and the DJ's home studio, to the prolific downloading of music for MP3 players and iPods. Arguably, all these innovations involve precisely the kind of reflexive, creative "amateur" that Hennion is interested in: a "public that is active – or rather 'acting', no longer 'frequenting'" (Hennion 2003b, p. 312). And they add up to a radically different relationship with art and arts institutions: "we are no longer talking here about a relationship with a facility, or with a clearly defined programme or content, and this totally transforms the way they [urban arts] can be problematised" (Hennion 2003b, p. 312). Like Hennion's own pragmatics, such practices subvert both the conventional dualism of a static, pre-fabricated aesthetic form faced with a static, objectified "public", and the conventional policy strategies built on this dualism. Strategies which, as he puts it, view cultural action in terms of ballistics, implying a need for movement between fixed points: "we have to make people go towards this or that; this practice is losing its momentum; that public is being targeted" (Hennion 2003b, p. 312). And, clearly, if we always measure cultural trends "ballistically", the findings will always be negative, as when surveys conclude that democratization has failed to bring new social groups to the theatre or opera. If, however, measurement begins with what ordinary people *are* doing rather than what they are not, a picture of intense activity emerges, "a proliferation of practices" (Hennion 2003b, p. 313). Sociological analysis needs to be "more sensitive to actual practices, and to the active role of that which presents itself less as a 'public' than as a varied spectrum of milieux, users and amateur enthusiasts, inventing their own ways of doing" (Hennion 2003b, p. 312). And the obvious conclusion for cultural agents to draw is that policy needs to be reconfigured accordingly, if it is to respond to these new cultural modalities.

Hennion's pragmatism also implies an ethics of cultural policy. He is at pains to avoid the word "pragmatic" being interpreted, as he puts it (Hennion 2005b), in the way his *concierge* might, implying political realism and opportunism. Instead, he takes pragmatism to mean that abstract principles – for example, that a particular form of music should be promoted for its intrinsic aesthetic merit – should be replaced by a concern with consequences. I interpret his reasoning here as being that, since music exists not as object but as process or event, what matters is not a declaration of principle regarding the worth of a particular genre, of the kind Lang was wont to utter about world music, rap, and later techno, but an on-going evaluation of the effects of a particular policy regarding that genre, which the policy agent must commit him/herself to constantly monitoring. As Hennion comments (2005b), "putting cultural policies through the mill of this pragmatic questioning […] seems to me to be a very good way of interrogating cultural policies".

Yet this is not a matter of evaluation for the sake of managerial efficiency or public accountability, for "there is a highly responsible definition of politics that pragmatism provides" (Hennion 2005b). At the furthest remove from his *concierge*'s use of the term, pragmatism leads ultimately to an existential sense of institutional responsibility for the socio-aesthetic world in which we live. Like all mediations, institutions such as ministries of culture and local authorities are constitutive of the objects of their discourses. They help write the narratives that constitute a particular music as a genre, one music as different from another, and, ultimately, music as music. For example, the intensity of debates engendered whenever institutions come up with inadequate and heavily connotative nomenclatures for pop music (current musics, amplified musics, musics of today) testifies to an acute awareness of what Hennion calls the "great performative importance" of words in the process of institutionalization (2002, p. 315, note 1). Such institutional interventions have also made the French pop world lose that indifference to legitimation and respectability that attracted him to study it in the 1970s, for the lure of state support has produced a new self-consciousness and a canny new language of self-presentation.

One policy issue that Hennion's pragmatism does not appear to shed light on is the lingering question of aesthetic judgments. To state that the pragmatics of music practice necessitates a flattening of the hierarchy of genre is one thing; but to say how aesthetic judgments are to be made once such a flattening has taken place, in the resulting wilderness of indiscrimination in which cultural agents will have to decide what is and is not worthy of support, is quite another. Hennion does address the issue diagnostically in a piece for the Ministry's History Committee, though with little by way of concrete proposals. He argues that the drift towards policies for professionalization has allowed the government to delegate aesthetic evaluation to professional bodies, leaving itself responsible only for overseeing the bodies themselves. This change he correctly interprets as a paradigm shift in French policy, away from state-driven cultural supply, to a policy responding much more to demand from local professionals and intermediaries. So, as things stand, the only choices available to state intervention are either to provide forms of support considered inappropriate for genres where conventional aesthetic judgments do not apply (such as rock or rap); or to provide support unselectively, which may appear to be a cheap substitute for a proper welfare policy for disadvantaged neighbourhoods (Hennion 2002, p. 317). But Hennion himself does not come down in favour of one or the other.

Can we, therefore, conclude that his sociology of culture implies an aesthetic relativism? He argues strenuously, and somewhat defensively, that it does not. Distancing himself from what he calls "relativist sociology", he brands his own approach "relational sociology". Relativist sociology derives from the reluctance of sociologists to address the aesthetic dimension, for fear of being accused of aestheticism. He clearly has in mind here the well established "art worlds" thesis of Howard Becker (1982), which, in Hennion's view, concentrates only on the human interactions influencing production and reception and ignores how qualitative distinctions between the different art worlds are drawn, be it rock, rap or Ravel. Crucial to relational sociology, on the other hand, "is the idea that elements do not have meanings in and of themselves, and that when a particular mediator [e.g. score, live performance, record, etc.] is chosen because of an aesthetic preference or a social meaning, the introduction of that element will initiate a whole sequence of changes in the values assigned to other intermediaries and will result in the production of very different musical genres." There is, therefore, "no global space to which music belongs" (Hennion 1997, pp. 432–433): there are only "pockets", or "aesthetic constituencies", each of which has its own definition of musical authenticity (Hennion 1997, pp. 432–433). For classical music, for example, the score represents the music's aesthetic truth, rather than the instrument or the recording, while "folk music values the instrument and condemns both the score and the recording" (Hennion 1997, p. 417). Such pockets are not, however, watertight; otherwise, genres would never change.

One might challenge the implication here that espousing relational sociology clears Hennion of the charge of relativism, for surely relativism is about aesthetics whereas relationalism is a matter of epistemology?[1] But for Hennion, I suggest, epistemology and aesthetics cannot be properly separated. The aesthetic is mediated, socially constructed, and therefore relational, which means that "taste, pleasure, and meaning are contingent, conjunctural, and hence transient" (Hennion 2003c, p. 84). Contingency, however, is not the same as relativity. After all, Hennion's music lovers make value judgments all the time in the course of their evolving aesthetic experiences. For him, pragmatism is in fact the only theoretical position to take such judgments seriously, by setting out to account for aesthetic pleasure *in situ*, experientially. And having studied such judgment-making at close quarters, as an ethnographer would, he claims to be confident that the amateur's evolving competence will make short work of distinguishing between Beethoven and Britney Spears (Hennion 2005c).

So can a policy position on aesthetic value be deduced from this view? Arguably, yes. What we can extrapolate is that, in the absence of this "global space to which music belongs", it is futile to evaluate one musical form in terms of another, to contend, for example, that assessments of aesthetic quality in classical music can be applied to popular music. Far more appropriate is the "good of its kind" argument that Jim McGuigan (1996, p. 45) advances: "a cultural performance may be deemed 'good' or 'bad' of its kind, that is, within its own discursive field". To this, McGuigan (1996, p. 45) adds a second, related argument: "the assumption that value and quality are also multiple and variable in relation to specific media, forms and socio-cultural contexts. There is no gold standard that applies to all cultural currency: value is various and variously contestable across different positions".

Conclusion

It would seem, then, that the first lesson that policy-makers can learn from Hennion is the need to rethink the ways in which music is institutionalized in the twentieth-first century. Policy should recognize all forms of musical practice, without seeking a universal standard for judging high and popular musics and without distinguishing too simplistically between production and consumption. Instead, it should be more responsive to what music does and how it is used, rather than focusing exclusively on music as a professionally produced "object" or on the "public" as a similarly objectified entity. This in turn implies that it must be better adapted to the ephemeralities of musical practices. Policy agents should also be aware of their existential responsibility in shaping and defining the nature of such practice.

But Hennion's sociology of music also has implications for policies for culture as a whole, even though his analysis of music's immateriality may sometimes appear to set it apart from the more material art works such as paintings and sculpture. Certainly, he sees the pragmatics of mediation and taste as applicable to artistic activities other than music, as his argument about music as a case study implies. But in his recent and ongoing collaborative research, supported by the Ministry of Culture, he goes further by drawing parallels between an informed passion for music (that of the "great amateur") and other forms of amateur attachment such as wine appreciation (a recurrent point of comparison in his work), gastronomy, reading, sport and collecting. His analysis of the music lover would thus seem to point more generally to what he has called a "theory of passion": an understanding of the heterogeneous means by which we develop tastes and enthusiasms. As he tentatively wrote in 2004:

> why not generalize this analysis of the amateur's competencies to far more varied forms of attachment? [...] What great amateurs enable us to see more easily, owing to their high level of engagement in a particular practice, is a range of social techniques that make us able to produce and continuously to adjust a creative relationship with objects, with others, with ourselves, and with our bodies; in other words, a pragmatic presence vis-à-vis the world that makes us and that we make. (Hennion 2004, p. 142)

However, for this theory of passion to contribute further to a theory of policy, one question that would need further clarification is what precisely is the relationship between the way in which cultural institutions help constitute their object and this passionate voluntarism, which apparently allows us to freely create our own cultural universes; as if, as Richard Middleton has put it in a brief discussion of Hennion, "actors can simply decide how to use music, outside the constraints and pressures of those frameworks that form both it and them" (Middleton 2003, p. 3)? Negus (1996, pp. 60–62) makes a related point about Hennion's early contention that, rather than the music industry imposing musical tastes on its passive audiences, there is an interactive relationship between the two, in which industry personnel empathetically intuit the tastes of the public, "feeling its pulse" and thus becoming, in Hennion's words, "politicians in a sort of imaginary democracy instituted by songs" (quoted in Le Guern 2003, p. 22). This foregrounding of the empathetic and intuitive over the organizational and structural, Negus believes, may rely too easily and uncritically on interviewees' unreflexive accounts – an objection that might be raised regarding Hennion's methodology as a whole, though it must be said that Negus's critique, like other Anglo-American assessments of Hennion's work, is based on a single translated extract from *Les Professionnels du disque* written some twenty-five years ago, which Hennion now repudiates.

What this institutional issue perhaps highlights above all is the need for an evolution in cultural studies, the interdiscipline where in my view Hennion belongs. Beginning with the study of cultural production, cultural studies moved on in the 1970s and 1980s to study reception – as Hennion himself did, making an important contribution to understanding the relationship between production and reception. But, considered from the specific standpoint of policy, his work might also indicate that now is the time to move on again, to a third phase in which the study of this relationship engages more directly with the institutional, political and discursive frameworks that emancipate or constrain, but at any event shape, cultural practices in everyday life.

ACKNOWLEDGEMENTS
I wish to thank the Arts and Humanities Research Council, the University of Leeds, and Antoine Hennion for their assistance with this article.

NOTE

1. I am particularly indebted to one of *The International Journal of Cultural Policy*'s anonymous referees for usefully drawing my attention to and discussing this point.

REFERENCES

AHEARNE, J. (2004) *Between Cultural Theory and Policy: The Cultural Policy Thinking of Pierre Bourdieu, Michel de Certeau and Régis Debray*, Research Papers, no. 7, Centre for Cultural Policy Studies, University of Warwick, Coventry.

BECKER, H. (1982) *Art Worlds*, University of California Press, Los Angeles and London.

BÉRA, M. & LAMY, Y. (2003) *Sociologie de la culture*, Armand Colin, Paris.

BERTHELOT, J.-M. (ed.) (2003) *La Sociologie française contemporaine*, 2nd edn, Quadrige/PUF, Paris.

BOURDIEU, P. (1984 [1979]) *Distinction: A Social Critique of the Judgement of Taste*, trans. R. Nice, Routledge and Kegan Paul, London; first published as *La Distinction: critique sociale du jugement*, Les Éditions de Minuit, Paris.

BOURDIEU, P. & DARBEL, A. (1990 [1966]) *The Love of Art: European Museums and Their Public*, trans. C. Beattie & N. Merriman, Stanford University Press, Stanford, USA; first published as *L'Amour de l'art: Les Musées d'art européens et leur public*, Éditions de Minuit, Paris.

DENORA, T. (2000) *Music in Everyday Life*, Cambridge University Press, Cambridge.

FRITH, S. (1996) *Performing Rites: Evaluating Popular Music*, Oxford University Press, Oxford and New York.

HENNION, A. (1981) *Les Professionnels du disque: Une Sociologie des variétés*, Métailié, Paris.

HENNION, A. (1990) 'The production of success: An antimusicology of the pop song, 1983', in *On Record: Rock, Pop and the Written Word*, eds S. Frith & A. Goodwin, Routledge, London and New York, pp. 185–206 (taken from Hennion 1981).

HENNION, A. (1993) *La Passion musicale: Une Sociologie de la médiation*, Métailié, Paris.

HENNION, A. (1996a) 'L'Amour de la musique aujourd'hui: Une Recherche en cours sur les figures de l'amateur', in *Musique et politique: Les Répertoires de l'identité*, ed. A. Darré, Presses Universitaires de Rennes, Rennes, pp. 41–50.

HENNION, A. (1996b) *Le Grand Écart entre la recherche et l'administration: Rapport au département des études et de la prospective*, unpublished report.

HENNION, A. (1997) 'Baroque and rock: music, mediators and musical taste', *Poetics*, vol. 24, pp. 415–435.

HENNION, A. (1999) 'Music industry and music lovers, beyond Benjamin: The return of the amateur', *Soundscapes: Online Journal on Media Culture*, vol. 2 (July), [online] available at http://www.icce.rug.nl/~soundscapes/DATABASES/MIE/Part2_chapter06.shtml.

HENNION, A. (2001) 'Music lovers: Taste as performance', *Theory, Culture and Society*, vol. 18 (October), pp. 1–22.

HENNION, A. (2002) 'La Musique, la ville et l'État. Plaidoyer pour des études de cas', in *Les Collectivités locales et la culture: Les Formes de l'institutionnalisation, 19e–20e siècles*, ed. P. Poirrier, Documentation Française, Paris, pp. 315–325.

HENNION, A. (2003a) 'Ce que ne disent pas les chiffres', in *Le(s) Public(s) de la culture: Politiques publiques et équipements culturels*, eds O. Donnat & P. Tolila, Presses de la Fondation Nationale des Sciences Politiques, Paris, pp. 287–304.

HENNION, A. (2003b) 'Éléments de synthèse', in *Le(s) Public(s) de la culture: Politiques publiques et équipements culturels*, eds O. Donnat & P. Tolila, Presses de la Fondation Nationale des Sciences Politiques, Paris, pp. 311–315.

HENNION, A. (2003c) 'Music and mediation: Towards a new sociology of music', in *The Cultural Study of Music: A Critical Introduction,* eds M. Clayton, T. Herbert & R. Middleton, Routledge, New York and London, pp. 80–91.

HENNION, A. (2004) 'Pragmatics of taste', in *The Blackwell Companion to the Sociology of Culture,* eds M. Jacobs & N. Hanrahan, Blackwell, Oxford, UK and Malden, USA, pp. 131–144.

HENNION, A. (2005a) 'Musiques, présentez-vous! Une comparaison entre le rap et la techno', in *Popular Music in France,* guest issue of *French Cultural Studies,* ed. D. Looseley, vol. 16 (June), pp. 121–134.

HENNION, A. (2005b), Interview with David Looseley, 12 April 2005.

HENNION, A. (2005c), Correspondence with David Looseley.

HENNION, A., MAISONNEUVE, S. & GOMART, E. (2000) *Figures de l'amateur: Formes, objets et pratiques de l'amour de la musique aujourd'hui,* Documentation Française, Paris.

LE GUERN, P. (2003) 'The study of popular music between sociology and aesthetics: A survey of current research in France', in *Popular Music in France from Chanson to Techno: Culture, Identity and Society,* eds H. Dauncey & S. Cannon, Ashgate, Aldershot, pp. 7–26.

LOOSELEY, D. L. (1995) *The Politics of Fun: Cultural Policy and Debate in Contemporary France,* Berg, Oxford and Washington DC.

LOOSELEY, D. L. (2003) *Popular Music in Contemporary France: Authenticity, Politics, Debate,* Berg, Oxford and New York.

LOOSELEY, D. L. (2004) 'The development of a social exclusion agenda in French cultural policy', *Cultural Trends,* vol. 50 (June), pp. 15–27.

LOOSELEY, D. L. (2005) 'The return of the social: Thinking postcolonially about French cultural policy', *International Journal of Cultural Policy,* vol. 11, no. 2, pp. 145–155.

MCGUIGAN, J. (1996) *Culture and The Public Sphere,* Routledge, New York and London.

MIDDLETON, R. (2003) 'Introduction: Music, modernization and popular identity', in *Popular Music in France from Chanson to Techno: Culture, Identity and Society,* eds H. Dauncey & S. Cannon, Ashgate, Aldershot, pp. 1–6.

NEGUS, K. (1996) *Popular Music in Theory: An Introduction,* Polity Press, Cambridge.

INDEX

Page numbers in **bold** represent figures. Page numbers in *italics* represent tables.

A Domestic Disgrace (Trznadel) 162
Addams, J. 21-34; influence of bullfighting on 24; legacy of 33; as "the woman of culture" 22-6
Adenauer, K. 180
Adorno, T. W. 97-8, 198, 228
advertising industry; development 63
Aesthetica (Baumgarten) 118
Agnew, S. 104
Ahearne, J. 9
americanisation: of immigrants 26, 31; multicultural policy of 30; of settlement movement 30-2
Amsterdam: and the culture of statistics 43-7; Jewish demography in 45
anarchism 98-9
Anderson, B. 75
Aristotle 116; Aristotelian "Prudence" 215
Arnold, M. 25, 217
Arnold, T. 25; headmastership of Rugby School 25
art: didactic function of 123-6; epistemological argument of 121-2; graduates and unemployment 91; guidelines for 168; influence of galleries 26; metaphysical argument of 120-1; new territories of 235; post-impressionist "sterile academicism" 168-9; psychological argument of 122-3; street 235; value of 90; visual artists 166-8
arts and crafts movement 38; and Fabianism 39; influence of 39
Arts Council of Great Britain 90; creation of 16
arts education 32; at Hull House 32; developing "play instinct" 32
Auschwitz 190-1
avant-garde movement 53
Averbakh, L. 149

Barnett, S. 23, 25; establishment of Toynbee Hall 23
Bassie, V. Lewis 102
Bauman, Z. 6
Beale, A. 58
Bebel, A. 178
Becker, H. 228, 236
Benda, J. 211
Berdyaev, N. 146
Berlage, H.P. 39, 41-2
Berland, J. 62
Berlin, I. 148-9
Beveridge, W. 27
Blair, T. 87
Bloch, E. 198
Blum Theses (Lukacs) 147-8
Bode, W. 50
Boekman, E. 37-54; Public dissertation defence (Amsterdam City University) **48**
Boekman Foundation 43-4
Bogart, H. 99
Bogdanov, A.A. 131-2, 138
Boll, H. 181
Bolshevism; and idealism 144-8
Bolshoi Theatre 138
Bourdieu, P. 219-20, 228; Bourdieusian sociology of taste 229
Braden, S. 90
Brebner, J.B. 59
Brecht, B. 152
Bretton Woods 101
British Broadcasting Corporation (BBC) 106
Bureau of Economics and Business Research 102
Burns, R. 177-203
Buxton, W. 59

Calvinism 51
Canada: cultural initiatives 57; federalism in 74; fur trade in 59; "national insecurity state" 57; nationalism in 58; Quebec 73-80; "Red Tory" stripe 58
Canadian Social Science Research Council 58
capitalism: attack on 196; cultural warfare against 148; global 17
Carey, J. 4, 58
Carson, M. 31
Casablanca 99
Catholicism 51
Caute, D. 212
Charlemagne 60
China; market culture in 108
Chirac, J. 186
Chomsky, N. 98
civilisation 16; suicides of 68
class: consciousness 145-7; embourgeoisement of 182; professional 182; working 182
Cogniot, G. 211
Cold War: culture 100; popular representations of 110
Cole, L. 111
Coleridge, S.T. 11
college: civic 22; effect of liberal curriculum 27; Smith College 22; Wellesley College 22; for women in America 22-3
communism: cultural 148-50; and deviationists 146; and education 139; in France 211; in Germany 178; and intellectuals 159-72
community: among urban poor 30; arts movement 26; concept of art 40-1; imagined 75; self-sacrifice as key to 31
consumerism; promotion of 99, 107
consumptionist populism 91
cultural change; anthropological model for 64
Cultural Commission for the Sixth Plan 219
cultural democratization: contemporary projects 32; project of 26
cultural diversity; exposure to 28
"cultural front" 149
cultural industries model 79
cultural inheritance; of social utility 27
cultural outreach: as "civilizing mission" 26; contradictions of 26-7
cultural policy: anti-political 212; Boekman on 48-53; and communist international 144-55; definition of 4, 8-10, 73; Dumont's stance on 78-80; and its discontents 73-6; ethics of 235; in France 228-38; instrumental 124; and intellectuals 3-18; intellectuals as the objects of 221-2; as liberal-rationalist venture 66; location-bound 66; in the Netherlands 37-54; and Plato's *Republic* 115-27; and the popular front 150-3; pragmatics of 233-7; in Quebec 73-80; and residual media 57-68; and romantics 3-18, 15-18; scope of 5; Soviet 132-40; and Stalinism 144-55; transformative 66
cultural politics; subliminal form of 210
cultural project; Bolshevism 131-3
culture: administration of the movement 67; and American Power 95-112; assumptions in 187; bourgeois concept of 200; capitalist hegemony 231; classless 139; Cold War 100; cultural theorism 195-8; democratization of 26; democratizing production 111; destruction of 201; and education 22; and empire 106-9; of European immigrants 28; high unemployment detrimental to 202; and history 60; impact of the Internet on 111; and imperialism 105; inclusive concept of 195-8; modern obsession with the immediate 64; pessimists towards 202; processed 92; reconstructing cultural commons 111-12; Russian 140; sociology of 200, 228; of statistics 43-7
Culture For Everyone project 201
culture populaire 77
culture savante 77
Curtiz, M. 99
Cuypers, P.J.H. 40

De Burcht: Building for the Dutch Diamond Factory Workers' Union (ANDB) **42**
de Certeau, M. 229, 232

De Kroniek (Tak) 39, 41
Debray, R. 215, 221
dédoublement; process of 77
Defence of Poetry (Shelley) 11
DeNora, T. 228
Derkinderen, A. 40-2; Mural Fragment (Den Bosch Town Hall) **40**
Derrida, J. 191, 194
Deutscher, I. 155
Dewey, J. 21, 28, 134
Dimitrov, G. 151, 154
Dominguez, V.R. 65
Donnat, O. 216
Dorland, M. 65-6
Dubois, V. 200-1, 217
Dumazedier, J. 218
dumbing down 4
Dumont, F. 3-80

education: and art 32; binding influence of 179-80; communist 139; and crisis 23-6; cultural 22; democratized schools 134; higher 180; liberal 23; as revolutionary tool 134; socialist 134-5; and television 103; vocational 22
Eichel, H. 201
Eisenhower, D. 95
Engels, F. 140
Enlightenment: in Germany 185; radicalized 164; Romanticism as a response to 10; suspension of legacy of 212
Enzensberger, H.M. 181
ethnic groups; greater autonomy for 74
European constitution: case for 191; necessity for 189
European Union (EU): common constitutional identity 186; mutual trust between countries in 186

Fabian Essays (Shaw) 38
Fabiani, J-L. 218
Fabianism: and the arts and crafts movement 39; influence of 39; in the Netherlands 38-43; as socialism "from above" 38
Fascism 148; barbarism of 152; role of bourgeois intellectuals in 151; Stalinist policy towards 154

France: *Cartel des Gauches* as Republic of the Professors 210; Communist Party in 211, 221; cultural policy in 209-22; development of cultural policy 233; intellectuals and cultural policy in 228-38; Ministry of Culture 233-4; Vichy regime 211
France, A. 152
Freud, S. 117
Frith, S. 228
Fuller, S. 88
Furedi, F. 4, 6-7, 88

Garnham, N. 9, 16
Gayme, L. 217, 220
Germany: Communist Party in 178; as cultural state 197; Enlightenment in 185; Federal Republic development of 184; Frankfurt 198; and philosophical idealism 185; revolutionary democracy of 153; Social-Democratic Party of 178; West 100
Giddens, A. 87
Gladstone, W. 16
global capitalism; aggressive forms of 17
global corporation; influence of 186
global market 108
global power; locus of 96
global terrorism; rise of 194
globalisation: American-controlled process of 187; commitment to international law 189; dumb expansion of corporate power 194
Gollancz, V. 153
Gorky, M. 131, 150, 154
Government and the Arts in the Netherlands (Boekman) 37
Government and the Value of Culture (Jowell) 125
Gramsci, A. 87
Graziadei, A. 146
Greater London Council 9, 17
Gros, F. 220

Habermas, J. 183-94, 198
Hall, S. 86
Halleck, D.D. 102

Hare, D. 91
Hartig, V. 196
Hennion, A. 218, 228-38
Herzberg, A.J. 47
Hoffmann, H. 183, 194-202
Hoggart, R. 86-94
Holocaust 190
Holst, R.R. 42, 53-4; Mural #1 (De Brucht) **44**; Mural #2 Holst **45**
Horkheimer, M. 97-8
Hull House: arts educational programmes at 32; Chicago 21, 25; early programme at 27-8
Hungary; bankruptcy of Marxism in 155

idealism; and Bolshevism 144-8
Ideologie and Utopie (Mannheim) 179
immigrant: Americanization of 26, 31; anti-immigrant backlash 31; culture of European 2; "upper tenth" 30; wartime 31
imperialism: American 67; cultural 105; and culture 106-9; modern 99
Innis, H. 57-68
Intellecktueller: negative polemical change 180; origin; context and use of word 177-8
intellectual: anti-intellectualism 91; autonomy 211; castigation of 202; and communism 159-72; as critic of power 209; as cultural agenda-setter 177-203; and cultural policy 3-18; cultural roles of 5; "dishonourable" 160; and French cultural policy 209-22, 228-38; good-bad 166-72; growing employment market for 8; "heroic" model of 6; as ideological free-float 179; interventions of 187-92; list of those in post 1945 Germany 180-1; as mediators of meaning 183; with moral integrity 162; oppositional 216; as optimistic theoretician of cultural politics 184-94; "organic" 179; as part of political and cultural landscape 180; petty-bourgeois intelligentsia 137; play and prestige 214-17; and policy analysis 1; in the policy process 217-21; postwar choices 161-6; as practitioner of cultural policy 194; pragmatic 37-54; public 87-8, 177, 210-11; as public protagonist in political debate 182-4; as reflexive elite 183; role of bourgeois intellectuals in Fascism 151; roles of 87-8, 137, 177-84; and Romantics 3-18; status as critic 188; status of in Quebec 75-7; theories of 179-80; and Utopianism 194-202
Internet: impact on culture 111; OhMyNews 111; Wikipedia 111
Iraq; illegal war in 186, 191
Islamic Fundamentalism 193

Janan, M. 117
Janaway, C. 124-5
Jansen, T. 52-3
Jeanson, F. 215
Jedlicki, J. 159-60
Jews: in Amsterdam 45; statistical explanation for problems of 47
Jhally, S. 63
Jowell, T. 125

Kautsky, K. 178
Kelley, A. 104
Kett, J. 28
Keynes, J.M. 16
Kingdon, J. 219
Kittler, F. 64-5
Koloski, L. 159-61
Konstan, D. 117
Korean War 67
Krakowska, G. 168, 171
Kraut, R. 117
Kriegel, B. 220
Krupskaya, N. 133
Kula, M. 165-6
Kulturpolitik 183-4
Kun, B. 146
Kwasniewski, A. 160

Laborier, P. 200-1
Labour Museum 28
Lady Chatterley's Lover (Lawrence) 86
Lang, J. 234
Langevin, P. 213
Lee, J. 8
Legutko, R. 163

Lenin, V. 133, 144
Les Professionnels du disque (Hennion) 229
Liebknecht, K. 178
Lovejoy, A.O. 10
Lukács, G. 144-55
Lunacharsky, A. 138
Lyrical Ballads (Wordsworth) 11

McCarthyism 101
McGuigan, J. 4, 9, 222, 237
McNeal, R. 133
Mackintosh, W.A. 61-3, 68
Malraux, A. 217, 233
Mann, H. 152-3
Mannheim, K. 151, 153
market: black 136; culture in China 108; employment for intellectuals 8
Marx, K. 18, 103, 140, 145
Marxism: bankruptcy of in Hungary 155; Hegelian 144; Western 155
Mass Communications and American Empire (Schiller) 103, 105
Matejko, J. 167
media: bias of 63; intellectuals 7; residual 57-68
Meirdieu, P. 214-15
Mercer, C. 65
Miller, T. 65-6
Miłosz, C. 161-2
Milton, J. 13
Monroe, J. 96
Morand, P. 211
Morin, E. 220
Morris, W. 18; obituary on 53
movement: arts and crafts 38, 39; avant-garde 53; community arts 26; nationalist 74; settlement 23-4, 30-2
Mulgan, G. 9
multiculturalism: Hoffman's commitment to 199; of Jane Addams 28-9; of policy of Americanization 30
Murdoch, I. 118
Murray, P. 117
museums: influence of 26; Labour Museum 28
music: definition of amateur 231; discomorphosis of listening 231-2; downloading of 235; expressive value of pop song 229; institutionalization of 237; and mediation 230; musicalisation 229; musicology of society 228-38; popular 233-5; and pragmatism 230

Naddaff, R. 115
nationalism: francophone 74; French-Canadian 74; greater autonomy for movement 74
Nazism 195; reinstatement of 181
Negus, K. 238
Netherlands: cultural policy in 37-54; Dutch Fabians 38-43
Nettleship, R. 116
New Economic Policy (NEP) 136, 138-40
New Labour 17
Niezsche, F. 117
Nizan, P. 149
Noirel, G. 216
Nolte, E. 190
nominal and relative expenditure of the central government on arts *50*

Ory, P. 211, 217

Pal, L. 68
Palumbo, P. 17
Paxton, R. 211
Peacock, T.L. 11
Peel, R. 16
Pfieffer, K. 64
philosophy: and disenfranchisement of art 119; German idealism 185; Patristic 126; Plato as inventor of 117
Plato 115-27; and censorship 123-7; influence over Western civilization 116; as "inventor of philosophy" 117; theories on poetry 116, 119-20, 123; theory of Forms 119; theory of Initiation 119
P. L. Takstraat (Amsterdam): early 1920s De Klerk Design for **43**
poetry 15; Plato's theories on 116, 119-20, 123; spirit of 16
Polak, H. 45-6

Poland: communism in 159-72; intellectuals in 159-72; postwar 159-72; struggle against foreign occupation 159
Policing the Crisis (Birmingham Centre) 89
political correctness 90, 182
Polytechnism 140
Pond, P. 59
Popular Front: anti-Fascist alliance 151-2; and cultural policy 150-3; influence of 153
populism: consumptionist 91; radical 96-8
pornography; copycat effect of 127
Posner, R. 6, 11-12, 88
poverty: of aspiration 125; cultural condition of 25; North-South line 101; urban 30
pragmatism 29; in intellectuals 37-54; philosophical 29
Pratt Institute 101
Prison Notebooks (Gramsci) 179
Proletarian Encyclopaedia 132
Proletarian University 132
Przewoznik, A. 160
public: contempt for the opinions of 13; cultural institutions 112; guardianship of criticism 186; intellectual 177, 210-11; morality 182; and the people 13; service broadcasting 112; trust in discourse 192
Public dissertation defence by Emanuel Boekman (Amsterdam City University) **48**

Quebec: cultural policy in 73-80; Dominion Textile 76-7; French-Canadian nationalism in 74; intellectual life in 76-7; status of intellectuals; journalists and artists in 75-6

Radbruch, G. 178, 195
Radvanayi, L. 150
Raphael 193
Reagan, R. 108
Recherches sociographiques 76
Republic (Plato) 115-27
revolution: conservative 178; cultural 136-7, 140; of culture in Soviet Union 136-7, 140; of democracy in Germany 153; education as tool for 134; proletarian 145; in Russia 133-5
Rieffel, R. 209
Rockefeller Foundation 58
Rogier, J. 52-3
Roland, H. 41
Rolland, R. 152-3
Romantic Movement; notion of 11
Romanticism 10-11; English 17; influence of today 17; as a response to Enlightenment 10
Romantics: and cultural policy 3-18; influence on state cultural policy 16; as intellectuals 11-15; vs. intellectuals 3-18
Rosenberg, A. 152
Roszkowski, W. 164
Russia: classics of culture 140; coronation of Tsar 40-1; oppression and impoverishment 40; revolution in 133-5

Said, E. 6, 88
satellite technology: potential of 102; regulation of 102; remote sensing 110
Schaper, E. 127
Schelsky, H. 181
Schiller, D. 103-4
Schiller, H. 95-112, 98
Schiller, Z. 104
Schroeder, G. 186
Scruton, R. 10
Second World War; American experience of 100
settlement movement 23-4; Americanization of 30-2; criticism of 30; English 24; failed idealism of 30-2; primary purpose of project 30
Sewell, W.H. 61-2
Shaw, G. 38
Shaw, R. 90
Shelley, M. 11-14, 16-18
Sinclair, U. 97
Sirinelli, J. 211, 217
Słabek, H. 164
Sloterdijk, P. 188
Smith, A. 7
Smith, C. 17
Smith College 22

Smythe, D. 103
social engineering 39, 135
social superiority 14
social utility; cultural inheritance of 27
Social-Democratic Party of Germany 178
socialism; aesthetic 43
socialist education 134-5
socialist realism 149
society: capitalist 196; musicology of 228-33
Society for Cultural Policy 200
sociology: of culture 228; of leisure 218; of music 228-38; of taste 229
Socrates 115, 119
Sollers, P. 214
Soviet Union: call for democratic dictatorship 147; collapse of 110; cultural policy in 132-40; cultural revolution in 136-7, 140; economic development in 136; Proletarian Encyclopaedia 132; Proletarian University 132
Stalin, J. 124, 150
Stalinism 144-55; appeal of cult 152; and Lukacs 154; policy towards Fascism 154
Stalinism and Polish Society (Swida-Ziemba) 165
Stamps, J. 61
Starr, E. 24
Stasi regime; criticism of 182
statistics: aims of 50; causal explanations from 47; culture of in Amsterdam 43-4; as lever for social change 46
Steiner, G. 127
Stern, J. 167-8; "The Construction Site" #1 (Muzeum Narodowe; Warsaw) **170**; "The Construction Site" #2 **171**; "Untitled" (1950) **172**
Stock Exchange 52
suffrage; universal 14
Szacki, J. 165-7
Sziklai, L. 150

Tak, P.L. 39-41
Tatian 126
Tawney, R.H. 27
technology: debunking new ideas 109; and innovation 109; romance of modern 140

television: BBC 106; Channel Four 106; commercial 105, 107; development of company 86; and education 103; expansion of interactive 110; participatory programming 109-10; pluralizing process 107; relations to violence 220
Thatcher, M. 90, 108
The Corporate Takeover of Public Expression (Schiller) 106
The Jungle (Sinclair) 97
The Love of Art (Bourdieu) 219
The Practice of Everyday Life (de Certeau) 219
The Uses of Literacy (Hoggart) 86
The Way We Live Now (Hoggart) 91
theory: free trade 107; of passion 238; of policy 238
Third World 99
Thompson, E.P. 38, 78, 86
Tischner, J. 165
Toynbee Hall: activities at 25; establishment by Samuel Barnett 23
transoceanic cable network; British domination of 102
Treaty of Brest-Litovsk 135
Trotsky, L. 148
Trudeau, P. 77
Truman, H. 100
Tsar; coronation of 40-1
Tusa, J. 5

Ulianov, V. 133
United Nations Educational, Scientific and Cultural Organization (UNESCO) 74, 87, 89, 101, 107
United States of America (USA): American Dream 98; American imperialism 67; American power 95-112; hegemony 191
university: growth of 7; Proletarian 132
University of California at San Diego (UCSD) 104
Utopianism; and intellectualism 194-202

Van Der Ploeg, R. 38
Van Der Will, W. 177-203
Van Gelderen, B. 46

Veblen, T.B. 60
Veth, J. 40-1

Walesea, L. 160
Wallmann, W. 201
Wallon, H. 213
Warpole, K. 9
Weber, M. 187
Wellesley College 22
West Germany; creation of 100
Where Have All The Intellectuals Gone? (Furedi) 4
Whitehead, A.N. 117
Wibaut, F.M. 39-43, 49
Wijnkoop, D. 47

Wikipedia 111
Williams, R. 6, 15, 16, 18, 63, 86, 196
Wittgenstein, L. 187
Woods, R. 31-2
Wordsworth, W. 11-13, 16, 18
Workerist discourse 137
World Trade Centre disaster 110, 193
Wright Mills, C. 97

Yudice, G. 65-6

Zinoviev, G. 146
Znak (The Sign) (Catholic monthly magazine) 163
Życiński, J. 164

9781138864634